An Introduction to Program Fa

An Introduction to Program Fault Tolerance

A Structured Programming Approach

ALI MILI
University of Tunis

With contributions by

Sayda, Ben Larbi, Laval University
Noureddine Boudriga, University of Tunis
Jules Desharnais, McGill University
Ali Jaoua, University of Sherbrooke
Fatma Mili, Oakland University
Paul Torrès, University of Tunis

FOREWORD BY
Professeur Gabrièle Saucier, Université de Grenoble, France

PRENTICE HALL
New York   London   Toronto   Sydney   Tokyo   Singapore

First published 1990 by
Prentice Hall International (UK) Ltd,
66 Wood Lane End, Hemel Hempstead,
Hertfordshire, HP2 4RG
A division of
Simon & Schuster International Group

Typeset in 10/12pt Times
by Best-set Typesetter, Hong Kong

Printed and bound in Great Britain by
BPCC Wheatons Ltd, Exeter

Library of Congress Cataloging-in-Publication Data

Mili, Ali.
    An introduction to program fault tolerance : a structured
programming approach / Ali Mili ... [et al.].
        p.   cm — (Prentice Hall international series in computer
science)
    Bibliography: p.
    ISBN 0-13-493511-X : $40.00
    1. Fault-tolerant computing.   2. Structured programming.
I. Title.   II. Series.
QA76.9.F38M55   1989   89-3560
004.2—dc19   CIP

British Library Cataloguing in Publication Data

Mili, Ali
    An introduction to program fault tolerance: a
    structural programming approach. — (Prentice Hall
    international series in computer sciences)
    1. Computer systems. Programs. Design faults. Tolerances
    I. Title   II. Larbi, Ben
    005.1'2

    ISBN 0-13-493511-X
    ISBN 0-13-493503-9   Pbk

1 2 3 4 5   94 93 92 91 90

Contents

viii   Contents

Foreword

Three sets of techniques are known and used nowadays to improve program reliability. These differ the ways that they deal with the potential appearance of a fault in the execution state of a program. *Fault avoidance* consists in constructing programs that are free of faults. As this goal is well known to be unachievable in general, we turn to another set of techniques, namely *Fault removal*. This consists of admitting the existence of faults in programs, and taking steps to remove them after programs are written. Even though it is less ambitious, this goal is hardly more achievable. Hence, it is necessary to turn to yet another set of techniques, namely *Fault tolerance*. This consists of admitting the existence of faults in programs, admitting that we cannot remove them all, but (as a last resort) taking steps to make sure that, by a combination of detection and recovery mechanisms, these faults do not cause programs to fail. Fault tolerance does seem to be a program's last line of defense; if anything, the next line of defense would be called *fault resignation*.

The text discusses program fault tolerance. It takes a structured programming approach to this subject, on the premise that *program fault tolerance* has more to do with *programs* than with *fault tolerance*. Indeed, the complexity of functions computed by programs, the redundancy of program states, and the non-determinacy of program specifications all contribute to give programs a complex pattern of fault tolerance.

This book can further be characterized by its algebraic approach to structured programming. It uses Tarski's relational algebra to represent program functions, program specifications, and the interactions between these. This approach yields results that are at the same time formal, intuitively appealing, and crisp.

In keeping with the traditional phase definitions of fault tolerance, this book covers in turn, following some background, the phases of error detection, damage assessment, and error recovery. Its theoretical developments are elucidated by numerous examples and exercises, and are illustrated by some sample programs.

The book is primarily a textbook, as it is written by an instructor, and stems from lecture notes. It can also be used by practicing software professionals since it remains close to its subject matter throughout, and is quite readable.

Professor Gabrièle Saucier
University of Grenoble, France

Preface

Nature is written in the language of Mathematics. (GALILEO, 1623)

Fault tolerance has become an important field of study in computer science. We illustrate its growth with two simple details. First, at the time of writing, eighteen annual international symposia on fault tolerant computing have been organized. Second, it is becoming more and more commonplace to find courses on fault tolerant computing in course catalogs. Many course descriptions found in university catalogs have one feature in common: they are oriented towards hardware fault tolerance, or system-level fault tolerance.

Yet, the study of software fault tolerance is both more critical and of greater interest. It is more critical because software problems are known to be more acute than hardware problems in today's technology. It is more interesting because programs are more information-rich, and carry more *natural redundancy*, a source of fault tolerance, than circuits.

The purpose of this book is to discuss aspects of program behavior in the presence of faults, and to propose possible approaches to addressing these aspects.

The book is based on course notes that I used during a course on fault tolerance which I taught at McGill University in Montreal, with Professor Vinod Agrawal. I have since used parts of the notes in courses that I have taught at the University of Tunis, FuDan University, the University of Adelaide, the University of Oran, and Laval University.

The text includes enough material for a regular fifteen week course, at the rate of three hours per week. This course can be taught at a senior undergraduate or graduate level of a computer science, computer engineering or software engineering curriculum. I have taught it at graduate level in all three kinds of curricula. It is best offered after a course on program proving or (mathematical) structured programming, using, e.g., Linger, Mills and Witt's *Structured Programming: theory and practice*. Nevertheless, the most critical prerequisite for this course, besides a familiarity with Pascal-like programming, is a course on discrete mathematics based, e.g., on C.L. Liu's *Elements of Discrete Mathematics*.

Each chapter ends with a set of problems that extend the material covered. These are labelled [A] if they are easy, [B] if they are difficult or long, and [C] if they are very difficult or very long. In addition, some research problems are labelled with [R]; they may range in magnitude from one week's research homework to a term project, and beyond. Each chapter has a section of bibliographic references, where suggestions for further reading are given. The references themselves are listed together at the end of the book; a special effort was made to include only the most synthetic references, and to include preferably those references that are most readily available.

Each section of a chapter ends with a set of exercises that apply and illustrate the material covered; they too are labelled [A], [B] or [C] depending on their length or level of difficulty. Some sections are marked with an asterisk and these can be skipped without interrupting the logical sequence of the book.

The material contained in the book has been the subject of research conducted over the past several years by the research group on heuristic and algorithmic programming, of the University of Tunis II; as such, it has benefited from the contributions of several members of the group. Particularly noteworthy is the participation of the contributing authors, whom we wish to gratefully acknowledge: S. Ben Larbi contributed to the derivation of the equations of forward error recovery under the hypothesis of non-deterministic specifications; N. Boudriga contributed to the study of regular relations and their usage as specifications; J. Desharnais contributed to the derivation of heuristics for programming under the hypothesis of deterministic specifications; A. Jaoua contributed to the study of damage assessment by executable assertions and the study of hybrid validation, as well as to the definition of regular relations; F. Mili contributed to the derivation of heuristics for programming under the hypothesis of deterministic and non-deterministic specifications; finally, P. Torrès contributed to the study of executable assertions, and self checking programs.

The author is indebted to the staff of Prentice Hall International for their cooperation in evaluating this book and then carrying it through its production. The author is also grateful to Dr Chris Marlin, from the University of Adelaide, for inviting him to Adelaide in the (southern) winter term of 1986, giving him the opportunity to teach a course related to this book's topic, and offering him the necessary conditions to start writing this book. Professor André Gamache, from Laval University, offered the author similar conditions in the (northern) spring term of 1987, while the book was in progress.

Professor Gabrièle Saucier, from the University of Grenoble, twice the author's doctoral supervisor (doctorat de troisième cycle, 1978; doctorat és-Sciences d'Etat, 1985), is further honoring her ever-devoted disciple by agreeing to write the foreword of this book.

Ali Mili
Tunis

Introduction

Is design fault tolerance necessary?
YES!
achieving perfection is difficult.
*   fault avoidance may not succeed totally.*
*   fault removal may not succeed completely.*
*   so fault tolerance will be needed.*
The 'Law of diminishing returns' supports using a range of techniques.
(TOM ANDERSON: Montréal, 1985)

The reliability of a program (or system) is measured by the probability that the program behaves properly for a given unit of time. High reliability is achieved through a combination of the three following sets of techniques:

1. *Fault avoidance* refers to the set of techniques for producing programs that are, by design, free of faults. This subsumes the combined use of formal specification techniques and structured programming techniques.
2. *Fault removal* refers to the set of techniques for removing faults from existing programs. This also subsumes the combined use of two techniques: (i) formal specifications, and (ii) program testing.
3. *Fault tolerance* refers to the set of techniques for continuing service despite the presence, and even the manifestation, of faults in the program. Primarily, this includes techniques for error detection and error recovery.

Program fault tolerance is the subject of this book. The orientation of the book can be characterized by the three following premises:

1. *We focus our attention on Pascal-like programs:* specifically, we concentrate on simple input–output programs that have no internal state; this is in contrast with other studies of fault tolerance which revolve around the notion of *system* (also referred to as a process, or a module).
2. *We take a structured-programming approach:* specifically, we use formal methods for program specification, analysis and construction.

3. *We take an algebraic approach* (Mills *et al.*, 1986; Linger *et al.*, 1979): specifically, we use relations to represent program specifications, and functions to represent program behavior; and we use relational algebra to capture the interaction between programs and their specifications.

The book is made up of five parts, organized as follows. Part I presents a mathematical background for structured programming, based primarily on an algebra of relations. Chapter 1 presents elements of discrete mathematics that are used throughout the book; in particular, it introduces a great deal of specific notation that is used throughout the book. Chapters 2 and 3 summarize the book's approach to structured programming: while Chapter 2 discusses program specifications, Chapter 3 briefly discusses program analysis, verification and design.

Part II presents fundamentals of program fault tolerance. The field of fault tolerance is sufficiently mature to have adopted a set of agreed upon models, concepts and terms. In Chapter 4, we adapt these models, concepts and terms to the particular scope of this book, and illustrate them. Chapter 5 further refines the notion of error in a program, by offering definitions of the key notion of state correctness, and highlighting its difference with program correctness. The discussions of Chapter 4 highlight four key phases in the process of fault tolerance: *error detection*, by which the current state is found to be distinct from the expected state; *damage assessment*, by which the extent of the damage is assessed to determine what must be done about this state; *fault removal*, by which the actual or hypothesized cause of the error is identified and removed from the running program; and *error recovery*, by which the current contaminated state is mapped into a correct state, before execution is allowed to resume. Error detection and damage assessment are discussed in Part III, while error recovery is discussed in Parts IV and V; as for fault removal, it is beyond the scope of this book.

Part III discusses techniques for error detection and damage assessment. In keeping with the orientation of this book, errors are detected using (program-controlled) executable assertions. Chapter 6 presents fundamentals of executable assertions, using relations; it then shows how executable assertions can be used for the purpose of error detection. Chapters 7 and 8 discuss damage assessment, by determining two significant boundaries of damage: when is the damage so limited that recovery is not even necessary (one can leave the program alone; it will recover spontaneously)? and, when is damage so extensive that recovery is not sufficient (critical information is lost from the current state; action is needed to retrieve another state)?

Once the extent of the damage to the current state is assessed, one must take action to erase the manifestation of this damage on the current state. Nowadays, two approaches to error recovery are known: backward error recovery, which consists of retrieving a previously saved correct state and resuming the computation from that state; forward error recovery, which consists of mapping the current contaminated state into a sufficiently correct state, and giving the control back to the program to continue.

Part IV discusses forward error recovery. Chapter 9 gives the equations of forward error recovery in the case of deterministic specifications, and illustrates them. Chapter 10 discusses the equations of forward error recovery in the case of non-deterministic specifications, and illustrates them. Finally, Chapter II presents case studies of programs designed hand-in-hand with their forward error recovery routines, and illustrates their behavior by means of a simple sorting program.

Part V discusses backward error recovery. Chapter 12 presents a basic structuring mechanism for backward error recovery: recovery blocks. Chapter 13 presents the mathematical formulas that govern the use of recovery blocks for the purpose of backward error recovery. Finally, Chapter 14 discusses the use of recovery blocks for the construction of self-checking programs.

List of Symbols

SET THEORY

$\in$:   is an element of
$\subseteq$:   is a subset of

$\cup$:   set union
$\cap$:   set intersection
$\times$:   cartesian product
P( ):   power set

$\varnothing$:   empty set
.:   composition of expressions

ARITHMETIC

$\leq$:   less than or equal
$\geq$:   greater than or equal

$*$:   multiplication
$/$:   real division

RELATIONS

$*$:   relational product
$^+$:   transitive closure
*:   reflexive transitive closure
.:   image set (s.R), antecedent set (R.s)

U( ):   universal relation

$V(\ )$:   diversity relation
$I(\ )$:   identity relation
ϕ: empty relation
Ω: 'absurd' relation

LOGICAL OPERATORS

$\wedge$:   logical 'and'
$\vee$:   logical 'or'
$\neg$:   logical 'not'
$\Rightarrow$:   logical implication
$\Leftrightarrow$:   logical equivalence
$\exists$:   there exists
$\forall$:   for all

Part I

Structured Programming: A Relational Approach

For, aside from the fact that the concepts occurring in this calculus possess an objective importance and are in these times almost indispensable in any scientific discussion, the calculus of relations has an intrinsic charm and beauty which makes it a source of intellectual delight to all who become acquainted with it. (ALFRED TARSKI, 1941)

As a preparation for a disciplined treatment of program fault tolerance, this part of the book introduces elements of structured programming. Specifically, we introduce elements of program specification, program verification and program construction. These are very wide subjects that deserve, and are getting, much attention of their own. The coverage we shall make of them is certainly insufficient by any standard: we shall cover just enough to enable us to carry out our discussions of program fault tolerance.

The approach that we take to our study of structured programming, and that we shall carry over to program fault tolerance, is based on Tarski's algebra of relations. We have found this algebra to be surprisingly effective in articulating ideas of program fault tolerance: in particular, it allows the interactions of the various parameters of program fault tolerance to be exhibited in a way that is at once formal, crisp, and intuitively appealing.

Chapter 1 discusses elements of discrete mathematics, with an emphasis on relational algebra. With few exceptions, it introduces no new concepts, but defines much of the specific notation and terms used through the book. Chapter 2 discusses program specifications, using an integrated relational methodology, including guidelines for specification generation and validation. Chapter 3 discusses program verification and construction, using relational manipulations.

CHAPTER 1

Discrete mathematics for programming

Throughout this book, we use discrete mathematics to formalize and discuss various problems of interest. In this chapter we present some elements of discrete mathematics pertaining, in particular, to sets, relations and functions. The chapter contributes few new results; for the most part it merely defines notation and terminology.

1.1 SETS

1.1.1 Definitions

A *set* is a collection of distinct, identifiable objects, called the *elements* of the set. We say that *s belongs* to set S, or that it is a *member* of set S if and only if s is an element of S. This is abbreviated to $s \in S$.

When a set S has a finite number of elements, we say that it is *finite*. The number of elements contained within a set is called the *cardinality* of the set and is a non-negative integer. A set with no elements is called an *empty set* and is denoted by $\emptyset$.

If all the elements of set S are in set S', we say that S is a *subset* of S' and denote it by $S \subseteq S'$; equivalently, we say that S' is a *superset* of S. If $S \subseteq S'$ and S' has a member that does not belong to S, we term S a *proper subset* of S'; equivalently, we say that S' is a *proper superset* of S.

We assume that predicates, their syntax and their semantics are known to the reader (see bibliographical notes). Given a predicate t on set S, we denote by $S|t$ the set of elements of S for which predicate t holds.

1.1.2 Operations on Sets

The *union* of two sets S and S' is the set of all elements which belong to S or to S' or to both; it is denoted by $S \cup S'$.

The *intersection* of two sets S and S' is the set of all elements which belong to S and to S'. It is denoted by $S \cap S'$.

The *difference* of set S' from set S is the set of elements which belong to S and do not belong to S'. It is denoted by $S - S'$.

The *cartesian product* of set S by set S' is the set of ordered pairs $\langle s, s' \rangle$ such that $s \in S$ and $s' \in S'$; it is denoted by $S \times S'$. If $U = S \times S'$ then S and S' are said to be *cartesian components* of U.

The nth *cartesian power* of set S is the set of ordered sequences $\langle s_1, s_2, \ldots, s_n \rangle$ such that for all k, $1 \le k \le n$, $s_k \in S$; it is denoted by S^n.

The *power set* of S is the set of subsets of S; it is denoted by $\mathbf{P}(S)$.

We say that we have defined a *partition* of S whenever we have defined a set of subsets of S, say $S_1, S_2, \ldots, S_n$, whose union equals S and whose pairwise intersections are empty.

1.1.3 Representing Sets

Most of the sets that we will be manipulating in this book fall into one of two categories, and sometimes into both: (i) finite sets, with a small cardinality; and (ii) subsets of cartesian products of pre-defined sets. We will discuss their representation in turn.

When a set is finite and has a reasonably small cardinality, it is easiest to represent it by listing all its members; hence, e.g. the set of vowels in the English alphabet can be represented as

$$\text{vowels} = \{\text{a, e, i, o, u, y}\}.$$

The order of the elements is irrelevant.

In programming, we often define sets as cartesian products of other pre-defined sets. The pre-defined sets we use in this book are as follows:

(a) **natural**, the set of natural numbers;
(b) **integer**, the set of integers;
(c) **real**, the set of real numbers;
(d) **char**, the set of characters;
(e) **boolean**, the set of truth values, **true** and **false**.

The set of triplets $\langle i, r, c \rangle$ such that i is an integer, r is a real and c is a character can be represented as

$$S = \textbf{integer} \times \textbf{real} \times \textbf{char}.$$

We can also represent it as

$$S = \{\langle i, r, c \rangle \,|\, i \in \textbf{integer} \wedge r \in \textbf{real} \wedge c \in \textbf{char}\}.$$

If we are interested in the subset S' of S such that, e.g., $i > r$ and c is a vowel, then we write

$S' = \{\langle i, r, c \rangle \,|\, i \in \textbf{integer} \land r \in \textbf{real} \land c \in \textbf{char} \land i > r \land c \in \text{vowels}\}.$

We may sometimes want to represent S' in a Pascal-like form, as follows:

```
S' = set
crt
   i: integer;
   r: real;
   c: crt;
sub
   i > r ∧ c ∈ vowels
end,
```

where **crt** stands for *cartesian product* and **sub** stands for *subset*. This notation is inspired by Pascal's **record** notation; it separates the two operations of performing the cartesian product (under **crt**) and taking a subset (under **sub**). Under the **crt** section we may write any Pascal-like variable declaration, while under the **sub** section we may write any logical predicate. When the predicate under **sub** is **true**, we may delete the whole section **sub** as well as the header **crt**.

Let s be an element of S'. We denote by $i(s)$, $r(s)$ and $c(s)$, respectively, the i-, r- and c-component of s; for example, if $s = \langle 4, 2.1, u \rangle$ then $i(s) = 4$, $r(s) = 2.1$ and $c(s) = u$. Clearly, we have $\langle i(s), r(s), c(s) \rangle = s$.

1.1.4 Expressions

In this section we discuss *expressions* on sets, formed by means of operators and variables. For the sake of readability, and because generalization is straightforward, we shall carry out most of our discussions on particular examples.

We consider the set of real numbers, along with the various unary $(-, \|, \log, \sin, \dots)$, binary $(+, *, -, /, \dots)$ and n-ary $(\max, \text{sum}, \min, \dots)$ operators that are known and commonly used on this set. The character strings $\log(s)$, $s + 3$, $(3 * s) + 1$, $(3/s) + 1$, $3/(s + 2)$ and $\min(3, 2 * s, s - 3)$ are *expressions* on S, with the *variable* s; a constant, such as $1/3$, could also be considered an expression with variable s, even though s does not appear in it. Let E be the expression $(3/s) + 1$; the *value* of expression E, say 2 for argument, is the **real** obtained by replacing s by 2 in expression E and effecting the prescribed operations;

hence we find $(3/2) + 1 = 5/2$. We denote the value of expression E for argument 2 by $E(2)$. The value of expression E may fail to be computable for all values of the argument s; for example, $(3/0) + 1$ cannot be computed. We call the *domain of definition* of E (abbreviation: **def**(E)) the set of arguments s for which the value of E can be computed; hence, for $E = \mathbf{log}$, we have $\mathbf{def}(E) = \{s \,|\, s > 0\}$, and for $E = (\ )^{1/2}$, $\mathbf{def}(E) = \{s \,|\, s \geq 0\}$.

We define three operations on expressions: composition, alternation and cartesian product as follows:

1. *Composition:* let E and E' be two expressions on S. The *composition* of E by E' is the expression denoted by $E \cdot E'$ obtained by replacing each occurrence of the variable of E by the expression $E'(s)$. For example, if $E(s) = (3/s) + 1$ and $E'(s) = s + 3$, then $E \cdot E'(s) = (3/(s+3)) + 1$ and $E' \cdot E(s) = ((3/s) + 1) + 3$.

2. *Alternation:* let E and E' be two expressions on S and let p be a predicate on S. The *alternation* of E and E' with respect to p is the expression on S represented by $\mathbf{alt}(p, E, E')$, whose value for all argument s is defined as follows: if $p(s)$ holds, then $E(s)$ else $E'(s)$.

3. *Cartesian product:* we consider the special case of expressions whose arguments and values are not necessarily in the same set. Let E_1 (resp E_2) be an expression on S (i.e. with arguments in S) whose values lie in S_1 (resp S_2). The *cartesian product* of E_1 by E_2 is the expression on S denoted by $E_1 \times E_2$, whose values in $S_1 \times S_2$ are defined by $E_1 \times E_2(s) = \langle E_1(s), E_2(s) \rangle$.

1.1.5   Exercises

1[A]   Say whether each of the following propositions hold:
    (a) $\varnothing \in \varnothing$.
    (b) $\varnothing \subseteq \varnothing$.
    (c) $\varnothing \in \{\varnothing\}$.
    (d) $\varnothing \subseteq \{\varnothing\}$.
    (e) $\varnothing \subset \{\varnothing\}$.

2[A]   Say whether each of the following propositions hold:
    (a) $\varnothing \in \mathbf{P}(\varnothing)$.
    (b) $\varnothing \subseteq \mathbf{P}(\varnothing)$.
    (c) $\varnothing \in \mathbf{P}(\{\varnothing\})$.
    (d) $\varnothing \subseteq \mathbf{P}(\{\varnothing\})$.
    (e) $\varnothing \subset \mathbf{P}(\{\varnothing\})$.

3[A]   Say whether each of the following propositions hold, where a and b are sets:

(a) $a \subseteq a$.

(b) $a \in a$.

(c) $a \in \{a\}$.

(d) $a \subseteq \{a\}$.

(e) $a \in \{\{\{a\}\}, \{a\}\}$.

4[A] Determine the cardinality of the following sets:

(a) $\varnothing$.

(b) $\{\varnothing\}$.

(c) $\{\{\varnothing\}\}$.

(d) $\varnothing \cup \{\varnothing\} \cup \{\varnothing\}$.

(e) $\{\varnothing \cup \{\varnothing\} \cup \{\varnothing\}\}$.

5[A] Determine the cardinality of the following sets:

(a) $\mathbf{P}(\varnothing)$.

(b) $\mathbf{P}(\{\varnothing\})$.

(c) $\mathbf{P}(\{\{\varnothing\}\})$.

(d) $\mathbf{P}(\varnothing \cup \{\varnothing\} \cup \{\varnothing\})$.

(e) $\mathbf{P}(\{\varnothing \cup \{\varnothing\} \cup \{\varnothing\}\})$.

6[B] Given the set S of cardinality n, determine the cardinality of the following sets:

(a) $S \cup \{S\}$.

(b) $\{S, \{S\}\}$.

(c) $\mathbf{P}(S)$.

(d) $\mathbf{P}(\mathbf{P}(S))$.

(e) The set of partitions of S.

7[A] Using the notation discussed in Section 1.1.3, give an adequate representation for the following sets:

(a) The set of trinomials, i.e. polynomials of degree 2.

(b) The set of polynomials of degree n, $n \geq 1$.

(c) The set of sorted character arrays, of size n, $n \geq 1$.

(d) The set of sorted arrays of variable size k, $1 \leq k \leq n$.

(e) The set of points in the cartesian plan that are at a distance d to the center, with $d < 1$.

8[A] Consider a non-empty set S and the operations $\cup$, $\cap$, $-$ and $\times$ on $\mathbf{P}(S)$. Show that any expression written on $\mathbf{P}(S)$ using the above operators has a domain of definition equal to $\mathbf{P}(S)$.

1.2 RELATIONS

1.2.1 Definitions

A *relation* R on set S is a subset of $S \times S$. Let (s, s') be an element of R; s is said to be an *argument* in R and s' is said to be an *image* in R.

The *domain* of relation R is the set of arguments of R; formally, $\text{dom}(R) = \{s \mid \exists s': (s,s') \in R\}$. The *range* of relation R is the set of images of R; formally, $\text{rng}(R) = \{s' \mid \exists s: (s,s') \in R\}$.

Among the constant relations on a set S, we mention the following: the *universal* relation $U(S) = S \times S$, the *identity* relation $I(S) = \{(s,s') \mid s \in S \ \& \ s' = s\}$, the *empty* relation $\emptyset = \{\ \}$ and the *diversity* relation $V(S) = U(S) - I(S)$. When S is implicit, we may represent $U(S)$, $I(S)$ and $V(S)$ by U, I and V respectively. In addition, we may – by abuse of notation – write $U(t)$, $I(t)$ and $V(t)$ to represent $U(S|t)$, $I(S|t)$ and $V(S|t)$, respectively, where t is a predicate on S.

A *relational* on set S is a relation on the set of binary relations on S.

In this book, we represent relations in one of two ways as follows: (i) finite relations with a small cardinality are represented by listing their elements (pairs); and (ii) other relations are represented as

$$\{(s,s') \mid p(s,s')\}$$

where $p(s,s')$ is a predicate characterizing those pairs to be included in R.

Remark. Let S be a set defined as a cartesian product of two sets, say, S_1 and S_2; and let R be a relation on S. Both S and R are cartesian products. Yet elements of S are represented using angle brackets ($\langle$, $\rangle$, see Section 1.1.3), whereas elements of R are represented using parentheses ((,), this section). While this is something of an abuse of notation, we use it whenever it is necessary to distinguish between the two levels of detail (the set level and the relation level).   □

1.2.2 Operations

The set-theoretic operations of *union*, *intersection* and *difference* can be applied to binary relations and are of interest. In addition, we define the following thirteen operations on relations:

1. *Complement:* the *complement* of relation R on S is the relation denoted by R^- and is equal to $U(S) - R$.
2. *Inverse:* the *inverse* of relation R is the relation denoted by $R^\wedge$ and is equal to $\{(s,s') \mid (s',s) \in R\}$.
3. *Cartesian product:* let S be the cartesian product of two sets, say S_1 and S_2, and let R_1 and R_2 be relations on S_1 and S_2 respectively. The *cartesian product* of R_1 by R_2 is the relation on $S = S_1 \times S_2$ denoted by $R = R_1 \times R_2$ and defined by

$$R = \{(\langle s_1, s_2\rangle, \langle s_1', s_2'\rangle) \mid (s_1, s_1') \in R_1 \wedge (s_2, s_2') \in R_2\}.$$

4. *Relational product:* let R and R' be two relations on S. The *relational product* of R by R' is the relation denoted by $R * R'$ and defined by

$$R * R' = \{(s, s') | \exists s'': (s, s'') \in R \land (s'', s') * R'\}.$$

Note that $\text{dom}(R * R') \subseteq \text{dom}(R)$.

5. *Relational power:* let R be a relation on S. The ith *relational power* of R for $i \geq 0$ is the relation denoted by R^i and defined by

$$R^0 = I(S),$$
$$R^i = R^{i-1} * R, \text{ for } i \geq 1.$$

Note that for all $i \geq 1$, $\text{dom}(R^i) \subseteq \text{dom}(R)$.

6. *Transitive closure:* let R be a relation on S. The *transitive closure* of R is the relation denoted by R^+ and defined by

$$R^+ = \{(s, s') | \exists i \geq 1: (s, s') \in R^i\}.$$

Note that we have $\text{dom}(R^+) = \text{dom}(R)$. If $T = R^+$, we say that R is a *transitive kernel* of T; if no proper subset of R is a transitive kernel of T, then R is said to an *irreducible transitive kernel* of T.

7. *Reflexive transitive closure:* the *reflexive transitive closure* of relation R on S is the relation denoted by R^* and equal to $I \cup R^+$.

8. *Pre-restriction:* let R be a relation on S and t be a predicate on S. The *pre-restriction* of R to t is the relation

$$t \backslash R = \{(s, s') | t(s) \land (s, s') \in R\}.$$

It is worth noting that this relation is nothing but $I(t) * R$.

9. *Post-restriction:* similarly, we define the post-restriction of relation R to predicate t on S to be

$$R / t = \{(s, s') | (s, s') \in R \land t(s')\}$$

and we note that this is nothing but $R * I(t)$. It is worth noting that for all relation R and predicate t defined on S, we have:

$$I(t) * R \cup I(\neg t) * R = R,$$
$$R * I(t) \cup R * I(\neg t) = R,$$

where $\neg t$ is the logical negation of t. These two formulas are called the *pre-projection* and the *post-projection* of relation R to predicate t (or $\neg t$) respectively.

10. *Pre-application:* the *pre-application* to $s \in S$ of relation R on S is the set denoted by $s \cdot R$ and defined by

$$s \cdot R = \{s' | (s, s') \in R\}.$$

By extension to this notation, if S' is a subset of S then we define $S' \cdot R$ to be the union of sets $s \cdot R$ for all $s \in S'$.

11. *Post-application:* the *post-application* to $s \in S$ of relation R on S is the set denoted by $R \cdot s$ and equal to $s \cdot R\hat{}$; also, the post-application to $S' \subseteq S$ of relation R on S is $R \cdot S' = S' \cdot R\hat{}$. We admit without proof that $s \cdot (R * R') = (s \cdot R) \cdot R'$ – a pseudo associativity; $dom(R) = R \cdot S$; $rng(R) = S \cdot R$. The proofs of these identities stem immediately from the definitions.

12. *Nucleus:* the *nucleus* of relation R is the relation

$$N(R) = R * R\hat{}.$$

This relation contains (s, s') if and only if s and s' share a common image.

13. *Kernel:* the *kernel* of relation R is the relation

$$K(R) = \{(s, s') | \emptyset \neq s' \cdot R \subseteq s \cdot R\}.$$

We take the following conventions regarding operator precedence: inversion, complement, relational power and transitive closure have the highest precedence (they are operated first); they are followed by relational product; then comes the set-theoretic operations of intersection, union and difference; finally comes the application operator ($\cdot$).

1.2.3   Properties of Relations

Equivalence Properties

Let R be a relation on S; R is said to be *reflexive* if and only if $I \subseteq R$; *symmetric* if and only if $R = R\hat{}$; *transitive* if and only if $R^2 \subseteq R$; an *equivalence* if and only if it is reflexive, symmetric and transitive. The *equivalence class* of element s in S *modulo* relation R is the set $s \cdot R$; equivalence classes of R on S define a partition of S.

Ordering Properties

Let R be a relation on S; R is said to be *antisymmetric* if and only if $R \cap R\hat{} \subseteq I$; *asymmetric* if and only if $R \cap R\hat{} = \emptyset$; *connected* if and only if $V(S) \subseteq R \cup R\hat{}$; *strongly connected* if and only if $U(S) \subseteq R \cup R\hat{}$.

Also, R is said to be a *partial ordering* if and only if it is reflexive, antisymmetric, and transitive (e.g. relation 'divides' on the set **natural**); a *total ordering* (also: *simple ordering*) if and only if it is a partial ordering that is strongly connected (e.g. relation 'is-less-than-or-equal-to' on the set **natural**); a *strict partial ordering* if and only if it is asymmetric and transitive (e.g. relation: 'divides-and-is-different-from' on the set **natural**); a *strict total ordering* (also: *strict simple ordering*) if and only if it is a partial ordering that is connected (e.g. 'less-than' on the set **natural**).

Lattices

Let R be a partial ordering relation on set S, and let S' be a subset of S. An element s of S' is said to be R-*maximal* in S' if and only if $s \cdot (R - I) \cap S' = \emptyset$, i.e. if there exists no t other than s in S' such that $(s, t) \in R$. Let S be the set **natural** and R be the relation 'divides'. The set $S' = \{2, 3, 6, 7, 9\}$ has three R-maximal elements, namely 6, 7 and 9. On the other hand, the set $S'' = \{2, 3, 6, 7, 9, 126\}$ has a unique R-maximal element, 126.

Let R be a partial ordering relation on set S, and let S' be a subset of S. An element s in S' is said to be R-*minimal* if and only if $(R - I) \cdot s \cap S' = \emptyset$. If we again take $S = $ **natural** and $R = divides$, then the set $S' = \{5, 6, 7, 10, 12, 14, 30\}$ has three R-minimal elements, namely 5, 6 and 7. For illustration purposes, we show that 6 is R-minimal:

$$
\begin{aligned}
R - I \quad &= \{(s, s') \,|\, s \text{ divides } s' \wedge s \neq s'\}. \\
(R - I) \cdot 6 &= \{s \,|\, s \text{ divides } 6 \wedge s \neq 6\} \\
&= \{1, 2, 3\}. \\
S' \qquad &= \{5, 6, 7, 10, 12, 14, 30\}.
\end{aligned}
$$

Clearly, we do have $(R - I) \cdot 6 \cap S' = \emptyset$; hence 6 is R-minimal in S'.

Let s and s' be two elements of S and let R be a partial ordering on S. The set of *upper-bounds* of s and s' is denoted by $ub(s, s')$ and defined as

$$
ub(s, s') = s \cdot R \cap s' \cdot R.
$$

Similarly, the set of *lower-bounds* of s and s' is denoted by $lb(s, s')$ and defined as

$$
lb(s, s') = R \cdot s \cap R \cdot s'.
$$

For $S = $ **natural** and $R = divides$, we find that $ub(6, 9)$ includes 18, 36, 54, 72, ..., while $lb(6, 9) = \{1, 3\}$.

Let s and s' be two elements of S, and let R be a partial ordering relation on S. An R-*least-upper-bound* of s and s', if it exists, is an R-*minimal* element of $ub(s, s')$; we denote it by $lub(s, s')$. Similarly, an R-*greatest-lower-bound* of s and s', if it exists, is an R-maximal element of $lb(s, s')$; we denote it by $glb(s, s')$. For $S = $ **natural** and $R = divides$, we find a unique glb for any pair (s, s'), namely $\gcd(s, s')$ and a unique lub for any pair (s, s'), namely the smallest common multiple of s and s'.

The above example notwithstanding, glb's and lub's are not necessarily unique for any given pair (s, s'). Let R be a partial ordering on S. We say that R is a *lattice* if and only if any pair (s, s') in S has a unique greatest-lower-bound and a unique least-upper-bound. The relation 'divides' on the set **natural** is a lattice. The relation 'is-less-than' on the set **natural** is also a lattice, with $\mathrm{glb}(s, s') = \min(s, s')$ and $\mathrm{lub}(s, s') = \max(s, s')$.

Well-Founded Orderings

Relation R is said to be *non-infinitely decreasing* if and only if for any s in S, there exists a natural number k (possibly dependent on s) such that $R^k \cdot s = \varnothing$; in other words, for all s there is no infinite decreasing (by R) sequence starting at s.

We present two propositions about non-infinitely-decreasing relations, prove them, and then explain their interest for our purposes:

- *Proposition 1*. If R is non-infinitely decreasing on S, then any subset S' of S has an R-minimal element.

Proof. Let m be an element of S'. If m is R-minimal, then we have established the result that we are seeking to prove. Otherwise, there exists an element n different from m such that $(n, m) \in R$. Letting n be re-named as m, we can again iterate the case analysis just shown. Because R is non-infinitely decreasing this process is bound to terminate, with m an R-minimal element of S'.   [QED]

- *Proposition 2*. If R is non-infinitely decreasing on S, then it is asymmetric.

Proof. Let R be a relation on S that is not asymmetric. Then $R \cap R^\smallfrown \neq \varnothing$. Let (x, y) be an element of $R \cap R^\smallfrown$, and let (s_i) be the sequence defined on S by

$$s_0 = x$$
$$s_1 = y$$
$$s_2 = x$$
$$s_3 = y$$
$$s_4 = x$$
$$\vdots$$

Then, $\forall i$, $R^i \cdot s_0$ is different from $\varnothing$ since it includes x or y. Hence R is not non-infinitely decreasing.   [QED]

A relation R is said to be a *well-founded ordering* if and only if it is transitive and non-infinitely decreasing.

The reader should be able to appreciate the interest of well-founded ordering relations in the study of program termination. By virtue of the first proposition above, we can use well-founded orderings for the purpose of induction: the existence of R-minimal elements enables us to carry out the *basis of induction* (see bibliography). By virtue of the second proposition above, we claim that if a relation is a well-founded ordering, then it is a strict partial ordering.

Measuring the images per argument ratio: Determinacy

In this section we wish to define a property that captures how deterministic a relation is in assigning images to arguments. Intuitively, we wish to think of a relation as being more-deterministic if it assigns fewer images to each argument (ultimately, one image per argument). One could measure the determinacy of finite relations by the numeric ratio of their number of images over their number of arguments; even then, such a measure is so abstract that it could hardly be of any use since it says very little about how arguments are mapped into images. We turn to a set-theoretic formulation of this notion:

Let R be a relation on S. We call the relation $T = R\hat{\ } * R$ the *co-nucleus* of R. Note that T is symmetric, and that $I(\mathrm{rng}(T)) \subseteq T$ (i.e. it is reflexive on its range). Interpreting the significance of $R\hat{\ } * R$, we find that a pair (s,s') belongs to $R\hat{\ } * R$ if and only if there exists s'' such that $(s'',s) \in R$ and $(s'',s') \in R$; in other words, $(s,s') \in R\hat{\ } * R$ if and only if s and s' are the images by R of a common argument, s''. By virtue of our intuitive interpretation of determinacy, we pose the definition: R is *more-deterministic* than R' if and only if $R\hat{\ } * R \subseteq R'\hat{\ } * R'$.

Note that if R is more-deterministic than R', then $\mathrm{rng}(R)$ is a subset of $\mathrm{rng}(R')$; $\mathrm{rng}(R)$ may be equal to $\mathrm{rng}(R')$ or it may be a strict subset of it.

Example 1. We let

$$R = \{(a,0), (b,1), (c,2), (d,2)\},$$
$$R' = \{(a,0), (a,1), (b,1), (b,2), (c,2), (c,3)\}.$$

While R associates one image to each of its arguments, R' associates two images to each argument; hence R appears to be more-deterministic than R'. We compute the co-nucleus of R and R' and match them:

$$R\hat{} * R = \{(0,0), (1,1), (2,2)\} \quad (= I(\text{rng}(R))),$$
$$R'\hat{} * R' = \{(0,0), (0,1), (1,0), (1,1), (1,2), (2,1), (2,2), (2,3), (3,2), (3,3)\}.$$

Clearly, the co-nucleus of R is a subset of the co-nucleus of R'. $\square$

A relation is said to be *deterministic* if and only if it is more-deterministic than I; its co-nucleus is a subset of $I\hat{} * I$, which is I. If R is deterministic, we say that it is a *function*.

Example 2. We again consider relations R and R' introduced in Example 1:

$$R = \{(a,0), (b,1), (c,2), (d,2)\},$$
$$R' = \{(a,0), (a,1), (b,1), (b,2), (c,2), (c,3)\}.$$

It is clear from observing the co-nuclei of R and R' (Example 1) that R is deterministic while R' is not. $\square$

We consider relation R of Example 2. One could permute its arguments at will without changing its co-nucleus; in fact one could even change its arguments completely (e.g. x, y, z, w, instead of a, b, c, d) without changing its co-nucleus. Hence the measure of determinacy – which rests on the definition of co-nucleus – does not provide a great deal of information about the relation involved. In the following section, we introduce another criterion, which is closer to the relations it measures.

Measuring the Information of a Relation: Definedness

Let A and B be two observers watching a deterministic input/output process; let R_a and R_b (given below) be their reports on the process observed:

$$R_a = \{(a,0), (b,1), (c,2), (d,3)\},$$
$$R_b = \{(a,0), (a,1), (a,2), (b,1), (b,2), (b,3), (c,2), (c,3), (c,4)\}.$$

By including, e.g. $(a,0)$, $(a,1)$ and $(a,2)$ in R_b, agent B means that for input a, he is not sure whether the output is 0, 1 or 2. Assuming that both A and B are faithful in their reports, which of them gives more information? The answer, of course, is A since: first, he knows about more inputs; second, for those inputs that B also knows about, A is more precise in his assignment of outputs to them. This suggests the following definition:

Let R and R' be two relations on S. We say that R is *more-defined* than R' if and only if:

$dom(R') \subseteq dom(R)$,

$\forall s \in dom(R'), s \cdot R \subseteq s \cdot R'$.

If R and R' have the same domain, then R is more-defined than R' if and only if $R \subseteq R'$; hence, $\{(a,0), (b,1)\}$, for example, is more-defined than $\{(a,0), (a,1), (b,1), (b,2)\}$.

On the other hand, if R and R' are deterministic, then R is more-defined than R' if and only if $R' \subseteq R$ (note the inversion of roles of R and R', with respect to the earlier hypothesis); hence, $\{(a,0), (b,1)\}$, for example, is more-defined than $\{(a,0)\}$. When a function R' is a subset of another function R, it is usual to state that R' is *less-defined* than R; the relational introduced here is a generalization to non-deterministic relations (in addition to being an inversion) of the relational *less-defined* which is traditionally discussed for deterministic relations (functions). relations (functions).

It is worth noting that if R' is a pre-restriction of R to some predicate, say t, then R is more-defined than R'. The proof is quite simple: clearly, $dom(R')$ is a subset of $dom(R)$, since $R' = I(t) * R$. Let s be an element of $dom(R')$; because $s \in dom(R')$, $t(s)$ holds, hence $s \cdot R = s \cdot I(t) * R = s \cdot R'$.

If we consider the second clause of the definition of the relational *more-defined*:

$$\forall s \in dom(R'), s \cdot R \subseteq s \cdot R',$$

we realize that it has a significance that is close to the definition of relational *more-deterministic*:

$$R^{\char`\^} * R \subseteq R'^{\char`\^} * R'.$$

Indeed, both of them tend to favour (as more-defined or more-deterministic) relations that have fewer images per argument. The exact relationship between these relationals is highlighted in the following proposition:

- *Proposition 3.* Let R and R' be two relations on set S such that R is more-defined than R' and $dom(R) = dom(R')$. Then R is more-deterministic than R'.

Proof. Because R is more-defined than R' and $dom(R) = dom(R')$, R is a subset of R'. It is immediately obvious that $R^{\char`\^} * R$ is subset of $R'^{\char`\^} * R'$.   [QED]

Example 3

$$R = \{(a,0), (b,1), (b,2)\},$$
$$R' = \{(a,0), (a,1), (b,1), (b,2)\}.$$

We have $\text{dom}(R) = \text{dom}(R')$. On the other hand,

$$a \cdot R = \{0\}, \qquad\qquad a \cdot R' = \{0,1\},$$
$$b \cdot R = \{1,2\}, \qquad\qquad b \cdot R' = \{1,2\}.$$

Hence $\forall s \in \text{dom}(R'), \ s \cdot R \subseteq s \cdot R'$. Then R is more-defined than R'. Since R and R' have the same domain, we deduce, by Proposition 3, that R is more-deterministic than R'. This can be verified easily:

$$R\hat{\ } * R \ = \{(0,0), (1,1), (2,2), (1,2), (2,1)\},$$
$$R'\hat{\ } * R' = \{(0,0), (1,0), (0,1), (1,1), (1,2), (2,1), (2,2)\}. \qquad \square$$

Clearly, a relation R can be more-deterministic than a relation R' without being more-defined than R'. Consider the following example:

Example 4

$$R \ = \{(a,0), (b,1), (c,2)\},$$
$$R' = \{(a,1), (b,2), (c,0), (c,2)\}.$$
$$R\hat{\ } * R = \{(0,0), (1,1), (2,2)\},$$
$$R'\hat{\ } * R' = \{(0,0), (1,1), (2,2), (0,2), (2,0)\},$$

Hence R is more-deterministic than R'. On the other hand, since $a \cdot R = \{0\}$ is not a subset of $a \cdot R' = \{1\}$, R is not more-defined than R'. $\qquad \square$

Measuring the Uniformity of a Relation: Regularity

Throughout the book, we frequently use structured-programming methods to address program fault tolerance problems. In all these problems, we deal with program specifications under the form of binary relations: the specification from which we derive a correct program; the specification with respect to which we plan error recovery; the specification with respect to which we make the program self-checking; and the specification of the recovery routine. In several instances, we find that our computations are dramatically facilitated if we accept the hypothesis that the specification at hand meets some property, which we define below.

We say that R is *regular* if and only if

$$R * R\hat{\ } * R \subseteq R.$$

It is worth noting that for all relation R, we have: $R \subseteq R * R\hat{} * R$, so that regularity can be equivalently defined as

$$R = R * R\hat{} * R.$$

In the future we shall use one formula or the other interchangeably.

It is something of a paradox that, even though *regularity* is a strong property (judging by the degree to which it simplifies our job, see Parts IV and V), it is also a general property; i.e. it is verified by a large class of relations. In particular, most ordinary specifications that we encounter in practice are regular. Below we discuss characterizations of regular relations which will elucidate why they are so general. We will, in turn, discuss sufficient conditions, necessary conditions, and then necessary and sufficient conditions of regularity.

- *Proposition 4.* If R is deterministic, then it is regular.

Proof. If R is deterministic, then

$$R\hat{} * R \subseteq I,$$

hence

$$R * R\hat{} * R \subseteq R. \hspace{4cm} \text{[QED]}$$

Example 5. Let S be the space defined by:

```
S = set
a, b: integer
end,
```

and let R be the following relation on S:

$$R = \{(s, s') \mid a(s') = a(s) + b(s) \land b(s') = 0\}$$

R is deterministic, so it is regular. $\hspace{3cm} \square$

- *Proposition 5.* If R is symmetric and transitive then it is regular.

Proof

$$
\begin{array}{ll}
R * R\hat{} * R & \\
\subseteq (R * R) * R & R \text{ is symmetric} \\
\subseteq (R) * R & R \text{ is transitive} \\
\subseteq R & R \text{ is transitive} \hspace{2cm} \text{[QED]}
\end{array}
$$

Example 6. Let S be

$\{0, 1, 2, 3, 4, 5, 6\}$,

and let R be

$\{(0,0),\ (0,1),\ (1,0),\ (1,1),\ (2,3),\ (2,2),\ (3,2),\ (3,3)\}$.

R is symmetric and transitive; hence it is regular. Notice that it is not reflexive since $(4,4)$, for example, is not in R.   □

A trivial corollary of the above proposition is that an equivalence relation is regular.

We say that relation R is *rectangular* if and only if it is of the form $R = A \times B$, where A and B are non-empty subsets of S:

• *Proposition 6*. If R is rectangular, then it is regular.

Proof. Let R be rectangular:

$R * R\hat{} * R$
$= (A \times B) * (B \times A) * (A \times B)$
$= (A \times A) * (A \times B)$
$= A \times B.$ [QED]

Example 7. We let:

S = **natural**.

$R = \{(s, s') \mid 3 \leq s \leq 9\}.$

R is rectangular because it can be written as $\{3, 4, 5, 6, 7, 8, 9\} \times S$. Hence it is regular.   □

• *Proposition 7*. If $R\hat{}$ is regular, then R is regular.

Proof. $R\hat{}$ is regular:

$\Rightarrow R\hat{} * R * R\hat{} \subseteq R\hat{}$
$\Rightarrow R * R\hat{} * R \subseteq R,$

then R is regular.   [QED]

Example 8. Let S be defined by

set
a, b: **integer**
end

and let R be

$$R = \{(s, s') \mid a(s) = a(s') + b(s') \wedge b(s) = 0\}.$$

The inverse of this relation is deterministic and hence is regular; thus so is R. □

- *Proposition 8.* If R is the cartesian product of two regular relations, then R is regular.

Proof. Let R be $(R_1 \times R_2)$:

$$
\begin{aligned}
&(R_1 \times R_2) * (R_1 \times R_2)\hat{} * (R_1 \times R_2) \\
&= (R_1 * R_1\hat{} * R_1) \times (R_2 * R_2\hat{} * R_2) \qquad \text{by definition} \\
&= R_1 \times R_2. \qquad R_1 \text{ and } R_2 \text{ are regular.} \qquad \text{[QED]}
\end{aligned}
$$

Example 9. Let S_1 and S_2 equal the set of naturals, and let R_1 and R_2 be

$$
\begin{aligned}
R_1 &= \{(a, a') \mid 2 \le a \le 12\} \\
R_2 &= \{(b, b') \mid 4 \le b' \le 6\}.
\end{aligned}
$$

Then the cartesian product of R_1 and R_2 is

$$
\begin{aligned}
R &= R_1 \times R_2 \\
&= \{(s, s') \mid 2 \le a(s) \le 12 \wedge 4 \le b(s') \le 6\}.
\end{aligned}
$$

R_1 and R_2 are regular because they are rectangular; and by virtue of this proposition, so is R. □

Because most of the spaces that we work on are cartesian products of simpler spaces, this proposition is frequently useful (as frequently as we find relations that respect the cartesian boundaries of the space).

- *Proposition 9.* If R is the intersection of two regular relations, then it is regular.

Proof. Let R be $(R_1 \cap R_2)$:

$$
\begin{aligned}
&(R_1 \cap R_2) * (R_1 \cap R_2)\hat{} * (R_1 \cap R_2) \\
&\subseteq R_i * R_i\hat{} * R_i \qquad \text{for } i = 1, 2 \\
&\subseteq R_i \qquad \text{for } i = 1, 2 \\
&\subseteq R_1 \cap R_2 \qquad\qquad\qquad\qquad\qquad\qquad \text{[QED]}
\end{aligned}
$$

Example 10. Let S be the set defined by

```
set
a, b, c: integer
end,
```

and let R be the relation defined by

$$R = \{(s,s') \mid a(s') = a(s) + b(s) \wedge b(s') = 0\}.$$

This relation can be written as $R = R_0 \cap R_1$, where

$$R_0 = \{(s,s') \mid a(s') + b(s') = a(s) + b(s)\},$$
$$R_1 = \{(s,s') \mid b(s') = 0\}.$$

R_0 is regular because it is an equivalence; relation R_1 is regular because it is rectangular; hence, by virtue of this proposition, so is R. □

The above proposition is useful since it is usual to encounter relations that are written as the intersection of an equivalence relation with a rectangular relation.

- **Proposition 10.** If R is thé right relational product of a regular relation by a function, then R is regular.

Proof. Let R be $f * R_1$, where f is a function and R_1 a regular relation:

$$
\begin{aligned}
R * R^{\wedge} * R = f * R_1 * R_1^{\wedge} * f^{\wedge} * f * R_1 & \\
\subseteq f * R_1 * R_1^{\wedge} * R_1 & \quad \text{because } f \text{ is a function} \\
\subseteq f * R_1 & \quad \text{because } R_1 \text{ is regular} \\
\subseteq R & \quad \text{by definition.} \quad \text{[QED]}
\end{aligned}
$$

Example 11. Let S be the space defined by

set
a, b, c: **integer**
end,

and let R be the relation

$$R = \{(s,s') \mid a(s') = b(s) + a(s)\}.$$

R may be written as the relational product of the function

$$f = \{(s,s') \mid a(s') = b(s) + a(s) \wedge c(s') = c(s) \wedge b(s') = b(s)\}$$

and the equivalence relation

$$R_1 = \{(s,s') \mid a(s') = a(s)\}.$$

Because R_1 is an equivalence relation, it is regular. Hence, by this proposition, so is R. □

The above proposition is useful since it is usual to encounter relations that are written as the conjunction of several predicates with the form

$$x(s') = h(s),$$

where x is a variable of the space at hand, and h is a function. If we have such a conjunct for each variable of state s', then the resulting relation is regular since it is deterministic. What this proposition provides is that we have a regular relation even when not all variables of state s' are specified.

Necessary conditions

- *Proposition 11.* If R is regular then $R * R\hat{}$ and $R\hat{} * R$ are transitive.

Proof. First we prove that if R is regular then $R * R\hat{}$ is transitive:

$$(R * R\hat{}) * (R * R\hat{}) \subseteq (R * R\hat{} * R) * R\hat{} \qquad \text{associativity}$$
$$\subseteq R * R\hat{} \qquad \text{regularity} \qquad \text{[QED]}$$

Second, we prove that if R is regular then $R\hat{} * R$ is transitive:

$$(R\hat{} * R) * (R\hat{} * R) \subseteq R\hat{} * (R * R\hat{} * R) \qquad \text{associativity}$$
$$\subseteq R\hat{} * R \qquad \text{regularity} \qquad \text{[QED]}$$

In practice, if we find that $R * R\hat{}$ or $R\hat{} * R$ are not transitive, then we can conclude that R is not regular. Also, by their very construction, relations $R * R\hat{}$ and $R\hat{} * R$ are symmetric and reflexive (on their domains). Hence, when R is regular, these relations are actually equivalences.

Necessary and sufficient conditions. Relation R on S is said to be *uniform* if and only if

$$(\forall u, v \in \text{dom}(R): u \cdot R \cap v \cdot R \neq \varnothing \Rightarrow u \cdot R = v \cdot R).$$

A uniform relation is one whose image sets, for any two elements, are either disjoint or identical.

- *Proposition 12.* R is regular if and only if it is uniform.

Proof of sufficiency. Let R be uniform, and let (s, s') be in $R * R\hat{} * R$. There exists u, v such that

$$(s, u) \in R \land (v, u) \in R \land (v, s') \in R.$$

Because it includes u, $s \cdot R \cap v \cdot R$ is not empty. By virtue of uniformity, we have

$$s \cdot R = v \cdot R.$$

Because $s' \in v \cdot R$, it also belongs to $s \cdot R$. Hence $(s, s') \in R$.   [QED]

Proof of necessity. Let R be regular and let u and v be two elements of its domain such that

$$u \cdot R \cap v \cdot R \neq \emptyset.$$

Let w be an element of $u \cdot R \cap v \cdot R$, and let z be an element of $u \cdot R$:

$(v, w) \in R,$
$(w, u) \in R\hat{},$
$(u, z) \in R.$

Hence $(v, z) \in R * R\hat{} * R$; because R is regular, $(v, z) \in R$. We have deduced $(v, z) \in R$ from $(u, z) \in R$. Hence $u \cdot R \subseteq v \cdot R$. Because u and v play symmetric roles, we have $u \cdot R = v \cdot R$.   [QED]

Example 12. Let S be the set of integer arrays (in the Pascal sense) of size n and let R be the relation

$$R = \{(s, s') | \text{sum}(s') = \text{sum}(s) \wedge \text{sorted}(s')\}.$$

Let u, v be elements of S such that

$$u \cdot R \cap v \cdot R \neq \emptyset.$$

Then,

$u \cdot R = \{s | (\text{sum}(s) = \text{sum}(u)) \wedge \text{sorted}(s)\},$
$v \cdot R = \{s | (\text{sum}(s) = \text{sum}(v)) \wedge \text{sorted}(s)\}.$

If $s_0 \in u \cdot R \cap v \cdot R$, then

$\text{sum}(s_0) = \text{sum}(u) \wedge \text{sorted}(s_0) \wedge \text{sum}(s_0) = \text{sum}(v) \wedge \text{sorted}(s_0)$
$\Rightarrow \text{sum}(u) = \text{sum}(v)$
$\Rightarrow u \cdot R = v \cdot R.$

Hence, this relation is regular.   □
   A relation R is said to be a *quasi-function* if and only if there exist two functions f and g such that $R = f * g\hat{}$.

● *Proposition 13*. Relation R is regular if and only it is a quasi-function.

Proof of sufficiency. Let R be written as $R = f * g\hat{}$. Then

$R * R\hat{} * R$
$= f * g\hat{} * g * f\hat{} * f * g\hat{}$
$\subseteq f * f\hat{} * f * g\hat{}$ since g is deterministic

$\subseteq f * g\hat{}$ since f is deterministic
$= R$ by assumption.   [QED]

Then, R is regular.

Proof of necessity. Let R be regular, and let k_R and k'_R be the following functions:

$$k_R = \{(s,p) \wedge p = s \cdot R\},$$

and

$$k'_R = \{(s,p) \wedge p = R \cdot s\}.$$

By definition, k_R maps each element of dom(R) into its image set by R, and k'_R maps each element of rng(R) into its antecedent set by R. We define the following relation on $\mathbf{P}(S)$ (the power set of S):

$$h = \{(p,p') | \exists s \in p, \ \exists s' \in p' : (s,s') \in R\}.$$

It is useful to note that h can be written simply as $k_R\hat{} * R * k'_R$. We pose:

$$f = k_R * h,$$
$$g = k'_R.$$

We must prove the two following lemmas:

(a) f is a function;
(b) $R = f * g\hat{}$.   [QED]

Proof of (a)

$f\hat{} * f = h\hat{} * k_R\hat{} * k_R * h$
$\quad\quad \subseteq h\hat{} * h$ determinacy of k_R
$\quad\quad \subseteq I$ determinacy of h.

The proof of the determinacy of h depends on the following property: $k_R\hat{} * R$ is deterministic due to the definition of k_R and to the uniformity of $R\hat{}$.   [QED]

Proof of (b)

$f * g\hat{}$
$= k_R * h * k'_R\hat{}$ by definition of f and g
$= k_R * k_R\hat{} * R * k'_R * k'_R\hat{}$ by definition of h
$= (R * R\hat{}) * R * (R\hat{} * R)$ by the definition of k_R, $k_R * k_R\hat{} = R * R\hat{}$
$= R$ by regularity of R.   [QED]

Remark. Regular relations were arrived at by three different directions, using three different definitions. The propositions above establish the equivalence of these definitions.   □

Remark. One of the most intriguing properties that we have found in regular relations is the capacity to be written as $f * g\hat{}$, where f and g are functions. This is intriguingly similar to the capacity of rational numbers to be written as p/q where p and q are integers. Hence, we would see a parallel between arbitrary relations and real numbers, deterministic relations (i.e. functions) and integers, and regular relations and rational numbers. The analogy goes even further: the decomposition given in the proof of Proposition 13 is minimal, in the sense that other decompositions can be obtained by posing

$$f' = f * l,$$
$$g' = g * l,$$

for some function l that meets some properties (not detailed here). This is similar to minimal decomposition of rational numbers to an irreducible fraction of two integers.   □

1.2.4   Relational Calculus

In this section, we define relational equations which will be used in the remainder of this book. It is not our intent to introduce an axiomatic definition of the relational calculus; the list given below is not supposed to be complete; nor is it minimal (i.e. free from redundancy). The arrangement of this list is inspired by Gries (1981).

1. *Commutative laws:*
   C1. $R \cap R' = R' \cap R$.
   C2. $R \cup R' = R' \cup R$.
2. *Associative laws:*
   A1. $(R \cap R') \cap R'' = R \cap (R' \cap R'')$.
   A2. $(R \cup R') \cup R'' = R \cup (R' \cup R'')$.
   A3. $(R * R') * R'' = R * (R' * R'')$.
3. *Distributive laws:*
   D1. $R * (R' \cap R'') = R * R' \cap R * R''$.
   D2. $R * (R' \cup R'') = R * R' \cup R * R''$.
   D3. $R \cup (R' \cap R'') = (R \cup R') \cap (R \cup R'')$.
   D4. $R \cap (R' \cup R'') = (R \cap R') \cup (R \cap R'')$.
4. *Identity laws:*
   I1. $R \cup \phi = R$.

I2. $R \cap U = R$.

I3. $R * I = R$.

I4. $I * R = R$.

5. *Inversion laws:*

V1. $R^{\smallfrown\smallfrown} = R$.

V2. $(R * R')^{\smallfrown} = R'^{\smallfrown} * R^{\smallfrown}$.

V3. $I^{\smallfrown} = I$.

V4. $U^{\smallfrown} = U$.

V5. $\phi^{\smallfrown} = \phi$.

6. *Absorption laws:*

S1. $R \cap \phi = \phi$.

S2. $R \cup U = U$.

S3. $R * \phi = \phi$.

S4. $\phi * R = \phi$.

7. *Monotonicity laws:*

M1. $R \subseteq R' \Rightarrow R * R'' \subseteq R' * R''$.

M2. $R \subseteq R' \Rightarrow R'' * R \subseteq R'' * R'$.

M3. $R \subseteq R' \Rightarrow R^{\smallfrown} \subseteq R'^{\smallfrown}$.

8. *Transitive closure laws:*

T1. $(R^{+})^{2} \subseteq R^{+}$.

T2. $I \cup (R^{*})^{2} \subseteq R^{*}$.

T3. $R * R \subseteq R \Rightarrow R^{+} = R \wedge R^{*} = I \cup R$.

T4. $I \cup R * R \subseteq R \Rightarrow R^{*} = R$.

9. *Restriction laws:*

R1. $I(\mathrm{dom}(R)) * R = R$.

R2. $R * I(\mathrm{rng}(R)) = R$.

R3. $\mathrm{dom}(R) \subseteq S' \Rightarrow I(S') * R = R$.

R4. $\mathrm{rng}(R) \subseteq S' \Rightarrow R * I(S') = R$.

R5. $\mathrm{dom}(R) \cap S' = \phi \Rightarrow I(S') * R = \phi$.

We will use these formulas throughout this book without explicit reference to them.

1.2.5 Exercises

1[A] Let S be $\{a, b, c, d, e, f\}$ and S' be $\{b, c, d, e\}$. Compute the following relations:

(a) $V(S)$.

(b) $V(S')$.

(c) $I(S) - U(S')$.

(d) $I(S) - V(S')$.

(e) $I(S') - U(S)$.

2[A]   Let S be $\{a,b,c,d,e,f\}$ and S' be $\{b,c,d,e\}$. Compute the following sets:
   (a) $b \cdot I(S) \cup b \cdot U(S) - b \cdot V(S)$.
   (b) $a \cdot U(S) - a \cdot U(S')$.
   (c) $a \cdot U(S'')$.
   (d) $c \cdot V(S'')$.
   (e) $\text{dom}(U(S'')) - \text{rng}(V(S''))$.

3[A]   Let S be **natural** and R be $\{(s,s')|s<s'\}$:
   (a) Compute R^-.
   (b) Compute $R^\wedge$.
   (c) Compute $R \cup R^\wedge$, and simplify.
   (d) Compute $R \cap R^\wedge$.
   (e) Compute R^2.

4[A]   Let S be **real** and R be $\{(s,s')|s<s'\}$:
   (a) Compute R^-.
   (b) Compute $R^\wedge$.
   (c) Compute $R \cup R^\wedge$, and simplify.
   (d) Compute $R \cap R^\wedge$.
   (e) Compute R^2.

5[A]   Let S be **natural** and R be $\{(s,s')|s'=s+1\}$:
   (a) Compute R^2.
   (b) Compute R^i, $i \geq 2$.
   (c) Compute R^+.
   (d) Compute R^*.

6[A]   Let S be **real** and R be $\{(s,s')|s'=s+1\}$:
   (a) Compute R^2.
   (b) Compute R^i, $i \geq 2$.
   (c) Compute R^+.
   (d) Compute R^*.

7[A]   Let S be $\{a,b,c,d,e\}$ and R be $\{(a,b),\ (b,c),\ (c,d),\ (d,e),\ (e,a)\}$:
   (a) Compute R^0, R^1, R^2, R^3, R^4 and R^5.
   (b) Deduce a formula for R^i, for $i \geq 0$.
   (c) Compute R^+, and simplify its expression.
   (d) Compute R^*, and simplify its expression.

8[A]   Let S be $\{a,b,c,d,e\}$ and R be $\{(a,b),\ (b,c),\ (c,d),\ (d,e)\}$:
   (a) Compute R^0, R^1, R^2, R^3, R^4 and R^5.
   (b) Deduce a formula for R^i, for $i \geq 0$.
   (c) Compute R^+, and simplify its expression.
   (d) Compute R^*, and simplify its expression.

9[B]   Let S be **natural** and R be $\{(s,s')|s'=s+1\}$:
   (a) Compute $\text{rng}(R)$ and $\text{dom}(R)$.

(b) Compute $R * R\hat{}$, and simplify its expression.

(c) Compute $R\hat{} * R$, and simplify its expression.

(d) For a given relation R, what can you say, in general, of $R * R\hat{}$?

(e) For a given relation R, what can you say, in general, of $R\hat{} * R$?

10[A] Let S be **natural** and R be $\{(s, s') | s \le s' \le s + 2\}$:

(a) Compute $\text{dom}(R)$, $\text{rng}(R)$.

(b) Compute $R\hat{}$, $\text{dom}(R\hat{})$ and $\text{rng}(R\hat{})$.

(c) Compute $R * R\hat{}$.

(d) Compute $R\hat{} * R$.

11[A] Let S be **natural** and R be $\{(s, s') | s' = s + 1\}$. Let *odd* and *even* be the predicates on S defined by

$$\text{odd}(s) = (s \bmod 2 = 1),$$
$$\text{even}(s) = (s \bmod 2 = 0).$$

(a) Compute $I(\text{odd}) * R$.

(b) Compute $I(\text{even}) * R$.

(c) Compute $R * I(\text{odd})$.

(d) Compute $R * I(\text{even})$.

(e) Compute $I(\text{odd}) * R \cup R * I(\text{odd})$.

12[A] Let S be **natural** and R be $\{(s, s') | s' = s + 4\}$. Let *gt3* be the predicate on S defined by

$$gt3(s) = (s > 3).$$

(a) Compute $I(gt3) * R$.

(b) Compute $R * I(gt3)$.

(c) Compute $I(gt3) * R\hat{} * R * I(gt3)$.

(d) Compute $I(gt3) * R\hat{} * R$.

(e) Compute $R\hat{} * I(gt3) * R$.

13[A] For each relation R below, compute the nucleus of R, $N(R)$, then the kernel of R, $K(R)$. Are they equal?

(a) $S = \{0, 1, 2, 3, 4, 5, 6\}$,
    $R = \{(0, 1), (0, 2), (0, 3), (3, 3), (3, 4), (4, 4), (4, 5), (4, 6)\}$.

(b) $S = \{0, 1, 2, 3, 4, 5, 6\}$,
    $R = \{(0, 0), (0, 1), (0, 2), (2, 0), (2, 1), (2, 2), (3, 3), (4, 3)\}$.

(c) S = **set**
      a, b, c: **integer**
    end,
    $R = \{(s, s') | a(s') = a(s)\}$.

(d) S = **set**
      a, b, c: **integer**

end,
$$R = \{(s, s') \mid a(s') \geq a(s)\}.$$
(e) S = **set**
   a, b, c: **integer**
   end,
$$R = \{(s, s') \mid a(s') + b(s') = a(s) + b(s)\}.$$

14[A] What equivalence properties (reflexivity, symmetry, transitivity or equivalence) do the following relations on S have?
(a) $V(S)$.
(b) ϕ.
(c) $U(S')$, where S' is a proper subset of S.
(d) $I(S) \cup V(S')$.
(e) $I(S') \cup V(S)$.

15[A] What equivalence properties (reflexivity, symmetry, transitivity or equivalence) do the following relations have?
(a) $R = \{(a, a), (b, b)\}$ on $S = \{a, b, c\}$.
(b) $R = \{(a, a), (b, b)\}$ on $S = \{a, b\}$.
(c) $R = \{(a, a), (a, b), (b, a), (b, b)\}$ on $S = \{a, b, c\}$.
(d) $R = \{(a, a), (a, b), (b, a), (b, b)\}$ on $S = \{a, b\}$.
(e) $R = \{(a, a), (a, b), (b, a), (b, b), (c, c)\}$ on $S = \{a, b, c\}$.

16[A] What equivalence properties (reflexivity, symmetry, transitivity or equivalence) do the following relations have on set

   S = **set**
      a, b, c: **natural**
   end?

(a) $R = \{(s, s') \mid a(s') = a(s)\}$.
(b) $R = \{(s, s') \mid a(s) + b(s) = a(s') + b(s')\}$.
(c) $R = \{(s, s') \mid a(s) + b(s) = a(s') + b(s') \wedge c(s') = c(s)\}$.
(d) $R = \{(s, s') \mid a(s') = a(s) + b(s) \wedge a(s) = a(s') + b(s')\}$.
(e) $R = \{(s, s') \mid a(s) = a(s) + b(s) \wedge a(s') = a(s') + b(s')\}$.

17[A] What ordering properties (antisymmetry, asymmetry, partial ordering, strict partial ordering, total ordering, strict total ordering) do the following relations on S have?
(a) ϕ.
(b) $V(S)$.
(c) $I(S)$.
(d) $I(S')$, where S' is a proper subset of S.
(e) $V(S) \cup I(S')$.

18[B] What ordering properties (antisymmetry, asymmetry, partial ordering, strict partial ordering, total ordering, strict total ordering) do the following relations have on set

```
S = set
  a, b, c: natural
end?
```

(a) $R = \{(s,s')|a(s) \leq a(s') \lor a(s') = a(s) \land b(s) \leq b(s') \lor$
$\qquad a(s') = a(s) \land b(s') = b(s) \land c(s) \leq c(s')\}$.

(b) $R = \{(s,s')|a(s) \leq a(s') \land b(s') = b(s) \land c(s) = c(s')\}$.

(c) $R = \{(s,s')|a(s) \leq a(s')\}$.

(d) $R = \{(s,s')|a(s) \leq b(s') \land b(s) = b(s') \land c(s') \leq c(s)\}$.

(e) $R = \{(s,s')|a(s) < b(s') \land b(s) < b(s') \land c(s) < c(s')\}$.

19[B] For each relation R given below, give a simple expression for $ub(s,s')$, $lb(s,s')$, $lub(s,s')$ and $glb(s,s')$, where s and s' are two elements of S. Say whether R is a lattice, and prove your claim:

(a) $S =$ **integer**; $R = \leq$.

(b) $S = \mathbf{P}(S')$, for some non-empty set S'; $R = \subseteq$.

(c) $S = \{\text{persons}\}$; $R = \{(s,s')|s' \text{ is an ancestor of } s\}$.

(d) $S = \{a,b,c,d,e,f\}$,
$\qquad R = \{(a,b),\ (b,c),\ (a,d),\ (b,e),\ (c,f),\ (d,e),\ (e,f)\}^*$.

(e) $S = \{a,b,c,d,e,f\}$,
$\qquad R = \{(c,a),\ (d,a),\ (d,b),\ (e,b),\ (f,c),\ (f,d),\ (g,d)\}^*$.

20[B] Give an example of relation R on some set S such that for any (s,s') $ub(s,s')$ and $lb(s,s')$ are not empty, but R is not a lattice.

21[A] Determine whether the following relations are well-founded orderings:

(a) $S =$ **natural**; $R = <$.

(b) $S =$ **natural**; $R = \leq$.

(c) $S =$ **natural**; $R = >$.

(d) $S =$ **natural**; $R = \{(s,s') \land s' = s + 1\}$.

(e) $S =$ **natural**; $R = \{(s,s') \land s = s' + 1\}$.

22[B] Determine whether the following relations are well-founded orderings:

(a) $S =$ **integer**; $R = <$.

(b) $S = \{\text{positive reals}\}$; $R = <$.

(c) $S = \{\text{positive reals}\}$; $R = \{(s,s')|s' = s + 1\}$.

(d) $S = \{\text{positive reals}\}$; $R = \{(s,s')|s' = s + 1\}^+$.

(e) $S = \{\text{positive reals}\}$; $R = \{(s,s')|s' = s + 1\}^*$.

23[B] Determine whether the following relations on set

```
S = set
  a, b, c: natural
end
```

are deterministic. In order to do so, compute their co-nuclei:

(a) $R = \{(s, s') \mid a(s') = a(s) \wedge b(s') = b(s) \wedge c(s') = a(s) + b(s)\}$.
(b) $R = \{(s, s') \mid a(s') = a(s) + b(s) \wedge a(s) = a(s') - b(s')$
$\wedge\; c(s') = a(s')\}$.
(c) $R = \{(s, s') \mid a(s) + b(s) = a(s') + b(s') \wedge c(s') = c(s)\}$.
(d) $R = \{(s, s') \mid a(s) = b(s) + c(s) \wedge a(s') = b(s') + c(s')\}$.
(e) $R = \{(s, s') \mid a(s') = 1 \wedge b(s') = 2 \wedge c(s') = 3\}$.

24[B] For

```
S = set
  a, b, c: natural
end,
```

and for each pair of relations R and R', compute the co-nuclei of R and R' and determine which one, if any, is more-deterministic than the other:

(a) $R = \{(s, s') \mid a(s') = a(s) \wedge b(s') = b(s) \wedge c(s')$
$= a(s) * b(s)\}$,
$R' = \{(s, s') \mid c(s') = a(s) * b(s)\}$.
(b) $R = \{(s, s') \mid a(s') = a(s) \wedge b(s') = b(s) \wedge c(s')$
$= a(s) * b(s)\}$,
$R' = \{(s, s') \mid c(s') = a(s) = b(s)\}$.
(c) $R = \{(s, s') \mid a(s') = a(s) \wedge c(s') = a(s) * b(s)\}$,
$R' = \{(s, s') \mid c(s') = c(s)\}$.
(d) $R = \{(s, s') \mid a(s) + b(s) = a(s') + b(s')\}$,
$R' = \{(s, s') \mid a(s') = a(s) \wedge b(s') = b(s)\}$.
(e) $R = \{(s, s') \mid a(s') = a(s) \wedge b(s') = b(s)\}$,
$R' = \{(s, s') \mid a(s') = a(s) \wedge c(s') = c(s)\}$.

25[B] Compare the following pairs of relations with respect to definedness. We take

```
S = set
  a, b, c: natural
end.
```

(a) $R = \{(s, s') \mid a(s') = a(s)\}$,
$R' = \{(s, s') \mid a(s') = a(s) \wedge b(s') = b(s)\}$.
(b) $R = \{(s, s') \mid a(s') = a(s)\}$,
$R' = \{(s, s') \mid a(s') = a(s) + 1\}$.
(c) $R = \{(s, s') \mid a(s') = a(s) \wedge b(s') = b(s)$
$\wedge\; c(s') = a(s) + b(s)\}$,
$R' = \{(s, s') \mid a(s) = b(s) \wedge a(s') = a(s) \wedge b(s') = b(s)$
$\wedge\; c(s') = a(s) + b(s)\}$.
(d) $R = \{(s, s') \mid a(s') = a(s) \wedge b(s') = b(s)$
$\wedge\; c(s') = a(s) + b(s)\}$,

$$R' = \{(s,s')\,|\,a(s') = a(s) \wedge b(s') = b(s) \wedge c(s')$$
$$= a(s) + b(s) \wedge c(s') > a(s')\}.$$

(e) $R = \{(s,s')\,|\,a(s') = a(s) \wedge c(s') = a(s) + b(s)\}$,
$R' = \{(s,s')\,|\,a(s') = a(s) \wedge c(s') = a(s) * b(s)\}$.

26[B] Compare the following pairs of relations on S = **real** with respect to definition:

(a) $R = \{(s,s')\,|\,s - 1 \leq s' \leq s + 2\}$; $R' = \{(s,s')\,|\,s \leq s' \leq s + 1\}$.

(b) $R = \{(s,s')\,|\,s > 0 \wedge s - 1 \leq s' \leq s + 2\}$;
$$R' = \{(s,s')\,|\,s - 1 \leq s' \leq s + 2\}.$$

(c) $R = \{(s,s')\,|\,s - 1 \leq s' \leq s + 2\}$;
$$R' = \{(s,s')\,|\,s > 0 \wedge s' = s + 2\}.$$

(d) $R = \{(s,s')\,|\,s \leq s' \leq s + 1\}$;
$$R' = \{(s,s')\,|\,s \leq s' \leq s + 1 \wedge s' > 0\}.$$

(e) $R = \{(s,s')\,|\,s \leq s' \leq s + 2\}$; $R' = \{(s,s')\,|\,s - 2 \leq s' \leq s\}$.

27[B] Determine whether the following relations are regular; if they are, give a possible decomposition as $f * g\hat{\ }$. We take

S = **set**
    a, b, c: **natural**
end.

(a) $R = \{(s,s')\,|\,a(s') + b(s') = a(s)\}$.

(b) $R = \{(s,s')\,|\,a(s') + b(s') = a(s) \wedge b(s) = 0\}$.

(c) $R = \{(s,s')\,|\,a(s') + b(s') = a(s) \wedge c(s') = 0\}$.

(d) $R = \{(s,s')\,|\,a(s') + b(s) = a(s) + b(s')\}$.

(e) $R = \{(s,s')\,|\,c(s') = a(s') + b(s') \wedge a(s) = b(s) + c(s)\}$.

28[B] Determine whether the following relations are regular; if they are, give a possible decomposition as $f * g\hat{\ }$:

(a) $S = \{0,1,2,3,4,5,6\}$,
$$R = \{(0,1),\,(0,2),\,(0,3),\,(3,3),\,(3,4),\,(4,4),\,(4,5),\,(4,6)\}.$$

(b) $S = \{0,1,2,3,4,5,6\}$,
$$R = \{(0,0),\,(0,1),\,(0,2),\,(2,0),\,(2,1),\,(2,2),\,(3,3),\,(4,3)\}.$$

(c) S = **set**
    a, b, c: **integer**
end,
$$R = \{(s,s')\,|\,a(s') = a(s)\}.$$

(d) S = **set**
    a, b, c: **integer**
end,
$$R = \{(s,s')\,|\,a(s') \leq a(s)\}.$$

(e) S = **set**
    a, b, c: **integer**
end,
$$R = \{(s,s')\,|\,a(s') + b(s') = a(s) + b(s)\}.$$

1.3 FUNCTIONS

1.3.1 Definition and Representation

A function f is, as we recall, a deterministic relation, i.e. a relation such that $f\hat{\ }*f \subseteq I$. We admit without proof that for a function f and a state s, $s \cdot f$ is a singleton. By abuse of notation, we use $s \cdot f$ to denote not only the singleton itself but also (sometimes) its unique element, commonly denoted by $f(s)$.

The function f on the set of natural numbers, defined by

$$f = \{(1,2),\ (2,3),\ (3,4),\ (4,5),\ (5,6)\}$$

cannot be represented merely by the *expression* $E(s) = s + 1$, because expression E does not carry information about the domain of f; we choose to represent f by the formula $[1 \le s \le 5,\ s + 1]$. Generally, we may want to represent a function f on S in the form $[p, E]$, where p is a predicate on S and E is an expression whose domain of definition is a subset of $S|p$. This representation is called the *pE-formula* of function f; it is defined as

$$[p, E] = \{(s, s')\,|\,p(s)\ \wedge\ s' = E(s)\}.$$

1.3.2 Operations on Functions

Among the operations on relations introduced in Section 1.2.2, three are particularly useful in the manipulation of functions. We describe them here using the *pE*-notation.

Union. The union of two functions $f = [p, E]$ and $f' = [p', E']$ is not a function unless the following condition is verified:

$$(\forall s, p(s)\ \wedge\ p'(s) \Rightarrow E(s) = E'(s)). \tag{C}$$

This condition means that f and f' map all states in $\text{dom}(f) \cap \text{dom}(f')$ into the same images. When this condition is satisfied, the union of f and f' is

$$[p, E] \cup [p', E'] = [p \vee p',\ \mathbf{alt}(p, E, E')].$$

It is easy to convince oneself that, under Condition (C), the expressions $\mathbf{alt}(p, E, E')$ and $\mathbf{alt}(p', E', E)$ are interchangeable in the operation above; hence the formula above is indeed symmetric with respect to f and f', as it should be. It is worth drawing the reader's attention to the distinction between the (set-theoretic) *union* of *functions* and the (algorithmic) *alternation* of *expressions*.

Example 13

S = **integer**

$$f = [-5 \leq s \leq 2, 3s^2],$$
$$f' = [0 \leq s \leq 8, s^3 + 2s].$$

Condition (C) is:

$$-5 \leq s \leq 2 \ \wedge \ 0 \leq s \leq 8 \Rightarrow 3s^2 = s^3 + 2s$$

$\Leftrightarrow$

$$0 \leq s \leq 2 \Rightarrow 3s^2 = s^3 + 2s$$

$\Leftrightarrow$

true.

The union of f and f' is then

$$[-5 \leq s \leq 8, \mathbf{alt}(-5 \leq s \leq 2, 3s^2, s^3 + 2s)]. \qquad \square$$

Intersection. The intersection of two functions $f = [p, E]$ and $f' = [p', E']$ is a function. We have

$$[p, E] \cap [p', E'] = [p \wedge p' \wedge E(s) = E'(s), E(s)].$$

In order for $s \in S$ to be in $\text{dom}(f \cap f')$, s has to be in $\text{dom}(f)$ (hence $p(s)$), and in $\text{dom}(f')$ (hence $p'(s)$); in addition, f and f' have to map s into the same image (hence $E(s) = E'(s)$). It is worth noting that the rightmost instance of expression $E(s)$ in the above equation can be replaced by $E'(s)$; hence the above formula is indeed symmetric with respect to f and f', as it should be.

Example 14

S = **integer**

$$f = [0 \leq s \leq 12, 3s^2],$$
$$f' = [0 \leq s \leq 5, s^3 + 2s].$$

Then $f \cap f'$

$$= [0 \leq s \leq 12 \ \wedge \ 0 \leq s \leq 5 \ \wedge \ 3s^2 = s^3 + 2s, 3s^2]$$
$$= [0 \leq s \leq 5 \ \wedge \ 3s^2 = s^3 + 2s, 3s^2]$$
$$= [0 \leq s \leq 2, 3s^2]$$

or, equivalently,

$$= [0 \leq s \leq 2, s^3 + 2s]. \qquad \square$$

Relational Product. The relational product of two functions $f = [p, E]$ and $f' = [p', E']$ is a function. We have

$$[p, E] * [p', E'] = [p(s) \land p'(E(s)), E' \cdot E(s)].$$

In order for s to belong to $\text{dom}(f * f')$, s must belong to $\text{dom}(f)$ (hence $p(s)$) and its image by f must belong to $\text{dom}(f')$ (hence $p'(E(s))$). As for $s \cdot f * f'$, it is computed by applying E to s then E' to the result, i.e. by applying $E' \cdot E$ to s. It is worth noting the distinction between the (set-theoretic) *relational product* of *functions f* and *f'* and the (algorithmic) *composition* of *expressions E* and *E'*. Note also that the composition of expressions is performed in reverse order of the relational product of functions.

Example 15

> S = **integer**
>
> $f = [0 \leq s \leq 5, s + 2]$,
> $f' = [0 \leq s \leq 5, s - 1]$,
> $f * f' = [0 \leq s \leq 5 \land 0 \leq s + 2 \leq 5, s + 1]$,
> $\quad\quad = [0 \leq s \leq 3, s + 1]$,
> $f' * f = [0 \leq s \leq 5 \land 0 \leq s - 1 \leq 5, s + 1]$
> $\quad\quad = [1 \leq s \leq 5, s + 1]$. □

In addition to the three operations given above which combine two functions in order to produce another function, we now introduce the operation of *nucleus* which generates a relation (an equivalence relation, in fact) from a function.

Nucleus. The nucleus of function f is, as we recall from Section 1.2.2,

$$N(f) = f * f^{\frown}.$$

This relation can be written (perhaps more expressively) as

$$N(f) = \{(s, s') \mid f(s) = f(s')\}.$$

It is straightforward to prove that $N(f)$ is an equivalence relation on $\text{dom}(f)$. The equivalence classes of $\text{dom}(f)$ modulo $N(f)$ are called the *level sets* of f; in each level set, all elements have the same image by f. It is trivial to see that if f is a function then the nucleus of f and the kernel of f are identical.

1.3.3 Properties of Functions

We wish to introduce a property that measures how *injective* a function is, i.e. how much f discriminates among its arguments. The more a function discriminates among its arguments, the more information the knowledge of $s \cdot f$ carries about s.

Example 16

$$f = \{(a,0), (b,1), (c,2), (d,3), (e,3)\},$$
$$f' = \{(a,0), (b,1), (c,1), (d,2), (e,2)\}.$$

Function f discriminates more among its arguments than does f'; e.g. if $s \cdot f = \{1\}$, then one can conclude that $s = b$, whereas if $s \cdot f' = \{1\}$, one can only conclude as much information as: $s \in \{b,c\}$.   □

Function f is said to be *more-injective* than function f' if and only if

$$N(f) \subseteq N(f').$$

Intuitive interpretation. If $(s,s') \in f*f^\wedge$, then $(s,s') \in f'*f'^\wedge$, i.e. if s and s' have the same image by f then they have the same image by f'; i.e. if f does not discriminate between s and s' then neither does f'. Note that f is more injective than f^1

$\Leftrightarrow$

$$f*f^\wedge \subseteq f'*f'^\wedge$$

$\Leftrightarrow$

$$(\forall s,s' \in \mathrm{dom}(f), f(s) = f(s') \Rightarrow f'(s) = f'(s'))$$

$\Leftrightarrow$

$$(\forall s,s' \in \mathrm{dom}(f), f'(s) \neq f'(s') \Rightarrow f(s) \neq f(s')).$$

Note that f is more-injective than f' if and only if $f^\wedge$ is more-deterministic than $f'^\wedge$.

Example 17. We consider functions f and f' of Example 16 and compute their nuclei, say R and R':

$$R = \{(a,a), (b,b), (c,c), (d,d), (e,d), (d,e), (e,e)\},$$
$$R' = \{(a,a), (b,b), (b,c), (c,b), (c,c), (d,d), (d,e), (e,d), (e,e)\}.$$

R is a subset of R'. The level sets of f are

$$\{a\}, \{b\}, \{c\}, \{d,e\},$$

whereas the level sets of f' are

$$\{a\}, \{b,c\}, \{d,e\}.$$ □

Let f and f' be two functions with the same domain. The intuition that one gets about the relational more-injective suggests that if f is more-injective than f', then f' can be obtained by multiplying (relational product) f to the right by some function k: if f discriminates between arguments x and y while f' does not, then k maps $f(x)$ and $f(y)$ into

$f'(x)(=f'(y))$. Function k will be all the more *injective* that the difference in injectivity between f and f' will be larger. The following proposition confirms this intuition and its proof gives a formula for k:

- *Proposition 14.* If $\text{dom}(f) = \text{dom}(f')$ and f is *more-injective* than f', then there exists a function k such that $f' = f * k$.

Proof. Let k be $f^\wedge * f'$. We wish to prove two lemmas: first, that k is deterministic; second, that $f' = f * k$.
Determinacy of k. We compute the co-nucleus of k:

$$
\begin{aligned}
&k^\wedge * k\\
&= f'^\wedge * f * f^\wedge * f' && \text{by the inversion laws}\\
&\subseteq f'^\wedge * f' * f'^\wedge * f' && \text{for } f \text{ is more injective than } f'\\
&\subseteq I && \text{for } f' \text{ is a function.}
\end{aligned}
$$

Now we prove that $f' = f * k$:

$$
\begin{aligned}
&f * k\\
&= f * f^\wedge * f' && \text{by definition of } k\\
&\subseteq f' && \text{because } f \text{ is a function.}
\end{aligned}
$$

On the other hand, let (s, s') be an element of f'; $s \in \text{dom}(f')$, then $s \in \text{dom}(f)$. Let s'' be in the same level set of f as s; we have $(s, s'') \in f * f^\wedge$. Because f is more-injective than f', we have $(s, s'') \in f' * f'^\wedge$. Hence $f'(s'') = f'(s) = s'$. From $(s, s'') \in f * f^\wedge$ and $(s'', s') \in f'$ we deduce $(s, s') \in f * f^\wedge * f'$, i.e. $(s, s') \in f * k$. We have deduced $(s, s') \in f * k$ from $(s, s') \in f'$. Hence $f' \subseteq f * k$.   [QED]

The relational *more-injective* (as a relation) is reflexive and transitive. The example below shows that it is not symmetric.

Example 18

$$
\begin{aligned}
f &= \{(a, 0), (b, 1), (c, 1)\},\\
f' &= \{(a, 1), (b, 0), (c, 0)\}.\\
f * f^\wedge &= \{(a, a), (b, b), (c, c), (c, b), (b, c)\},\\
f' * f'^\wedge &= \{(a, a), (b, b), (c, c), (c, b), (b, c)\}.
\end{aligned}
$$

We do have $f * f^\wedge \subseteq f' * f'^\wedge$ and $f' * f'^\wedge \subseteq f * f^\wedge$; yet $f \neq f'$.   □

A function f is said to be *injective* if and only if it is *more-injective* than I; in other words, f is injective if and only if $f * f^\wedge \subseteq I$.

Example 19

$$
f = \{(a, 0), (b, 1), (c, 2)\}; \quad f * f^\wedge = \{(a, a), (b, b), (c, c)\} \subseteq I;
$$
f is injective.

$f' = \{(a,0),\ (b,1),\ (c,1)\};$
$f' * f'^\wedge = \{(a,a),\ (b,b),\ (b,c),\ (c,b),\ (c,c)\} \nsubseteq I;$
f' is not injective.   □

Note that a function f is injective if and only if its inverse $f^\wedge$ is deterministic.

When f is more-injective than f' and f' is more-injective than f and $\mathrm{dom}(f) = \mathrm{dom}(f')$, we say that f and f' are equally injective; we cannot conclude that f and f' are identical. The precise nature of the relationship linking f and f' is highlighted in the following proposition.

● *Proposition 15.* If f and f' are equally injective, then there exists an injective function k such that $f' = f * k$.

Proof. In reference to the proof of Proposition 14, we merely prove that $k = f^\wedge * f'$ is injective. We compute its nucleus:

$k * k^\wedge$
$= f^\wedge * f' * f'^\wedge * f$ by definition of k
$\subseteq f^\wedge * f * f^\wedge * f$ because f' is more-injective than f
$\subseteq I.$ because f is deterministic.   □

1.3.4 Exercises

1[A] Determine, by computing their co-nuclei, whether the following relations on

       S = **set**
         a, b, c: **natural**
       end

are functions. If they are, give their pE-formula:
(a) $R = \{(s,s')\,|\,a(s') = a(s) \wedge b(s') = b(s) - 1$
$\wedge\ c(s') = c(s) + a(s)\}.$
(b) $R = \{(s,s')\,|\,a(s') + b(s') = a(s) + b(s) - 1$
$\wedge\ c(s') = c(s) + a(s)\}.$
(c) $R = \{(s,s')\,|\,a(s') = 0 \wedge b(s') = b(s) - 1$
$\wedge\ c(s') = c(s) + a(s)\}.$
(d) $R = \{(s,s')\,|\,a(s) + b(s) + c(s) = a(s') + b(s') + c(s')$
$\wedge\ a(s) + c(s) = a(s') + c(s')\}.$
(e) $R = \{(s,s')\,|\,a(s) + b(s) = a(s') + b(s')$
$\wedge\ a(s) - b(s) = a(s') - b(s')$
$\wedge\ a(s) + c(s) = a(s') - c(s')\}.$

2[B] Determine, by computing their co-nuclei, whether the following

relations on S = **real** are functions. If they are, write their *pE*-formulas:
(a) $R = \{(s, s') \mid s > 1 \wedge \log_2(s) < 1 \wedge s' = \log_2(1/s)\}$.
(b) $R = \{(s, s') \mid s > 0 \wedge s'^2 = s\}$.
(c) $R = \{(s, s') \mid s'^2 = s\}$.
(d) $R = \{(s, s') \mid s'^2 = s \wedge s' > 0\}$.
(e) $R = \{(s, s') \mid s'^2 = s^2 \wedge s' < 0\}$.

3[A]   Find a *pE*-formula for the following functions on S = **natural**:
(a) $f = \{(0, 1), (1, 2)\}$.
(b) $f = \{(0, 1), (1, 2), (2, 5), (3, 10), (4, 17)\}$.
(c) $f = \{(0, 0), (1, 0)\}$.
(d) $f = \{(0, -1), (1, 0), (2, 3), (3, 8), (4, 15)\}$.
(e) $f = \{(-1, -1), (0, 0), (1, 1), (2, 512)\}$.

4[A]   If the following pairs of functions on S = **natural** have a deterministic union, then compute it using in turn (i) the set-theoretic representation, and (ii) the *pE*-notation:
(a) $f = \{(0, 1), (1, 2), (2, 3)\}, f' = \{(10, 15), (11, 16), (12, 17)\}$.
(b) $f = \{(-3, 3), (-2, 2), (-1, 1), (0, 0)\},$
     $f' = \{(1, 1), (2, 2), (3, 3)\}$.
(c) $f = \{(-3, 3), (-2, 2), (-1, 1), (0, 0)\},$
     $f' = \{(0, 0), (1, 1), (2, 2), (3, 3)\}$.
(d) $f = \{(-3, 3), (-2, 2), (-1, 1), (0, 0), (1, 1)\},$
     $f' = \{(-1, 1), (0, 0), (1, 1), (2, 2), (3, 3)\}$.
(e) $f = \{(-3, -3), (-2, -2), (-1, -1), (0, 0), (1, 1)\},$
     $f' = \{(-1, 1), (0, 0), (1, 1), (2, 2), (3, 3)\}$.

5[A]   Determine whether the following pairs of functions on S = **natural** have a deterministic union, and eventually compute it using the *pE*-notation:
(a) $f = [0 \le s \le 9, s + 3]; f' = [-10 \le s \le 0, 3]$.
(b) $f = [0 \le s \le 3, s^4 + 11s^2]; f' = [0 \le s \le 3, 6s^3 + 6s]$.
(c) $f = [-9 \le s \le 3, s^4 + 11s^2]; f' = [0 \le s \le 12, 6s^3 + 6s]$.
(d) $f = [-2 \le s \le 10, s^5 + 4s]; f' = [-10 \le s \le 2, 5s^3]$.
(e) $f = [-2 \le s \le 10, 5s^3]; f' = [-10 \le s \le 2, s^5 + 4s]$.

6[A]   Compute the intersection on the following functions on S = **integer**:
(a) $f = [s \ge 0, s^2]; f' = [s < 0, s]$.
(b) $f = [s \ge 0, s^2]; f' = [s \le 0, s]$.
(c) $f = [s \ge 0, s^2]; f' = [s \le 4, s]$.
(d) $f = [s < 1, s^4 + 16]; f' = [s > -1, 17s^2]$.
(e) $f = [s < 5, s^4 + 16]; f' = [s > -5, 17s^2]$.

7[A]   Compute the intersections of the following functions on S = **integer**:

(a) $f = [s \geq -4, s^4 + 26s + 120]$; $f' = [s < -4, 2s^3 + 25s^2]$.
(b) $f = [s \geq -4, s^4 + 26s + 120]$; $f' = [s < -2, 2s^3 + 25s^2]$.
(c) $f = [s \geq -4, s^4 + 26s + 120]$; $f' = [s < +3, 2s^3 + 25s^2]$.
(d) $f = [s \geq -4, s^4 + 26s + 120]$; $f' = [s < +5, 2s^3 + 25s^2]$.
(e) $f = [s \geq -4, s^4 + 26s + 120]$; $f' = [s < 10, 2s^3 + 25s^2]$.

8[A]   For each pair of functions f and f' on set S = **natural**, compute
$f * f'$ then $f' * f$, using (i) the definition of relative product, and
(ii) the pE-formula. Match the results:

(a) $f = \{(2,2), (3,3), (4,4), (5,5)\}$,
$\qquad f' = \{(0,2), (1,3), (2,4), (3,5), (4,6)\}$.

(b) $f = \{(2,2), (3,3), (4,4), (5,5)\}$,
$\qquad f' = \{(0,4), (1,5), (2,6), (3,7), (4,8)\}$.

(c) $f = \{(2,2), (3,3), (4,4), (5,5)\}$,
$\qquad f' = \{(0,6), (1,7), (2,8), (3,9), (4,10)\}$.

(d) $f = \{(0,0), (1,1), (2,2), (3,3), (4,4)\}$,
$\qquad f' = \{(0,6), (1,7), (2,8), (3,9), (4,10)\}$.

(e) $f = \{(6,6), (7,7), (8,8), (9,9), (10,10)\}$,
$\qquad f' = \{(0,6), (1,7), (2,8), (3,9), (4,10)\}$.

9[A]   For each pair of functions f and f' on set S = **natural**, compute
$f * f'$ then $f' * f$, using (i) the definition of relational product, and
(ii) the pE-formula of relational product. Match the results:

(a) $f = \{(0,4), (1,5), (2,6), (3,7)\}$,
$\qquad f' = \{(8,4), (9,5), (10,6), (11,7)\}$.

(b) $f = \{(0,4), (1,5), (2,6), (3,7)\}$,
$\qquad f' = \{(7,3), (8,4), (9,5), (10,6)\}$.

(c) $f = \{(0,4), (1,5), (2,6), (3,7)\}$,
$\qquad f' = \{(6,2), (7,3), (8,4), (9,5)\}$.

(d) $f = \{(0,4), (1,5), (2,6), (3,7)\}$,
$\qquad f' = \{(5,1), (6,2), (7,3), (8,4)\}$.

(e) $f = \{(0,4), (1,5), (2,6), (3,7)\}$,
$\qquad f' = \{(4,0), (5,1), (6,2), (7,3)\}$.

10[A]   Let S be the set

```
S = set
  a, b, c: natural
end.
```

For each pair of functions below, compute $f * f'$ then $f' * f$, using
(i) the definition of relational product, and (ii) the pE-formula
of relational product:

(a) $f = \{(s,s') \mid a(s') = a(s) + b(s) \wedge b(s') = 0 \wedge c(s') = c(s)\}$,
$\qquad f' = \{(s,s') \mid a(s') = a(s) + 1 \wedge b(s') = b(s) - 1$
$\qquad\qquad\qquad \wedge c(s') = c(s)\}$.

(b) $f = \{(s,s') \mid b(s) \neq 0 \wedge a(s') = a(s) + b(s) \wedge b(s') = 0$
$\wedge\ c(s') = c(s)\}$,
$f' = \{(s,s') \mid a(s') = a(s) + 1 \wedge b(s') = b(s) - 1$
$\wedge\ c(s') = c(s)\}$.

(c) $f = \{(s,s') \mid a(s') = a(s) \wedge b(s') = 0$
$\wedge\ c(s') = c(s) + a(s) * b(s)\}$,
$f' = \{(s,s') \mid a(s') = a(s) \wedge b(s') = b(s) - 1$
$\wedge\ c(s') = c(s) + a(s)\}$.

(d) $f = \{(s,s') \mid a(s') = a(s) \wedge b(s') = 0$
$\wedge\ c(s') = c(s) + a(s) * b(s)\}$,
$f' = \{(s,s') \mid b(s) \neq 0 \wedge a(s') = a(s) \wedge b(s') = b(s) - 1$
$\wedge\ c(s') = c(s) + a(s)\}$.

(e) $f = \{(s,s') \mid b(s) \neq 0 \wedge a(s') = a(s) + 1 \wedge b(s') = b(s) - 1$
$\wedge\ c(s') = c(s)\}$,
$f' = \{(s,s') \mid a(s') = a(s) - 1 \wedge b(s') = b(s) + 1$
$\wedge\ c(s') = c(s)\}$.

11[A] For each relation R given below on set

    S = **set**
    a, b, c: **natural**
    end

determine whether R is a function (using its co-nucleus), then, eventually, whether it is invertible (using its nucleus):

(a) $R = \{(s,s') \mid a(s') = a(s) \wedge b(s') = a(s) + 1 \wedge c(s') = c(s)\}$.

(b) $R = \{(s,s') \mid a(s') = a(s) + b(s) \wedge b(s') = a(s) - b(s)$
$\wedge\ c(s') = c(s) - b(s)\}$.

(c) $R = \{(s,s') \mid a(s') + b(s') = a(s) + b(s)$
$\wedge\ b(s') + c(s') = b(s) + c(s)\}$.

(d) $R = \{(s,s') \mid a(s') = a(s) \wedge b(s') = a(s) + b(s) \wedge c(s') = 0\}$.

(e) $R = \{(s,s') \mid a(s') = a(s) \wedge b(s') = a(s) * b(s)\}$.

12[B] Compare the injectivity of the following pairs of functions on set

    S = **set**
    a, b, c: **integer**
    end.

If they are equally injective, find the function that separates them:

(a) $f = \{(s,s') \mid a(s') = a(s) \wedge b(s') = a(s) - b(s)$
$\wedge\ c(s') = c(s)\}$,
$f' = \{(s,s') \mid a(s') = b(s) \wedge b(s') = a(s) - b(s)$
$\wedge\ c(s') = c(s)\}$.

(b) $f = \{(s,s') \mid a(s') = a(s) + c(s) \wedge b(s') = a(s) - b(s)$
$\wedge\ c(s') = c(s)\}$,

$$f' = \{(s,s') \mid a(s') = a(s) + c(s) \wedge b(s') = a(s) - b(s)$$
$$\wedge \; c(s') = 0\}.$$

(c) $f = \{(s,s') \mid a(s') = a(s) + b(s) \wedge b(s') = b(s) + c(s)$
$\qquad \wedge \; c(s') = 0\}$,
$\quad f' = \{(s,s') \mid a(s') = 0 \wedge b(s') = b(s) + c(s)$
$\qquad \wedge \; c(s') = a(s) + b(s)\}$.

(d) $f = \{(s,s') \mid a(s') = a(s) + c(s) \wedge b(s') = b(s)$
$\qquad \wedge \; c(s') = 1\}$,
$\quad f' = \{(s,s') \mid a(s') = 1 \wedge b(s') = a(s) + c(s) \wedge c(s') = b(s)\}$.

(e) $f = \{(s,s') \mid a(s') = a(s) + b(s) \wedge b(s') = b(s) + c(s)$
$\qquad \wedge \; c(s') = c(s) + a(s)\}$,
$\quad f' = \{(s,s') \mid a(s') = b(s) \wedge b(s') = c(s) \wedge c(s') = a(s)\}$.

13[B] Compare the injectivity of the following pairs of functions on

```
S = set
  a, b, c: integer
end.
```

If they are equally injective, find the function that separates them:

(a) $f = \{(s,s') \mid a(s') = c(s) \wedge b(s') = a(s) \wedge c(s') = b(s)\}$,
$\quad f' = \{(s,s') \mid a(s') = b(s) \wedge b(s') = c(s) \wedge c(s') = a(s)\}$.

(b) $f = \{(s,s') \mid a(s') = c(s) \wedge b(s') = a(s) \wedge c(s') = b(s)\}$,
$\quad f' = \{(s,s') \mid a(s') = a(s) \wedge b(s') = b(s) \wedge c(s') = 0\}$.

(c) $f = \{(s,s') \mid a(s') = c(s) \wedge b(s') = a(s) \wedge c(s') = b(s)\}$,
$\quad f' = \{(s,s') \mid a(s') = 0 \wedge b(s') = 0 \wedge c(s') = 0\}$.

(b) $f = \{(s,s') \mid a(s') = a(s) + b(s) \wedge b(s') = a(s) + b(s)$
$\qquad \wedge \; c(s') = 0\}$,
$\quad f' = \{(s,s') \mid a(s') = a(s) + b(s) \wedge b(s') = 0 \wedge c(s') = 0\}$.

(e) $f = \{(s,s') \mid a(s) = a(s') + b(s') \wedge b(s') = a(s)$
$\qquad \wedge \; c(s') = b(s)\}$,
$\quad f' = \{(s,s') \mid a(s') = a(s) + b(s) \wedge b(s') = b(s) \wedge c(s') = 0\}$.

14[B] Characterize the level sets of each of the following functions on set

```
S = set
  a, b: integer;
end,
```

and determine their (the level sets') cardinality:

(a) $f = \{(s,s') \mid -3 \le a(s) \le 3 \wedge -4 \le b(s) \le 4 \, a(s') = a(s) + b(s) \wedge b(s') = a(s) - b(s)\}$.

(b) $f = \{(s,s') \mid -3 \le a(s) \le 3 \wedge -4 \le b(s) \le 4 \, a(s') = a(s) + b(s) \wedge b(s') = 0\}$.

(c) $f = \{(s,s') \mid -3 \le a(s) \le 3 \wedge -4 \le b(s) \le 4 a(s') = 0 \wedge$
$\quad b(s') = a(s) - b(s)\}.$

(d) $f = \{(s,s') \mid -3 \le a(s) \le 3 \wedge -4 \le b(s) \le 4 a(s') = a(s) \wedge$
$\quad b(s') = 0\}.$

(e) $f = \{(s,s') \mid -3 \le a(s) \le 3 \wedge -4 \le b(s) \le 4 a(s') = 0 \wedge$
$\quad b(s') = b(s)\}.$

1.4 PROBLEMS

1[A]   Determine the domain of definition of expression

$$\mathbf{alt}(p, E, E')$$

as a function of the definition domains of E and E', and of p.
Under what condition is this domain equal to S?

2[A]   Determine the domain of definition of expression

$$E \cdot E'$$

as a function of the definition domains of E and E'. Under what
condition is this domain equal to S?

3[A]   Determine the domain of definition of expression

$$(E \times E')$$

as a function of the definition domains of E and E'. Under what
condition is this domain equal to S?

4[B]   Let $\mathbf{R}(S)$ be the set of binary relations on set S. We define the
relations $\mathcal{MF}$ and MF on $\mathbf{R}(S)$, as follows:

$$\mathcal{MF} = \{(R, R') \mid R' \text{ is more-defined than } R\}.$$
$$\mathrm{MF} = \mathcal{MF} - I(\mathbf{R}(S)).$$

Investigate the properties of relations $\mathcal{MF}$ and MF.

5[B]   Let $\mathbf{R}(S)$ be the set of binary relations on set S. We define the
relations $\mathcal{MT}$ and MT on $\mathbf{R}(S)$, as follows:

$$\mathcal{MT} = \{(R, R') \mid R' \text{ is more-deterministic than } R\}.$$
$$\mathrm{MF} = \mathcal{MT} - I(\mathbf{R}(S)).$$

Investigate the properties of relations $\mathcal{MT}$ and MT.

6[B]   Let R be a relation on S such that $\mathrm{dom}(R) = S$; and let $N(R)$ and
$K(R)$ be the nucleus and kernel of R respectively:
(a) Show that $N(R)$ is reflexive and symmetric.
(b) Show that $K(R)$ is reflexive and transitive.
(c) Show that if R is regular then $N(R) = K(R)$.

(d) Deduce that if R is regular then $N(R)$ and $K(R)$ are equivalences.

(e) Interpret the significance of this equivalence relation.

7[C] Let R be a relation on S such that $N(R) = K(R)$. Is R necessarily regular? Prove your claim.

8[B] Is the set of regular relations closed with respect to the union? Give the weakest possible condition under which the union of two regular relations is regular.

9[A] Let f be an invertible function on set S:

(a) Write the (relational) algebraic properties that f verifies.

(b) Assume, further, that $\text{dom}(f) = S$. What additional properties does this hypothesis give us? How do we solve the equation

$$x * f = g$$

in the unknown x under this hypothesis?

(c) Assume, further, that $\text{rng}(f) = S$. What additional properties does this hypothesis give us? How do we solve the equation

$$f * x = g$$

in the unknown x under these hypotheses?

1.5   BIBLIOGRAPHICAL NOTES

For propositional and predicate logic, the reader is referred to Larson (1983), Mendelson (1964), Kleene (1968), Suppes (1957), Quine (1961), Manna (1974) or Gries (1981); in the latter two references, logic is introduced for the specific purpose of program analysis and/or design.

For additional reading on set theory, the reader is referred to Suppes (1972) and Liu (1977). Computer science oriented books on set theory also include Stanat and McAllister (1977), Tremblay and Manohar (1975), Manna (1974) and Stone (1973).

For additional reading on relations and functions, and their use in programming, the reader is referred to Sanderson (1980), Linger *et al.* (1979), Mills *et al.* (1986) and Manna (1974). For more information on regular relations, consult Boudriga *et al.* (1989).

CHAPTER 2

Program specifications

2.1 AN INTRODUCTION TO SPECIFICATIONS

Specifications play a key role in the study of program fault tolerance because, as we shall see in Chapter 4, they are at the very basis of defining what a fault is, and when a program is said to tolerate a fault.

2.1.1 The Nature of Specifications

The process and the product. It is an accident of linguistics that the word *specification* refers both to a process and to a product. *Webster's New Collegiate Dictionary* (1980 edition) gives two definitions of the word:

1. the act or process of specifying.
2. a detailed precise presentation of something.

In software engineering, the contrast between *process* and *product* is quite recurrent; so much so that it is one of the main pillars of commonly adopted software engineering goal structures.

As a process, the specification is the phase where the requirements imposed on software to be produced are formulated and recorded. As a product, it is the document that records these requirements; it may record several aspects of the proposed software, such as its functional properties, its precision, its response time, its resource utilization, or the equipment on which it is run.

The specification product. As a product, a specification plays two key roles: first, it is a *contract* between the user (whose requirements it defines) and the programmer (whose obligations it defines); second, it is a primary *design document* for the programmer.

As a contract, a specification is used to check the validity of candidate

44

solutions; this subsumes the existence of a precise criterion by which we can judge whether a given (by definition, formal) program is correct with respect to a (hopefully, formal) specification.

As a design document the specification undergoes a stepwise refinement process, whose every step consists of decomposing a (sub-) specification into several component specifications arranged in some form of hierarchy. This refinement process assumes the existence and use of a notation which encompasses both the representation of specifications and the representation of hierarchy among subspecifications.

The specification process. For the sake of argument, we adopt the following scenario for the specification process: we are given a user group, a specifier group, and a verification and validation group; while the first group is familiar with the application domain of the projected software product, the latter two groups are familiar with writing and manipulating specifications. We define two steps in the specification process as follows:

1. *Specification generation:* where requirements are formulated by the specifier group, on the basis of information given by the user group in a written document or via live interaction; the specifier acquaints himself with user requirements, and then attempts to capture his understanding of the specification in a formal description.
2. *Specification validation:* where the verification and validation group checks the derived specification for completeness and consistency against redundant specification information provided by the user group.

Forms of specifications Software is being introduced in various domains of application, to perform widely differing functions, so widely differing that it is hardly conceivable that their functional descriptions have the same form. Indeed, it is useful to distinguish between three forms of specifications: procedural specifications; data-type specifications; and continuous process specifications. We discuss them in turn below.

Procedural specifications describe programs that map a given input into an output; successive invocations of such programs do not interfere with each other, so that for a given input the program will always return the same output. This is the most traditional kind of programs; examples of such programs are a sort package, a sine function or a tree traversal program.

Data specifications describe the behavior of a machine that has an internal state which can be changed or probed using pre-defined procedures and functions. Typical examples of such systems are an abstract data type or a data base.

Continuous process specifications describe programs that perform a stimulus–response mechanism. Examples of such programs include on-board flight packages, industrial process monitoring packages, and operating systems.

2.1.2 Properties of Specifications

In order to fulfil its function in a complete and minimal manner, a specification must possess a number of properties. Several researchers have in the past provided sets of properties; see the bibliography. Despite their apparent variety, these sets actually reflect a fairly wide consensus on the desirable properties of specifications. We provide a brief list of such properties, distinguishing between properties of the product and those of the process. We identify three properties of the specification as a product – formality, simplicity, and abstraction:

1. *Formality:* specifications must be formal so as to make possible such activities as *specification validation* (ensuring that the specification incorporates user requirements) and *program verification* (ensuring that the program is correct with respect to the specification). Formality can be achieved through the use of mathematics.
2. *Simplicity:* specifications must be as simple as possible, so as to promote such activities as reading, analyzing, and understanding; simplicity can be achieved by the appropriate use of structure and abstraction mechanisms.
3. *Abstraction:* the specification must not carry any design hint, or any bias towards a particular structure of solution programs. The specification must limit itself to expressing *what* functional properties are required from the candidate programs, leaving the programmer to decide *how* the desired functional properties are to be achieved.

We also identify two properties of the process – completeness and minimality:

1. *Completeness:* a specification must reflect all the user requirements. Completeness is achieved through good communication with the user, which is itself facilitated by simplicity.
2. *Minimality:* the specification language/model must not force the user to be any more specific than he/she wishes. Just as it is important to reflect *all* the user requirements, it is important that a specification expresses *nothing but* the user requirements. This property is also called *non-determinacy*.

2.1.3   Specifications: A Definition

As a product, a specification of a program is the expression of requirements formulated by a user about a program that he wishes to acquire. In its most general form, a specification expresses functional requirements (pertaining to the functional capabilities expected from candidate programs) as well as performance requirements (pertaining to the resources available to candidate programs). In this chapter, we (drastically) reduce the scope of our study by considering functional requirements only. We also consider simple input/output programs, with no internal memory.

We say that we have defined a *specification*, say Sp, when we have provided two elements:

(a) a set S, called the *space* of the specification;
(b) a relation R on S, called the *relation* of the specification.

In compliance with the principle of *minimality*, a specification's relation may be arbitrarily non-deterministic (in the sense used in Chapter 1). Any element s of S is called a *state* of the specification; any element s of $dom(R)$ is called an *initial state* (or *input* state) of Sp; any element s of $rng(R)$ is called a *final state* (or *output* state) of Sp. When space S is implicit from the context of our discussions, we may drop it from the description and represent Sp simply as R.

2.1.4   Specifications: Semantics

In its general form, a specification has two components: the space S and the relation R.

The space S defines the variables to be manipulated by candidate programs. It is conceivable that candidate programs manipulate additional variables to those defined in S, for the purposes of storing intermediate results; for the sake of simplicity, and because it would not enrich our study, we shall not concern ourselves with this possibility.

Relation R contains all the input/output pairs that the user considers correct. Specifically, it contains the following:

1. $dom(R)$ contains all the *legal* input states that the user can possibly submit.
2. For any input state s, $s \cdot R$ contains all the *correct* output states that the user considers acceptable for input s.

It stems from this definition that if s is a state outside $dom(R)$ (i.e. $s \cdot R = \emptyset$), then the user does not consider s to be a possible input state;

candidate programs need not make provisions for such a state, and their behavior on such states is not relevant to the verification activity. On the other hand, if for some state s we have $s \cdot R = S$, then the user considers s to be a legal input state, for which candidate programs must make provision; nevertheless, the user does not care what output state s' in S is returned for input s, so long as it (i.e. the output s') is defined. Example 1 below illustrates this distinction.

Example 1. We consider specification $Sp = (S, R)$,

> S = **real**
> $R = \{(s, s') | s \geq 0 \wedge s' = s^{1/2}\}.$

The specifier does not consider -1, for example, to be a possible input state; hence he does not include it in $\text{dom}(R)$. A candidate program will not be liable for its behavior on input state -1.

Now, we consider $Sp' = (S', R')$, where

> S' = **real**
> $R' = \{(s, s') | s \geq 0 \wedge s' = s^{1/2}\} \cup \{(s, s') | s < 0\}.$

The specifier considers that -1 is a possible input state; nevertheless he imposes no condition on the value of the output for input state -1. He does, however, impose the condition that candidate programs produce a defined output state for input state -1.

Finally, we consider $Sp'' = (S'', R'')$, where

> S'' = **real**
> $R'' = \{(s, s') | s \geq 0 \wedge s' = s^{1/2}\} \cup \{(s, s') | s < 0 \wedge s' = -2\}.$

The specifier is being even more specific here: he considers -1 to be a legal input state, and -2 to be the only acceptable output state for input state -1, possibly reading -2 as an error message.

Note that R'' is more-defined than R', which is in turn more-defined than R.

Special specifications on space S include: the *empty* specification ϕ, which is satisfied by any program; the *total* specification U, which is satisfied by any program that is defined for all s in S; the *identity* specification, which is satisfied by the empty program on space S. In the traditional relational formalism, there exists no **false** specification, i.e. a specification that no program can satisfy; we could, however, by a stretch of the imagination, adopt for this purpose the specification Ω that is defined as:

$$\Omega = S \times \emptyset.$$

2.1.5 Exercises

1[A] Determine whether the following specifications on

  S = **set**
    a, b, c: **integer**
  end

are deterministic.
(a) $R = \{(s,s') | a(s) = a(s') \wedge b(s) = a(s') \wedge b(s) = b(s')\}$.
(b) $R = \{(s,s') | a(s) = a(s') + b(s') \wedge b(s) = a(s') - b(s') \wedge c(s) = c(s') + a(s')\}$.
(c) $R = \{(s,s') | a(s) + b(s) = a(s') + b(s') \wedge c(s') = c(s)\}$.
(d) $R = \{(\langle 0,1,2\rangle, \langle 2,1,1\rangle), (\langle 1,2,0\rangle, \langle 2,1,1\rangle), (\langle 0,2,1\rangle, \langle 1,2,1\rangle)\}$.
(e) $R = \{\langle 0,1,0\rangle, \langle 1,0,1\rangle, \langle 0,0,1\rangle, \langle 1,1,0\rangle\}^2$.

2[B] What are the legal input states of the following specifications on space S defined by

  S = **set**
    a, b, c: **integer**
  end?

(a) $R = \{(s,s') | a(s') = b(s) + c(s) \wedge b(s') = a(s) + c(s) \wedge c(s') = a(s) + b(s)\}$.
(b) $R = \{(s,s') | a(s') + b(s') = a(s) \wedge b(s') = b(s) \wedge a(s') = c\}$.
(c) $R = \{(s,s') | a(s') - b(s') = a(s) \wedge b(s') = b(s) \wedge a(s') - b(s') = c(s)\}$.
(d) $R = \{(s,s') | a(s') - b(s') = a(s) \wedge a(s') - b(s') = c(s)\}$.
(e) $R = \{(s,s') | a(s') + b(s') = a(s) \wedge b(s') = b(s) \wedge a(s') = b(s)\}$.

3[A] Let S be the space defined as

  S = **set**
    a, b, c: **integer**
  end.

Write the following specifications on S. For each specification you write, state whether it is deterministic, and whether it is regular (see Chapter 1). Give its domain.
(a) R preserves a and b while decreasing c.
(b) R preserves a while decreasing b and c.
(c) R preserves a while decreasing the sum of b and c.
(d) R preserves the sum of a and b, the sum of b and c, and the sum of c and a.

   (e) *R* preserves the sum of *a* and *b* and the sum of *b* and *c*, and
       decreases the sum of *c* and *a*.

4[B]   Let *S* be the space defined as

   S = **set**
      a, b, c: **integer**
   end.

Write the following specifications on *S*. For each specification
you write, state whether it is deterministic, and whether it is
regular. Give its domain:

   (a) *R* preserves the maximum of *a*, *b*, *c* and the sum of *a*, *b*, *c*.
   (b) *R* preserves the minimum of *a*, *b*, *c*, preserves *a*, and sets
       b to the sum of *a* and *c*.
   (c) *R* increases the maximum of *a*, *b*, *c*, decreases the minimum
       of *a*, *b*, *c*, and preserves *b*.
   (d) *R* increases the maximum of *a*, *b*, *c*, decreases the minimum
       of *a*, *b*, *c*, and preserves the sum of *a*, *b*, *c*.
   (e) *R* preserves the sum of *a*, *b*, *c*, as well as the sum of the
       maximum of *a*, *b*, *c* and the minimum of *a*, *b*, *c*.

5[A]   On the space S = **real**, derive the following specifications. State
whether they are deterministic, and whether they are regular.
Give their domain:

   (a) *R* computes the square root of positive reals, within a
       precision of Y, Y > 0.
   (b) *R* computes the square root of non-negative reals, within a
       precision of Y, Y > 0.
   (c) *R* computes the exact square root of non-negative reals.
   (d) *R* computes the exact square root of non-negative reals, and
       is defined for negative reals.
   (e) *R* computes the exact square root of non-negative reals, and
       returns the input if it is negative.

2.2 SPECIFICATIONS: GENERATION

Specifications are potentially complex formulas. Thus, it is not reasonable to assume that a specifier can, at any stage of the specification
process, conceive his/her specification in all its detail and complexity.
Rather, it is only reasonable to expect the specifier to work on one
aspect of the specification at a time. If one analyzes the intellectual
process that takes place during the phase of specification generation
(as defined in Section 2.1.1), one can discern two orthogonal strategies

that are used alternately or in combination. These problem-solving strategies aim at breaking down the target specification into intellectually manageable (sub-) specifications. We discuss these two strategies in turn.

2.2.1   Union Strategy: Specification by Case Analysis

In order to generate a specification R on space S, one generates the specifications $R_1, R_2, \ldots, R_k$ whose domains are disjoint and then pose

$$R = R_1 \cup R_2 \cup \ldots \cup R_k.$$

This strategy is suitable for those cases where the specification can best be articulated by partitioning its input space and considering one partition at a time.

Because the condition that the domains of the R_is be disjoint is too restrictive in practice, we replace it by the weaker condition that for all i, j in $\{1, 2, 3, 4, \ldots, k\}$ and for all s in S,

$$s \in (\mathrm{dom}(R_i) \cap \mathrm{dom}(R_j)) \Rightarrow s \cdot R_i = s \cdot R_j;$$

this (weaker) condition allows two domains ($\mathrm{dom}(R_i)$ and $\mathrm{dom}(R_j)$) (U) to have elements (s) in common, provided these elements have the same image sets by R_i and by R_j.

Example 2

Space, S = $\{\langle a, b, c\rangle \mid a \in$ **natural** $\wedge$ b $\in$ **natural** $\wedge$ c $\in$ **natural**$\}$.

We want to write a specification for a program to permute the values of variables a, b and c in such a way that a is less than or equal to b, which is in turn less than or equal to c. One possible approach to this specification is the following:

$R_0 = \{(s, s') \mid a(s) \le b(s) \le c(s) \wedge s' = s\},$
$R_1 = \{(s, s') \mid a(s) \le c(s) \le b(s) \wedge s' = \langle a(s), c(s), b(s)\rangle\},$
$R_2 = \{(s, s') \mid b(s) \le a(s) \le c(s) \wedge s' = \langle b(s), a(s), c(s)\rangle\},$
$R_3 = \{(s, s') \mid b(s) \le c(s) \le a(s) \wedge s' = \langle b(s), c(s), a(s)\rangle\},$
$R_4 = \{(s, s') \mid c(s) \le a(s) \le b(s) \wedge s' = \langle c(s), a(s), b(s)\rangle\},$
$R_5 = \{(s, s') \mid c(s) \le b(s) \le a(s) \wedge s' = \langle c(s), b(s), a(s)\rangle\}.$

This example is, of course, purely illustrative; it is to be compared with Example 3 which deals with the same specification by using the intersection strategy. Note that the domains of R_0, R_1, R_2, R_3, R_4 and R_5 are not disjoint, but they satisfy the weaker condition given above.   □

2.2.2   Intersection Strategy: Combining Weak Properties

In order to generate specification R on space S, one generates the specifications $R_1, R_2, \ldots, R_k$, all of whose domains are S, and then poses

$$R = R_1 \cap R_2 \cap \ldots \cap R_k.$$

This strategy is suitable for those cases where the specification can best be articulated as the conjunction of several weaker properties.

The requirement that, for all R_i, $\text{dom}(R_i) = S$, proves not to be very restrictive in practice. Furthermore, if some R_i has a domain smaller than S, one can replace it by

$$R_i' = R_i \cup I(t_i) * U(S),$$

where $t_i(s) \Leftrightarrow s \notin \text{dom}(R_i)$, and $U(S)$ is the universal relation on S; we admit without proof that this change does not alter the message of R_i as a specification. See Problem 1, Chapter 3.

Example 3

$$S = \{\langle a, b, c \rangle \,|\, a \in \textbf{natural} \wedge b \in \textbf{natural} \wedge c \in \textbf{natural}\}.$$

We write the same specification as that of Example 2, only this time we use the intersection strategy. We assume given the functions from S to **natural**:

min(s):   minimum value of $a(s)$, $b(s)$ and $c(s)$.
max(s):   maximum value of $a(s)$, $b(s)$ and $c(s)$.
sum(s): $a(s) + b(s) + c(s)$.

The target specification can be developed stepwise as follows: First, the output is sorted;

$$R_0 = \{(s, s') \,|\, a(s') \leq b(s') \leq c(s')\}.$$

In order to show that the three values $\langle a, b, c \rangle$ are preserved, we can show that their maximum, their minimum and (to ensure the preservation of their middle element) their sum are preserved.

$$R_1 = \{(s, s') \,|\, \max(s) = \max(s')\}.$$
$$R_2 = \{(s, s') \,|\, \min(s) = \min(s')\}.$$
$$R_3 = \{(s, s') \,|\, \text{sum}(s) = \text{sum}(s')\}.$$

Now, we pose

$$R = R_0 \cap R_1 \cap R_2 \cap R_3. \qquad \square$$

2.2.3 Specification Generation: A Mathematical Justification

In Sections 2.2.1 and 2.2.2, we have presented strategies for dealing with the complexity of specification generation. In this section, we show the rationale of these two strategies, *a posteriori*, by analyzing the relationship between the derived relations (R_i) and the target relation R. We analyze this relationship in the case of the two strategies in turn.

Union. In the union strategy, $R_i \subseteq R$, hence $\text{dom}(R_i) \subseteq \text{dom}(R)$. Let s be an element of $\text{dom}(R_i)$; we are interested in $s \cdot R$.

$$s \cdot R = s \cdot R_1 \cup s \cdot R_2 \cup \ldots \cup s \cdot R_k$$
$$= s \cdot R_i \cup s \cdot R_{j_1} \cup s \cdot R_{j_2} \cup \ldots \cup s \cdot R_{j_l},$$

where $R_{j_1}, R_{j_2}, \ldots R_{j_l}$ are the relations other than R_i to whose domains s belongs. By virtue of condition (U), we deduce

$$s \cdot R = s \cdot R_i.$$

This, in conjunction with $\text{dom}(R_i) \subseteq \text{dom}(R)$, leads to the conclusion that R is more-defined than R_i, for any R_i.

Intersection. In the intersection strategy, all relations R_i have a domain equal to S. For R (the intersection of all the R_is) to have a smaller domain than S, means that there exists an input state s such that

$$(\forall i, s \cdot R_i \neq \emptyset),$$

yet

$$s \cdot R = \emptyset.$$

This case occurs when the R_is contradict each other. This abnormal case notwithstanding, we assume $\text{dom}(R) = S$; hence $\text{dom}(R_i) = \text{dom}(R)$. Now, let s be some element of $\text{dom}(R_i)$; because $R \subseteq R_i$, $s \cdot R \subseteq s \cdot R_i$. This, in conjunction with $\text{dom}(R_i) \subseteq \text{dom}(R)$, leads to the conclusion that R is more-defined than R_i, for any R_i.

In both strategies, the specifier constructs a complex specification (R) by means of a set of less-defined specifications (R_i). The rationale behind these strategies is that less-defined specifications carry less input–output information and hence are easier to generate.

2.2.4 Heuristics for Specification Generation

Because of the creative nature of specification generation, the strategies given above cannot be considered sufficient in themselves. Below we present three heuristics for specification generation, and we justify their use by means of intuitive arguments.

H1: Separate Binary Properties from Unary Properties. It is common for specifications to be a conjunction of two kinds of properties: binary properties, linking input states (s) to output states (s'); and unary properties, describing features of output states (s'). A good strategy of separation of concerns is to distinguish between these two types of properties. More specifically, it is fruitful to reduce binary properties to their simplest possible expression, abstracting away any hint of unary properties.

Usually, a binary property has the form of an equivalence relation, and expresses some form of preservation. In contrast, the unary property serves to reduce the range of the relation, and expresses the property that we desire to produce in the output. A simple illustration of such a distinction between binary and unary properties is given in Example 3, where $R_1 \cap R_2 \cap R_3$ captures the binary properties of the specification, while R_0 captures the unary properties.

H2: Use Only Binary and Unary Properties. The keyword of this heuristic is *only*. Some specifications can conceivably be formulated in the following terms: 'given s, find s' that maximizes $f(s')$ under the constraint $p(s, s')$'. The fact that s' maximizes function f is not a property linking s' to s; rather it is a property linking s' to other possible occurrences of s' that satisfy $p(s, s')$. As such, it does not fit well into the relational formalism, which is best suited for describing binary properties of s and s', and unary properties of s'. The key to obviating this difficulty is to re-formulate the specification in such a way that the maximality of $f(s')$ is expressed as a property of s' alone – thus fitting into the mould of a unary property – or as a property of s and s' – thus fitting into the mould of a binary property.

H3: Avoid Structuring Specifications as Relational Products. Specifications structured as relational products present a number of intrinsic weaknesses, which we explain below:

1. A specification that is structured as a relational product is a virtual order to the designer to structure his program solution as a sequence of blocks, one for each term of the expression. Because this dictates a specific design to the programmer, it is in clear violation to the principle of *abstraction* (Section 2.1.2).
2. In a specification structured as a relational product, one cannot see

any relationship between inputs and outputs (the only kind of relationship of interest to the user) until one has fully grasped all the relations involved in the relational product – a severe challenge to readability.
3. The analysis-related activities performed on the specification (e.g. validation) require that one computes – mentally or otherwise – the relational product of the component relations; not exactly an easy exercise.

In the light of these remarks, it does seem reasonable to avoid, whenever possible, structuring specifications as relational products.

2.2.5 Exercises

1[A] Use the union strategy to derive the following specifications on space S = **real**:
   (a) R maps input states into their absolute value.
   (b) R maps input states between 0 and 2.9 into their floor.
   (c) R maps input states between 0.1 and 3 into their ceiling.
   (d) R maps s into the maximum of the absolute value of s and the exponential of s.
   (e) R maps s into the maximum of zero and $s^2 - 9$. Do not use function max.

2[B] Let S be

```
set
crt
    a, b, c: real;
    x', x": real;
sub
    a ≠ 0
end.
```

Use the union strategy to derive the following specification: R eventually stores in x' and x'' the roots, if they exist, of polynomial

$a * x^2 + b * x + c.$

3[A] Let S be

```
set
    a, b, c: integer
end.
```

Use the union strategy to write the following specification: R stores in c the maximum of a, b, c.

4[A]   Let S be

    set
    crt
      a, b: **integer**
    sub
      $a > 0 \wedge b > 0$
    end.

Use the intersection strategy to derive the following specifications:

(a) R computes the greatest common divisor of a and b in a and preserves b.

(b) R computes the greatest common divisor of a and b in a and b.

(c) R computes the smallest common multiple of a and b in b.

(d) R computes the greatest common divisor of a and b in a and preserves the product of a by b.

(e) R computes the greatest common divisor of a and b in a and the smallest common multiple of a and b in b.

5[A]   Use the intersection strategy to write the following specification on space $S = $ **real**: R maps input s into the floor of s.

6[A]   Use the intersection strategy to write the following specification on space $S = $ **real**: R maps input s into the floor of s.

7[A]   Let S be

    set
      a: **array** [indextype] of **real**;
      i: indextype
    end,

where indextype $= 1..n$, for some $n \geq 1$. Use the intersection strategy to derive a specification that sorts array a in increasing order.

2.3   SPECIFICATIONS: VALIDATION

Specification *validation* is the phase where *properties* that must be met by a specification are first proposed and then the specification is checked against them to establish *validity*.

This definition immediately raises two questions: (i) What is a property? (ii) How does one check the validity of a specification with respect to a property? We address these questions in turn.

2.3.1 What is a Property?

The verification and validation group, whose task it is to generate (from the requirements, and by interaction with the user) properties to be met by specification R asks questions of the form:

- Does R express that for input states s satisfying the predicate $q(s)$, output states s' must satisfy the predicate $q'(s, s')$?

Such a question can in effect be captured in the relation

$$V_0 = \{(s, s') | q(s) \wedge q'(s, s')\}.$$

Hence the definition: a *property* is a relation.

In order to breathe some life into this abstract definition, we give below instances of properties that one could derive for the specifications generated in Examples 2 and 3.

Example 4

$\quad$ S = $\{\langle a, b, c \rangle | a \in$ **natural** $\wedge$ b $\in$ **natural** $\wedge$ c $\in$ **natural**$\}$.

- Writing a specification for a program to permute the values of variables a, b, and c in such a way that the sequence $\langle a, b, c \rangle$ be sorted in non-decreasing order.

Using this text (*not* the written formal specifications) one may choose to propose the following properties, ranked from the most specific (in relational terms: the most-defined) to the most general (in relational terms: the least-defined):

0: The specification must imply that $\langle 3, 1, 2 \rangle$ is mapped onto $\langle 1, 2, 3 \rangle$.
1: The specification must imply that if $a(s) = 3$ (s: input), then $a(s') = 3$ or $b(s') = 3$ or $c(s') = 3$ (s': output).
2: The specification must imply that if the input is sorted, then the output is identical to the input.
3: The specification must imply that the max of $\langle a, b, c \rangle$ is preserved.
4: The specification must imply that the output is sorted.

These properties can be captured by the following relations:

$$V_0 = \{(\langle 3, 1, 2 \rangle, \langle 1, 2, 3 \rangle)\}.$$
$$V_1 = \{(s, s') | a(s) = 3 \wedge (a(s') = 3 \vee b(s') = 3 \vee c(s') = 3)\}.$$
$$V_2 = \{(s, s') | a(s) \le b(s) \le c(s) \wedge s' = s\}.$$
$$V_3 = \{(s, s') | \max(s) = \max(s')\}.$$
$$V_4 = \{(s, s') | a(s') \le b(s') \le c(s')\}. \qquad \qquad \square$$

2.3.2   How do we Check Validity?

Checking that a specification R is valid with respect to a property V amounts to checking the following:

1. The set of input states associated with property V is included in the set of input states associated with specification R.
2. Whenever applicable, the set of output states acceptable by V includes the set of output states acceptable by R.

Formally, these conditions can be written as

1. $\mathrm{dom}(V) \subseteq \mathrm{dom}(R)$.
2. $\forall s \in \mathrm{dom}(V), \; s \cdot R \subseteq s \cdot V$.

In other words, R is more-defined than V, hence the following definition:

- *Definition.* Let R be a specification and V be a property, both on space S. Specification R is said to be *valid* with respect to property V if and only if R is more-defined than V.

In the example given below, we check the validity of the specification proposed in Example 3 against the properties proposed in Example 4.

Example 5

$$S = \{\langle a,b,c \rangle \,|\, a \in \textbf{natural} \wedge b \in \textbf{natural} \wedge c \in \textbf{natural}\}$$
$$R = R_0 \cap R_1 \cap R_2 \cap R_3,$$

where

$$R_0 = \{(s,s') \,|\, a(s') \leq b(s') \leq c(s')\}.$$
$$R_1 = \{(s,s') \,|\, \max(s) = \max(s')\}.$$
$$R_2 = \{(s,s') \,|\, \min(s) = \min(s')\}.$$
$$R_3 = \{(s,s') \,|\, \mathrm{sum}(s) = \mathrm{sum}(s')\}.$$

We pose $\mathrm{mid}(s) = \mathrm{sum}(s) - \min(s) - \max(s)$; $\mathrm{mid}(s)$ designates the middle element of s.

For each V_i, we must prove that

$$\mathrm{dom}(V_i) \subseteq \mathrm{dom}(R),$$
$$\forall s \in \mathrm{dom}(V_i), \; s \cdot R \subseteq s \cdot V_i.$$

Because $\mathrm{dom}(R) = S$, we only have to prove the second clause, which we rewrite as

$$s \in \mathrm{dom}(V_i) \wedge (s,s') \in R \Rightarrow (s,s') \in V_i.$$

For V_0:

$$s = \langle 3,1,2 \rangle \wedge a(s') \leq b(s') \leq c(s') \wedge \max(s') = 3 \wedge \min(s') = 1$$
$$\wedge\ a(s') + b(s') + c(s') = 6$$
$$\Rightarrow s = \langle 3,1,2 \rangle \wedge c(s') = 3 \wedge a(s') = 1 \wedge b(s') = 2$$
$$\Rightarrow s = \langle 3,1,2 \rangle \wedge s' = \langle 1,2,3 \rangle$$
$$\Rightarrow (s,s') \in V_0.$$

For V_1:

$$a(s) = 3 \wedge a(s') \leq b(s') \leq c(s') \wedge \max(s) = \max(s')$$
$$\wedge\ \min(s) = \min(s') \wedge \mathrm{sum}(s) = \mathrm{sum}(s')$$
$$\Rightarrow a(s) = 3 \wedge a(s') \leq b(s') \leq c(s') \wedge \max(s) = c(s')$$
$$\wedge\ \min(s) = a(s') \wedge \mathrm{mid}(s) = b(s').$$

By considering three cases, namely $a(s) = \min(s)$, $a(s) = \max(s)$ and $a(s) = \mathrm{mid}(s)$, we reach three alternatives, namely $a(s') = 3$, $c(s') = 3$ or $b(s') = 3$, whence we deduce

$$\Rightarrow (s,s') \in V_1.$$

For V_2:

$$a(s) \leq b(s) \leq c(s) \wedge a(s') \leq b(s') \leq c(s') \wedge \max(s') = \max(s)$$
$$\wedge\ \min(s') = \min(s) \wedge \mathrm{sum}(s) = \mathrm{sum}(s')$$
$$\Rightarrow a(s') = a(s) \wedge c(s') = c(s) \wedge b(s') = b(s) \wedge a(s) \leq b(s) \leq c(s)$$
$$\Rightarrow s' = s \wedge a(s) \leq b(s) \leq c(s)$$
$$\Rightarrow (s,s') \in V_2.$$

For V_3:

$$a(s') \leq b(s') \leq c(s') \wedge \max(s) = \max(s') \wedge \min(s) = \min(s')$$
$$\wedge\ \mathrm{sum}(s) = \mathrm{sum}(s')$$
$$\Rightarrow \max(s') = \max(s)$$
$$\Rightarrow (s,s') \in V_3.$$

For V_4:

$$a(s') \leq b(s') \leq c(s') \wedge \max(s') = \max(s) \wedge \min(s') = \min(s)$$
$$\wedge\ \mathrm{sum}(s') = \mathrm{sum}(s)$$
$$\Rightarrow a(s') \leq b(s') \leq c(s')$$
$$\Rightarrow (s,s') \in V_4. \qquad \square$$

2.3.3   Exercises

1[A]   For each specification described in Exercise 3, Section 2.1.5, propose two properties.

2[A]   For each specification described in Exercise 4, Section 2.1.5, propose two properties.

3[A]   For each specification described in Exercise 5, Section 2.1.5, propose two properties.

4[A]   For each specification described in Exercise 1, Section 2.2.5, propose two properties.

5[A]   Propose five properties for the specification described in Exercise 2, Section 2.2.5.

6[A]   Propose five properties for the specification described in Exercise 3, Section 2.2.5.

7[A]   For each specification described in Exercise 4, Section 2.2.5, propose two properties.

8[A]   Propose five properties for the specification described in Exercise 5, Section 2.2.5.

9[A]   Propose five properties for the specification described in Exercise 6, Section 2.2.5.

10[A]   Propose five properties for the specification described in Exercise 7, Section 2.2.5.

11[B]   We consider the space

$$S = \textbf{set}$$
$$a, b, c: \textbf{natural}$$
$$\textbf{end};$$

Let the user requirement be:

Specification R must express that

(i) a contains the minimum of a and c,
(ii) c contains the maximum of a and c,
(iii) the sum of a and b is preserved.

Let R be

$$R = \{(s,s') | (a(s') = a(s) \lor a(s') = c(s)) \land a(s') \leq a(s)$$
$$\land\ a(s') \leq c(s) \land a(s) + c(s) = a(s') + c(s')$$
$$\land\ a(s) + b(s) = a(s') + b(s')\}.$$

For each property V proposed below, prove or disprove that R is valid with respect to V:

(a) The sum of a, b, and c is preserved.
(b) The sum of b and c is preserved.
(c) If a is less than c then it is preserved.
(d) c contains the maximum of a and c.
(e) If a is less than c then b is preserved.

12[B]   Same question as above:
   (a) If the input is $\langle 2,1,3 \rangle$, then the output is $\langle 2,1,3 \rangle$.
   (b) If a equals c, then s is preserved.
   (c) The sum of a and c is preserved.
   (d) If the input is sorted $(a(s) \leq b(s) \leq c(s))$, then so is the output $(a(s') \leq b(s') \leq c(s'))$.
   (e) If the input is sorted, then it is equal to the output.

13[B]   Let S be **real**, and let the user requirement be expressed as follows:

> Specification R must express that for negative inputs, output -1 is returned, and that for non-negative input s, the square root of s is returned.

Let specification R be:

$$R = \{(s,s')|s < 0 \wedge s' = -1\} \cup \{(s,s')|s \geq 0 \wedge s' = s^{1/2}\}.$$

For each property V given below, state whether R is valid with respect to V:
   (a) For all negative initial states, R expresses that the final state is negative.
   (b) For all initial states greater than 4, R expresses that the final state is less than the initial state.
   (c) For all initial states between 1 and 6 inclusive, specification R expresses that the final state is the square root of the initial state.
   (d) For all initial states between -1 and 1 inclusive, specification R expresses that the absolute value of the final state is not greater than 1.
   (e) Specification R is defined for all positive initial states.
   (f) Specification R is defined for all initial states.

14[B]   Validate the specification of Example 2 against the properties generated in Example 4.

2.4 PREDICATE-BASED SPECIFICATIONS

2.4.1 Definitions and Notation

In the predicate-based (vs. relation-based) logic of programming, specifications are represented as pairs of predicates, namely an *input predicate* and an *output predicate*. In this section, we briefly describe the link between our relation-based specifications and predicate-based specifications.

We say that we have defined a *predicate-based specification* when we have given the following:

(a) a set S, called the *space* of the specification;
(b) a predicate p on S, called the *input predicate* of the specification;
(c) a predicate q on S, called the *output predicate* of the specification.

To reflect this definition, we represent predicate-based specifications by $Sp = (S, p, q)$, or, if S is implicit, by $Sp = (p, q)$.

2.4.2 Transformation Formulas

Given a specification (S, R), we can write it under *predicate-based* form as

$$(S, p_R, q_R),$$

where

$$p_R(s) = s = s_0 \land s \in \operatorname{dom}(R),$$

and

$$q_R(s) = (s_0, s) \in R,$$

where s_0 is some constant state.

On the other hand, given a predicate-based specification under the form (S, p, q), we transform it into a relation-based specification defined as $(S, R_{p,q})$, where

$$R_{p,q} = \{(s, s') \mid \exists s_0 \colon p(s) \land q(s')\};$$

it is assumed, of course, that s_0 is the constant state used in the formulas of q and q'.

Example 6. We are given the space

```
S = set
   a, b: integer
end.
```

Specification (p, q), where

$$p(s) = (a(s) > 0 \land b(s) > 0 \land s = s_0)$$

and

$$q(s) = (a(s) = \gcd(a(s_0), b(s_0)))$$

can be mapped into

$$R = \{(s, s') \mid a(s) > 0 \wedge b(s) > 0 \wedge a(s') = \gcd(a(s), b(s))\}.$$

Conversely, specification

$$R = \{(s, s') \mid a(s') = a(s) + b(s)\}$$

can be mapped into the predicate-based form

$$(s = s_0, a(s) = a(s_0) + b(s_0)). \qquad \qquad \square$$

2.4.3 Exercises

1[A]   Write the predicate-based equivalent of the specifications given in Exercise 1, Section 2.1.5.

2[A]   Write the predicate-based equivalent of the specifications given in Exercise 2, Section 2.1.5.

3[A]   Write the predicate-based equivalent of the specification given in Exercise 11, Section 2.3.3.

4[A]   Write the predicate-based equivalent of the specification given in Exercise 13, Section 2.3.3.

5[A]   Write the relational equivalent of the following specifications:

(a)   S = **real**

p: $s = s_0 \wedge s > 0$,
q: $s = \log(s_0)$.

(b)   S = **set**
    a, b, c: **integer**
end,

p: $s = s_0$,
q: $a(s) + b(s) = a(s_0) \wedge a(s) + b(s) = b(s_0)$.

(c)   S = **set**
    a, b, c: **integer**
end,

p: $s = s_0$,
q: $a(s) = a(s_0) + b(s_0)$.

(d)   S = **set**
    a, b, c: **integer**
end,

p: $s = s_0$,
q: $a(s) = 5 \land b(s) + c(s) = -1$.

(e) S = **set**
    a, b, c: **integer**
end,

p: $s = s_0$,
q: $a(s) = 9 \land b(s) = 4 \land a(s) = b(s) + a(s_0)$.

2.5 PROBLEMS

1[A] Analyze the specification model/language given in Section 2.1.3 vis-à-vis the principles of good specification given in Section 2.1.2.

2[A] *Defensive programming* consists of checking that the input submitted to the program is legal (with respect to the specification at hand) and of casting appropriate error messages if it is not:

(a) Briefly comment on the practical interest of the defensive programming approach.

(b) Explain why, from the standpoint of the semantic definition given in Section 2.1.4, a program that provides for non-legal inputs is no better than a program that does not.

3[B] The specification generation techniques of Section 2.2 lead to structuring specifications as unions or intersections. To what extent is this structuring a violation of the criterion of *abstraction*? Is not any form of structuring a violation of this criterion?

4[B] Comment on the use of structure and abstraction in specification generation. Can we talk of *abstracted specifying* to parallel *structured programming*?

2.6 BIBLIOGRAPHICAL NOTES

Several lists of specification properties can be found in the literature: Parnas (1972) advocates (if we may paraphrase him) completeness, minimality, formality and relevance; Liskov and Zilles (1977) advocate formality, constructibility, comprehensibility, minimality, applicability and extensibility, Caplain (1978) advocates (if we may translate him) clarity, ambiguity–tolerance, simplicity, rigor and usability; Balzer and Goldman (1979) mention (if we may paraphrase them) abstraction, generality, completeness, understandability, executability, ambiguity–tolerance, and modularity; referring to them colorfully as *the seven sins of the specifier*, Meyer (1985) proscribes noise, silence, overspecification, contradiction, ambiguity, forward reference, and wishful thinking.

General topics on predicate-based specifications can be found in Hoare (1969), Gries (1981) and Manna (1974). General topics on relational specifications can be found in Abrial *et al.* (1980), Jones (1980), Jones (1986), Linger *et al.* (1979), Mills *et al.* (1986), Sanderson (1980) and Mili *et al.* (1986).

Recent theoretical developments in the field of program specifications can be found in *IEEE* (1979) and Yeh (1977). The *pulse* of the general field of software specification can be read in the proceedings of the current series of *International Workshops on Software Specification and Design*: Ohno (1982), Babb and Mili (1984), Hennell (1985), Harandi (1987) and Potts (1989).

CHAPTER 3

Program verification and construction

In this book, we take a *structured-programming* approach to program fault tolerance. Specifically, we use a relational/functional form of structured programming. In this chapter, we introduce the basic ingredients of this approach which allow us to formulate problems, and then we derive and interpret solutions to the topic of our interest.

In Section 3.1, we study the generation of the function computed by a program. In Section 3.2, we study the verification of the correctness of a program with respect to a given specification. In Section 3.3, we discuss summarily how to construct a program from a given specification, in terms of the relational level of abstraction.

The language that we have selected for the purpose of our discussions is a simple subset of Pascal. While this choice is somewhat arbitrary, it is also of little consequence; indeed, we have made every effort to make the programming language used as transparent as possible to the developments of this book. Specifically, the results of this book are transportable, at minimal cost, to other languages that have the following features: the notion of execution state can be defined, and can be interpreted as carrying the history of past computations; the notion of program function can be defined, and can be interpreted as mapping inputs to outputs; program functions are defined/computed inductively by means of iteration or recursion; the constructs of the language can be captured by relational operators. As the reader can appreciate, these conditions are hardly restrictive, and hold for a large class of languages.

3.1 THE FUNCTIONAL ANALYSIS OF PROGRAMS

The approach that we take to the functional analysis of programs is deductive: the function of a complex program is computed from the functions of its components.

3.1.1 Functional Abstraction: Definitions

Let P be a program on variables a, b, c of types A, B, C. If we are only interested in the values of a, b, c that verify some predicate $q(a, b, c)$, then we define the *space* of program P as the set:

```
S = set
crt
   a: A;
   b: B;
   c: C;
sub
   q(a, b, c)
end.
```

Elements of S are called the *states* of program P; when program P starts its execution with initial values a_0 for a, b_0 for b and c_0 for c, we say that $s_0 = \langle a_0, b_0, c_0 \rangle$ is an *initial state* of the program; when program P terminates its execution with final values a_f for a, b_f for b and c_f for c, we say that $s_f = \langle a_f, b_f, c_f \rangle$ is a *finite state* of program P.

When P is executed on some initial state s, one of several conditions may occur, as follows:

1. P terminates normally after a finite amount of time (a finite number of steps) in some final state s'.
2. P engages in an infinite loop – so that it produces no definable final state.
3. P attempts some undefined operation such as the logarithm of a negative number, the division by zero, the attempt to read beyond an end of file, etc.
4. P causes an unexpected event such as overflow, parity error, under-flow, etc.

We say that, in the first case, execution of P takes place under *normal* conditions, whereas in the other cases it takes place under *exceptional* conditions. In this book, we assume that the arithmetic of our machine is perfect, so that the only exceptional conditions with which we concern ourselves with are the infinite loop and the invocation of an undefined operation.

The *functional abstraction* of program P is the function denoted by $[P]$ and defined by:

$$[P] = \{(s, s') | \text{If } P \text{ is executed on initial state } s \text{ then it terminates normally in final state } s'\}.$$

If *f* is the functional abstraction of *P*, we say that *P computes f*. It stems from the definition of functional abstraction that:

dom([*P*]) = {*s*|If *P* is executed on state *s* then it terminates normally}.

Example 1. We give below – without proof – some examples of *functional abstractions*:

S = **real**; P = **begin** s := 1/(1 − s); s := log(s) **end**;
[*P*] = [*s* < 1, −log(1 − *s*)]; dom([*P*]) = {*s*|*s* < 1}.
S = **real**; P = **begin if** s < 4 **then** s := s + 6 **else** s := s − 5;
               if s < 6   **then** s := s + 2 **else** s := s − 1 **end**;
[*P*] = [*s* < 0, *s* + 8] ∪ [0 ≤ *s* < 4, *s* + 5] ∪ [4 ≤ *s* < 11, *s* − 3]
    ∪ [*s* ≥ 11, *s* − 6];
dom([*P*]) = S.
S = **set**
   a, b: **integer**
end;
P = **while** b ≠ 0 **do begin** a := a + 1; b := b − 1 **end**;
[*P*] = [*b*(*s*) ≥ 0, ⟨*a*(*s*) + *b*(*s*), 0⟩]; dom([*P*]) = {*s*|*b*(*s*) ≥ 0}.   □

3.1.2   Functional Abstraction: Generation

In this section we introduce a set of axioms that are useful for the generation of functional abstractions of Pascal programs. In particular, we are interested in the following eight programming constructs:

1. *Assignment* statements, of the form

   ⟨variable⟩ := ⟨expression⟩.

2. *Sequence* statements, of the form

   ⟨statement⟩; ⟨statement⟩.

3. *Alternation* statements, of the form

   if ⟨expression⟩ **then** ⟨statement⟩ **else** ⟨statement⟩.

4. *Iteration* statements, of the form

   while ⟨expression⟩ **do** ⟨statement⟩.

5. *Concurrency* statements, of the form

   cobegin ⟨statement⟩, ⟨statement⟩ **coend**.

6. *Procedure* calls, of the form

   ⟨procedure-name⟩.

7. *Parameter passing mechanisms*, such as by name and by value.
8. *Recursion*, of the form

   f(s) := **if** ⟨expression⟩ **then** ⟨expression⟩ **else** ⟨expression⟩.

For each of the programming constructs given above, we present an axiom that allows us to compute its functional abstraction; the system of axioms obtained in this manner will be adopted as our semantic definition of the programming language involved. We attempt to convince the reader of the consistency of these axioms with the operational semantics associated with the constructs at hand. Because the last four constructs (concurrency, procedure calls, parameter passing, and recursion) will not be used in the remainder of the book, their study in this chapter is not critical to the continuity of the book. However, their description is given in Section 3.4.

Assignment

Assignment statements have the form $s := E(s)$, where s is the global state of the program and E is an expression on the (whole) state of the program at hand (i.e. potentially involving all its variables). Before we interpret assignment statements, we need to give an interpretation of expressions. We discuss in turn, arithmetic expressions (on the sets **natural**, **integer** and **real**), then logical expressions (on the set **boolean**). Because we assume that Pascal's arithmetic is perfect, and because we adopt the same notations as Pascal (+ for addition, − for subtraction, ∗ for multiplication, etc.), the only difference between a Pascal expression E and its mathematical interpretation (which we denote by $[E]$) is in its reference to program variables: the interpretation of variable x appearing in expression E at state s is $x(s)$. Hence, for example, the interpretation of expression

$$x * z + y * z - x * y$$

is

x(s) ∗ z(s) + y(s) ∗ z(s) − x(s) ∗ y(s).

As this difference is minor, we will in general (whenever this does not cause confusion), identify a Pascal arithmetic expression with its mathematical interpretation. As for the interpretation of logical expressions, it is worth noting that the logical connectives of Pascal (**and, or, not**) are distinct from those used in mathematics (∧, ∨, ⌐). Hence the following definition of Pascal's logical expressions, where $[E]$ denotes the interpretation of E:

- If E is an atom, then $[E] = E(s)$, where s is the current state.
- If E is a conjunction, say $E = (E_1$ **and** $E_2)$, then $[E] = [E_1] \wedge [E_2]$.
- If E is a disjunction, say $E = (E_1$ **or** $E_2)$, then $[E] = [E_1] \vee [E_2]$.
- If E is a negation, say $E = $ **not** E', then $[E] = \neg[E']$.

Again, for the sake of readability, and because these transformations are straightforward, we may, when it does not affect understanding identify a Pascal logical expression with its mathematical interpretation.

We define, axiomatically,

Assignment axiom. $[\mathsf{s} := \mathsf{E}(\mathsf{s})] = [\in \mathsf{def}(\mathsf{E}), \mathsf{E}(\mathsf{s})]$.

In order for statement $s := E(s)$ to be normally executable, the initial state must be in the domain of definition of expression E; in addition, the final state generated by the execution of this statement on s is then $E(\mathsf{s})$.

Example 2. Let S be

```
set
    a, b: real
end
```

and P be

```
begin b := log(a + b) end.
```

Then we interpret this statement as having the form

$$s := E(s)$$

where

$$s = \langle a(s), b(s) \rangle$$

and

$$E(s) = \langle a(s), \log(a(s) + b(s)) \rangle;$$

we have

$$\mathsf{def}(E) = \{s \mid a(s) + b(s) > 0\};$$

hence

$$[P] = [a(s) + b(s) > 0, \langle a(s), \log(a(s) + b(s)) \rangle] \qquad \square$$

Sequence

Sequence axiom. $[\mathsf{P1}; \mathsf{P2}] = [\mathsf{P1}] * [\mathsf{P2}]$.

A pair of states (s, s') belongs to the function $[P_1; P_2]$ if and only if there exists an intermediate state s'' such that $(s, s'') \in [P_1]$ and $(s'', s') \in [P_2]$.

Example 3

S = **real**; P = **begin** s := s + 1; s := s * s **end**.
$[P]$ = [**true**, $s + 1$] * [**true**, s^2]
   = [**true**, $(s + 1)^2$].
S = **real**; P = **begin** s := 1/(1 − s); s := log(s) **end**.
$[P]$ = [$s \neq 1$, $1/(1 - s)$] * [$s > 0, \log(s)$]
   = [$s \neq 1 \wedge (1 - s) > 0$, $-\log(1 - s)$]
   = [$s < 1$, $-\log(1 - s)$].
S = **real**; P = **begin** s := s * s + 4; s := log(3 − s) **end**.
$[P]$ = [**true**, $s^2 + 4$] * [$3 - s > 0$, $\log(3 - s)$]
   = [**true** & $3 - s^2 - 4 > 0$, $\log(3 - s^2 - 4)$]
   = ϕ.   □

Alternation

Alternation axiom. [**if** t **then** tc **else** ec] = I(def(t)) * (I(t) * [tc] ∪ I(⌐t) * [ec]).

We first interpret the expression

$$(I(t) * [tc] \cup I(\neg t) * [ec]),$$

then the factor $I(\mathrm{def}(t))$. Given that the logical expression t is defined, the set of pairs that constitutes the function

[**if** t **then** tc **else** ec]

is the union of two disjoint sets: the set of pairs (s, s') such that $t(s)$ holds and $s' = [tc](s)$; and the set of pairs (s, s') such that $\neg t(s)$ holds and $s' = [ec](s)$. Now, clearly, the alternation statement is not defined unless expression t can be computed; hence the restrictive factor $I(\mathrm{def}(t))$ on the left. Whenever t is defined on all S, $I(\mathrm{def}(t))$ is identified with I, and can be dropped totally from the above expression.

From the alternation axiom we can deduce the axiom that treats the particular case of the conditional statement: **if** t **then** tc.

Conditional axiom. [**if** t **then** tc] = I(def(t)) * (I(t) * [tc] ∪ I(⌐t)).

Statement (**if** t **then** tc) is equivalent to (**if** t **then** tc **else**), and the functional abstraction of the empty statement following **else** is the identity function.

Example 4. This example combines the alternation axiom with those of assignment and sequence:

S = **real**; P = **begin if** s < 4 **then** s := s + 6 **else** s := s − 5;
      if s < 6 **then** s := s + 2 **else** s := s − 1 **end**.

$$[P] = ([s < 4, s + 6] \cup [s \geq 4, s - 5]) * ([s < 6, s + 2]$$
$$\cup [s \geq 6, s - 1])$$
$$= [s < 4 \wedge s + 6 < 6, s + 8] \cup [s < 4 \wedge s + 6 \geq 6, s + 5] \cup$$
$$[s \geq 4 \wedge s - 5 < 6, s - 3] \cup [s \geq 4 \wedge s - 5 \geq 6, s - 6]$$
$$= [s < 0, s + 8] \cup [0 \leq s < 4, s + 5] \cup [4 \leq s \leq 11, s - 3]$$
$$\cup [s \geq 11, s - 6].$$ □

Iteration

Iteration axiom. **[while** t **do** b] = (I(def(t)) * I(t) * [b])* * I(def(t)) * I($\neg$t).

Of course, the factor $I(\text{def}(t))$ plays the same role as in the axioms of alternation and conditional; in the forthcoming discussions we assume t to be defined on all S, so that the expressions we discuss is:

$$(I(t) * [b])^* * I(\neg t).$$

The term $I(t)$ in the above formula represents the execution of a test of condition t, with a **true** outcome; $I(t) * [b]$ represents the sequence of testing condition t (and finding it to be **true**) then executing block b; $(I(t) * [b])^*$ represents the possibility that the test-t-execute-b sequence be repeated an arbitrary number of times; the factor $I(\neg t)$ represents the fact that this iteration process is interrupted when testing condition t yields a **false** outcome.

Even though it is constructive, this definition of the loop function is of little help in practice − for the determination of the transitive closure is potentially complex. Below, we propose an alternative definition of [w] which is often more useful in practice − once a good guess is found for the function computed by the loop.

● *Theorem of the **while** statement*. Original version due to Mills *et al.* (1986). Let $w = (\textbf{while } t \textbf{ do } b)$ be a while statement on space S and let f be a function on S. Then $[w] = f$ if and only if:

p0: $I(\neg t) * f = I(\neg t)$,
p1: $I(t) * f = I(t) * [b] * f$,
p2: $\text{dom}(f) = \text{dom}([w])$.

Proof. The proof of necessity is quite simple: If $[w] = f$ then p0 and p1 can be verified using the iteration axiom, and p2 is a tautology. As for the sufficiency of premises p0, p1 and p2, one can prove it as follows: let s be an element of dom($[w]$), by p2, $s \in$ dom(f); we wish to prove that $s \cdot f = s \cdot [w]$. If $\neg t(s)$ holds, then $(s \cdot f = s \cdot [w])$ stems from p0 and from the operational semantics of while loops. Suppose that $t(s)$ holds; by the operational semantics of while loops there exists $i > 0$ such that $s \cdot [w] = s \cdot (I(t) * [b])^i$. We apply $I(\neg t)$ on the right-hand side of the equality:

$$s \cdot [w] * I(\neg t) = s \cdot (I(t) * [b])^i * I(\neg t).$$

Now, because rng($[w]$) $\subseteq S|\neg t$, we have $[w] * I(\neg t) = [w]$; hence

$$s \cdot [w] = s \cdot (I(t) * [b])^i * I(\neg t).$$

By premise p0, we can write

$$s \cdot [w] = s \cdot (I(t) * [b])^i * (I(\neg t) * f).$$

Because t does not hold for the final state $s \cdot (I(t) * [b])^i$ we obtain

$$s \cdot (I(t) * [b])^i * I(\neg t) = s \cdot (I(t) * [b])^i,$$

whence

$$s \cdot [w] = s \cdot (I(t) * [b])^i * f.$$

We factor out $(I(t) * [b])$:

$$s \cdot [w] = s \cdot (I(t) * [b])^{i-1} * (I(t) * [b] * f).$$

By premise p1, we obtain

$$s \cdot [w] = s \cdot (I(t) * [b])^{i-1} * (I(t) * f).$$

By definition of i, $s \in$ dom$((I(t) * [b])^i)$; hence $s \cdot (I(t) * [b])^{i-1} \in$ dom($I(t) * [b]$). Now, dom($I(t) * [b]$) $\subseteq$ dom($I(t)$) $= S|t$; hence $s \cdot (I(t) * [b])^{i-1}$ verifies t and we obtain

$$s \cdot [w] = s \cdot (I(t)[b])^{i-1} * f.$$

Factoring out all the $i - 1$ factors $(I(t) * [b])$ as we just did, we obtain

$$s \cdot [w] = s \cdot f. \hspace{4cm} \text{[QED]}$$

Given a **while** statement w = (**while** t **do** b), we can determine its functional abstraction in one of two ways:

1. The formula $[w] = (I(t) * [b])^* * I(\neg t)$,
2. The formula $[w]$ = the function that verifies premises p0, p1, and p2.

In the remainder of this book, we will use one formula or the other, depending on our needs. Below, we give two simple examples of the application of these two formulas.

Example 5

$$S = \textbf{set}$$
$$\text{x, y, z: } \textbf{integer}$$
$$\textbf{end},$$
$$w = \textbf{while } y \neq 0 \textbf{ do begin } y := y - 1; \ z := z + x \textbf{ end}.$$

We use the formula $[w] = (I(t) * [b])^* * I(\neg t)$.

$$I(t) = \{(s, s') \mid s' = s \land y(s) \neq 0\}.$$
$$[b] = \{(s, s') \mid x(s') = x(s) \land y(s') = y(s) - 1 \land z(s') = z(s) + x(s)\}.$$
$$I(t) * [b] = \{(s, s') \mid y(s) \neq 0 \land x(s') = x(s) \land y(s') = y(s) - 1$$
$$\land \ z(s') = z(s) + x(s)\}.$$

The transitive closure of this relation is

$$(I(t) * [b])^+ = \{(s, s') \mid \exists i > 0: (\forall k, 0 \leq k \leq i \Rightarrow y(s) - k \neq 0)$$
$$\land \ x(s') = x(s) \land y(s') = y(s) - i$$
$$\land \ z(s') = z(s) + i * x(s)\}.$$
$$(I(t) * [b])^+ * I(\neg t) = \{(s, s') \mid \exists i > 0: (\forall k, 0 \leq k < i \Rightarrow y(s) - k \neq 0)$$
$$\land \ x(s') = x(s) \land y(s') = y(s) - i$$
$$\land \ z(s') = z(s) + i * x(s) \land y(s') = 0\}$$
$$= \{(s, s') \mid (\forall k, 0 \leq k < y(s) \Rightarrow y(s) - k \neq 0)$$
$$\land \ x(s') = x(s) \land y(s') = 0$$
$$\land \ z(s') = z(s) + y(s) * x(s)\}$$
$$= \{(s, s') \mid y(s) > 0 \land x(s') = x(s)$$
$$\land \ y(s') = 0 \land z(s') = z(s) + y(s) * x(s)\}.$$

Because for any relation A, $A^* = A^+ \cup I$, we obtain

$$(I(t) * [b])^* * I(\neg t) = (I(t) * [b])^+ * I(\neg t) \cup I(\neg t)$$
$$= \{(s, s') \mid y(s) > 0 \land x(s') = x(s) \land y(s') = 0$$
$$\land \ z(s') = z(s) + y(s) * x(s)\}$$
$$\cup$$
$$\{(s, s') \mid y(s) = 0 \land s' = s\}$$
$$= \{(s, s') \mid y(s) > 0 \land x(s') = x(s) \land y(s') = 0$$
$$\land \ z(s') = z(s) + x(s) * y(s)\}$$
$$\cup$$
$$\{(s, s') \mid y(s) = 0 \land x(s') = x(s) \land y(s') = 0$$
$$\land \ z(s') = z(s) + x(s) * y(s)\}$$
$$= \{(s, s') \mid y(s) \geq 0 \land x(s') = x(s) \land y(s') = 0$$
$$\land \ z(s') = z(s) + x(s) * y(s)\}.$$

Interpretation: statement w is defined for non-negative y only; when it terminates, it cancels y, adds $x(s) * y(s)$ to z and preserves x.   □

Even though this program is quite simple, computing its functional abstraction does prove difficult – due to the transitive closure. In the following example, application of the constructive method would prove nearly impossible. We will then resort to characterizing $[w]$ by premises p0, p1 and p2.

Example 6

```
S = set
crt
   x, y: integer;
sub
   x > 0 ∧ y > 0
end.
w = while x ≠ y do if x > y then x := x − y else y := y − x.
```

We denote by $\gcd(s)$ the greatest common divisor of $x(s)$ and $y(s)$. We pose

$$f = [\textbf{true}, \langle \gcd(s), \gcd(s) \rangle]$$

and we verify that f satisfies premises p0, p1 and p2 of the **while** statement theorem; we will then deduce $[w] = f$.

p0: $I(x(s) = y(s)) * f = [x(s) = y(s), \langle \gcd(s), \gcd(s) \rangle]$;
it is a well-known property of the gcd function that if $x = y$, then $\gcd(x, y) = x = y$.
$= [x(s) = y(s), \langle x(s), y(s) \rangle]$
$= I(x(s) = y(s))$.

p1: $I(x(s) \neq y(s)) * [b] * f$
$= [x(s) \neq y(s), s] * ([x(s) > y(s), \langle x(s) - y(s), y(s) \rangle]$
$\quad \cup\ [x(s) \leq y(s), \langle x(s), y(s) - x(s) \rangle]) * f$
$= [x(s) \neq y(s), s] * [x(s) > y(s), \langle x(s) - y(s), y(s) \rangle] * f$
$\quad \cup$
$\quad [x(s) \neq y(s), s] * [x(s) \leq y(s), \langle x(s), y(s) - x(s) \rangle] * f$
$= [x(s) > y(s), \langle \gcd(x(s) - y(s), y(s)), \gcd(x(s) - y(s), y(s)) \rangle]$
$\quad \cup$
$\quad [x(s) < y(s), \langle \gcd(x(s), y(s) - x(s)), \gcd(x(s), y(s) - x(s)) \rangle]$.
Using Euclid's identities, we get
$= [x(s) > y(s), \langle \gcd(s), \gcd(s) \rangle] \cup [x(s) < y(s), \langle \gcd(s), \gcd(s) \rangle]$
$= [x(s) \neq y(s), \langle \gcd(s), \gcd(s) \rangle]$
$= I(x(s) \neq y(s)) * f$.

p2: $\operatorname{dom}(f) = S$; on the other hand, w terminates for any initial state in S, hence $\operatorname{dom}([w]) = S$.   □

3.1.3   Exercises

1[A]   Using the axioms of Section 3.1.2, compute the following functional abstractions:

    (a) S = **real**;
        p = **begin** s := 1/s; s := 1/(1 − s) **end**.
    (b) S = **real**;
        p = **begin** s := 1/(1 − s); s := 1/s **end**.
    (c) S = **real**;
        p = **begin** s := s * s; **if** s < 0 **then** s := s + 1 **end**.
    (d) S = **real**;
        p = **begin if** s < 0 **then** s := s + 1; s := s * s **end**.
    (e) S = **real**;
        p = **begin** s := s * s + 1; **if** s > 0 **then** s := log(1 − s) **end**.

2[A]   Using the axioms of Section 3.1.2, compute the following functional abstractions on S = **integer**:

    (a) p = **if** s > 0 **then** s := sqrt(s + 1) **else** s := sqrt(−s + 1).
    (b) p = **if** s > 0 **then** s := sqrt(s + 1) **else** s := sqrt(s − 1).
    (c) p = **if** s > 0 **then** s := sqrt(−s − 1) **else** s := sqrt(s).
    (d) p = **if** s > 0 **then** s := sqrt(−s) **else** s := sqrt(s).
    (e) p = **if** s > 0 **then** s := sqrt(−s − 1) **else** s := sqrt(s − 1).

3[A]   Using the axioms of Section 3.1.2, compute the following functional abstractions on S = **integer**:

    (a) p = **begin if** s > 0 **then** s := s + 8 **else** s := s − 8;
              if s * s < 4 **then** s := s + 4 **else** s := sqrt(−s * s + 8)
              end.
    (b) p = **begin if** s > 0 **then** s := s + 4 **else** s := s − 4;
              if s > 16 **then** s := s − 4 **else** s := sqrt(s − 25) **end**.
    (c) p = **begin if** s > 0 **then** s := s + 2 **else** s := s − 2;
              if s > 0 **then** s := s + 4 **else** s := s − 4 **end**.
    (d) p = **begin if** s > 0 **then** s := s + 2 **else** s := s − 2;
              if s > 8 **then** s := s + 2 **else** s := s − 2 **end**.
    (e) p = **begin if** s > 0 **then** s := s − 6 **else** s := s + 6;
              if s > 2 **then** s := s − 2 **else** s := s + 2 **end**.

4[A]   Use the *iteration axiom* to constructively compute the functional abstraction of the following statement on S:

     set
     x, y: **integer**
     end,
     w = **while** y ≠ 0 **do begin** x := x + 1; y := y − 1 **end**.

To do so, take the following steps sequentially:
(a) Compute $[b]$, then $I(t) * [b]$.
(b) Compute $(I(t) * [b])^2$ then deduce a formula for $(I(t) * [b])^i$.
(c) Compute $(I(t) * [b])^+$, then $(I(t) * [b])^+ * I(\neg t)$.
(d) Compute $(I(t) * [b])^* * I(\neg t)$.
(e) As an additional step, consider the formula

$$f = (I(t) * [b])^* * I(\neg t).$$

Briefly verify the conditions of the iteration theorem on this expression of f.

5[A] Use the *iteration axiom* to compute constructively the functional abstraction of the following statements on $S = $ **integer**:

(a) **while** s = 10 **do** s := s + 1;
(b) **while** s ≠ 10 **do** s := s + 1;
(c) **while** s < 10 **do** s := s + 1;
(d) **while** s > 10 **do** s := s + 1;
(e) **while false do** s := s + 1.

6[A] Using the iteration theorem (henceforth implicit), derive the functional abstraction of the following programs on $S = $ **integer**:

(a) **while** s = 10 **do** s := s + 1;
(b) **while** s ≠ 10 **do** s := s + 1;
(c) **while** s < 10 **do** s := s + 1;
(d) **while** s > 10 **do** s := s + 1;
(e) **while false do** s := s + 1.

7[A] Compute the functional abstraction of the following programs on

    S = **set**
      x, y, z: **integer**
    end.
(a) **while** y > 0 **do begin** y := y − 1; z := z + x **end**.
(b) **begin** y := 10; **while** y > 0 **do begin** y := y − 1; z := z + x **end end**.
(c) **begin** z := 0; **while** y > 0 **do begin** y := y − 1; z := z + x **end end**.
(d) **begin** z := 0; y := 10;
       while y > 0 **do begin** y := y − 1; z := z + x **end end**.
(e) **begin** z := 0; y := −1;
       while y > 0 **do begin** y := y − 1; z := z + x **end end**.

8[A] Compute the functional abstraction of the following programs on

    S = **set**
      x, y, z: **natural**
    end.

(a) **while** x ≥ y **do begin** x := x − y; z := z + 1 **end.**
(b) **begin** z := 0; **while** x ≥ y **do begin** x := x − y; z := z + 1 **end end.**
(c) **begin** z := 0; y := 0;
    while x ≥ y **do begin** x := x − y; z := z + 1 **end end.**
(d) **begin** x := 0; **while** x ≥ y **do begin** x := x − y; z := z + 1 **end end.**
(e) **begin** z := 0; y := 1;
    while x ≥ y **do begin** x := x − y; z := z + 1 **end end.**

3.2 PROGRAM CORRECTNESS

Now that we have defined the functional abstraction and the specification of a program, we discuss how we can match a program against a specification in order to determine whether the program is correct with respect to the specification.

3.2.1 Correctness: An Illustration

Let S be the space $\{a,b,c,d,e,f\}$ and let R be the relation defined on S by

$$R = \{(a,a), (a,b), (a,c), (b,b), (b,c), (b,d), (c,c), (c,d), (c,e),$$
$$(d,d), (d,e), (d,f)\}.$$

Let p be the program on S whose functional abstraction is:

$$[p] = \{(a,c), (b,c), (c,c), (d,f), (e,f), (f,f)\}.$$

Function $[p]$ is defined for all states in $\mathrm{dom}(R)$; in addition, for each s in $\mathrm{dom}(R)$, $[p](s)$ is one of the final states that R considers correct for s. We then say that p is *totally correct* with respect to R.

Let p' be a program on space S such that

$$[p'] = \{(a,a), (b,b), (c,c), (f,f)\}.$$

One can see that $[p']$ is not defined for all s in $\mathrm{dom}(R)$ since it is not defined for $s = d$. However, wherever $[p']$ is defined, it behaves as recommended by R. We then say that p' is *partially correct* with respect to R. The notion of partial correctness is arbitrarily weak since a program p' whose functional abstraction is empty, i.e. which fails to terminate for all its initial states, is partially correct with respect to any specification.

Let p'' be a program on space S such that

$$[p''] = \{(a,a), (b,a), (c,c), (d,c), (e,e), (f,e)\}.$$

One can see that $[p'']$ is defined for all s in $dom(R)$; $[p''](s)$ may (as in the case of a) or may not (as in the case of b) belong to $s \cdot R$. We then say that p'' is *defined* with respect to R, or that it *terminates* with respect to R.

3.2.2   Correctness: Formal Presentation

The mathematical formulas given below reflect the informal explanations given in the preceding section.

- *Definition – total correctness.* A program p is said to be *totally correct* with respect to specification R if and only if

$$(\forall s, s \in dom(R) \Rightarrow s \in dom([p]) \land (s, [p](s)) \in R).$$

When the context does not lend to confusion, we may sometimes omit the adverb *totally*.

- *Definition – partial correctness.* Program p is said to be *partially correct* with respect to specification R if and only if

$$(\forall s, s \in dom(R) \land s \in dom([p]) \Rightarrow (s, [p](s)) \in R).$$

The difference between this and the previous definition is that clause $s \in dom([p])$ has changed sides with respect to the $\Rightarrow$ sign, whereas in the definition of total correctness clause $s \in dom([p])$ results from the pre-condition $s \in dom(R)$; in definition of partial correctness clause $s \in dom([p])$ must be conjuncted with $s \in dom(R)$ to yield the post-condition $(s, [p](s)) \in R$.

- *Definition – termination.* Program p is said to be *defined* (or: to *terminate*) with respect to specification R if and only if

$$(\forall s, s \in dom(R) \Rightarrow s \in dom([p])).$$

It is worth noting that these definitions are equivalent to the usual definitions given in the program correctness literature, even though they are formally different. For all their ease of interpretation, these formulas are nevertheless difficult to use and below we give equivalent formulas which are easier to use in practice.

- *Proposition 1* (due to Mills *et al.* 1986). Program p is correct with respect to specification R if and only if

$$dom(R \cap [p]) = dom(R).$$

Proof. Because $\operatorname{dom}(R \cap [p]) \subseteq \operatorname{dom}(R)$ is a tautology, the formula above is equivalent to $\operatorname{dom}(R) \subseteq \operatorname{dom}(R \cap [p])$. We have to prove the equivalence of

$$\operatorname{dom}(R) \subseteq \operatorname{dom}(R \cap [p]) \tag{a}$$

and

$$(\forall s, s \in \operatorname{dom}(R) \Rightarrow s \in \operatorname{dom}([p]) \wedge (s, [p](s)) \in R). \tag{b}$$

$a \Rightarrow b$: let s be in $\operatorname{dom}(R)$; by (a), $s \in \operatorname{dom}(R \cap [p])$; hence there exists s' such that $(s, s') \in R \wedge (s, s') \in [p]$; hence $s \in \operatorname{dom}([p])$ and $(s, [p](s)) \in R$.

$b \Rightarrow a$: let s be in $\operatorname{dom}(R)$; by (b), $(s, [p](s)) \in R$ and by definition $(s, [p](s)) \in [p]$; hence $(s, [p](s)) \in R \cap [p]$ and $s \in \operatorname{dom}(R \cap [p])$.

[QED]

- *Proposition 2.* Program p is partially correct with respect to R if and only if

  $$\operatorname{dom}(R \cap [p]) = \operatorname{dom}(R) \cap \operatorname{dom}([p]).$$

Proof. Because $\operatorname{dom}(R \cap [p]) \subseteq \operatorname{dom}(R) \cap \operatorname{dom}([p])$ is a tautology, we shall prove the equivalence of

$$\operatorname{dom}(R) \cap \operatorname{dom}([p]) \subseteq \operatorname{dom}(R \cap [p]) \tag{a}$$

and

$$(\forall s, s \in \operatorname{dom}(R) \wedge s \in \operatorname{dom}([p]) \Rightarrow (s, [p](s)) \in R). \tag{b}$$

$a \Rightarrow b$: let s be an element of $\operatorname{dom}(R)$ and $\operatorname{dom}([p])$; by (a), $s \in \operatorname{dom}(R \cap [p])$, i.e. there exists s' such that $(s, s') \in R \cap [p]$; hence $(s, s') \in R$ and $(s, s') \in [p]$. From the latter conjunct we deduce $s' = [p](s)$, which we replace in the former conjunct to obtain $(s, [p](s)) \in R$.

$b \Rightarrow a$: let s be an element of $\operatorname{dom}(R) \cap \operatorname{dom}([p])$; by (b), $(s, [p](s)) \in R$, whence $(s, [p](s)) \in R$ and $(s, [p](s)) \in [p]$, i.e. $(s, [p](s)) \in R \cap [p]$. Therefore $s \in \operatorname{dom}(R \in [p])$.   [QED]

- *Proposition 3.* Program p is defined with respect to specification R if and only if

  $$\operatorname{dom}(R) \cap \operatorname{dom}([p]) = \operatorname{dom}(R).$$

Proof. In fact this condition is equivalent to $\operatorname{dom}(R) \subseteq \operatorname{dom}([p])$, which is itself a paraphrase of the definition of termination.   [QED]

The reason why we have chosen to characterize termination by the relatively complex formula

$$\text{dom}(R) \cap \text{dom}([p]) = \text{dom}(R)$$

rather than the simple formula

$$\text{dom}(R) \subseteq \text{dom}([p])$$

is that we wish to highlight the fact that the conjunction of partial correctness and termination yields total correctness.

Below, we give, without proof, another series of three propositions for total correctness, partial correctness, and termination of programs; these propositions are based on the notion of definedness:

- *Proposition 4.* Program p is totally correct with respect to specification R if and only if $[p]$ is more-defined than R.

- *Proposition 5.* Program p is partially correct with respect to specification R if and only if $[p]$ is more-defined than $I(\text{dom}([p])) * R$.

- *Proposition 6.* Program p is defined with respect to specification R if and only if $[p]$ is more-defined than $R * U(S)$.

3.2.3   Proof of Correctness: Illustrative example

In order to prove the correctness of program p with respect to relation R, we shall compute the functional abstraction of p, then confront it against the given specification by means of the formula of Proposition 1. As an example, we consider a program that checks whether two given arrays, a and b, have some element in common. In this section we compute the functional abstraction of the program by means of the formulas given in Section 3.1; we then match this functional abstraction against some specifications and judge the correctness of p with respect to these.

Computing a Functional Abstraction: An Example

We consider the following program, whose functional abstraction we wish to compute. The parts that, for the sake of generality or simplicity, we do not wish to take into account are embedded as comments:

```
program intersection (input, output);
{const
   n = 5; m = 6;
```

```
type
  item = integer;}
var
  a: array [1..n] of item;
  b: array [0..m] of item;
  i: integer; x: item; u: boolean {found};
  procedure loadata;
  var i: integer;
  begin
  for i := 1 to n do readln(a[i]);
  for i := 1 to m do readln(b[i]);
  end;
  procedure search (y: item);
  var j: integer;
  begin j := m; b(0) := y;
  while b[j]⟨⟩y do j := j − 1;
  u := u or (j⟨⟩0)
  end;
begin
{loadata;}
i := 1; u := false;
while i ≤ n do
  begin
  x := a[i];
  search(x);
  i := i + 1
  end;
{writeln(u)}
end.
```

In the remainder of this example, we denote by $a[i..j]$ the sequence $(a[i]..a[j])$ if $i \le j$ or the empty sequence if $i > j$. In addition, if x is an item and $a[i..j]$ a subarray, we represent by $x \cdot a[i..j]$ the concatenation of x to the subarray $a[i..j]$.

First of all, we compute the functional abstraction of the body of procedure search (see Sections 3.4.2 and 3.4.3 for the procedure call rule and the call by value rule). The space of this procedure is

```
S = set
  a: array [1..n] of item;
  b: array [0..m] of item;
  i, j: integer;
  x, y: item; u: boolean
```

end.
$$[j := m; \; b[0] := y] = \{(s, s') \mid a(s') = a(s) \land b(s') = y \cdot b(s)[1..m]$$
$$\land \; i(s') = i(s) \land j(s') = m$$
$$\land \; x(s') = x(s) \land y(s') = y(s)$$
$$\land \; u(s') = u(s)\}$$
$$= [\textbf{true}, \; \langle a(s), y \cdot b(s)[1..m], i(s), m, x(s), y(s), u(s) \rangle].$$

In order to compute the functional abstraction of the **while** loop, we must propose a candidate function f, and then verify premises p0, p1 and p2 of the **while** statements theorem. We propose:

$$f = \{(s, s') \mid (0 \le j(s) \le m \land (\exists k: 0 \le k \le j(s) \land b(s)[k] = y(s)))$$
$$\land \; a(s') = a(s) \land b(s') = b(s)$$
$$\land \; i(s') = i(s) \land j(s') = h(s)$$
$$\land \; x(s') = x(s) \land y(s') = y(s)$$
$$\land \; u(s') = u(s)\},$$

where $h(s)$ is the greatest index between 0 and $j(s)$, inclusive, such that $b(s)[h(s)] = y(s)$. The first clause (in parentheses) defines the domain of function f (for an interpretation of this clause, see the proof of premise p3); the other clauses express that j takes value $h(s)$ while all other variables remain unchanged:

p0: Let s be a state verifying $b(s)[j(s)] = y(s)$. It is simple to verify that we then have $(s, s) \in f$.

p1: Let s be a state verifying $b(s)[j(s)] \ne y(s)$. We must show that its images by f and by $[j := j - 1] * f$ are identical. This results immediately from the definition of $h(s)$ and the hypothesis $b(s)[j(s)] \ne y(s)$: If $b(s)[j(s)] \ne y(s)$, then the greatest index between 0 and $j(s)$ such that $b(s)[h(s)] = y(s)$ is identical to the greatest index between 0 and $j(s) - 1$ such that $b(s)[h(s)] = y(s)$.

p2: The domain of f is

$$\{s \mid 0 \le j(s) \le m \land (\exists k: 0 \le k \le j(s) \land b(s)[k] = y(s))\}.$$

Indeed, the while statement terminates normally only if $j(s)$ is a legal index $(0 \le j(s) \le m)$ and the termination condition is guaranteed to hold after a finite number if iterations.

We then have

$$[\textbf{while } b[j] \langle \rangle y \textbf{ do } j := j - 1]$$
$$= \{(s, s') \mid (0 \le j(s) \le m \land (\exists k: 0 \le k \le j(s) \land b(s)[k] = y(s)))$$
$$\land \; a(s') = a(s) \land b(s') = b(s)$$
$$\land \; i(s') = i(s) \land j(s') = h(s)$$
$$\land \; x(s') = x(s) \land y(s') = y(s) \land u(s') = u(s)\},$$

which we write under pE form as

$$= [0 \le j(s) \le m \land (\exists k: 0 \le k \le j(s) \land b(s)[k] = y(s)),$$
$$\langle a(s), b(s), i(s), h(s), x(s), y(s), u(s) \rangle].$$

It stems from the sequence axiom that:

$$[j := m; b[0] := y; \textbf{while } b[j]\langle \rangle y \textbf{ do } j := j - 1]$$
$$= [\textbf{true}, \langle a(s), y(s) \cdot b(s)[1 .. m], i(s), m, x(s), y(s), u(s) \rangle]$$
$$* [0 \le j(s) \le m \& (\exists k: 0 \le k \le j(s) \land b(s)[k] = y(s)),$$
$$\langle a(s), b(s), i(s), h(s), x(s), y(s), u(s) \rangle].$$

We use the formula of relative product:

$$= [\textbf{true} \& 0 \le m \le m \& (\exists k: 0 \le k \le m$$
$$\& (y(s) \cdot b(s)[1 .. m])[k] = y(s)),$$
$$\langle a(s), y(s) \cdot b(s)[1 .. m], i(s), H(s), x(s), y(s), u(s) \rangle],$$

where $H(s)$ is the greatest index between 0 and m such that $b(s)[k] = y(s)$. If we observe that $(0 \le m \le m)$ holds and that $k = 0$ verifies condition $(0 \le 0 \le m \land (y(s) \cdot b(s)[1 .. m])[0] = y(s))$, we can write:

$$= [\textbf{true}, \langle a(s), y(s) \cdot b(s)[1 .. m], i(s), H(s), x(s), y(s), u(s) \rangle].$$

On the other hand,

$$[u := (u \text{ or } j\langle \rangle 0)]$$
$$= [\textbf{true}, \langle a(s), b(s), i(s), j(s), x(s), y(s), u(s) \lor (j(s) \ne 0) \rangle].$$

We deduce, by the rule of sequence and the formula of relative product

$$[j := m; b[0] := y; \textbf{while } b[j]\langle \rangle y \textbf{ do } j := j - 1; u := u \text{ or } (j\langle \rangle 0)]$$
$$= [\textbf{true}, \langle a(s), y(s) \cdot b(s)[1 .. m], i(s), H(s), x(s), y(s),$$
$$u(s) \lor (H(s) \ne 0) \rangle].$$

Expression $H(s) \ne 0$ can be interpreted as follows: the greatest index between 0 and m such that $b(s)[H(s)] = y(s)$ is different from zero. This is equivalent to $y(s) \in b(s)[1 .. m]$. So that, if we call c the body of procedure *search*, we have:

$$[c] = [\textbf{true}, \langle a(s), y(s) \cdot b(s)[1 .. m], i(s), H(s), x(s), y(s),$$
$$u(s) \lor y(s) \in b(s)[1 .. m] \rangle]$$

or, equivalently

$$= \{(s, s') \mid a(s') = a(s) \land b(s') = y(s) \cdot b(s)[1 .. m] \land i(s') = i(s)$$
$$\land j(s') = H(s) \land x(s') = x(s) \land y(s') = y(s)$$
$$\land u(s') = u(s) \lor y(s) \in b(s)[1 .. m]\}.$$

We must now compute the functional abstraction of the procedure called *search (x)*, with parameter passing by value. The state of program *intersection* where this procedure call takes place is

```
S = set
   a: array [1..n] of item;
   b: array [0..m] of item;
   i: integer; x: item; u: boolean;
end.
```

Note that this definition of S involves a modification in the interpretation of variable s used so far: we will no longer talk of $j(s)$ and $y(s)$ henceforth; in keeping with the notation introduced in the parameter passing axiom, $y(s)$ will be represented by t and $j(s)$ by ι. We have

$$
\begin{aligned}
&[\text{search}(x)]\\
&= \{(s,s')\,|\,\exists t,\iota,t',\iota': x(s) = t \wedge (\langle s,t,\iota\rangle, \langle s',t',\iota'\rangle) \in [c]\}\\
&= \{(s,s')\,|\,\exists t,\iota,t',\iota': t = x(s) \wedge a(s') = a(s) \wedge b(s') = t \cdot b(s)[1..m]\\
&\qquad \wedge\, i(s') = i(s) \wedge \iota' = H(s) \wedge x(s') = x(s) \wedge t = t'\\
&\qquad \wedge\, u(s') = (u(s) \vee t \in b(s)[1..m])\}\\
&= \{(s,s')\,|\,a(s') = a(s) \wedge b(s') = x(s) \cdot b(s)[1..m] \wedge i(s') = i(s)\\
&\qquad \wedge\, x(s') = x(s) \wedge u(s') = (u(s) \vee x(s) \in b(s)[1..m])\\
&\qquad \wedge\, (\exists t,\iota,t',\iota': t = x(s) \wedge \iota' = H(s) \wedge t = t')\}\\
&= \{(s,s')\,|\,a(s') = a(s) \wedge b(s') = x(s) \cdot b(s)[1..m] \wedge i(s') = i(s)\\
&\qquad \wedge\, x(s') = x(s) \wedge u(s') = (u(s) \vee x(s) \in b(s)[1..m])\}.
\end{aligned}
$$

The pE-form of this function is

$$
= [\textbf{true}, \langle a(s), x(s) \cdot b(s)[1..m], i(s), x(s),
$$
$$
u(s) \vee x(s) \in b(s)[1..m]\rangle].
$$

On the other hand,

$$
[x := a[i]] = [\textbf{true}, \langle a(s), b(s), i(s), a(s)[i(s)], u(s)\rangle]
$$

and

$$
[i := i+1] = [\textbf{true}, \langle a(s), b(s), i(s) + 1, x(s), u(s)\rangle].
$$

Therefore

$$
\begin{aligned}
&[x := a[i]; \text{search}(x); i := i+1]\\
&= [\textbf{true}, \langle a(s), b(s), i(s), a(s)[i(s)], u(s)\rangle]\\
&* [\textbf{true}, \langle a(s), x(s) \cdot b(s)[1..m], i(s), x(s), u(s) \vee x(s) \in b(s)[1..m]\rangle]\\
&* [\textbf{true}, \langle a(s), b(s), i(s) + 1, x(s), u(s)\rangle]\\
&= [\textbf{true}, \langle a(s), a(s)[i(s)] \cdot b(s)[1..m], i(s), a(s)[i(s)],\\
&\qquad u(s) \vee a(s)[i(s)] \in b(s)[1..m]\rangle]
\end{aligned}
$$

$* [\textbf{true}, \langle a(s), b(s), i(s)+1, x(s), u(s) \rangle]$
$= [\textbf{true}, \langle a(s), a(s)[i(s)] \cdot b(s)[1..m], i(s)+1, a(s)[i(s)],$
$(u(s) \lor a(s)[i(s)] \in b(s)[1..m]) \rangle].$

In order to compute the functional abstraction of the while loop, we must propose a candidate function for which we verify premises p0, p1 and p2. We propose

$f = \{(s,s') \mid 0 \le i(s) \le n \land a(s') = a(s) \land b(s') = a(s)[n] \cdot b(s)[1..m]$
$\qquad \land\; i(s') = n+1 \land x(s') = a(s)[n] \land$
$\qquad u(s') = u(s) \lor (\exists k: i(s) \le k \le n \land a(s)[k] \in b(s)[1..m])\}$
$\cup$
$\{(s,s') \mid i(s) > n \land s' = s\}.$

We write the pE-form of this function as follows:

$f = [0 \le i(s) \le n, \langle a(s), a(s)[n] \cdot b(s)[1..m], n+1, a(s)[n],$
$\qquad u(s) \lor (\exists k: i(s) \le k \le n \land a(s)[k] \in b(s)[1..m]) \rangle]$
$\cup$
$[i(s) > n, s].$

p0: Clearly, $I(i(s) > n) * f = I(i(s) > n).$
p1: We must prove that

$$I(i(s) \le n) * [x := a[i]; \text{search}(x); i := i+1] * f = I(i(s) \le n) * f.$$

We write

$I(i(s) \le n) * [x := a[i]; \text{search}(x); i := i+1] * f$
$= [i(s) \le n, \langle a(s), a(s)[i(s)] \cdot b(s)[1..m], i(s)+1, a(s)[i(s)],$
$\qquad u(s) \lor a(s)[i(s)] \in b(s)[1..m] \rangle]$
$\quad * [0 \le i(s) \le n, \langle a(s), a(s)[n] \cdot b(s)[1..m], n+1, a(s)[n],$
$\qquad u(s) \lor (\exists k: i(s) \le k \le n \land a(s)[k] \in b(s)[1..m]) \rangle]$
$\cup$
$[i(s) \le n \land i(s)+1 > n, \langle a(s), a(s)[i(s)] \cdot b(s)[1..m], i(s)+1,$
$\qquad a(s)[i(s)], u(s) \lor a(s)[i(s)] \in b(s)[1..m] \rangle]$
$= [i(s) \le n \land 0 \le i(s)+1 \le n, \langle a(s), a(s)[n] \cdot b(s)[1..m], n+1,$
$\qquad a(s)[n], u(s) \lor a(s)[i(s)] \in b(s)[1..m]$
$\qquad \lor (\exists k: i(s)+1 > k > n \land a(s)[k] \in b(s)[1..m]) \rangle]$
$\cup$
$[i(s) = n, \langle a(s), a(s)[n] \cdot b(s)[1..m], n+1, a(s)[n],$
$\qquad u(s) \lor a(s)[n] \in b(s)[1..m] \rangle]$
$= [0 \le i(s) \le n-1, \langle a(s), a(s)[n] \cdot b(s)[1..m], n+1, a(s)[n],$
$\qquad u(s) \lor (\exists k: i(s) \le k \le n \land a(s)[k] \in b(s)[1..m]) \rangle]$
$\cup$
$[i(s) = n, \langle a(s), a(s)[n] \cdot b(s)[1..m], n+1, a(s)[n],$

$$u(s) \ \lor \ (\exists k: i(s) \leq k \leq n \ \land \ a(s)[k] \in b(s)[1..m])\rangle]$$
$$= [0 \leq i(s) \leq n, \ \langle a(s), a(s)[n] \cdot b(s)[1..m], n+1, a(s)[n],$$
$$u(s) \ \lor \ (\exists k: i(s) \leq k \leq n \ \land \ a(s)[k] \in b(s)[1..m])\rangle]$$
$$= I(i(s) \leq n) * f.$$

p2: The domain of f is S; on the other hand, it is clear that the **while** statement terminates normally for any initial state.

We consider the initialization segment:

$$[i := 1; \ u := \textbf{false}]$$
$$= [\textbf{true}, \ \langle a(s), b(s), 1, x(s), \textbf{false}\rangle].$$

We apply the sequence axiom to compute the functional abstraction of the whole program:

$$[\textbf{true}, \ \langle a(s), b(s), 1, x(s), \textbf{false}\rangle]$$
$$* \ [0 \leq i(s) \leq n, \ \langle a(s), a(s)[n] \cdot b(s)[1..m], n+1, a(s)[n],$$
$$u(s) \ \lor \ (\exists k: i(s) \leq k \leq n \ \land \ a(s)[k] \in b(s)[1..m])\rangle]$$
$$\cup$$
$$[\textbf{true}, \ \langle a(s), b(s), 1, x(s), \textbf{false}\rangle] * [i(s) > n, s]$$
$$= [0 \leq 1 \leq n, \ \langle a(s), a(s)[n] \cdot b(s)[1..m], n+1, a(s)[n],$$
$$(\exists k: 1 \leq k \leq n \ \land \ a(s)[k] \in b(s)[1..m])\rangle]$$
$$\cup$$
$$[1 > n, \ \langle a(s), b(s), 1, x(s), \textbf{false}\rangle].$$

Since we suppose that n is greater than or equal to 1, we can write

$$= [\textbf{true}, \ \langle a(s), a(s)[n] \cdot b(s)[1..m], n+1, a(s)[n],$$
$$(\exists k: 1 \leq k \leq n \ \land \ a(s)[k] \in b(s)[1..m])\rangle].$$

The expression of the final value of u can be written – perhaps more elegantly – as follows:

$$= [\textbf{true}, \ \langle a(s), a(s)[n] \cdot b(s)[1..m], n+1, a(s)[n],$$
$$a(s) \cap b(s)[1..m] \neq \varnothing\rangle].$$

In set-theoretic terms, this function can be written as:

$$= \{(s,s') \mid a(s') = a(s) \ \land \ b(s') = a(s)[n] \cdot b(s)[1..m]$$
$$\land \ i(s') = n+1 \ \land \ x(s') = a(s)[n]$$
$$\land \ u(s') = (a(s) \cap b(s)[1..m] \neq \varnothing)\}.$$

Using one representation or the other, the reader can convince himself that this function is, effectively, the function computed by the given program.   □

Matching Against Specifications

The first specification with respect to which we match the above program is

$$R = \{(s,s') \,|\, u(s') = (a(s) \cap b(s)[1..m] \neq \varnothing)\}.$$

Specification R expresses what a user is most likely to be interested in, whereas $[p]$ captures all the functional properties of program p. In this particular instance, we have $[p] \subseteq R$, hence $R \cap [p] = [p]$, and $\mathrm{dom}(R \cap [p]) = \mathrm{dom}([p]) = S$. On the other hand, $\mathrm{dom}(R) = S$. Hence p is correct with respect to R.

We consider another specification, namely:

$$R' = \{(s,s') \,|\, a(s)[1] = b(s)[1] \wedge u(s') = \textbf{true}\}.$$

This specification expresses that for all initial states s such that $a(s)[1] = b(s)[1]$, the final value of variable u is **true** (which it should be):

$$\mathrm{dom}(R') = \{s \,|\, a(s)[1] = b(s)[1]\}.$$

On the other hand,

$$
\begin{aligned}
&R' \cap [p] \\
&= \{(s,s') \,|\, a(s') = a(s) \wedge b(s') = a(s)[n] \cdot b(s)[1..m] \wedge i(s') = n+1 \\
&\qquad \wedge x(s') = a(s)[n] \wedge u(s') = (a(s) \cap b(s)[1..m] \neq \varnothing) \\
&\qquad \wedge a(s)[1] = b(s)[1] \wedge u(s') = \textbf{true}\} \\
&= \{(s,s') \,|\, a(s)[1] = b(s)[1] \wedge a(s') = a(s) \\
&\qquad \wedge b(s') = a(s)[n] \cdot b(s)[1..m] \wedge i(s') = n+1 \\
&\qquad \wedge x(s) = a(s)[n] \wedge u(s') = \textbf{true}\}.
\end{aligned}
$$

Hence,

$$\mathrm{dom}(R \cap [p]) = \{s \,|\, a(s)[1] = b(s)[1]\}.$$

Note that R is more-defined than R', so that we could have deduced the correctness of p with respect to R' from the correctness of p with respect to R (by transitivity of relational *more-defined*).

We now consider a third specification, namely

$$R'' = \{(s,s') \,|\, u(s') = \textbf{false}\}.$$

We have $\mathrm{dom}(R'') = S$. On the other hand,

$$
\begin{aligned}
&\mathrm{dom}(R'' \cap [p]) \\
&\quad = \mathrm{dom}(\{(s,s') \,|\, a(s') = a(s) \wedge b(s') = a(s)[n] \cdot b(s)[1..m] \\
&\qquad\qquad \wedge i(s') = n+1 \\
&\qquad\qquad \wedge x(s') = a(s)[n] \\
&\qquad\qquad \wedge u(s') = (a(s) \cap b(s)[1..m] \neq \varnothing) \\
&\qquad\qquad \wedge u(s') = \textbf{false}\}) \\
&\quad = \{s \,|\, a(s) \cap b(s)[1..m] = \varnothing\}.
\end{aligned}
$$

Hence p is not correct with respect to R''.

3.2.4 Exercises

1[A] Characterize the following programs on space S:
   (a) Program p is correct with respect to specification $U(S)$.
   (b) Program p is partially correct with respect to specification $U(S)$.
   (c) Program p is correct with respect to specification $I(S)$.
   (d) Program p is defined with respect to specification $I(S)$.
   (e) Program p is correct with respect to specification ϕ.

2[A] Let p be the program

while $b \neq 0$ **do begin** $c := c + a;\ b := b - 1$ **end**

on space

    S = **set**
      a, b, c: **integer**
    end.

Say whether p is correct, partially correct, or defined with respect to the following specifications:
   (a) $R = \{(s,s') \mid c(s') = c(s) + a(s) * b(s)\}$.
   (b) $R = \{(s,s') \mid b(s) = 0 \land c(s') = c(s) + a(s) * b(s)\}$.
   (c) $R = \{(s,s') \mid b(s) \geq 0 \land c(s') = a(s) * b(s)\}$.
   (d) $R = \{(s,s') \mid b(s) \geq 0 \land c(s) = 0 \land c(s') = a(s) * b(s)\}$.
   (e) $R = \{(s,s') \mid b(s) \geq 0 \land b(s') \geq 0\}$.

3[A] Let p be the program

while $b > 0$ **do begin** $c := c + a;\ b := b - 1$ **end**

on space

    S = **set**
      a, b, c: **integer**
    end.

Say whether p is correct, partially correct, or defined with respect to the following specifications.
   (a) $R = \{(s,s') \mid a(s') = a(s) \land b(s') = 0\}$.
   (b) $R = \{(s,s') \mid b(s) \neq 0 \land b(s') = 0\}$.
   (c) $R = \{(s,s') \mid b(s) \geq 0 \land c(s') = c(s) + a(s) * b(s)\}$.
   (d) $R = \{(s,s') \mid b(s) < 0 \land c(s') = c(s) + a(s) * b(s)\}$.
   (e) $R = \{(s,s') \mid b(s) < 0\}$.

4[A] We consider the program

    p = **while** n ≠ 0 **do**
          begin

```
                    fc := fc * n;
                    n := n − 1
                  end
```

on space

```
      S = set
          fc, n: natural
      end.
```

For each specification below, say whether the program is correct, partially correct or defined:
(a) $R = \{(s,s') \,|\, n(s) \geq 0 \,\wedge\, fc(s') = n(s)!\}$.
(b) $R = \{(s,s') \,|\, fc(s') = fc(s) * n(s)!\}$.
(c) $R = \{(s,s') \,|\, n(s) \geq 0 \,\wedge\, fc(s) = 1 \,\wedge\, fc(s') = n(s)!\}$.
(d) $R = \{(s,s') \,|\, n(s) \geq 0 \,\wedge\, fc(s') = fc(s) * n(s)!\}$.
(e) $R = \{(s,s') \,|\, n(s) \leq 1 \,\wedge\, fc(s') = 1\}$.

5[A]   We consider the program

```
      p = while a < b do a := a + 1
```

on space

```
      S = set
          a, b: integer
      end.
```

For each specification below, say whether the program is correct, partially correct or defined:
(a) $R = \{(s,s') \,|\, \max(s) = \max(s')\}$.
(b) $R = \{(s,s') \,|\, a(s') = \max(s)\}$.
(c) $R = \{(s,s') \,|\, a(s) > b(s) \,\wedge\, \min(s) = \min(s')\}$.
(d) $R = \{(s,s') \,|\, \min(s) = \min(s')\}$.
(e) $R = \{(s,s') \,|\, a(s) \leq b(s) \,\wedge\, a(s) = b(s')\}$.

6[A]   Let p be the program

```
      begin c := 0; while b ≠ 0 do begin c := c + a; b := b − 1 end end
```

on space

```
      S = set
          a, b, c: integer
      end.
```

Say whether p is correct, partially correct, or defined with respect to the following specifications:
(a) $R = \{(s,s') \,|\, a(s') = a(s) \,\wedge\, b(s') = 0\}$.

(b) $R = \{(s,s')|b(s) \neq 0 \land b(s') = 0\}$.
(c) $R = \{(s,s')|b(s) \geq 0 \land c(s') = c(s) + a(s) * b(s)\}$.
(d) $R = \{(s,s')|b(s) < 0 \land c(s') = c(s) + a(s) * b(s)\}$.
(e) $R = \{(s,s')|b(s) < 0\}$.

7[A] Let p be the program

```
begin c := 0; b := 10;
   while b ≠ 0 do begin c := c + a; b := b - 1
   end end
```

on space

```
S = set
   a, b, c: integer
end.
```

Say whether p is correct, partially correct, or defined with respect to the following specifications:
(a) $R = \{(s,s')|a(s') = a(s) \land b(s') = 0\}$.
(b) $R = \{(s,s')|b(s) \neq 0 \land b(s') = 0\}$.
(c) $R = \{(s,s')|b(s) \geq 0 \land c(s') = c(s) + a(s) * b(s)\}$.
(d) $R = \{(s,s')|b(s) > 0 \land c(s') = c(s) + a(s) * b(s)\}$.
(e) $R = \{(s,s')|b(s) < 0\}$.

8[A] Let p be the program

```
while b ≠ 0 do begin a := a + 1; b := b - 1 end
```

on space

```
S = set
   a, b: integer
end.
```

Say whether p is correct, partially correct, or defined with respect to the following specifications:
(a) $R = \{(s,s')|b(s') \geq 10 \land b(s') = 10\}$.
(b) $R = \{(s,s')|b(s) \geq 0 \land b(s') = 0\}$.
(c) $R = \{(s,s')|b(s) \geq 0 \land a(s') \geq a(s)\}$.
(d) $R = \{(s,s')|b(s) > 0 \land a(s') > a(s) \land b(s') = 0\}$.
(e) $R = U(S)$.

9[A] We consider the space

```
S = set
   a, b, c: integer
end
```

and the specification

$$R = \{(s,s')|b(s) \geq 0 \land c(s') = a(s) * b(s)\}.$$

Say whether the programs below are correct, partially correct or defined with respect to the specification above:

(a) p = **while** b ≠ 0 **do begin** c := c + a; b := b − 1 **end**.
(b) p = **begin** b := 15;
    while b ≠ 0 **do begin** c := c + a; b := b − 1 **end end**.
(c) p = **begin** b := 0;
    while b ≠ 0 **do begin** c := c + a; b := b − 1 **end end**.
(d) p = **begin** b := 15; c := 0;
    while b ≠ 0 **do begin** c := c + a; b := b − 1 **end end**.
(e) p = **begin** b := 10; c := 0;
    while b ≠ 0 **do begin** c := c + a; b := b − 1 **end end**.

10[A] Characterize specification R that verifies the following conditions:
(a) Any program is correct with respect to R.
(b) Any program is partially correct with respect to R.
(c) Any program is defined with respect to R.
(d) The empty program (whose abstraction is I) is correct with respect to R.
(e) A program whose abstraction is $I(t)$, for some predicate t on S is correct with respect to R.

3.3   PROGRAM CONSTRUCTION

In this section we address the problem of program construction. We take a relational approach to this problem, formalizing each design decision in terms of relational manipulations.

3.3.1   Construction Model

Because a specification is a relation, the stepwise refinement of a program from a specification consists in a progressive transformation of a relation, say R, into a program. A natural pattern to this activity is the following:

• *Construct(R).* If R is *sufficiently simple*
  then   extract a correct program from R
  else derive one or more relations from R apply the construction process to them

The construction process described above immediately raises three crucial questions, namely: (i) How do we define the simplicity of a relation; in particular, when do we say that a relation is simple enough? (ii) How do we extract a correct program from a given specification? (iii) What does it mean to 'derive one or more relations' from a given relation R?

The first question, along with extensions of it, will be discussed in Section 3.3.2. The second question stems readily from our definition of program correctness; it will be discussed briefly in Section 3.3.3. As for the third question, we have found that there are two classes of rules for deriving one or more relations from a given relation R:

1. The *decomposition rules*, which map specification R into one or two simpler (in a sense to be defined; see Section 3.3.2) specifications. These will be discussed in Section 3.3.4.
2. The *generalization rule*, which maps specification R into a more general (in a sense to be defined) specification. This rule will be discussed in Section 3.3.5.

3.3.2 Simplicity of a Relation

The notion of simplicity of a relation (interpreted as a specification) resists easy formal definition. It is reasonable to view the property of simplicity as the disjunction of several independent criteria of simplicity. We have identified two of these criteria and they are the subject of the next two sections.

Simplicity: Intrinsic Criterion

In this section we discuss a criterion of simplicity that depends on the very set of pairs that the relation contains, rather than how the relation is represented. We call this an *intrinsic criterion* of simplicity. Before we define this criterion, we wish to illustrate it with a simple example. Let a, b, c, d, e be *abstract* names of elements (i.e. there is no successor relationship between a and b, b and c, ...) and let S be the set $\{a, b, c, d, e\}$. Let R and R' be the following two relations:

$$R = \{(a,b), (b,c), (c,d), (d,e), (e,a)\}$$

and

$$R' = \{(a,b), (a,c), (a,d), (b,c), (b,d), (b,e), (c,d), (c,e), (c,a),$$
$$(d,e), (d,a), (d,b)\}.$$

If a programmer were given the choice between solving (i.e. finding a program correct with respect to) specification R or solving specification R', which should he choose? We suggest that he should choose R', for the two following reasons:

1. R' has a smaller domain; in other words the programmer has fewer initial states to consider (and worry about).
2. For any given argument, R' has a larger image set; in other words, for any initial state, the programmer has a wider choice of final states to map the initial state into.

The two conditions above can be written formally as follows:

$$\mathrm{dom}(R') \subseteq \mathrm{dom}(R).$$
$$\forall s \in \mathrm{dom}(R'),\ s \cdot R \subseteq s \cdot R'.$$

Whence the definition:

- *Definition.* Relation R' is said to be *intrinsically simpler* than relation R if and only if R' is less-defined than R.

In Chapter 2, we were shown that a relation (specification) is all the simpler to *generate* because it is less-defined. According to this definition (and the discussion that has led to it), a relation is all the simpler to *solve* because it is less-defined.

The purpose of the following proposition is to give an additional justification for the definition above. It shows that a specification is all the more intrinsically simple because it has more solutions (in the form of correct programs).

- *Proposition 7.* If R' is intrinsically simpler than R, then any program correct with respect to R is correct with respect to R'.

Proof. Let p be a program correct with respect to R; then $[p]$ is more-defined than R. Because R' is simpler than R, R is more-defined than R'. Hence $[p]$ is more-defined than R'.   [QED]

In the light of the above proposition, one can further motivate the choice of the least-defined specification by the following argument: when given the choice between two specifications, choose the one that has more programs correct with respect to it (then one will have an easier time finding one of them!).

Simplicity: Representational Criterion

We have identified a criterion of simplicity which resists a set-theoretic formulation; rather, it is defined on the basis of the notation used to represent relations: we call this a *representational criterion* of simplicity.

Because we have not been successful in capturing this criterion in a formal definition, we content ourselves with illustrating it by means of simple examples.

Example 7. Let R and R' be the relation on $S = $ **natural** defined as:

$$R = \{(0,2), (1,3), (2,4), (3,5)\ldots\},$$
$$R' = \{(0,1), (1,2), (2,3), (3,4)\ldots\}.$$

We suppose that the only available arithmetic operation that is available to us for the purpose of providing a closed form for these relations is the incrementation by 1. Using this arithmetic operation we can represent R' as

$$R' = \{(s,s') | s' = \text{inc}(s)\}, \text{ where } \text{inc}(s) = s + 1.$$

As for R, we represent it as $R' * R'$. Then it is reasonable to consider that R' is (representationally) simpler than R.   □

Example 8. We consider the same relations R and R' as in Example 7, but this time we consider that the only arithmetic operations available are the incrementation by 2 and the decrementation by 1. Using this arithmetic, we represent R as follows:

$$R = \{(s,s') | s' = \text{inc2}(s)\}, \text{ where } \text{inc2}(s) = s + 2.$$

In order to represent R', we introduce relation D defined as

$$D = \{(s,s') | s' = \text{dec}(s)\}, \text{ where } \text{dec}(s) = s - 1,$$

and we pose $R' = R * D$. Then it is reasonable to consider that R is (representationally) simpler than R'.   □

Examples 7 and 8 show how the same relation R may seem simpler or more complex than relation R', depending on representational conventions chosen. Here we are witnessing a measure of complexity which does not depend on the set-theoretic properties of the relation at hand; rather, it depends on how we represent relations.

The arithmetic and logical operations of a given programming language define a measure of representational simplicity; a programming language affects the program construction process through the measure of representational simplicity that it defines.

3.3.3 Assignment Rule

This is the rule that extracts a program from a specification in a single step. Specifically, it extracts an assignment statement from a representationally simple specification.

- *Rule.* Given relation R on S, find expression E on S such that $[\in \mathrm{def}(E), E]$ is more-defined than R.

- *Proposition 8.* If E is so chosen, then $(s := E(s))$ is correct with respect to R.

Proof. This is straightforward from the semantic definition of the assignment statement and from the definition of correctness.   [QED]

Example 9

$S = \textbf{integer};$

$$R = \{(s,s') \mid 0 \le s \le 9 \wedge s - 1 \le s' \le s + 2\}$$
$$\cup$$
$$\{(s,s') \mid 10 \le s \le 19 \wedge s + 1 \le s' \le s + 4\}.$$

We pose $E(s) = s + 2$; then

$$
\begin{aligned}
f &= [\in \mathrm{def}(E), E] \\
  &= [\textbf{true}, s + 2] \\
  &= \{(s,s') \mid s' = s + 2\}.
\end{aligned}
$$

Then,

$$
\begin{aligned}
R \cap f &= \{(s,s') \mid 0 \le s \le 9 \wedge s - 1 \le s' \le s + 2 \wedge s' = s + 2\} \\
&\quad \cup \\
&\quad \{(s,s') \mid 10 \le s \le 19 \wedge s + 1 \le s' \le s + 4 \wedge s' = s + 2\} \\
&= \{(s,s') \mid 0 \le s \le 19 \wedge s' = s + 2\}.
\end{aligned}
$$

Clearly, $\mathrm{dom}(R)$ and $\mathrm{dom}(R \cap f)$ are equal, since they both equal $\{s \mid 0 \le s \le 19\}$. $\square$

3.3.4 Decomposition Rules

These rules consist of transforming a (complex) specification into one or more simpler specifications. The specifications generated can be either intrinsically simpler or representationally simpler than the original specification.

A complex relation can be decomposed into the *union* of simpler relations, the *intersection* of simpler relations, the *relative product* of simpler relations of the *transitive closure* of a simpler relation. The decomposition rule by intersection proves to be of limited interest in practice, and can only be applied under very restrictive conditions. Hence we will not show it, contenting ourselves with mentioning two of its salient features: (i) it corresponds to the programming construct of concurrency; and (ii) it derives intrinsically simpler specifications than the original specification. The other three rules are given below.

Each decomposition rule will be given two names which will be used interchangeably throughout the remainder of this book: a name referring to the (Pascal-like) programming language construct defined by the decomposition; and a name referring to the relational operator defined by the decomposition. Each rule will be labelled by a superscript (r) or an (i) depending on whether the specifications generated by the rule are, respectively, representationally or intrinsically simpler than the original specification.

A: Sequence Rule (Relative Product Rule)$^{(r)}$

This rule decomposes a relation R into the relative product of two representationally simpler relations, R_1 and R_2.

- *Rule.* Given relation R on S, find R_1 and R_2 such that

  (i) $R = R_1 * R_2$;
  (ii) $\operatorname{rng}(R_1) \subseteq \operatorname{dom}(R_2)$.

- *Proposition 9.* If p_1 is correct with respect to R_1 and p_2 is correct with respect to R_2, then

  $$p = (p_1; p_2)$$

  is correct with respect to R.

Proof. Let s be in $\operatorname{dom}(R)$; by (a), $s \in \operatorname{dom}(R_1)$; because p_1 is correct with respect to R_1, we assert:

$$s \in \operatorname{dom}([p_1]) \tag{a1}$$

and

$$(s, [p_1](s)) \in R_1. \tag{b1}$$

Because of (b1), we know $[p_1](s) \in \operatorname{rng}(R_1)$; by virtue of (ii), we have $[p_1](s) \in \operatorname{dom}(R_2)$; by the correctness of p_2 with respect to R_2, we can assert

$$[p_1](s) \in \operatorname{dom}([p_2]) \tag{a2}$$

and

$$([p_1](s), [p_2]([p_1](s))) \in R_2. \tag{b2}$$

From (a1) and (a2), we deduce

$$s \in \text{dom}([p_1] * [p_2]).\hspace{4cm}\text{(a3)}$$

From (b1) and (b2), we deduce

$$(s, [p_1] * [p_2](s)) \in R_1 * R_2.\hspace{3cm}\text{(b3)}$$

Due to the semantic definition of the sequence statement, the definition of R and the definition of p, clauses (a3) and (b3) can be rewritten as

$$s \in \text{dom}([p])\hspace{5cm}\text{(a)}$$

and

$$(s, [p](s)) \in R.\hspace{5cm}\text{(b)}$$

Because (a) and (b) are the logical conclusions of $s \in \text{dom}(R)$, p is correct with respect to R.   [QED]

Example 10

  $S = \textbf{real}$,

  $R = \{(s, s') | \log(s^2 + 1) \le s' \le 2 * \log(s^2 + 1)\}.$

We pose

  $R_1 = \{(s, s') | s' = s^2 + 1\},$
  $R_2 = \{(s, s') | s > 0 \land \log(s) \le s' \le 2 * \log(s)\}.$

Now,

  $R_1 * R_2$
  $= \{(s, s') | \exists s'': s'' = s^2 + 1 \land s'' > 0 \land \log(s'') \le s' \le 2 * \log(s'')\}$
  $= \{(s, s') | s^2 + 1 > 0 \land \log(s^2 + 1) \le s' \le 2 * \log(s^2 + 1)\}$
  $= \{(s, s') | \log(s^2 + 1) \le s' \le 2 * \log(s^2 + 1)\}.$

On the other hand, we have

  $\text{rng}(R_1) = \{s | s \ge 1\},$
  $\text{dom}(R_2) = \{s | s \ge 0\},$

hence $\text{rng}(R_1) \subseteq \text{dom}(R_2)$. Hence the decomposition of R into R_1 and R_2 is valid.

Another acceptable decomposition is:

  $R_1 = \{(s, s') | s^2 + 1 \le s' \le (s^2 + 1)^2\},$
  $R_2 = \{(s, s') | s > 0 \land s' = \log(s)\}.$

It is simple to verify that $R = R_1 * R_2$. We briefly check the condition $\text{rng}(R_1) \subseteq \text{dom}(R_2)$:

$$\text{rng}(R_1) = \{s | \exists x: x^2 + 1 \le s \le (x^2 + 1)^2\}$$
$$= \{s | \exists x \ge 1: x \le s \le x^2\};$$
$$\text{dom}(R_2) = \{s | s > 0\}.$$

Clearly, we do have $\text{rng}(R_1) \subseteq \text{dom}(R_2)$. $\square$

B: Alternation Rule (Union Rule)[i]

This rule decomposes a relation R into the union of two intrinsically simpler relations TC (then-clause) and EC (else-clause).

- *Rule.* Given relation R, find relations TC and EC such that:

  (i) $R = TC \cup EC$,
  (ii) $\text{dom}(TC) \cap \text{dom}(EC) = \emptyset$.

- *Proposition 10.* If tc is correct with respect to TC and ec is correct with respect to EC, then

  p = **if** t **then** tc **else** ec

  is correct with respect to R, where $t(s) = s \in \text{dom}(TC)$.

Proof. Because tc is correct with respect to TC, we have

$$\text{dom}(TC) \subseteq \text{dom}([tc]) \tag{t1}$$
$$\forall s \in \text{dom}(TC), (s, [tc](s)) \in TC. \tag{t1$'$}$$

Because ec is correct with respect to EC, we have

$$\text{dom}(EC) \subseteq \text{dom}([ec]) \tag{e1}$$
$$\forall s \in \text{dom}(EC), (s, [ec](s)) \in EC. \tag{e1$'$}$$

From (t1) and (e1), we deduce

$$\text{dom}(I(t) * TC) \subseteq \text{dom}(I(t) * [tc]) \tag{t1}$$
$$\text{dom}(I(\neg t) * EC) \subseteq \text{dom}(I(\neg t) * [ec]). \tag{e2}$$

By definition of t, t2 and e2 can be written as

$$\text{dom}(TC) \subseteq \text{dom}(I(t) * [tc]), \tag{t3}$$
$$\text{dom}(EC) \subseteq \text{dom}(I(\neg t) * [ec]). \tag{e3}$$

Using clause (a) and the semantic definition of alternation, we deduce from t3 and e3 that

$$\text{dom}(R) \subseteq \text{dom}([p]). \tag{te}$$

Let s be in $\text{dom}(R)$. From (t1$'$) and (e1$'$), clause (a), and from the semantic definition of alternation, we deduce – by a case analysis on t – that

$$(s, [p](s)) \in R. \tag{te'}$$

From (te) and (te') we deduce the correctness of p with respect to R.

[QED]

Example 11

```
S = set
   a, b, c: integer
end
```

$$R = \{(s, s') \mid c(s') = \max(a(s), b(s))\}.$$

We may pose

$$TC = \{(s, s') \mid a(s) \geq b(s) \wedge c(s') = a(s)\},$$
$$EC = \{(s, s') \mid a(s) < b(s) \wedge c(s') = b(s)\}.$$

It is simple to check conditions (i) and (ii) of the alternation rule. □

C: Iteration Rule (Transitive Closure Rule)[r]

This rule decomposes a (complex) relation into the transitive closure of a (representationally) simpler relation. It can be applied only when the original specification meets some feasibility condition.

- *Rule.* Let R be a relation on S such that $\operatorname{dom}(R) = S$. If R verifies the *feasibility condition*

$$I(\operatorname{rng}(R)) * R = I(\operatorname{rng}(R)) \tag{F}$$

then find relation B such that

(i) $\operatorname{dom}(B) = S - \operatorname{rng}(R)$,
(ii) B^+ is a well-founded ordering,
(iii) $R = B^* * I(\operatorname{rng}(R))$.

- *Proposition 11*

(a) If R does not meet condition (F), then no relation B verifies (i), (ii) and (iii) simultaneously.
(b) If R verifies condition (F) then there exists a relation B verifying (i), (ii) and (iii), and for all b correct with respect to B, statement

$$w = \textbf{while } t \textbf{ do } b$$

is correct with respect to R, where $t(s) = s \in \text{dom}(B)$.

Proof. First of all, we admit without proof that the hypothesis $\text{dom}(R) = S$ does not affect the generality of our study; it is worth noting that this hypothesis implies, by virtue of (i), that $\neg t(s) = s \in \text{rng}(R)$. In order to prove clause (a) of the proposition, we prove that if there existed B verifying conditions (i), (ii) and (iii), then (F) is verified.

$$
\begin{aligned}
&I(\neg t) * R \\
&= I(\neg t) * B^+ * I(\neg t) \cup I(\neg t) * I(\neg t) \qquad \text{by virtue of (iii)} \\
&= \phi * I(\neg t) \cup I(\neg t) \qquad\qquad\qquad\quad \text{by virtue of (i)} \\
&= I(\neg t).
\end{aligned}
$$

Let R be a relation verifying (F). We pose $B = I(S - \text{rng}(R)) * R$ and we verify in turn all the clauses (i), (ii) and (iii) for this relation:

Clause (i). This clause stems readily from the hypothesis $\text{dom}(R) = S$ and the definition of B.

Clause (ii). In order to compute B^+, we first compute B^2; we obtain

$$
\begin{aligned}
B^2 &= I(S - \text{rng}(R)) * R * I(S - \text{rng}(R)) * R & \text{definition} \\
&= I(S - \text{rng}(R)) * (R * I(S - \text{rng}(R))) * R & \text{associativity} \\
&= I(S - \text{rng}(R)) * \phi * R & \text{rng}(R) \cap S - \text{rng}(R) \\
& & = \varnothing \\
&= \phi & \text{absorption}
\end{aligned}
$$

Therefore $B^+ = B = I(t) * R$. From $B^2 = \phi$, we deduce both that B is transitive and that it is non-infinitely-decreasing. Hence it is indeed a well-founded ordering.

Clause (iii). From $B^2 = \phi$ we deduce $B^* = I \cup B$. Hence

$$
\begin{aligned}
&B^* * I(\text{rng}(R)) \\
&= B * I(\text{rng}(R)) \cup I(\text{rng}(R)) \\
&= I(S - \text{rng}(R)) * R * I(\text{rng}(R)) \cup I(\text{rng}(R)) & \text{definition of } B \\
&= I(S - \text{rng}(R)) * R \cup I(\text{rng}(R)) & \text{post-restriction} \\
&= I(S - \text{rng}(R)) * R \cup I(\text{rng}(R)) * R & \text{condition (F)} \\
&= (I(S - \text{rng}(R)) \cup I(\text{rng}(R))) * R & \text{factoring} \\
&= R. & I * R = R \quad \text{[QED]}
\end{aligned}
$$

Let b be a program correct with respect to B. In order to prove that $w = (\textbf{while } t \textbf{ do } b)$ is correct with respect to R, we use the *subgoal induction theorem* (see the bibliography). A modified version of this theorem is given below:

Let $w = (\textbf{while } t \textbf{ do } b)$ be a program and let R be a relation on S such that $\text{dom}(R) = S$; if

(a) $\mathrm{dom}([w]) = S$,
(b) $\neg t(s) \Rightarrow (s,s) \in R$,
(c) $t(s) \wedge ([b](s),s^*) \in R \Rightarrow (s,s^*) \in R$,

then w is correct with respect to R.

In order to prove (a), it suffices to prove that w terminates for all s in S: this stems from condition (ii) and from the hypothesis that b is correct with respect to B. In order to prove (b), it suffices to notice that $\neg t(s) \Rightarrow (s,s) \in I(\neg t) \Rightarrow (s,s) \in R$. As for (c), one can prove it is follows: We must deduce $(s,s^*) \in R$ from the following hypotheses:

$$t(s) \tag{0}$$
$$([b](s),s^*) \in R \tag{1}$$
$$s \in \mathrm{dom}(B) \Rightarrow s \in \mathrm{dom}([b]) \wedge (s,[b](s)) \in B. \tag{2}$$

From (0) and (2), and from the definition of $t(s)$ (as $s \in \mathrm{dom}(B)$), we deduce

$$s \in \mathrm{dom}([b]) \wedge (s,[b](s)) \in B. \tag{3}$$

Combining (1) and (3), we obtain

$$(s,s^*) \in B * R.$$

Now,

$$\begin{aligned} B * R &= B * B^* * I(\neg t) \\ &= B^+ * I(\neg t) \\ &\subseteq R. \end{aligned}$$

Hence $(s,s^*) \in R$.   [QED]

We give three simple examples of application of this rule; we use them merely for the purpose of illustrating the iteration rule (rather than to show its applicability).

Example 12

```
S = set
crt
   a, b, c: integer;
sub
   b ≥ 0
end
```

$$R = \{(s,s') \,|\, a(s') = a(s) \wedge b(s') = 0 \wedge c(s') = c(s) + a(s) * b(s)\}.$$

We verify the condition of feasibility for R: $\mathrm{rng}(R) = \{s \,|\, b(s) = 0\}$; then

$$I(\text{rng}(R)) * R$$
$$= \{(s,s') \mid b(s) = 0 \wedge a(s') = a(s) \wedge b(s') = b(s) \wedge c(s') = c(s)\}$$
$$= I(\text{rng}(R)).$$

We are now assured of the existence of relation B. We consider clauses (i), (ii) and (iii), and we attempt to generate B in the light of these conditions. We propose

$$B = \{(s,s') \mid b(s) \neq 0 \wedge a(s') = a(s) \wedge b(s') = b(s) - 1$$
$$\wedge \; c(s') = c(s) + a(s)\}.$$

We check conditions (i), (ii) and (iii) in turn:

(i) $\text{dom}(B) = \{s \mid b(s) \neq 0\} = S - \{s \mid b(s) = 0\} = S - \text{rng}(R).$

(ii) $B^+ = \{(s,s') \mid \exists i > 0 \colon b(s) \neq 0 \wedge a(s') = a(s) \wedge b(s') = b(s) - i$
$$\wedge \; c(s') = c(s) + i * a(s)\}$$
$$\subseteq \{(s,s') \mid \exists i > 0 \colon b(s') = b(s) - i\}$$
$$= \{(s,s') \mid b(s') < b(s)\}.$$

On set S, this relation is non-infinitely decreasing, hence so is B^+ which contains it. Because B^+ is also transitive, by construction, it is a well-founded ordering.

(iii) $B^+ = \{(s,s') \mid b(s) \neq 0 \wedge a(s') = a(s) \wedge (\exists \, i > 0 \colon b(s') = b(s) - i$
$$\wedge \; c(s') = c(s) + i * a(s))\}$$
$$= \{(s,s') \mid b(s) \neq 0 \wedge a(s') = a(s) \wedge b(s') < b(s)$$
$$\wedge \; c(s') = c(s) + a(s) * (b(s) - b(s'))\}.$$
$$B^+ * I(\neg t) = \{(s,s') \mid b(s) \neq 0 \wedge a(s') = a(s) \wedge b(s) > 0$$
$$\wedge \; c(s') = c(s) + a(s) * b(s) \wedge b(s') = 0\}.$$

By definition of S, it is clear that $b(s) \neq 0$ and $b(s) > 0$ are equivalent predicates. Then

$$B^+ * I(\neg t) = \{(s,s') \mid b(s) \neq 0 \wedge a(s') = a(s) \wedge b(s') = 0$$
$$\wedge \; c(s') = c(s) + a(s) * b(s)\}.$$

As for $I(\neg t)$, we can well write it as

$$I(\neg t) = \{(s,s') \mid b(s) = 0 \wedge a(s') = a(s) \wedge b(s') = b(s) \wedge c(s') = c(s)\}$$
$$= \{(s,s') \mid b(s) = 0 \wedge a(s') = a(s) \wedge b(s') = 0$$
$$\wedge \; c(s') = c(s) + a(s) * b(s)\}.$$

Hence,

$$B^* * I(\neg t)$$
$$= B^+ * I(\neg t) \cup I(\neg t)$$
$$= \{(s,s') \mid a(s') = a(s) \wedge b(s') = 0 \wedge c(s') = c(s) + a(s) * b(s)\}$$
$$= R.$$

Hence B is a valid decomposition of R. $\square$

Example 13

$$S = \{0, 1, 2, 3, 4, 5, 6\},$$
$$R = \{(6,0), (5,1), (4,0), (3,1), (2,0), (1,1), (0,0)\}.$$

We have $\text{dom}(R) = S$ and $\text{rng}(R) = \{0, 1\}$; clearly, condition [F] is valid. We choose

$$B = \{(6,4), (5,3), (4,2), (3,1), (2,0)\};$$

then $\text{dom}(B) = \{2, 3, 4, 5, 6\}$, and condition (i) is valid. On the other hand

$$\begin{aligned}
B^* = \{ &(6,6), (6,4), (6,2), (6,0), \\
&(5,5), (5,3), (5,1), \\
&(4,4), (4,2), (4,0), \\
&(3,3), (3,1), \\
&(2,2), (2,0), \\
&(1,1), \\
&(0,0)\}.
\end{aligned}$$

Then $B^* * I(\urcorner t) = \{(6,0), (5,1), (4,0), (3,1), (2,0), (1,1), (0,0)\} = R$. Hence B is a valid decomposition of R.   □

Example 14

$$S = \textbf{natural},$$

$$R = \{(s,s') \mid s > 4 \wedge s' \leq 4\} \cup \{(s,s') \mid s \leq 4 \wedge s' = s\}.$$

Clearly, $\text{dom}(R) = S$. On the other hand, $\text{rng}(R) = \{s \mid s \leq 4\}$; let R_1 and R_2 be the two terms in the expression of R as given above. The condition of feasibility stems easily from the remarks that $I(\text{rng}(R)) * R_1 = \phi$ and $I(\text{rng}(R)) * R_2 = I(\text{rng}(R))$. We propose $B = \{(s,s') \mid s > 4 \wedge s - 4 \leq s' \leq s - 1\}$. Then $\text{dom}(B) = \{s \mid s > 4\}$, hence condition (i) is verified. In addition, we have

$$B^+ = \{(s,s') \mid s > 4 \wedge s' < s\},$$
$$B^+ * I(\urcorner t) = \{(s,s') \mid s > 4 \wedge s' \leq 4\},$$
$$B^+ * I(\urcorner t) = \{(s,s') \mid s > 4 \wedge s' \leq 4\}, \cup \{(s,s') \mid s \leq 4 \wedge s' = s\}.$$

Interpretation: If $s \leq 4$, R maps it to itself, else it maps it to an image $s' \leq 4$; B expresses that this image can be found from s by consecutive decrements of 1, 2, 3, or 4.   □

Remark. One can imagine that the search of a relation B verifying clauses (i), (ii) and (iii) is carried out in two steps:

Step 1: find a relation X such that
    (i) $\text{dom}(X) = S - \text{dom}(R)$,
    (ii) X is a well-founded ordering,
    (iii) $R = X * I(\neg t) \cup I(\neg t)$;
Step 2: find a transitive kernel B of X.

The trade-offs involved in the choice of B once X is chosen are the following:

1. One can choose for B an irreducible transitive kernel of X, as was done in Examples 12 and 13. It seems from analyzing Examples 12 and 13 that this solution leads to representationally simpler options for B.
2. One can choose for B an arbitrarily large transitive kernel of X. Note that $\text{dom}(B) = \text{dom}(X)$, hence the larger B is, the less-defined (and less-deterministic) it is because its domain is fixed (equal to $\text{dom}(X)$). Thus this solution leads clearly to intrinsically simpler values for B. This was the choice made in Example 14; a choice that is representationally simpler and intrinsically more complex than Example 14 is, for example, $B' = \{(s, s') | s > 4 \wedge s' = s - 1\}$.

It follows from the foregoing discussion that the derivation of B from X depends heavily on whether we favor an intrinsic or a representational criterion of simplicity for B. In Example 12 we adopted option 1 by choosing B as an irreducible transitive kernel of X; another transitive kernel of X that we could have chosen is

$$B' = \{(s, s') | b(s) > 0 \wedge a(s') = a(s) \wedge b(s') = b(s) - 1$$
$$\wedge \ c(s') = c(s) + a(s)\}$$
$$\cup$$
$$\{(s, s') | b(s) > 1 \wedge a(s') = a(s) \wedge b(s') = b(s) - 2$$
$$\wedge \ c(s') = c(s) + 2 * a(s)\}.$$

B' is intrinsically simpler than B; it is easy to convince oneself that – in our mode of representation – B is representationally simpler than B'. In Example 14, we adopted policy 2 by choosing B rather large – hence (because its domain is necessarily $\{s | s > 4\}$) intrinsically rather simple.   □

3.3.5 The Generalization Rule

The generalization rule generates no programming language construct; rather, it maps a relation into a less intrinsically simple relation. This paradoxical rule is an instance of the well-known pattern of problem-solving that bears the same name: given a specific problem P, solve a more general problem P', and deduce the solution of P as a particular instance. Perhaps is it better described by a logician (Larson, 1983):

- It may seem paradoxical but it is often the case that a problem can be simplified, and made more tractable and understandable, when it is generalized... A more general setting provides a broader perspective, strips away nonessential features, and provides a whole new arsenal of techniques.

The programming equivalent of this problem-solving pattern is discussed below.

- *Rule.* Given relation R, find a relation R' that is more-defined than R.

- *Proposition 12.* If p is correct with respect to R', then it is correct with respect to R.

Proof. If p is correct with respect to R', then $[p]$ is more-defined than R', hence $[p]$ is more-defined than R.   [QED]

Example 15

$$S = \{(0,1,2,3,4,5,6\},$$
$$R = \{(6,0),\ (5,1),\ (4,0),\ (3,1),\ (2,0)\}.$$

Clearly, the iterative statement

$$w = \textbf{while } s > 1 \textbf{ do } s := s - 2$$

(that we could derive from Example 13) is correct with respect to R; it is then reasonable to think that one can derive w from R by applying the iteration rule. It turns out not to be the case, for relation R does not meet the condition of feasibility:

$$I(\mathrm{rng}(R)) = \{(0,0),\ (1,1)\},$$
$$I(\mathrm{rng}(R)) * R = \phi.$$

Yet, it is a simple matter to apply the generalization rule to R, mapping it to

$$R' = \{(6,0),\ (5,1),\ (4,0),\ (3,1),\ (2,0),\ (1,1),\ (0,0)\}.$$

Now, R' does meet the feasibility condition and the iteration rule can be applied to it. In this first example, R' was obtained from R by enlarging its domain; one could conceive another scenario, where the generalization rule deduces the output per input ratio – while preserving the domain:

$$R = \{(6,0), (5,1), (4,0), (3,1), (2,0), (1,1), (1,0), (0,1), (0,0)\}.$$

Again, $I(\text{rng}(R)) = \{(1,1), (0,0)\}$ and $I(\text{rng}(R)) * R = \{(0,1)\}^2$ is not equal to $I(\text{rng}(R))$. The generalization rule can map R onto

$$R' = \{(6,0), (5,1), (4,0), (3,1), (2,0), (1,1), (0,0)\}. \qquad \square$$

3.3.6 Exercises

1[B] Consider an arithmetic on the set of integers that has only two binary operations: the division by 2 and the remainder by 2. Give an example of two relations R and R' such that R is representationally simpler than R'. Derive an arithmetic in which R' is representationally simpler than R.

2[B] Devise an arithmetic on the set of integers, and give an example of two distinct relations R and R' such that R is intrinsically simpler than R' and R' is representationally simpler than R.

3[B] Apply the relative product rule to the following specifications on $S = \textbf{real}$:
   (a) $R = \{(s,s') | \exp(s^2) \le s' \le \exp(s^2)^2\}$.
   (b) $R = \{(s,s') | \text{sqrt}(s^2 + 1) \le s' \le \text{sqrt}(s^2 + 4)\}$.
   (c) $R = \{(s,s') | 2 * \text{sqrt}(s) \le s' \le 4 * \text{sqrt}(s) + 2\}$.
   (d) $R = \{(s,s') | (s^2 + 1)^2 - 1 \le s' \le (s^2 + 1)^2 + 1\}$.
   (e) $R = \{(s,s') | (s^2 - 1)^2 + 1 \le s' \le (s^2 + 1)^2 + 1\}$.

4[A] Apply the union rule to the following specifications:
   (a) $S = \textbf{real}$,
       $R = \{(s,s') | (s' = s^2 - 4 \lor s' = 4 - s^2) \land s' \ge 0\}$.
   (b) $S = \textbf{real}$,
       $R = \{(s,s') | s \, \text{div} \, 2 = s' \, \text{div} \, 2 \land s' \, \text{mod} \, 2 = 0\}$.
   (c) $S = \textbf{set}$
       a, b, c: **integer**
       end,
       $R = \{(s,s') | c(s') \ge a(s) \land c(s') \ge b(s)$
       $\qquad \land \ (c(s') = a(s) \lor c(s') = b(s))\}$.
   (d) $S = \textbf{set}$
       a, b, c: **integer**
       end,
       $R = \{(s,s') | (a(s) \ge b(s) \Rightarrow a(s') = b(s) \land b(s') = a(s))$
       $\qquad \land \ (a(s) \le b(s) \Rightarrow s' = s)\}$.

(e) S = **set**
     a, b, c: **integer**
    end,
    $$R = \{(s,s') \mid a(s) + b(s) = a(s') + b(s')$$
    $$\land \ (a(s') = a(s) \lor a(s') = b(s))\}.$$

5[B]   Apply the iteration rule to the following specification on

    S = **set**
      a, b, c: **natural**
    end:
    $$R = \{(s,s') \mid a(s') = a(s) \land b(s') = 0 \land c(s') = c(s) * a(s)^{b(s)}\}.$$

6[A]   Apply the generalization rule to the following specification on the same space as 5, in order that it meets the feasibility condition of the iteration rule:

$$R = \{(s,s') \mid c(s') = c(s) * a(s)^{b(s)}\}.$$

3.4   ADDITIONAL FUNCTIONAL ABSTRACTIONS[*]

3.4.1   Concurrency

In this section, we cover three constructs of concurrency, namely:

1. *Interference-free concurrency* between two independent programs.
2. The *synchronization* of two programs through a shared boolean variable. To this effect we use the control structure

    (**await** . . . **then** . . .)

    whose semantics we describe summarily here: the program executing (**await** t **then** b) is blocked until t is made true by some action of some other program; when that occurs, b is executed. The whole statement (test of t, execution of b) is indivisible.
3. *Communication* between two programs is the mechanism whereby a sender sends some data to a receiver, waits for an acknowledgement of receipt from the receiver, then continues.

Interference-free concurrency. The study of concurrency necessitates that we generalize the notion of functional abstraction. In a sequential programming environment, a program is deterministic because it controls the values of all the variables, even those which it does not modify and which then remain unchanged. By contrast, each program in a concurrent programming environment controls only some of the variables that are attached to it; hence its functional abstraction is potentially non-deterministic. For example, let S be

set
  x, y: **integer**
end

and P be

$$x := x + 1;$$

then in a sequential programming environment the functional abstraction of P is

$$[P]_1 = \{(s, s') \mid x(s') = x(s) + 1 \land y(s') = y(s)\},$$

whereas in a concurrent programming environment, assuming that x is attached to P and y is attached to some other program, the functional abstraction of P is

$$[P]_2 = \{(s, s') \mid x(s') = x(s) + 1\}.$$

Clearly, $[P]_1$ is deterministic, whereas $[P]_2$ is not.

The functional abstraction of a program in a concurrent programming environment is formally defined as follows: space S is the cartesian product of two spaces S_1 and S_2, i.e. $S = S_1 \times S_2$; space S_1 is controlled by program P while S_2 is controlled by some other program. The *functional abstraction* of P is the relation

$$[P] = \{(\langle s_1, s_2 \rangle, \langle s_1', s_2' \rangle) \mid \text{If execution of } P \text{ starts in a state whose } S_1$$
$$\text{component is } s_1, \text{ then it terminates in a}$$
$$\text{state whose } S_1 \text{ component is } s_1'\}.$$

On the basis of this definition, we define the semantics of Interference-free concurrency by the following axiom:

• *Interference-free concurrency axiom*

    [cobegin P1, P2 **coend]** = [P1] ∩ [P2].

This axiom can be interpreted as follows: when P_1 and P_2 have no interference, their total effect is the conjunction (in relational terms: the intersection) of their individual effects.

Example 16

  S = **set**
    x, y: **integer**
  end,
  $P_1 = (x := x + 1),$
  $P_2 = (y := y - 1).$

Then we have

$$[P_1] = \{(s,s')|x(s') = x(s) + 1\},$$
$$[P_2] = \{(s,s')|y(s') = y(s) - 1\}.$$
[cobegin P1, P2 **coend]**
$$= [P_1] \cap [P_2]$$
$$= \{(s,s')|x(s') = x(s) + 1 \wedge y(s') = y(s) - 1\}. \qquad \Box$$

Synchronization. We consider two programs P_1 and P_2, controlling spaces S_1 and S_2, and we pose $S = S_1 \times S_2$. We have

```
P1 = begin              P2 = begin
       P11;
       b := true;              await b then;
                               P22
     end                     end;
```

where b is a shared boolean variable, initialized to **false**. Segment P_{11} accesses and modifies S_1 only, whereas P_{22} accesses all of S but modifies only S_2. The purpose of this synchronization is to make sure that P_{22} reads the variables of S_1 only after P_1 has set them properly. The semantics of synchronization is captured in the following axiom:

- *Synchronization axiom*

    [cobegin begin P11; b := **true end,**

                begin await b **then;** P22 **end coend]**
    $$= ([P_{11}] \cap I'(S_2)) * (I'(S_1) \cap [P_{22}]),$$

where $I'(S_1)$ and $I'(S_2)$ are relations defined on $S = S_1 \times S_2$ as follows:

$$I'(S_1) = \{(\langle s_1, s_2 \rangle, \langle s_1', s_2' \rangle)|s_1 = s_1'\},$$
$$I'(S_2) = \{(\langle s_1, s_2 \rangle, \langle s_1', s_2' \rangle)|s_2 = s_2'\}.$$

It is easy to understand this axiom, if one realizes that $I'(S_1)$ is the functional abstraction of the empty statement between ($b :=$ **true**) and **end** in P_1, while $I'(S_2)$ is the functional abstraction of the empty statement between **begin** and **await** in P_2.

Example 17

```
S1 = integer; S2 = integer;
S = set
    x: S1;
    y: S2
end.
```

```
P1 = begin                    P2 = begin
      x := 3 * x + 1;
      b := true;                    await b then;
                                    y := y + x - 1
      end                       end.
```

By the axiom of synchronization, we have

[cobegin P1, P2 coend]
$$= ([x := 3 * x + 1] \cap I'(S_2)) * (I'(S_1) \cap [y := y + x - 1])$$
$$= (\{(s,s') | x(s') = 3 * x(s) + 1\} \cap \{(s,s') | y(s') = y(s)\})$$
$$\quad * (\{(s,s') | x(s') = x(s)\} \cap \{(s,s') | y(s') = y(s) + x(s) - 1\})$$
$$= \{(s,s') | x(s') = 3 * x(s) + 1 \wedge y(s') = y(s)\}$$
$$\quad * \{(s,s') | x(s') = x(s) \wedge y(s') = y(s) + x(s) - 1\}$$
$$= \{(s,s') | x(s') = 3 * x(s) + 1 \wedge y(s') = y(s) + 3 * x(s)\}. \qquad \square$$

Communication. We consider two programs P_1 and P_2 operating on spaces S_1 and S_2 (respectively) and we pose $S = S_1 \times S_2$.

```
P1 = begin                    P2 = begin
      P11;                          P21;
      send := true;                 await send then;
                                    l2;
      await acknowledge then;       acknowledge := true;
      P12                           P22
      end                           end
```

where *send* and *acknowledge* are shared boolean variables initialized to **false**. Segments P_{11} and P_{12} access the modify only S_1; segments P_{21} and P_{22} access and modify only S_2; segment l2 accesses S_1 and S_2 but modifies S_2 only.

● *Axiom of communication*

[cobegin begin P11; send := true; await acknowledge then; P12 end,
           begin P21; await send then; l2; acknowledge := true; P22 end
coend]
$$= ([P_{11}] \cap [P_{21}]) * (I'(S_1) \cap [l2]) * ([P_{12}] \cap [P_{22}]).$$

Example 18

```
S1 = integer; S2 = integer;
S = set
  x: S1;
```

```
        y: S2
    end.
    P1 = begin                          P2 = begin
        x := 4;                             y := y − 2;
        send := true;                       await send then;
                                            y := 2 * y + x;
        await acknowledge then;             acknowledge := true;
        x := 2 * x                          y := ymod2
        end                                 end.
```

We have

[cobegin P1, P2 end]
$= ([x := 4] \cap [y := y − 2]) * (I'(S_1) \cap [y := 2 * y + x])$
$\quad * ([x := 2 * x] \cap [y := ymod2])$
$= \{(s, s') \mid x(s') = 4 \wedge y(s') = y(s) − 2\}$
$\quad * \{(s, s') \mid x(s') = x(s) \wedge y(s') = 2 * y(s) + x(s)\}$
$\quad * \{(s, s') \mid x(s') = 2 * x(s) \wedge y(s') = y(s)\mathbf{mod}2\}$
$= \{(s, s') \mid x(s') = 4 \wedge y(s') = 2 * y(s)\}$
$\quad * \{(s, s') \mid x(s') = 2 * x(s) \wedge y(s') = y(s)\mathbf{mod}2\}$
$= \{(s, s') \mid x(s') = 8 \wedge y(s') = 0\}.$ □

3.4.2 Procedure Calls

In this section, we discuss parameter-less procedure calls, reporting parameter passing to the next section. Let P be a program on space S, and p be a procedure declared as follows:

procedure p;
type   T = ⟨type-declaration⟩;
var   t:T;
begin ⟨code involving variables of S and T⟩ **end**.

Let c be the body of procedure p (executable code between **begin** and **end**); the space of c is $S \times T$, while the space of the procedure call 'p' is S.

- *Procedure call axiom.* Let p be the procedure:

    procedure p; **var** t:T; **begin** c **end**.

    Then

    $$[p] = \{(s, s') \mid \exists t, t': (\langle s, t \rangle, \langle s', t' \rangle) \in [c]\}.$$

When procedure p is invoked, the state of the program is augmented with t; in effect a cartesian product is performed on S to get $S \times T$. Execution of c transforms $\langle s, t \rangle$ into $\langle s', t' \rangle$; the return from the procedure call applies a projection of $S \times T$ on S.

Example 19

> S = **set**
>   a, b, c: **integer**
> **end**,
> **procedure** powers;
> **var** t: **integer**;
> **begin** t := a; b := t * t; t := b; c := t * t **end**.

Then:

$$[c] = \{(\langle s, t \rangle, \langle s', t' \rangle) \mid a(s') = a(s) \wedge b(s') = t' \wedge c(s') = t'^2$$
$$\wedge\ t' = a(s)^2\}.$$

Hence

$$[\text{powers}] = \{(s, s') \mid \exists t, t' : a(s') = a(s) \wedge b(s') = t' \wedge c(s') = t'^2$$
$$\wedge\ t' = a(s)^2\}$$
$$= \{(s, s') \mid a(s') = a(s) \wedge b(s') = a(s)^2 \wedge c(s') = a(s)^4$$
$$\wedge\ \exists t, t' : t' = a(s)^2\}$$
$$= \{(s, s') \mid a(s') = a(s) \wedge b(s') = a(s)^2 \wedge c(s') = a(s)^4\}. \quad \square$$

3.4.3   Parameter Passing

Value Parameters

Let P be a program on space S and p be a procedure declared in P under the form:

> **procedure** p($\iota : \mathcal{T}$);
> **type** T = $\langle$type-declaration$\rangle$;
> **var** t:T;
> **begin** c **end**.

In a call-by-value, procedure p initializes state ι from s; during its execution, segment c is likely to affect the state of P through references to the global variables of P; upon the return of the procedure, states t and ι are simply ignored.

- *The axiom of value parameters.* Let p be the procedure:

> **procedure** p($\iota : \mathcal{T}$); **var** t : T; **begin** c **end**.

Then

$$[p(E(s))] = \{(s,s') \mid \exists \iota, t, \iota', t' : \iota = E(s)$$
$$\wedge\ (\langle s, \iota, t \rangle, \langle s', \iota', t' \rangle) \in [c]\},$$

where $E(s)$ is the expression that corresponds to the actual parameters of the call.

Example 20

```
S = set
    a, b, c: integer
end,
procedure average(x, y: integer); var k1, k2: real;
begin k1 := 2.1; k2 := 1.9; c := (k1 * x + k2 * y)/(k1 + k2) end.
```

We compute $[\text{average}(a, b)]$

$$= \{(s,s') \mid \exists (x,y), (k_1,k_2), (x',y'), (k_1',k_2'): x = a(s) \wedge y = b(s)$$
$$\wedge\ (\langle s, x, y, k_1, k_2 \rangle, \langle s', x', y', k_1', k_2' \rangle) \in [c]\}$$
$$= \{(s,s') \mid \exists (x,y), (k_1,k_2), (x',y'), (k_1',k_2'): x = a(s) \wedge y = b(s)$$
$$\wedge\ a(s') = a(s) \wedge b(s') = b(s) \wedge c(s') = (k_1 * x + k_2 * y)/4$$
$$\wedge\ x' = x \wedge y' = y \wedge k_1' = 2.1 \wedge k_2' = 1.9\}$$
$$= \{(s,s') \mid a(s') = a(s) \wedge b(s') = b(s)$$
$$\wedge\ c(s') = (2.1 * a(s) + 1.9 * b(s)\exists/4$$
$$\wedge\ \exists (x,y), (k_1,k_2), (x',y'), (k_1',k_2'): x = a(s)$$
$$\wedge\ y = b(s) \wedge x = x' \wedge y' = y \wedge k_1' = 2.1 \wedge k_2' = 1.9\}$$
$$= \{(s,s') \mid a(s') = a(s) \wedge b(s') = b(s)$$
$$\wedge\ c(s') = (2.1 * a(s) + 1.9 * b(s))/4\}. \qquad \square$$

Call by Name

Let P be a program on space S and p be a procedure declared in P under the form:

procedure p(**var** $\iota :\mathscr{T}$); **var** t:T; **begin** c **end**.

In a call-by-name, procedure p initializes state ι with actual parameters taken from $s \in S$, and establishes an identity of names between formal parameters and actual parameters; during its execution, procedure p affects the global state of P either through explicit references to the variables of P or through implicit references via the identity of names between formal parameters and actual parameters; when procedure p terminates its execution, t is ignored without leaving a trace, whereas ι is ignored while leaving its values in the actual parameters with which the procedure was invoked.

- *The axiom of call by name.* Let p be

    procedure p(**var** $\iota :\mathcal{T}$); **var** t:T; **begin** c **end**.

Then

$$[p(a(s))] = \{(s,s')|\exists t,t': (\langle s,t\rangle, \langle s',t'\rangle) \in [c(\iota, !a(s))]\},$$

where $c(\iota, !a(s))$ is the program obtained from c by replacing all formal parameters (ι) by actual parameters $(a(s))$.

Example 21

    S = **set**
        x, y, z: **integer**
    end,
    procedure sort(**var** x, y: **integer**);
    var t: **integer**;
    begin if x > y **then begin** t := x; x := y; y := t **end end**.

We wish to compute $[\text{sort}(y,z)]$.

    c(^(x,y), !(y,z)) = **if** y > z **then begin** t := y; y := z; z := t **end**.

Then

$$[c(^(x,y),\ !(y,z))]$$
$$= \{(\langle s,t\rangle, \langle s',t'\rangle)|y(s)\leq z(s) \wedge s'=s \wedge t'=t\}$$
$$\cup$$
$$\{(\langle s,t\rangle, \langle s',t'\rangle)|y(s)>z(s) \wedge x(s')=x(s) \wedge y(s')=z(s)$$
$$\wedge z(s')=y(s) \wedge t'=y(s)\}.$$

Hence

$$[\text{sort}(y,z)]$$
$$= \{(s,s')|\exists t,t': (\langle s,t\rangle, \langle s',t'\rangle) \in [c(^(x,y), !(y,z))]\}$$
$$= \{(s,s')|y(s)\leq z(s) \wedge s'=s\}$$
$$\cup$$
$$\{(s,s')|y(s)>z(s) \wedge x(s')=x(s) \wedge y(s')=z(s)$$
$$\wedge z(s')=y(s)\}. \qquad \Box$$

3.4.4 Recursion

In this section we briefly show how to define the semantics of a recursive (Pascal) **function**. Note that if a function (in the mathematical sense of the term) has its arguments in one set – say A – and its images in another set – say B – then one can still consider that all its arguments and images are in the same set, namely $S = A \cup B$. Hence it is without loss of generality that we restrict our study to Pascal **functions** whose header reads as

function f(s : S) : S.

In addition, we adopt the following format for the body of the function:

begin if t **then** f := E(s) **else** f := K(f)(s) **end**,

where $E(s)$ is an expression on S and K is a functional on S (hence $K(f)$ is a function on S). We transform the above segment into the following functional equation:

$$f = I(t) * e \ \cup \ I(\neg t) * K(f),$$

where $e = [\in \text{def}(E), E]$. If we pose

$$H = \{(f, f') | f' = I(t) * e \ \cup \ I(\neg t) * K(f)\}$$

then the above equation becomes

$$f = H(f).$$

- *Axiom of recursion.* Let f be the recursive **function** defined by

  function f(s : S) : S; **begin if** t **then** f := E(s) **else** f := K(f)(s) **end**

  and let H be the functional derived from it (as shown above). Then

  $[f] = $ The least-defined function, if it exists, that verifies $f = H(f)$.

Note that on the set of functions, *less-defined* is synonymous with *subset*. This axiom can be formulated as: the smallest function f such that $f = H(f)$. Such a function, when it exists, is called the least fixpoint of functional H.

Example 22

    function f(s: **integer**): **integer**;
    begin if false then f := 0 **else** f := f(s) **end**.

We derive the following recursive equation:

$$f = I(\textbf{false}) * [\textbf{true}, 0] \ \cup \ I(\textbf{true}) * f$$

$\Leftrightarrow$

$$f = f.$$

Any f is a solution of this equation; the smallest is ϕ.   □

Example 23

```
function f(s: integer): integer;
begin if s = 0 then f := 1 else f := f(s) end.
```

Recrusive equation:

$$f = I(s = 0) * [\textbf{true}, 1] \ \cup \ I(s \neq 0) * f$$

$$\Leftrightarrow$$

$$f = \{(0, 1)\} \ \cup \ I(s \neq 0) * f.$$

Any function containing $(0, 1)$ is solution to this equation; the least defined among these is $\{(0, 1)\}$.

3.5 PROBLEMS

1[B] Consider the transformation proposed in Section 2.2.2 of Chapter 2 as:

$$R' = R \ \cup \ I(t) * U(S),$$

where $t(s) = (s \notin \mathrm{dom}(R))$. We wish to prove the validity of this transformation, in a sense to be defined:
(a) Prove that $\mathrm{dom}(R') = S$.
(b) Prove that if a program p is correct with respect to R, then it is correct with respect to R'.
(c) Prove that if a program p is correct with respect to R', then it is correct with respect to R.
(d) Conclude: in what sense is this transformation correctness-preserving?

2[A] Check that the function f proposed in the iteration axiom verifies the conditions of the iteration theorem.

3[B] Prove Propositions 4, 5 and 6.

4[B] Let P be a program on space S. Program P is said to be *robust* with respect to specification R if and only if P is correct with respect to R and $\mathrm{dom}([P]) = S$. Given R, construct a specification R' such that P is robust with respect to R if and only if it is correct with respect to R'. Conclude.

5[A] Let R and R' be two relations such that $R' \subseteq R$ and $\mathrm{dom}(R') \cap \mathrm{dom}(R - R') \neq \emptyset$. Show that R' is intrinsically simpler than R. Deduce that the union rule decomposes specifications along intrinsic simplicity lines. Show, by means of Examples 8 and 9, that there is also a representational dimension in this rule.

3.6   BIBLIOGRAPHICAL NOTES

Standard references on the programming language Pascal include Jensen and Wirth (1974) and Wirth (1976). References on semantic definitions of Pascal-like programming languages can be found in DeBakker (1980), Linger *et al.* (1979), Mills *et al.* (1986), Sanderson (1980) and Stoy (1977).

Textbook references on program-solving include Gries (1981), Berg *et al.* (1981), Loekx *et al.* (1984), Linger *et al.* (1979), Manna (1974), Mili (1984) and Mills *et al.* (1986). Textbook references on program design include Dijkstra (1976), Gries (1981), Linger *et al.* (1979) and Mills *et al.* (1986).

The subgoal induction theorem, referred to in Section 3.3.4, is due to Morris and Wegbreit (1977); for a recent version of it which is consistent with our notation, consult Mili (1984). The **await then** construct referred to in the Section 3.4.1 is due to Owicki and Gries; the interested reader is referred to Chapter 11 of Gries (1978) for further study.

Part II
Fundamental Definitions

Is it (fault tolerance) a mature technology?
YES!
Well developed and ready for exploitation.
  Range of techniques.
  Established mechanisms.
  7 reliability models.
  Applicable in real-time, concurrent and distributed systems.
                              (Tom Anderson: Montréal, 1985)

The field of fault tolerance is sufficiently mature to have its own, agreed upon, set of models, concepts, and terms. In Chapter 4 we shall present these, after adapting them to the specific scope and orientation of this book. In Chapter 5, we take the concepts introduced in Chapter 4 and refine them further; we have found these refinements to be both significant and critical in the study of program fault tolerance. In particular, we define the conditions under which a final state is sufficiently correct to be considered failure-free. We also define the conditions under which an intermediate state is sufficiently correct to still be recoverable, and the conditions under which it is sufficiently correct to be considered error-free. These conditions are of prime importance for an understanding of the remainder of the book.

CHAPTER 4

Fundamental definitions

In this chapter we introduce some models, concepts and terms pertaining to fault tolerance in general, and to program fault tolerance in particular. They have been adapted from general references in the field of fault tolerance to match the concerns and orientations of this book. Other concepts and terms are introduced for the specific purposes of this book, and are most significant in the study of *program* fault tolerance.

4.1 EXECUTION MILESTONES

4.1.1 Labels and Milestones

Let p be a program on space S, and let L be a label in the text of p. We observe the execution of program p on some initial state s_0, and we are interested in the state of the program at label L. Because label L may appear in the loop body of a **while** statement, it may then be reached more than once for any given execution; hence we cannot speak of the state of program p *at label L*. Instead, we shall speak of the state of the program at the vth visit to label L, for $v \geq 1$. Hence we have the following definition.

- *Definition.* Let p be a program on space S, and let L be a label in the text of p. A *milestone* of program p at label L is the pair (v, L) where v is a positive integer.

Milestone (v, L) represents the vth visit to label L. The range of values that v may take depends not only on where L appears in the text of program p, but also on the initial state s_0 that is being considered. The examples below illustrate various ranges for v.

Example 1

```
S = set
   a, b: natural
end;
p1 = begin a := a + 1; L: b := b – 1 end.
```

Regardless of the initial state s_0, label L may be reached once and only once: The only milestone at label L is $m = (1, L)$

```
p2 = while b ≠ 0 do begin a := a + 1; L: b := b – 1 end.
```

For initial state $s_0 = \langle 4, 3 \rangle$, there are only three possible milestones at label L, namely: $(1, L)$, $(2, L)$ and $(3, L)$. The states of program p at these milestones are, respectively: $\langle 5, 3 \rangle$, $\langle 6, 2 \rangle$ and $\langle 7, 1 \rangle$.   □

Remark 1. Labeling While Loops. As we study **while** statements, we realize that the most interesting place at which we wish to place a label is inside the loop, right before the test of the iteration; see Figure 4.1. The question that we address is: in a Pascal **while** loop, where should we write the label to reflect the flowchart of Figure 4.1? We use the convention of writing label L immediately before the keyword **while**, i.e.

   L: **while** t **do** b.

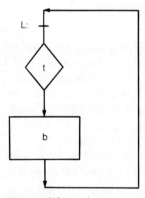

Figure 4.1

Whenever we want to place label L upstream of the statement, to be reached only once, before the iteration starts (see Figure 4.2), then we write:

   L: ; **while** t **do** b.

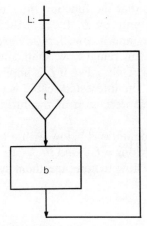

Figure 4.2

4.1.2   Past and Future

Let p be a program on space S and let L be a label in the text of p. Let $m = (v, L)$ be a milestone on label L. At milestone m, two functions are of interest: (i) the function that the program defines between initial states and current states; and (ii) the function that the program defines between current states and final states. Hence we have the following definitions:

● *Definition.* Let $m = (v, L)$ be a milestone defined on label L of program p on space S. The function *past* at milestone m is defined as follows:

$$pst_{v,L} = \{(s, s') | \text{if execution of } p \text{ starts in state } s, \text{ then it reaches milestone } (v, L) \text{ in state } s'\}.$$

When, from the context, v is implicit we shall talk of the function past *at label L*, rather than *at milestone (v, L)*; we then denote it by pst_L. When label L is also implicit from the context, we shall merely talk of the function *past*.

● *Definition.* Let (v, L) be a milestone defined on label L of program p on space S. The function *future* at milestone (v, L) is defined as follows:

$$ftr_{v,L} = \{(s, s') | \text{if execution of } p \text{ starts from label } L \text{ in state } s, \text{ then it terminates in state } s'\}.$$

It is important to note that the function $ftr_{v,L}$ is *by definition* independent of v; it depends only on L. Indeed, the definition given above makes no mention of v, and it considers any execution that starts from label L. As a result of this remark, we shall consider the notation $ftr_{v,L}$ an ftr_L to be interchangeable. Also, if L is implicit, we shall merely talk of the function *future*. The interested reader is referred to Problem 3 of this chapter, where this definition of the function future is discussed further.

We illustrate these definitions below with a few simple examples. In the examples, the functions $pst_{v,L}$ and $ftr_{v,L}$ are given without proof. In Section 4.1.3 we show how to compute them systematically.

Example 2

Space S; program p = **begin** p1; L: p2 **end**.

There exists a unique milestone at label L, namely $m = (1, L)$. We have, clearly,

$$pst_m = [p_1];$$
$$ftr_m = [p_2].$$

Space S; program p = **begin** L; **while** t **do** b **end**.

We consider milestone $m = (3, L)$.

$$pst_m = (I(t) * [b])^2,$$
$$ftr_m = [\textbf{while } t \textbf{ do } b].$$

Interestingly, function *future* equals the functional abstraction of the whole loop. One can explain it as follows: because $ftr_{v,L}$ does not depend on v, it is equal to $ftr_{1,L}$, which is precisely [**while** t **do** b].

Space S = **set**
    a, b: **integer**
  end,
Program p = **begin** L: **while** b ≠ 0 **do begin** a: = a + 1; b: = b − 1 **end**
        end.

Let m be milestone $(3, L)$. Then

$$pst_m = \{(s,s') \mid b(s) \neq 0 \land b(s) \neq 1 \land a(s') = a(s) + 2 \land b(s') = b(s) - 2\},$$
$$ftr_m = \{(s,s') \mid b(s) \geq 0 \land a(s') = a(s) + b(s) \land b(s') = 0\}. \qquad \square$$

4.1.3 Past and Future Paths

Let $m = (v, L)$ be a milestone defined on a program p. In order to compute functions *past* and *future* we must first exhibit the sequence of statements which is executed (respectively) upstream of m, and downstream of it, and which we call the *past path* and the *future path*. This is the purpose of this section.

The statements executed upstream of milestone $m = (v, L)$ may include any of the following:

(a) assignment statements;
(b) structured programming constructs, such as **if-then-else**, **while-do** or **begin-end**;
(c) test statements, appearing in alternative or iterative constructs, and which we represent by (t?**true**) and (t?**false**), depending on the outcome of testing condition t.

The statements executed downstream of milestone $m = (v, L)$ may include any of the following:

(a) assignment statements;
(b) structured programming constructs, such as **if-then-else**, **while-do** or **begin-end**.

When the label under consideration is deep within a nested control structure, determining a past path at milestone $m = (v, L)$ may pose some difficulties, because it depends on v, the order of the visit. Let us consider two illustrative examples:

```
P = begin
      L: while t do
         begin
         b1;
         M: while u do b21;
         b3
         end.
    end
Q = begin
      L: while t do
         begin
         b1;
         if u then tc else M:ec;
         b3
         end.
    end.
```

Milestone $(2, M)$ in program P can be reached in at least two ways: (i) either by the sequence of labels (L, M, M), i.e. the outer loop body is entered once and the second visit to M takes place after the inner loop has iterated once; (ii) or the sequence (L, M, L, M), i.e. the outer loop body is entered twice, and the first time it is entered the inner loop does not iterate. As another example, milestone $(1, M)$ in program Q can be reached in infinitely many ways, of which we mention two: (i) either by the sequence of labels (L, M), i.e. the first time the loop body is entered, the **else** branch of the alternation statement is taken; or (ii) by the sequence of labels (L, L, M), i.e. it is only at the second iteration that the **else** branch is taken.

Because this problem has no general simple solution, because in most cases we use a single label in a program, and because past paths are not of great interest in practice (see Chapter 5), we consider this problem to be beyond our scope of interest. We content ourselves in this book with avoiding defining milestones inside such nested structures, or, if we cannot do so, we make enough simplifying hypotheses; the interested reader is referred to Problems 1 and 2 at the end of this chapter.

The example below shows instances of past paths and future paths.

Example 3

   P = **begin** p1; L: p2 **end**.

The past path at milestone $(1, L)$ is P_1, while the future path at milestone $(1, L)$ is p_2.

   P = **begin** p1; **if** t **then begin** tc1; L: tc2 **end end**.

The past path at milestone $(1, L)$ is

   pp = **begin** p1; (t?**true**); tc1 **end**,

while the future path at milestone $(1, L)$ is fp = tc2.

   P = **begin**
       p1;
       while t **do begin** b1; L: b2 **end**;
       p2
       end.

The past path at milestone $(3, L)$ is:

   pp = **begin**
       p1; (t?**true**); b1;
       L: b2; (t?**true**); b1;

```
    L: b2; (t?true); b1;
    L:
    end,
```

while the future path at milestone $(3, L)$ (or at label L) is:

```
fp = begin
     L: b2;
     while t do begin b1; L: b2 end;
     p2
     end.
```

4.1.4   Computing Past and Future Functions

We admit without proof that the function *past* at milestone m is the functional abstraction of the past path at milestone m, and that the function *future* at milestone m is the functional abstraction of the future path at milestone m. This immediately begs the question of how we compute the functional abstraction of test nodes, such as

    (t?**true**),

and

    (t?**false**).

We pose the following axioms:

    [(t?**true**)] = I(t)

and

    [(t?**false**)] = I($\lnot$t).

The example below shows instances of functions past and future, computed systematically using the above formulas.

Example 4

```
S = set
    a, b, c: natural
end.
p = begin
    c := 0;
    while b ≠ 0 do begin c := c + a; L: b := b − 1 end;
    b := c
    end.
```

The past path of p at milestone $(3, L)$ is

```
pp = begin
      c := 0; (b ≠ 0?true); c := c + a;
      L: b := b − 1; (b ≠ 0?true); c := c + a;
      L: b := b − 1; (b ≠ 0?true); c := c + a;
      L:
     end,
```

while the future path of p at milestone $(3, L)$ is

```
fp = begin
      L: b := b − 1;
      while b ≠ 0 do begin c := c + a; L: b := b − 1 end;
      b := c
     end.
```

Whence we compute

$$
\begin{aligned}
pst &= [c := 0; (b \neq 0?\textbf{true}); c := c + a] \\
&\quad * [b := b - 1; (b \neq 0?\textbf{true}); c := c + a]^2 \\
&= [\textbf{true}, \langle a(s), b(s), 0 \rangle] \\
&\quad * I(b(s) \neq 0) \\
&\quad * [\textbf{true}, \langle a(s), b(s), c(s) + a(s) \rangle] \\
&\quad * ([\textbf{true}, \langle a(s), b(s) - 1, c(s) \rangle] \\
&\qquad * I(b(s) \neq 0) \\
&\qquad * [\textbf{true}, \langle a(s), b(s), c(s) + a(s) \rangle])^2 \\
&= [b(s) \neq 0, \langle a(s), b(s), a(s) \rangle] \\
&\quad * ([b(s) \neq 1, \langle a(s), b(s) - 1, c(s) + a(s) \rangle] \\
&\qquad * [b(s) \neq 1, \langle a(s), b(s) - 1, c(s) + a(s) \rangle]) \\
&= [b(s) \neq 0, \langle a(s), b(s), a(s) \rangle] \\
&\quad * [b(s) \neq 1 \wedge b(s) - 1 \neq 1, \langle a(s), b(s) - 2, c(s) + 2 * a(s) \rangle] \\
&= [b(s) \geq 3, \langle a(s), b(s) - 2, 3 * a(s) \rangle].
\end{aligned}
$$

In summary, execution of p can reach milestone $(3, L)$ only if $b(s) \geq 3$; when it does reach the milestone, b has been decremented by 2 and c equals three times a, while a is preserved.

Also, we compute function ftr at milestone $(3, L)$:

$$
\begin{aligned}
ftr &= [b := b - 1] \\
&\quad * [\textbf{while } b \neq 0 \textbf{ do begin } c := c + a; L: b := b - 1 \textbf{ end}] \\
&\quad * [b := c] \\
&= [\textbf{true}, \langle a(s), b(s) - 1, c(s) \rangle] \\
&\quad * [\textbf{true}, \langle a(s), 0, c(s) + a(s) * b(s) \rangle] \\
&\quad * [\textbf{true}, \langle a(s), c(s), c(s) \rangle]
\end{aligned}
$$

$$= [\textbf{true}, \langle a(s), 0, c(s) + a(s) * (b(s) - 1) \rangle]$$
$$* [\textbf{true}, \langle a(s), c(s), c(s) \rangle]$$
$$= [\textbf{true}, \langle a(s), c(s) + a(s) * (b(s) - 1), c(s) + a(s) * (b(s) - 1) \rangle].$$
$$\square$$

4.1.5 Exercises

1[A] Consider the following program on space S defined by

```
S = set
    a, b: natural
  end,
p = begin L: while b ≠ 0 do begin a := a + 1; b := b − 1 end end.
```

For each initial state shown below, say which milestones one can define at label L:
(a) $s_0 = \langle 3, 0 \rangle$.
(b) $s_0 = \langle 5, 0 \rangle$.
(c) $s_0 = \langle 3, 5 \rangle$.
(d) $s_0 = \langle 5, 5 \rangle$.
(e) $s_0 = \langle 2, b_0 \rangle$.

2[B] Consider the following program on space S defined by

```
S = set
    a, b: natural
  end
p = while a ≠ b do if a > b then a := a − b else L: b := b − a.
```

For each initial state shown below, say which milestones one can define at label L:
(a) $s_0 = \langle 25, 45 \rangle$.
(b) $s_0 = \langle 30, 40 \rangle$.
(c) $s_0 = \langle 30, 30 \rangle$.
(d) $s_0 = \langle 10, 30 \rangle$.
(e) $s_0 = \langle 5, 55 \rangle$.

3[A] Show the past path and the future path of the following program, at the milestones given:

```
p = begin
    p1;
    L: while t do begin b1; M: b2 end;
    p2
    end.
```

(a) $m = (1, L)$.
(b) $m = (3, L)$.
(c) $m = (1, M)$.
(d) $m = (3, M)$.
(e) $m = (5, M)$.

4[B]   Show the past path and the future path of the following program, at the milestones given:

```
p = begin
    p1;
    L: while t do
        begin
        b1;
        M: if u then tc else ec;
        N: b2
        end;
    p2
end.
```

(a) $m = (2, L)$.
(b) $m = (3, L)$.
(c) $m = (1, M)$.
(d) $m = (2, M)$.
(e) $m = (2, N)$.

5[B]   Show the past path and the future path of the following program, at the milestones given:

```
p = begin
    p1;
    while t do
        begin
        b1;
        L: while u do begin b21; M: b22 end;
        b3
        end;
    p2
end.
```

(a) $m = (1, L)$.
(b) $m = (3, L)$.
(c) $m = (1, M)$.
(d) $m = (2, M)$.
(e) $m = (3, M)$.

6[B]   Re-do Example 4, Section 4.1.4, with the space S defined as

```
S = set
      a, b, c: integer
end.
```

(Hint: if b is no longer **natural**, *then* $b \neq 0 \wedge b \neq 1 \wedge b \neq 2$ no longer means $b \geq 3$; check also *ftr*.)

7[B]   Compute functions past and future on program p, at each of the given milestones:

```
S = set
crt
      a, b: natural
sub
      a ≠ 0 & b ≠ 0
end.
p = begin
      L: while a ≠ b do
         begin
         M: if a > b then a := a − b else b := b − a;
         N:
         end
      end.
```

(a) $m = (1, L)$.
(b) $m = (3, L)$.
(c) $m = (1, M)$.
(d) $m = (2, M)$.
(e) $m = (3, N)$.

8[B]   Compute functions past and future on program p, at each of the given milestones:

```
S = set
      a: array [0 .. n] of integer;
      x: integer;
      f : boolean;
      k: 0 .. n;
end,
p = begin
      a[0] := x; k := n;
      L: while x ≠ a[k] do M: k := k − 1;
      f := (k ≠ 0)
end.
```

(a) $m = (1, L)$.
(b) $m = (3, L)$.

(c) $m = (1, M)$.
(d) $m = (2, M)$.
(e) $m = (n, M)$.

9[C]   Compute functions past and future on program p, at each of the given milestones:

```
S = set
      a : array [0 .. n] of integer;
      m: integer;
      j, k, l: 0 .. n;
   end,
p = begin
      k := 1;
      L: while k < n do
         begin
         m := a[k]; j := k + 1; l := k;
         M: while j ≤ n do
            begin
            if a[j] < m then
               begin
               m := a[j]; l := j
               end;
            j := j + 1
            end;
         a[l] := a[k]; a[k] := m; k := k + 1
         end
   end.
```

(a) $m = (1, L)$.
(b) $m = (2, L)$.
(c) $m = (1, M)$, suppose $n \geq 2$.
(d) $m = (2, M)$, suppose $n \geq 3$.
(e) $m = (3, M)$, suppose $n \geq 4$.

4.2 FAILURE, ERROR AND FAULT

4.2.1 Definitions

We consider a program p on space S, and a specification R on S. We assume that p is expected to be correct with respect to R. Let p be executed on initial state s_0, such that $s_0 \in \text{dom}(R)$; we observe the output of the program for input s_0, if any.

- *Definition.* A *failure* occurs when we observe a behavior of program p that is inconsistent with the correctness of p with respect to R.

Let us remember that p is correct with respect to R if and only if:

$$(\forall s: s \in \operatorname{dom}(R) \Rightarrow s \in \operatorname{dom}([p]) \wedge (s, [p](s)) \in R).$$

Hence a failure is observed if any one of the following two conditions arises:

1. the program fails to terminate, i.e. $s_0 \notin \operatorname{dom}([p])$;
2. the program does terminate, but fails to produce a correct output, i.e. the output state s is outside $s_0 \cdot R$ $((s_0, s) \notin R)$.

This definition will be further refined in the next chapter.

Let m be a milestone on program p, and let pst_m be the past function of program p at milestone m. We observe the state of the program at milestone m. The designer of the program has a specific expectation as to what the state of the program should be at milestone m for initial state s_0.

- *Definition.* An *error* occurs at milestone m when we observe that

$$s_m \neq pst_m(s_0),$$

where s_m is the expected state at milestone m for input state s_0, and pst is the actual *past* function of program p at milestone m.

While a failure is observable by a user, on the basis of information available to the user (specifications, user manual), an error is observable only by a designer, for it requires information that is only available to a designer (the structure of the program, the expected function of its parts). The difference between the expected state at milestone m (namely state s_m) and the actual state (namely $pst_m(s_0)$) results from the actual past function pst_m being different from the expected past function, which the designer meant to compute, and which we denote by PST_m. Hence an error occurs at milestone m for initial state s_0 if and only if

$$pst_m(s_0) \neq PST_m(s_0).$$

An error at milestone m may be propagated to the output to generate a failure, or it may be *masked* by the future function, in case $ftr_m(s_m)$ happens to be identical to $ftr_m(pst_m(s_0))$. The definition of error will also be refined in the next chapter.

Now we observe the past path of program p at milestone m:

- *Definition.* A *fault* exists in the past path of program p at milestone m if the actual past function of p at m differs from the expected past function of p at m.

A fault exists as soon as the actual past function pst_m is different from the expected past function PST_m: it takes the right s_0 to transform the fault into an error, i.e. an s_0 such that $pst_m(s_0) \neq PST_m(s_0)$. By and large, we designate by *fault* the identified or hypothesized cause of the error, and possibly the failure.

It is usual in fault tolerant computing literature to distinguish between *anticipated faults* and *unanticipated faults*. In our context, anticipated faults are all those that could be predicted by the designer of the program. Program testing literature contains a large number of classifications of such faults: missing path fault, faulty path, inappropriate path condition, incomplete specification, is a typical classification.

Unanticipated faults are those that the designer could not predict at program design time. Typical unanticipated faults in hardware are those that stem from physical wear and deterioration due to age. In our context, unanticipated faults are those of the virtual machine, i.e. the aggregate made up of the Pascal compiler, the operating system, and the hardware. Any deviation of the Pascal machine from its expected behavior (as defined by Pascal's semantics) which causes the actually computed past function to be different from the expected past function is an unanticipated fault. Examples of unanticipated faults are: an overflow or underflow (the value computed does not fit); a memory failure (the value retrieved from a variable is not the value stored in it); a CPU failure (the value computed is not correct); a communication failure (the value received on a bus is not the value sent on it). Other, more general examples could be taken.

Example 5. We consider space $S = \textbf{real}$, and specification

$$R = \{(s,s')\,|\,(s+1)^2 - 1 \leq s' \leq (s+1)^2 + 1\}.$$

Also, we consider the input state $s_0 = 2$.

Let p be a program on space S; we observe the execution of p on s_0. If p fails to terminate or if it returns a value outside the interval $[8, 10]$, then there is a failure.

Now we look inside program p.

```
p = begin
    p1;
    L: p2
    end.
```

We assume that the expected past function of program p at milestone $m = (1, L)$ is

$$PST = \{(s, s') | s' = s + 1\},$$

so that for input $s_0 = 2$, the expected state at milestone m is $s = +3$. If the actual state is $s = -3$, then the error is masked and will not lead to a failure. If the error is different from both $+3$ and -3, then the error will not be masked and will lead to a failure.

If the actual function computed by p_1 is different from PST then there is a fault. If the Pascal machine is correct and p_1 is

$$s := s + 2,$$

then we are dealing with an anticipated fault (inappropriate path). On the other hand, if p_1 is correct, i.e.

$$s := s + 1,$$

but the Pascal virtual machine is not correct (e.g. computes $s - 1$ instead of $s + 1$), then we are dealing with an unanticipated fault.   □

4.2.2 Fault Tolerance

The terms defined in Section 4.2.1 afford us a precise definition of program fault tolerance.

- *Definition* (adapted from Avizienis, 1985). A *fault tolerant program* is a program that has provisions to avoid failure after faults have caused errors.

It is usual to define four phases, as follows, in the fault tolerance process, by which we avoid that an error causes a failure:

1. *Error detection:* when the presence of the error is detected.
2. *Fault removal:* when the fault is removed from the program.
3. *Damage assessment:* when the extent of the damage done to the state is assessed.
4. *Error recovery*, when the error is removed from the state of the program.

4.2.3 Exercises

1[A] We consider space S = **real**,
      specification $R = \{(s, s') | (s + 3)^2 \leq s' \leq (s + 3)^4\}$, and a program p of the form

      p = **begin** p1; L: p2 **end**.

Give examples of:
(a) a failure;
(b) a maskable error at milestone $m = (1, L)$, if any;
(c) an unmaskable error at milestone $m = (1, L)$;
(d) an anticipated fault;
(e) an unanticipated fault.

2[A]   Same as exercise 1, for S = **real**,

$$R = \{(s, s') \mid (s + 3)^2 \le s' \le (s + 3)^3\},$$

and a program of the same form. (Hint: compute the domain of R.)

4.3 PROBLEMS

1[C]   Consider the following program on space S:

while t **do if** u **then** tc **else** L: ec.

We are interested in computing function $pst_{1,L}$:
(a) Show a possible past path for milestone $(1, L)$.
(b) Show the general form of past paths for milestone $(1, L)$.
(c) Suppose that u becomes **false** before t does, in the sequence of iterants obtained from the initial state. Propose a formula for $pst_{1,L}$.
(d) Under similar conditions, which you must define, express $pst_{v+1,L}$ as a function of $pst_{v,L}$.
(e) Give a general formula for $pst_{v,L}$ for the above program, under the appropriate hypothesis.

2[C]   Following the pattern of problem 1, consider how to compute function *past* at milestone (v, L) for the following program:

P = **begin while** t **do while** u **do** L: b **end**.

3[B]   Consider the following definition of function future as:

$$ftr'_{v,L} = \{(s, s') \mid \text{if execution of } p \text{ starts from } milestone \text{ } m \text{ in} $$
$$\text{state } s \text{ then it terminates in state } s'\}.$$

Notice that it differs from the definition of Section 4.1.2 by the fact that it has *milestone* instead of *label*:
(a) Compare $ftr_{v,L}$ and $ftr'_{v,L}$ from the viewpoint of inclusion.
(b) Let $q_{v,L}$ be the predicate defined on S by $q_{v,L}(s)$: if execution of p starts in state s, then it reaches milestone (v, L). Write $ftr'_{v,L}$ as a function of $ftr_{v,L}$ and $q_{v,L}$.

(c) Compare $pst_{v,L} * ftr_{v,L}$ and $pst_{v,L} * ftr'_{v,L}$. Interpret.

(d) Why is $ftr_{v,L}$ a better formula than $ftr'_{v,L}$?

4[C] Let P be a program and let (v, L) be a milestone on P. Let pst and ftr be the functions past and future defined at milestone (v, L) and let q be the predicate defined as in Problem 3 above:

(a) What inclusion relationship is there between $[P]$ and $pst * ftr$?

(b) What equation links $[P]$, q, and $pst * ftr$?

(c) The equation of question (a) could be called the 'triangular axiom'. Explain.

(d) Interpret the equation of question (b).

5[B] How do we compute the expected past function of a program

p = **begin** p1; L: p2 **end**

at milestone $m = (1, L)$ under the hypothesis of

(a) anticipated faults;

(b) unanticipated faults.

6[B] Same as Problem 5, for the actual past function.

7[R] Consider a language of logic programming (e.g. Prolog), and a standard semantic interpretation of logic programs, using, for example, Herbrand models. Define the logic programming equivalent of:

(a) an execution state, an initial state, a final state;

(b) a milestone, a past path, a future path;

(c) a functional abstraction;

(d) function past, and function future;

(e) failure, fault, error.

8[R] Same as Problem 7, for a functional programming language (e.g. Lisp, ML, Lucid, etc.), and a standard interpretation thereof (using, e.g. least fixpoints).

9[R] Same as Problem 7, for a concurrent programming language (e.g. Concurrent Euclid), and the relational interpretation of concurrency, as defined in Section 3.4 of the preceding chapter (this may involve a dramatic reduction in the use of the language; take hypotheses as necessary).

4.4 BIBLIOGRAPHICAL NOTES

The fundamental definitions of fault tolerance are adapted from earlier work by, among others, Anderson and Lee (1981), Avizienis (in Agrawal, 1985) and Anderson (in Agrawal, 1985).

CHAPTER 5

State correctness: Degrees of failure and degrees of error

In the preceding chapter, we have introduced the notions of *failure* and *error*, and have used these notions to give a definition of fault tolerance. In this chapter, we refine the definitions of failure and error, in preparation for a detailed study of program fault tolerance.

Specifically, we distinguish between two degrees of failure which we define and illustrate in Section 5.1. We then distinguish between six degrees of error which we classify into two categories: three degrees of correctness, the subject of Section 5.2; and three degrees of recoverability, the subject of Section 5.3. In Section 5.4, we give several perspectives of the degrees of error, for the sake of illustration.

5.1 DEGREES OF FAILURE

5.1.1 Definitions

Let p be a program on space S, let L be a label on program p; and $m = (v, L)$ be a milestone on L. Let s_0 be an initial state of program p. Let P be the expected function of program p. Unless we indicate otherwise, we assume that P is computed as the functional abstraction of program p (this assumption is, in fact, legitimate under the hypothesis of unanticipated faults, when the program at hand is considered correct). Let R be the specification that program p is supposed to meet (i.e. that it is constructed to meet, and is judged against).

Ideally, program p is supposed to compute function P; on input state s_0, it is supposed to produce $P(s_0)$. We naturally pose the following definition:

- *Definition.* We observe the execution of program p on state s_0. A *strict failure* occurs if and only if the final state is distinct from $P(s_0)$.

Now, the following observation leads us to seek a less restrictive definition: the choice of P as the expected function of program p is not the user's choice, since the user only imposed specification R; rather, it is partly the designer's choice. Hence the ultimate requirement is not for p actually to *compute* function P; rather it is for p merely to *be correct* with respect to R.

- *Definition*. We observe the execution of program p on state s_0. A *specificationwise failure* occurs if and only if the final state is outside $s_0 \cdot R$.

Because R is potentially (and most generally) non-deterministic, the set $s_0 \cdot R$ is potentially large. There are potentially a large number of strict failures that are not specificationwise failures. See Figure 5.1 below.

5.1.2 Exercises

1[A] For the given space, program, initial state and specification, perform the following:
   (a) Compute function P (as the functional abstraction of the program p).
   (b) Characterize strict failure for initial state s_0.
   (c) Characterize specificationwise failure with respect to R.
   (d) Interpret your results in terms of the non-determinacy of R.

```
S = set
      a, b: natural
end.
P = begin
      L: while b ≠ 0 do
         begin
            a := a + 1;
            b := b − 1
         end
    end.
```

$$s_0 = \langle 5, 9 \rangle.$$
$$R = \{(s, s') \mid a(s') = a(s) + b(s)\}.$$

2[A] Use the same space, program, specification and initial state as exercise 1, and use the following specification:
$$R = \{(s, s') \mid b(s') = 0\}.$$

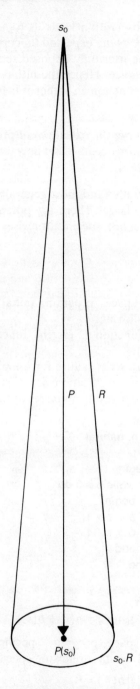

Figure 5.1

5.2   DEGREES OF ERROR: LEVELS OF CORRECTNESS

When an error appears in the state of a program at some milestone m, one needs to assess the damage of the state before taking action. For instance, it is important to know whether the error in the state can be masked or not. If the error can be masked, then no error recovery is necessary to avoid failure. In this section we define three degrees of error which we also refer to as levels of state correctness. State correctness differs from program correctness in several important ways: while the former is a statement about the program, the latter is a statement about a particular execution of the program for a particular initial state at a particular milestone; while the former is a statement about the overall input/output behavior of the program, the latter is a statement about the state of the program at a given stage in its execution; while the former is relative to the functional specification of the program, the latter is relative to the internal structure and design of the program.

Let p be a program on space S. Let L be a label on program p; and let $m = (v, L)$ be a milestone on L. Let s_0 be an initial state of program p. Let P be the expected function of program p. We propose to observe the state of program p at milestone m.

Normally, the state of program p at milestone $m = (v, L)$ is

$$s = PST_{v,L}(s_0),$$

where $PST_{v,L}$ is the expected past function of program p at milestone $m = (v, L)$. However, a fault in the past path of program p at milestone m may cause the actual past function $pst_{v,L}$ to differ from the expected past function $PST_{v,L}$; in addition, the initial state s_0 may sensitize this difference if it verifies the equation

$$PST_{v,L}(s_0) \neq pst_{v,L}(s_0).$$

5.2.1   Definitions

When the execution of program p on initial state s_0 proceeds normally from the beginning up to milestone $m = (v, L)$, then we reach milestone m in a state that is correct in the strict sense of the word.

- *Definition.* State s is said to be *strictly correct* (s-correct, for short) at milestone (v, L) vis-à-vis initial state s_0 if and only if

$$s = PST_{v,L}(s_0),$$

where $PST_{v,L}$ is the expected past function of program p at milestone $m = (v, L)$.

For a given initial state s_0 there exists a unique s-correct state at milestone (v, L). This definition of state correctness is far too restrictive; indeed, a state may fail to be strictly correct, yet be sufficiently close to the strictly correct state so that function $ftr_{v,L}$ maps them both to the same final state. Whence the following definition arises:

- *Definition.* State s is said to be *loosely correct* (l-correct) at milestone (v, L) vis-à-vis initial state s_0 if and only if

$$ftr_{v,L}(s) = P(s_0).$$

In the remainder of this chapter (and most of this book), we assume that the actual future function of program p at milestone m is identical to the expected future function at the same milestone. This function will be denoted by $ftr_{v,L}$ or, if no ambiguity arises, by ftr. Given that execution of program p on initial state s_0 reaches milestone m, we have, by definition,

$$P(s_0) = ftr_{v,L}(PST_{v,L}(s_0)).$$

Hence the equation of the above definition can be written as

$$ftr_{v,L}(s) = ftr_{v,L}(PST_{v,L}(s_0)).$$

If we denote by x the strictly correct state at milestone (v, L), we can rewrite this as

$$ftr_{v,L}(s) = ftr_{v,L}(x),$$

which is equivalent to

$$(s, x) \in ftr_{v,L} * \hat{ftr}_{v,L}.$$

In other words, s is l-correct at milestone (v, L) if and only if it belongs to the same level set of $ftr_{v,L}$ as the strictly correct state at that milestone. The larger the level sets of $ftr_{v,L}$ are, i.e. the less-injective $ftr_{v,L}$ is, the more l-correct states exist at milestone $m = (v, L)$. This same relationship can be exhibited from the equation of the definition of loose correctness, from which we can write the set of l-correct states as

$$(s_0 \cdot P) \cdot \hat{ftr}_{v,L}.$$

The less-deterministic $\hat{ftr}_{v,L}$ is, i.e. the less-injective $ftr_{v,L}$ is, the more l-correct states exist at milestone $m = (v, L)$. Notice that it is common in practice to deal with very non-injective functions, i.e. functions with several arguments per image. For example, a sort program working on an array of 100 distinct cells maps $(100!)$ initial arrays into a single sorted array. Level sets of such a function have (100!) elements each, i.e. nearly 10^{100}.

According to the definitions of strict and loose correctness, it is clear that strictly correct states as well as loosely correct states allow us to avoid strict failure. If it is not necessary for us to avoid strict failure, and it suffices to avoid specificationwise failure, then the current state may even fail to be l-correct, and still be considered correct. This remark inspires the following definition:

- *Definition.* State s is said to be *specificationwise correct* (sp-correct) at milestone (v, L) vis-à-vis initial state s_0 with respect to specification R if and only if

  $$ftr_{v,L}(s) \in s_0 \cdot R.$$

The set of all sp-correct states can be written as:

$$(s_0 \cdot R) \cdot \hat{ftr}_{v,L}.$$

The size of this set is dependent on two factors: (i) the non-determinacy of R; and (ii) the non-determinacy of $\hat{ftr}_{v,L}$, i.e. the non-injectivity of $ftr_{v,L}$. The less-deterministic R is, and the less-injective $ftr_{v,L}$ is, the more sp-correct states exist at milestone $m = (v, L)$. In the discussions surrounding the specification of loose correctness, we pointed out that commonly used functions can be very non-injective. Let us add here that commonly used specifications can be very non-deterministic: if relation R fails to specify the final value of a single variable, say z, then for any initial state s_0, the set $s_0 \cdot R$ contains as many elements as z can take values, namely (potentially) inifinitely many. In practice, it is common to see a specification fail to specify the final values of several variables. See Figure 5.2 and Example 1 for further illustration of sp-correctness.

5.2.2 Illustration

Example 1

Space:
S = **set**
    n, f, k **natural**
end.
Program:
p = **begin**

```
    k := 1; f := 1;
    L: while k ≠ n + 1 do
       begin
          f := f * k;
          k := k + 1
       end
    end.
```

Specification:

$$R = \{(s, s') \mid f(s') = n(s)!\}.$$

Initial state:

$$s_0 = \langle 5, 3, 9 \rangle.$$

Milestone:

$$m = (3, L).$$

Note that even though it expresses the most significant functional feature of this program, relation R is not deterministic. In fact, it is very non-deterministic, since there are two variables whose final values are not specified by R, namely n and k. This non-determinacy will be reflected in the definition of sp-correct states.

Function past at milestone m. The past path at milestone $(3, L)$ is

```
pp_{v,L} = begin
             k := 1; f := 1;
             L: (k ≠ n + 1?true); f := k * f; k := k + 1;
             L: (k ≠ n + 1?true); f := k * f; k := k + 1;
             L:
          end.
```

Hence

$$
\begin{aligned}
pst_{v,L} &= [\textbf{true}, \langle n(s); 1, 1 \rangle] \\
&\quad * [k(s) \neq n(s) + 1, \langle n(s), k(s) + 1, k(s) * f(s) \rangle]^2 \\
&= [\textbf{true}, \langle n(s), 1, 1 \rangle] \\
&\quad * [k(s) \neq n(s) + 1 \wedge k(s) + 1 \neq n(s) + 1, \\
&\qquad \langle n(s), k(s) + 2, (k(s) + 1) * k(s) * f(s) \rangle] \\
&= [1 \neq n(s) + 1 \wedge 2 \neq n(s) + 1, \langle n(s), 3, 2 \rangle] \\
&= [n(s) \geq 2, \langle n(s), 3, 2 \rangle].
\end{aligned}
$$

Milestone $m = (3, L)$ is reached only if $n(s) \geq 2$; when it is reached, $n(s)$ is preserved, $k(s)$ equals 3 and $f(s)$ equals 2.

Function future at milestone *m*. The future path at milestone (v, L) is the whole **while** statement, whose function we take as

$$W = [k(s) \leq n(s) + 1, \ \langle n(s), n(s) + 1, f(s) * n(s)! * k(s)/k(s)! \rangle].$$

We use premises p0, p1 and p2 of the **while** statement theorem (Section 3.1.2 of Chapter 3), to check that this is indeed the function of the **while** loop:

p0: $\text{dom}(W) = \{s \mid k(s) \leq n(s) + 1\}$, by inspection of function W.
    $\text{dom}([w]) = \{s \mid k(s) \leq n(s) + 1\}$, by inspection of statement w.

p1: $I(k(s) = n(s) + 1) * W$
    $= [k(s) = n(s) + 1, \ \langle n(s), n(s) + 1, f(s) * (n(s) + 1)!/(n(s) + 1)! \rangle]$
    $= [k(s) = n(s) + 1, \ \langle n(s), k(s), f(s) \rangle]$
    $= I(k(s) = n(s) + 1).$

p2: $I(t) * [b] * W$
    $= I(k(s) \neq n(s) + 1) * [f := f * k; \ k := k + 1]$
    $\quad * [k(s) \leq n(s) + 1, \ \langle n(s), n(s) + 1, f(s) * n(s)! * k(s)/k(s)! \rangle]$
    $= [k(s) \neq n(s) + 1, \ \langle n(s), k(s) + 1, f(s) * k(s) \rangle]$
    $\quad * [k(s) \leq n(s) + 1, \ \langle n(s), n(s) + 1, f(s) * n(s)! * k(s) * k(s)/k(s)! \rangle]$
    $= [k(s) \leq n(s), \ \langle n(s), n(s) + 1,$
    $\quad (f(s) * n(s)! * k(s) * (k(s) + 1)/(k(s) + 1)! \rangle]$
    $= [k(s) \leq n(s), \ \langle n(s), n(s) + 1, f(s) * n(s)! * k(s)/k(s)! \rangle]$
    $= I(k(s) \neq n(s) + 1)$
    $\quad * [k(s) \leq n(s) + 1, \ \langle n(s), n(s) + 1, f(s) * n(s)! * k(s)/k(s)! \rangle]$
    $= I(t) * W.$

Hence $[w] = W$. From which we deduce

$$ftr_{v,L} = [k(s) \leq n(s) + 1, \ \langle n(s), n(s) + 1, f(s) * n(s)! * k(s)/k(s)! \rangle].$$

Function P. We have already computed the function of the **while** statement; it is now a simple matter to multiply it on the left by the function of the initialization segment.

$$\begin{aligned}
P &= [k := 1; \ f := 1] * [w] \\
&= [\textbf{true}, \ \langle n(s), 1, 1 \rangle] \\
&\quad * [k(s) \leq n(s) + 1, \ \langle n(s), n(s) + 1, f(s) * n(s)! * k(s)/k(s)! \rangle] \\
&= [\textbf{true}, \ \langle n(s), n(s) + 1, n(s)! \rangle].
\end{aligned}$$

S-correct state. Function $pst_{3,L}$ is defined for initial state $s_0 = \langle 5, 3, 9 \rangle$; we have

$$pst_{3,L}(\langle 5, 3, 9 \rangle) = \langle 5, 3, 2 \rangle.$$

This is the only strictly correct state at milestone $(3, L)$.

L-correct states. The set of l-correct states at milestone $m = (3, L)$ is $s_0 \cdot (P * ftr^\wedge_{3,L})$. We first compute $(P * ftr^\wedge_{3,L})$, then we apply it to state s_0:

$$
\begin{aligned}
P * ftr^\wedge &= \{(s, s') \mid n(s') = n(s) \wedge k(s') = n(s) + 1 \wedge f(s') = n(s)!\} \\
&\quad * \{(s, s') \mid n(s') = n(s) \wedge n(s') + 1 = k(s) \\
&\qquad \wedge f(s) = f(s') * n(s')! * k(s')/k(s')! \\
&\qquad \wedge k(s') \leq n(s') + 1\} \\
&= \{(s, s') \mid n(s') = n(s) \wedge f(s') * n(s')! * k(s')/k(s')! = n(s')! \\
&\qquad \wedge k(s') \leq n(s') + 1\} \\
&= \{(s, s') \mid n(s') = n(s) \wedge f(s') * k(s') = k(s')! \\
&\qquad \wedge k(s') \leq n(s') + 1\}.
\end{aligned}
$$

Notice that if $k(s') = 0$, then the second conjunct becomes $f(s') * 0 = 1$, which cannot be satisfied. Hence we can write this as:

$$
\begin{aligned}
&= \{(s, s') \mid n(s') = n(s) \wedge f(s') * k(s') = k(s')! \\
&\qquad \wedge 1 \leq k(s') \leq n(s') + 1\}.
\end{aligned}
$$

Simplifying by $k(s')$ on both sides of the second conjunct, we obtain

$$
\begin{aligned}
&= \{(s, s') \mid n(s') = n(s) \wedge f(s') = (k(s') - 1)! \\
&\qquad \wedge 1 \leq k(s') \leq n(s') + 1\}.
\end{aligned}
$$

Now,

$$
\begin{aligned}
s_0 \cdot (P * ftr^\wedge) \\
&= \{s \mid n(s) = n(s_0) \wedge f(s) = (k(s) - 1)! \wedge 1 \leq k(s) \leq n(s) + 1\} \\
&= \{s \mid n(s) = 5 \wedge f(s) = (k(s) - 1)! \wedge 1 \leq k(s') \leq 6\} \\
&= \{\langle 5, 1, 1, \rangle, \langle 5, 2, 1 \rangle, \langle 5, 3, 2 \rangle, \langle 5, 4, 6 \rangle, \langle 5, 5, 24 \rangle, \\
&\qquad \langle 5, 6, 120 \rangle\}.
\end{aligned}
$$

This is the set of all the l-correct states at label L; if execution proceeds from label L on any of the following states, it will terminate in the correct final state. Note that $\langle 5, 3, 2 \rangle$, the s-correct state at milestone $(3, L)$, is among the l-correct states.

Sp-correct States. The set of sp-correct states is $s_0 \cdot (R * ftr^\wedge)$. We compute $(R * ftr^\wedge)$, then apply it to s_0.

$$
\begin{aligned}
R * ftr^\wedge &= \{(s, s') \mid \exists t: (s, t) \in R \wedge (s', t) \in ftr\} \\
&= \{(s, s') \mid \exists t: f(t) = n(s)! \wedge k(s') \leq n(s') + 1 \wedge n(t) = n(s') \\
&\qquad \wedge k(t) = n(s') + 1 \\
&\qquad \wedge f(t) = f(s') * n(s')! * k(s')/k(s')!\} \\
&= \{(s, s') \mid n(s)! = f(s') * n(s')! * k(s')/k(s')! \\
&\qquad \wedge k(s') \leq n(s') + 1\}.
\end{aligned}
$$

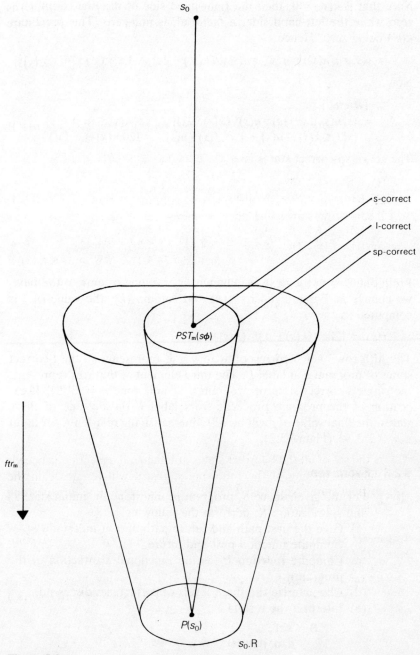

Figure 5.2

Note that if $k(s') = 0$, then the right-hand side of the first conjunct is zero while the left-hand side, a factorial, is non-zero. This precludes $k(s')$ being zero. Hence

$$= \{(s,s') \mid n(s)! = f(s') * n(s')!/(k(s') - 1)! \, \wedge \, 1 \leq k(s') \leq n(s') + 1\}.$$

Now,

$$\begin{aligned} s_0 \cdot (R * ftr\hat{}) \\ &= \{s \mid n(s_0)! = f(s) * n(s)!/(k(s) - 1)! \, \wedge \, 1 \leq k(s) \leq n(s) + 1\} \\ &= \{s \mid 1 \leq k(s) \leq n(s) + 1 \, \wedge \, f(s) * n(s)! = 120 * (k(s) - 1)!\}. \end{aligned}$$

The set of sp-correct states is:

$$\begin{aligned} \{&\langle 1,1,120 \rangle, \langle 1,2,120 \rangle, \\ &\langle 2,1,60 \rangle, \quad \langle 2,2,60 \rangle, \quad \langle 2,3,120 \rangle, \\ &\langle 3,1,20 \rangle, \quad \langle 3,2,20 \rangle, \quad \langle 3,3,40 \rangle, \quad \langle 3,4,120 \rangle, \\ &\langle 4,1,5 \rangle, \quad \langle 4,2,5 \rangle, \quad \langle 4,3,10 \rangle, \quad \langle 4,4,30 \rangle, \quad \langle 4,5,120 \rangle, \\ &\langle 5,1,1 \rangle, \quad \langle 5,2,1 \rangle, \quad \langle 5,3,2 \rangle, \quad \langle 5,4,6 \rangle, \quad \langle 5,5,24 \rangle, \quad \langle 5,6,120 \rangle, \\ &\qquad\qquad\qquad\qquad\qquad\quad \langle 6,4,1 \rangle, \quad \langle 6,5,4 \rangle, \quad \langle 6,6,20 \rangle, \quad \langle 6,7,120 \rangle \} \end{aligned}$$

From one row to the next, we change n; from one column to the next, we change k. For a given row (n) and column (k), the value of f is computed as

$$f(s) = 120 * (k(s) - 1)! / (n(s))!.$$

The fifth row, which corresponds to $n = 5$, represents all the l-correct states of program p at label L. The third element of that row represents the single s-correct state of program p at milestone $m = (3, L)$. If execution of the program proceeds from label L on any one of these states, the final value of f will be 120, thus satisfying relation R for input $s_0 = \langle 5,3,9 \rangle$ (Figure 5.2).

5.2.3 Exercises

1[A] For the given space S, program p, milestone m, initial state s_0 and specification R, perform the following.
(a) Give the past path and future path of p at milestone m.
(b) Compute function past and future.
(c) Compute function P (as the functional abstraction of the program).
(d) Characterize the three levels of correctness discussed.
(e) Interpret the results.

>   S = **set**
>   a, b: **natural**
>   **end**.

```
p = begin
   L: while b ≠ 0 do
      begin
         a := a + 1;
         b := b − 1
      end
   end.
```

$m = (3, L).$
$s_0 = \langle 5, 9 \rangle.$
$R = \{(s, s') \mid a(s') = a(s) + b(s)\}.$

2[A] Use the same space, program, milestone and initial state as exercise 1, and use the following specification:

$$R = \{(s, s') \mid b(s') = 0\}.$$

3[B] Same as Exercise 1, for the following space, program, milestone, initial state and specification:

```
S = set
crt
   a, b: natural;
sub
   a ≠ 0 ∧ b ≠ 0
end.
p = begin
   L: while a ≠ b do
      if a > b then a := a − b else b := b − a
   end.
```

$m = (3, L),$
$s_0 = \langle 35, 50 \rangle,$
$R = \{(s, s') \mid a(s') = \gcd(s)\},$

where $\gcd(s)$ is the greatest common divisor of $a(s)$ and $b(s)$.

4[B] Use the same space, program, milestone and initial state as Exercise 3, and use the following specification:

$$R = \{(s, s') \mid a(s') = b(s')\}.$$

5[B] Same as Exercise 1 for the following space, program, milestone, initial state and specification:

```
S = set
   a, b, c: natural
end.
```

```
p = begin
    c := 0;
    L: while b ≠ 0 do
       begin
       b := b − 1;
       c := c + a
       end;

    b := c
end;
```

$m = (3, L)$.
$s_0 = \langle 5, 8, 3 \rangle$.
$R = \{(s, s') \mid b(s') = a(s) * b(s)\}$.

6[B] Use the same space, program, milestone and initial state as Exercise 5, and use the following specification:

$$R = \{(s, s') \mid c(s') = b(s')\}.$$

[B]   Consider Example 1, in Section 5.2.2:
(a) Compute $f = pst_{3, L} * ftr_{3, L}$.
(b) Compare f to P. What can you say?
See also Problem 4 of Chapter 4.

8[C] Same as Exercise 1, for the following space, program, milestone, initial state and specification:

```
S = set
    a, b, c: natural
end.
p = begin
c := 1;
L: while b ≠ 0 do
     if b mod 2 = 0 then
        begin
        a := a * a; b := b/2
        end
     else
        begin
        c := c * a; b := b − 1
        end;
     b := c
end,
```

$m = (3, L)$,
$s_0 = \langle 2, 13, 5 \rangle$,
$R = \{(s, s') \mid b(s') = a(s)^{b(s)}\}$.

9[C]   Same as Exercise 1, for the following space, program, milestone, initial state and specification:

```
S = set
      a: array [0 .. n] of integer;
      x: integer;
      f: boolean;
      k: 0 .. n;
end,
p = begin
      a[0] := x; k := n;
      L: while x ≠ a[k] do M: k := k − 1;
      f := (k ≠ 0)
      end.
```

$m = (5, L).$

s_0 defined by
$$a(s_0) = [3, 5, 2, 19, 12, 10, 7, 3, 29, 8, 5].$$
$$x(s_0) = 19.$$
$$f(s_0) = \textbf{true}.$$
$$k(s_0) = 0.$$

$R = \{(s, s') \mid a(s') = a(s) \land a(s)[k(s')] = x(s)\}.$

10[C]   Use the same space, program, milestone and initial state as
Exercise 9, and use the following specification:

$$R = \{(s, s') \mid a(s)[k(s')] = x(s)\}.$$

Then the following specification:

$$R = \{(s, s') \mid a(s')[k(s')] = x(s')\}.$$

Compare your results, and interpret them.

11[C]   Use the same space, program, milestone and initial state as
Exercise 9, and use the following specification:

$$R \{(s, s') \mid f(s') \lor (\forall h: a(s)[h] \neq x(s))\}.$$

12[C]   Same as Exercise 1, for the following space, program, milestone, initial state and specification:

```
S = set
      a: array [0 .. n] of integer;
      m: integer;
      j, k, l: 0 .. n;
end,
```

where $n > 4$.

```
p = begin
    k := 1;
    L: while k < n do
       begin
       m := a[k]; l := k; j := k + 1;
       M: while j ≤ n do
          begin
          if a[j] < m then
             begin
             m := a[j]; l := j
             end;
          j := j + 1
          end;
       a[l] := a[k]; a[k] := m; k := k + 1
       end
    end.
```

$m = (4, L)$.

s_0 defined by:

$$a(s_0) = [12, 5, 14, 2, 21, 17].$$
$$j(s_0) = 1.$$
$$k(s_0) = 6.$$
$$l(s_0) = 5.$$
$$m(s_0) = -1.$$
$$R = \{(s, s') \mid a(s') \text{ is sorted}\}.$$

Interpret your results.

5.3   DEGREES OF ERROR: LEVELS OF RECOVERABILITY

Let p be a program on space S, L a label on p, and s_0 an initial state of program p. We run program p on initial state s_0 and observe the state of p at milestone (v, L), for some **natural** v.

The state of p at milesone (v, L) may fail to be correct, by any of the definitions given above, yet it may still contain all the necessary information to complete the execution of p without failure; we then say that s is *recoverable*, in the sense that we can retrieve a correct state from it. Let us consider state s of program p at milestone (v, L). Because state s is not correct, execution of p may not proceed without some form of intervention; because such a state contains all the necessary information, it is possible, using some form of intervention, to generate a correct state from it, at milestone (v, L) and to let the execution proceed. Such intervention takes the form of a *recovery routine*.

5.3.1 Definitions

A state of program p at milestone (v, L) may fail to be s-correct, yet contain all the necessary information to generate an s-correct state. Hence we have the following definition:

- *Definition*. State s is said to be *strictly recoverable* (s-recoverable) at milestone (v, L) vis-à-vis initial state s_0 if and only if there exists a Pascal program r, such that $[r](s)$ is s-correct.

Program r is called a *recovery routine*; it must, of course, be independent of s_0. A state is s-recoverable if and only if there exists r such that

$$[r](s) = pst_{v,L}(s_0).$$

The set of all s-recoverable states is

$$s_0 \cdot (pst_{v,L} * [r]\hat{\ }).$$

Because $[r]$ is potentially (and typically) non-injective, $[r]\hat{\ }$ is non-deterministic, and this set is potentially larger than a singleton. See Figure 5.3 for a graphical representation of s-recoverable states; and see Example 2 below for an illustration of s-recoverability. See Section 5.4 for a discussion of the relationships between correctness and recoverability levels.

- *Definition*. State s is said to be *loosely recoverable* (l-recoverable) at milestone (v, L) vis-à-vis initial state s_0 if and only if there exists a Pascal program r, such that $[r](s)$ is l-correct.

In other words, a state is l-recoverable if and only if

$$ftr([r](s)) = P(s_0).$$

The set of l-recoverable states is

$$s_0 \cdot (P * ftr\hat{\ } * [r]\hat{\ }).$$

This set is typically very large, as $ftr\hat{\ }$ and $[r]\hat{\ }$ are typically non-deterministic, i.e. ftr and $[r]$ are non-injective. See Figure 5.3 for a graphical representation of l-recoverable states; see Example 2 below

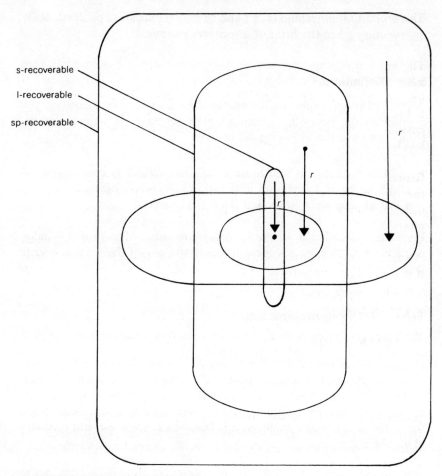

Figure 5.3   Levels of recoverability

for an illustration of l-recoverability. See Section 5.4 for a discussion of the relationship between correctness and recoverability levels.

- *Definition.* State *s* is said to be *specificationwise recoverable* (sp-recoverable) at milestone (v, L) vis-à-vis initial state s_0 if and only if there exists a Pascal program *r*, such that $[r](s)$ is sp-correct.

In other words, a state is sp-recoverable if and only if

$$ftr([r](s)) \in s_0 \cdot R.$$

The set of sp-recoverable states is

$$s_0 \cdot (R * ftr\hat{\ } * [r]\hat{\ }).$$

The more R is non-deterministic and ftr and $[r]$ are non-injective, the more sp-recoverable states exist at milestone $m = (v, L)$. See Figure 5.3 for a graphical representation of sp-recoverable states; see Example 2 below for an illustration of sp-recoverability. See Section 5.4 for a discussion of the relationship between correctness and recoverability levels.

Remark 2. In the remainder of this chapter, and this book, we may use the term *levels of correctness*, as it pertains to states, to mean two different things: the three levels of correctness defined in Section 5.2, or all six levels of correctness and recoverability defined in Sections 5.2 and 5.3. The context can usually distinguish between the two meanings. Also, following traditional terminology, we say that a state is *maskable* if it is l-correct or sp-correct.   □

5.3.2   Illustration

We illustrate the three definitions above with a program similar to that of Example 1, Section 5.2. The clause

    ... there exists a Pascal program r ...

precludes a systematic construction of the sets of recoverable states (strictly, largely, or specificationwise recoverable). In Example 5.2 below, we derive these sets on the basis of informal arguments.

Example 2. The program used here is similar to that of Example 1, except for a minor – artificial – detail, whose interest will become clear later:

Space:

```
S = set
    n, f, k: natural;
    a: natural
end.
```

Program:

```
p = begin
    k := 1; f := 1;
```

```
L: while k ≠ n + 1 do
   begin
   f := f * k; k := k + 1
   end
end.
```

Specification:

$$R' = \{(s,s') \mid k(s') = n(s') + 1 \wedge a(s') = a(s)\}.$$

Milestone:

$$m = (v, L).$$

Initial state:

$$s_0.$$ ☐

We give, without proof, the main functions of interest. For details of how these functions are derived, see Example 1, which is quite similar:

$$P = \{(s,s') \mid n(s') = n(s) \wedge k(s') = n(s) + 1 \wedge f(s') = n(s)! \\ \wedge a(s') = a(s)\}.$$
$$pst_{v,L} = \{(s,s') \mid n(s) \geq v - 1 \wedge n(s') = n(s) \wedge k(s') = v \\ \wedge f(s') = (v-1)! \wedge a(s') = a(s)\}.$$
$$ftr_{v,L} = \{(s,s') \mid k(s) \leq n(s) + 1 \wedge n(s') = n(s) \wedge k(s') = n(s) + 1 \\ \wedge f(s') = f(s) * n(s)! * k(s)/k(s)! \wedge a(s') = a(s)\}.$$

S-recoverable states. Given that execution of p on s_0 has reached milestone (v, L), i.e. that $n(s_0) \geq v - 1$, the s-correct state at milestone (v, L) is

$$s = \langle n(s_0), v, (v-1)!, a(s_0) \rangle.$$

Even though state s has four components, it has only three independent components. For example, if the value of $f(s)$ (i.e. $(v-1)!$) has been lost, one can retrieve it using the value of $k(s)$ (i.e. v). Consequently, it seems reasonable to characterize s-recoverable states by the equations

$$n(s) = n(s_0) \wedge k(s) = v \wedge a(s) = a(s_0).$$

A satisfactory recovery routine would compute the factorial of $(k(s) - 1)$ into variable f, so as to generate the s-correct state.

L-recoverable states. By inspection of Example 1, we can characterize l-correct states of p at milestone (v, L) by the following relations:

$$n(s) = n(s_0) \wedge 1 \leq k(s) \leq n(s_0) + 1 \wedge f(s) = (k(s) - 1)! \wedge a(s) = a(s_0).$$

In order to generate a state that verifies this condition, it suffices to know $n(s_0)$ and $a(s_0)$. Hence we can characterize l-recoverable states by

$$n(s) = n(s_0) \wedge a(s) = a(s_0).$$

Notice that we can lose the value of both k and f, and still have an l-recoverable state. A possible recovery routine would pick a value for k between 1 and $n + 1$, then compute the factorial of $(k - 1)$ into f.

Sp-recoverable states. First, let us characterize sp-correct states with respect to R'. We compute $R' * ftr\hat{\ }$, then apply it to s_0:

$$
\begin{aligned}
R' & * ftr\hat{\ } \\
&= \{(s, s') \,|\, \exists t\colon (s, t) \in R' \wedge (s', t) \in ftr\} \\
&= \{(s, s') \,|\, \exists t\colon k(t) = n(t) + 1 \wedge a(t) = a(s) \wedge k(s') \le n(s') + 1 \\
&\qquad \wedge\ n(t) = n(s') \wedge k(t) = n(s') + 1 \\
&\qquad \wedge\ f(t) = f(s') * n(s')! * k(s)/k(s')! \\
&\qquad \wedge\ a(t) = a(s')\} \\
&= \{(s, s') \,|\, k(s') \le n(s') + 1 \wedge a(s) = a(s')\}.
\end{aligned}
$$

Hence

$$s_0 \cdot (R' * ftr\hat{\ }) = \{s \,|\, k(s) \le n(s) + 1 \wedge a(s) = a(s_0)\}.$$

A state is sp-correct at milestone $m = (v, L)$ with respect to R' vis-à-vis s_0 if

$$k(s) \le n(s) + 1 \wedge a(s) = a(s_0).$$

In order to generate a state that verifies this condition, it suffices to know $a(s_0)$. Hence sp-recoverable states can be characterized by

$$a(s) = a(s_0).$$

Notice that we can lose the values of all of n, k and f and still have an sp-recoverable state. A satisfactory recovery routine could pick an arbitrary value for n, choose a value for k which is at most equal to $n + 1$, choose arbitrary values for f, and finally preserve a.

Non-sp-recoverable states. Notice that if the values of a is damaged, we no longer have an sp-recoverable state since specification R' requires the preservation of variable a.

We recapitulate

It is worth noting that this state may lose three variables out of four and still remain (sp-) recoverable. Of course, such spectacular ratios are not common. The following example is contrived for purposes of illustration.

	a	n	k	f	Lost
s-correct	$a(s_0)$	$n(s_0)$	v	$(v-1)!$	None
s-recoverable	$a(s_0)$	$n(s_0)$	v	–	f
l-recoverable	$a(s_0)$	$n(s_0)$	–	–	f,k
sp-recoverable	$a(s_0)$	–	–	–	f,k,n
Non sp-recoverable	–	–	–	–	All

5.3.3 Exercises

1[A] Consider Exercise 1 of Section 5.2.3. From the characterizations of
   s-correctness,
   l-correctness,
   sp-correctness,
derive characterizations for
   s-recoverability,
   l-recoverability,
   sp-recoverability.

2[A] Consider Exercise 2 of Section 5.2.3. From the characterizations of
   s-correctness,
   l-correctness,
   sp-correctness,
derive characterizations for
   s-recoverability,
   l-recoverability,
   sp-recoverability.

3[B] Consider Exercise 3 of Section 5.2.3. From the characterizations of
   s-correctness,
   l-correctness,
   sp-correctness,
derive characterizations for
   s-recoverability,
   l-recoverability,
   sp-recoverability.

4[B] Consider Exercise 4 of Section 5.2.3. From the characterizations of

    s-correctness,
    l-correctness,
    sp-correctness,
  derive characterizations for
    s-recoverability,
    l-recoverability,
    sp-recoverability.

5[B] Consider Exercise 5 of Section 5.2.3. From the characterizations of
    s-correctness,
    l-correctness,
    sp-correctness,
  derive characterizations for
    s-recoverability,
    l-recoverability,
    sp-recoverability.

6[B] Consider Exercise 6 of Section 5.2.3. From the characterizations of
    s-correctness,
    l-correctness,
    sp-correctness,
  derive characterizations for
    s-recoverability,
    l-recoverability,
    sp-recoverability.

7[C] Consider the program of Exercise 9, with the specifications given in Exercises 9, 10 and 11 of Section 5.2.3. From the characterizations of
    s-correctness,
    l-correctness,
  derive characterizations for
    s-recoverability,
    l-recoverability,
Similarly, for each characterization of sp-correctness obtained from each specification, derive a characterization of sp-recoverability. Interpret your results.

8[B] Consider the following factorial program:

```
S = set
      n, f: natural
    end,
p = begin
```

```
        f := 1;
        L: while n ≠ 0 do
           begin
             f := f * n;
             n := n − 1
           end
        end.
```

$$R = \{(s, s') \mid f(s') = n(s)!\}.$$

(a) Characterize s-correct states, l-correct states and sp-correct states at milestone (v, L) vis-à-vis initial state s_0 with respect to R. Compare your findings with Example 2.

(b) Characterize s-recoverable states, l-recoverable states and sp-recoverable states at milestone (v, L) vis-à-vis s_0 with respect to R. Compare your findings with Example 2.

(c) Disregarding variable a (of Example 2), discuss the trade-offs of parsimony (in number of variables) versus redundancy (between variables), and their impact on the potential for recoverability.

9[B]   Construct an example similar to Example 2, in that you go from s-correctness to s-recoverability to l-recoverability to sp-recoverability to non-sp-recoverability by losing 0, 1, 2, 3 or 4 variables out of four.

10[B]   We consider the following space and program:

```
        S = set
            a: array [1..n] of real;
            sum: real;
            k: 1..n + 1
        end.
        p = begin
            sum := 0; k := 1;
            L: while k ≠ n + 1 do
               begin
                 sum := sum + a[k];
                 k := k + 1
               end
        end.
```

(a) Characterize s-recoverable states, l-recoverable states and sp-recoverable states at milestone (v, L) vis-à-vis s_0 with respect to specification:

$$R = \{(s,s')\,|\,a(s') = a(s) \wedge \text{sum}(s') = \Sigma_{i=1}^{n}\,a(s')[i]\}.$$

(b) Same question, with the specification

$$R = \{(s,s')\,|\,\text{sum}(s') = \Sigma_{i=1}^{n}\,a(s')[i]\}.$$

(c) Same question, with the specification

$$R = \{(s,s')\,|\,k(s') = n(s') + 1\}.$$

11[C] We consider the following space and program:

```
S = set
    a: array [0..n] of integer;
    m: integer;
    j, k, l: 0..n;
end,
p = begin
    k := 1;
    L:  while k < n do
    begin
    m := a[k]; l := k; j := k + 1;
    M: while j ≤ n do
        begin
        if a[j] < m then
            begin
            m := a[j]; l := j
            end;
        j := j + 1
        end;
    a[l] := a[k]; a[k] := m; k := k + 1
    end
end.
```

(a) Characterize its s-correct and s-recoverable states at milestone (v, L), for $v \leq n + 1$.
(b) Characterize its l-correct and l-recoverable states at milestone (v, L), for $v \leq n + 1$.
(c) Characterize its sp-correct and sp-recoverable states at milestone (v, L), with respect to specification

$$R = \{(s,s')\,|\,\text{prm}(s,s') \wedge \text{ord}(s')\},$$

where $\text{prm}(s,s')$ means that $a(s')$ is some permutation of $a(s)$, and $\text{ord}(s')$ means that $a(s')$ is sorted.
(d) Same question as (c), with specification

$$R = \{(s,s')\,|\,\text{ord}(s')\}.$$

(e) Same question as (c), with specification

$$R = \{(s,s')|\text{prm}(s,s')\}.$$

5.4 HIERARCHY OF CORRECTNESS LEVELS

In this section we take a global view of correctness and recoverability levels, and exhibit their interrelationships. We take three different views in turn.

5.4.1 Correctness Levels

Figure 5.4 shows the inclusion relationships among the sets of correct states.

Clearly, if a state s is s-correct, then it is s-recoverable; also, if a state is l-correct, then it is l-recoverable; finally, if a state is sp-correct, then it is sp-recoverable. For all these cases, the empty program – whose functional abstraction is the identity – is an adequate recovery routine.

Note that there is no inclusion relationship between the set of l-correct states and the set of s-recoverable states, although they are not disjoint; their intersection includes the l-correct states that contain all the necessary information to retrieve the s-correct state. Also, there is no inclusion relationship between the set of sp-correct states and the set of l-recoverable states, although they are not disjoint; their intersection includes the sp-correct states that contain the necessary information to retrieve l-correct states.

5.4.2 The Lattice of Correctness Levels

Figure 5.5 shows the hierarchy of correctness levels by means of a lattice-like network. The higher a node, the weaker the property it represents, the larger the set of states that meet the property.

5.4.3 The three Dimensions of Correctness

Three factors are involved in the definition of a correctness level: (i) the non-injectivity of the future function ftr; (ii) the non-injectivity of the recovery routine, r; (iii) the non-determinacy of the specification, R. The six levels of correctness/recoverability can in fact be defined by determining which of these three factors is or is not involved in the

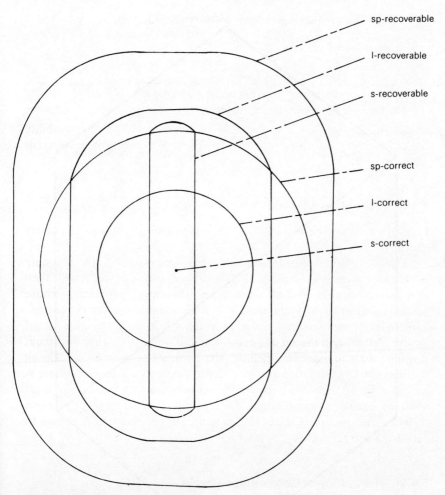

sp-recoverable

l-recoverable

s-recoverable

sp-correct

l-correct

s-correct

Figure 5.4   Inclusion relationships

definition. This situation can be illustrated on a three-dimensional cartesian space with boolean axes (see Figure 5.6).

In the definition of s-correctness, none of these factors intervenes; we obtain the point $(0,0,0)$. In the definition of l-correctness, only the non-injectivity of ftr intervenes; we obtain the point $(1,0,0)$. In the definition of s-recoverability, only the non-injectivity of $[r]$ intervenes; we obtain the point $(0,1,0)$. In the definition of l-recoverability, both the non-injectivity of ftr and $[r]$ intervene; we obtain the point $(1,1,0)$. In

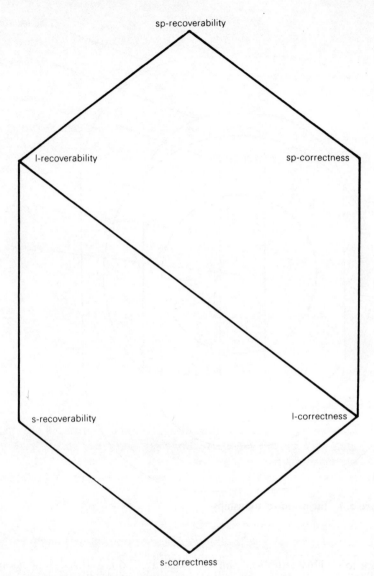

Figure 5.5   Lattice of correctness levels

the definition of sp-correctness, both the non-injectivity of *ftr* and the non-determinacy of R intervene; we obtain the point $(1, 0, 1)$. Finally, in the definition of sp-recoverability, all three factors intervene; we obtain the point $(1, 1, 1)$.

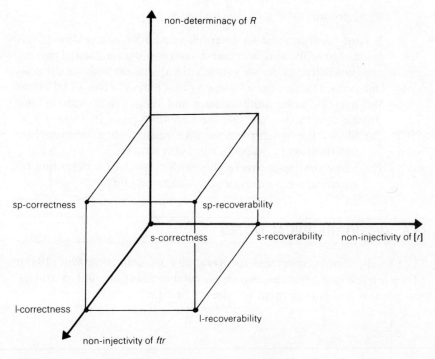

Figure 5.6 The three dimensions of state correctness

5.4.4 Exercises

1[A] Consider Example 2 of Section 5.3.2, and Figure 5.4. In each area of Figure 5.4 (intersection, set difference, etc.), give an example of state.

2[B] Same as Exercise 1, using the program of Exercise 9 in Section 5.2 instead of Example 2.

3[B] Same as Exercise 1, using the program of Exercise 12 in Section 5.2 instead of Example 2.

4[A] Give a physical interpretation of least upper bound and greatest lower bound in the lattice of Figure 5.5.

5[A] What simple relationship is there between Figures 5.5 and 5.6?

6[A] Explain why two points are missing in the cube of Figure 5.6.

5.5 PROBLEMS

1[R] The definitions of recoverability levels (Section 5.3) depend on a predicate of the form

∃ program r: . . . .

It is of great interest to determine under what conditions (sufficient, possibly also necessary) such a program exist. Ignoring computability issues, we can ask the question: under what condition does there exist a function f that plays the rôle of $[r]$? Pose the question with finite domain and range, then with infinite domain and range. See also the Examples given in Section 5.3.

2[C]   (a) Show that sp-correctness with respect to a deterministic specification is equivalent to l-correctness.

(b) Show that sp-recoverability with respect to a deterministic specification is equivalent to l-recoverability.

5.6   BIBLIOGRAPHICAL NOTES

The levels of correctness and recoverability are defined in Mili (1985). They are relevant to discussions on executable assertions and to damage assessment and containment (Anderson and Lee, 1981).

Part III

Error Detection and Damage Assessment

The most certain and effectual check upon errors which arise in the process of computation, is to cause the same computation to be made by separate and independent computers; and this check is rendered still more decisive if they make their computations by different methods.

(DIONYSIUS LARDNER, 1834)

In Part II, we have identified four phases in the process of fault tolerance, whereby we prevent a fault causing a failure:

1. *Error detection:* when the manifestation of the fault, i.e. the error, is detected.
2. *Damage assessment:* when the extent of the damage done to the state is assessed.
3. *Fault removal:* when the fault is diagnosed then removed from the (text of the) program.
4. *Error recovery:* when the error is removed from the state of the program.

Fault removal is beyond the scope of this book; it deals with program testing and debugging, a very large field in its own right. Error detection and damage assessment is the subject of this part, while error recovery is the subject of the next two parts.

The purpose of this part is to discuss techniques for detecting errors in running programs, and to assess their extent in terms of the taxonomy presented in the preceding part. In keeping with the orientation of the book, we use executable assertions for these purposes which have two advantages: first, the detection of errors is made by the program, under its own control (rather by external agents, such as e.g. watchdog processors); second, the formalism that we use to capture the semantics of executable assertions is the same as that used for other aspects of our problem (specifications, program functions, etc.).

In Chapter 6, we introduce the use of executable assertions in structured programs; then we discuss how executable assertions can be used for error detection. In Chapters 7 and 8 we discuss the use of executable assertions for damage assessment: Chapter 7, subtitled 'when is recovery necessary?' discusses under what condition the extent of the damage is sufficiently large that the error is not maskable (in which case recovery is necessary); Chapter 8, subtitled 'when is recovery sufficient?' discusses under what condition the damage is sufficiently limited that the state still contains sufficient information to be recovered (in which case recovery is sufficient).

CHAPTER 6

Error detection by executable assertions

In this chapter we discuss the nature and properties of executable assertions. Then we discuss the use of executable assertions for the purpose of *error detection*, i.e. determining when a state fails to be strictly correct at some milestone.

6.1 ON THE NATURE OF EXECUTABLE ASSERTIONS

6.1.1 Syntax of Executable Assertions

An executable assertion is a statement that checks whether a particular condition holds among the variables of the program, and takes some action in case it does not hold. Although several modern programming languages provide special constructs for executable assertions, we shall content ourselves with Pascal's **if-then-else** for this purpose, so that in their simplest form, executable assertions take the form

    if not assertion **then** action,

where *assertion* is a Pascal boolean expression, and *action* is a Pascal procedure.

We consider such an executable assertion at label L of program P.

    L: **if not** a **then** action.

If assertion a refers only to the present state of the program, then it is bound to be limited in terms of the functional aspects that it can check: in fact the strongest property that assertion a can check, provided that it refers only to the current state, is

$$a(s) = s \in \text{rng}(PST_m),$$

where $m = (v, L)$ is the current milestone, and PST_m is the expected past function of program P at milestone m.

In its most general form, an assertion must refer not only to the current state, but also to some previous state. Among the possible choices for this previous state, we mention the following two:

(a) the initial state, s_0;
(b) some intermediate state between s_0 and the current state which was reached along the past path.

Three reasons call for choosing an intermediate state rather than the initial state:

1. *Modularity:* it is best to think of the assertion a as checking a local program segment b by referring to the state of the program before execution of b, and after; hence the program segment b and its assertion checking facilities form a modular unit that is context independent, in the sense that it does not depend on where it is in the program.
2. *Time parsimony:* block b can be arbitrarily short, and the function it computes arbitrarily simple. Hence the assertion that checks it can be arbitrarily easy to compute, and arbitrarily time efficient. By contrast, referring to s_0 means that, at milestone m, we check functional properties of function PST_m, whose complexity we do not choose.
3. *Space parsimony:* block b can be arbitrarily short, and the variables it affects arbitrarily few. Hence the memory space required to save the variables modified by block b is arbitrarily small. By contrast, referring to s_0 means that sufficient memory space must be set aside to save all of s_0, whose size we do not choose.

As a consequence of our choice, executable assertions must be looked at along with the block that they check, and the statement that saves (part of) the previous state. This whole aggregate we call an *elementary asserted block (eab)*. Its general form is:

```
ŝ := s;
b {modifies s, but not ŝ};
if not a(ŝ, s) then action.
```

The assignment statement $(\hat{s} := s)$ refers to the act of saving state s in $\hat{s}$; in practice one may want to save only some variables, e.g. those that are going to be modified by b and/or those that are involved in the expression of assertion a.

Example 1
For S = **integer** and $b = (s := s * s)$, we take three assertions:

```
bea1: ŝ := s;
      b;
```

```
        if not (s = ŝ²) then action;
bea2: ŝ := s;
        b;
        if not (ŝ > 1 ⇒ s > ŝ) then action;
bea3: ŝ := s;
        b;
        if not (s > 0) then action;
```

These are simple examples, used for illustrative purposes; in practice, b would typically be an intricate block of code that is difficult to analyse and $a(\hat{s}, s)$ would be a simple assertion.   □

6.1.2 Semantics of Executable Assertions

We consider the following elementary asserted block:

```
eab: begin
        ŝ := s;
        b;
        if not a(ŝ, s) then action
     end.
```

The executable assertion of this eab is naturally captured by the binary relation

$$R = \{(s, s') \mid a(s, s')\}.$$

The behavior of this whole eab can then be captured by the following formula:

$$(\forall s: s \in \mathrm{dom}(R) \land s \in \mathrm{dom}([b]) \land (s, [b](s)) \notin R$$
$$\Rightarrow \mathrm{invoked}(\mathrm{action})),$$

where invoked(action) means that procedure *action* is invoked. In other words, for any state $\hat{s}$ in $\mathrm{dom}(R)$, for which b is defined ($s \in \mathrm{dom}([b])$) and yields a final state ($[b](s)$) that does not meet assertion $a((s, [b](s)) \notin R)$, we are ensured that the procedure named *action* is invoked.

6.1.3 Strength of an Assertion

An executable assertion can be arbitrarily stringent in its checking the functional properties of its block. Hence assertion a in the following eab:

```
ŝ := s;
b;
if not a(ŝ, s) then action
```

can be as stringent as

$$a(\hat{s}, s) = (\hat{s}, s) \in B,$$

where B is the expected function of block b. It can also be as weak as

$$a(\hat{s}, s) = s \in \text{rng}(B),$$

and even weaker

$$a(\hat{s}, s) = \textbf{true}.$$

Of course, a wide range of possibilities exist between these.

We define the strength of an assertion in terms of the relation that the assertion defines. Specifically, let a and a' be two assertions, and R and R' be the relations associated with them. We say that a is stronger than a' if and only if R is more-defined than R'. The rationale behind this definition is, of course, that a relation is all the more defined that it carries more input/output information. The example given below illustrates this definition.

Example 2
$S = \textbf{integer}$; let b be a block of Pascal code on space S.

```
eab:  ŝ := s;
      b;
      if not (s = ŝ + 1) then action;
eab': ŝ := s;
      b;
      if not (ŝ ≤ s ≤ ŝ + 3) then action;
eab": ŝ := s;
      b;
      if not (ŝ > 3 ∧ s = ŝ + 1) then action;
```

If we let a, a' and a'' be the assertions defined by these three elementary asserted blocks, we can easily prove that a is stronger than both a' and a'', and that a' and a'' are not comparable.   □

Note that in general,

   a is stronger than a'

is not synonymous with

   a logically implies a';

nor is it synonymous with

   a is more difficult to check than a'.

The implications of this remark are discussed in the next section; but, first, here is an illustrative example.

Example 3. Let a be:

$$a(\hat{s}, s) = \hat{s} \leq s \leq \hat{s} + 2$$

and a' be:

$$a'(\hat{s}, s) = \hat{s} \geq 3 \land \hat{s} \leq s \leq \hat{s} + 2.$$

Assertion a is stronger than a'; yet it neither implies a' nor is more complex than a'. $\qquad\qquad\square$

6.1.4 Assertions with Fixed Domain

The relational *more-defined*, that we use to define the strength of assertions, is fairly difficult to manipulate. In addition, it is rather counterintuitive, as shown by the concluding remark of the preceding section. We remember, however, that this relational takes on a simple form when it compares two relations with the same domain. Specifically, if R and R' have the same domain, then R is more-defined than R' if and only if

$$R \subseteq R'.$$

In this frame of discussion, assertion a is stronger than assertion a' if and only if a logically implies a'. Furthermore, if a conjunctive form is used (by means of *and*'s) then there is a strong connection between the strength of an assertion and the complexity of checking it.

Hence, for the sake of simplicity, it is best to have assertions with the same domain. For the sake of uniformity, we shall assume (unless specified otherwise) that all assertions used define relations whose domain is S. Some of the assertions we shall use stem from relational equations, and may have domains that are smaller than S. We know of two techniques for transforming such relations into relations whose domain is S.

Pushing the domain back. This simple technique is best illustrated by an example.

Example 4

```
p: ŝ := s;
   b1;
```

```
if not a1(ŝ, s) then action(1);
ŝ := s;
b2;
if not (ŝ > 3 ∧ s = ŝ + 1) then action(2);
```

The second assertion defines a relation whose domain is not S, but $D = \{s \mid s > 3\}$; we transform this assertion program to become

```
p': ŝ := s;
b1;
if not a1(ŝ, s) ∧ (s > 3) then action(1);
ŝ := s;
b2;
if not (s = ŝ + 1) then action(2).
```

Now the domain of the second assertion is S. Notice that we gain another advantage by this manipulation: the assertion (>3) is checked about a current state ($s > 3$) rather than a previous state ($\hat{s} > 3$); hence it is less costly, in terms of time and space. □

Reasoning by Equivalence. Let S_m be the set of states that are reachable at milestone m, and let R and R' be two relations that represent two possible assertions, say a and a', that we may want to check at milestone m. We admit the following trivial result: If

$$I(S_m) * R = I(S_m) * R'$$

then assertions a and a' are interchangeable at milestone m. A simple illustration of this result is given below.

Example 5
Let S be **integer**, and let the set of reachable states at milestone m be $S_m = \{s \mid s > 3\}$. Let the relation to be checked at milestone m be

$$R = \{(s, s') \mid s \geq 1 \wedge s' = s + 9\}.$$

We want to know whether we can find a simpler (to write) relation that is interchangeable with R at milestone m. This relation, say R', is subject to the following equation

$$I(S_m) * R = I(S_m) * R'$$

$$\Leftrightarrow$$

$$\{(s, s') \mid s > 3 \wedge s' = s + 9\} = I(s > 3) * R'.$$

We take, naturally,

$$R' = \{(s, s') \mid s' = s + 9\}.$$

This relation corresponds to the assertion

$$a'(\hat{s}, s) = (s = (\hat{s} + 9)). \qquad \square$$

In general, we prefer to use the second technique whenever it is applicable because it is self-contained (it does not involve other eab's).

6.1.5 Exercises

1[A] Consider space $S = $ **integer**, and let b be the program segment whose expected function is

$$B = \{(s, s') | s' = s^2 + 1\}.$$

Give five increasingly strong assertions, that one may want to check about block b.

2[B] Same as Exercise 1, with

$$B = \{(s, s') | s \ge 0 \land s' = s^2 + 1\}.$$

3[B] Same as Exercise 1, with

$$B = \{(s, s') | s' = s^2 + 1 \land s' \le 10\}.$$

4[B] Same as Exercise 1, with

$$B = \{(s, s') | s \ge 0 \land s' = s^2 + 1 \land s' \le 10\}.$$

6.2 ERROR DETECTION

6.2.1 Position of the Problem

We consider a program p on space S which we run on some initial state s_0; and we observe its state at milestone m. According to the definitions of Chapters 4 and 5, there is an error in the current state of the program if and only if it is not strictly correct.

One cannot use executable assertions, as they are presented here, to check the strict correctness of the current state using the formula

$$s = PST_m(s_0),$$

because the executable assertion is not supposed to refer to s_0; rather, it refers to an intermediate state between the initial state and the current state. In keeping with the definitions of the preceding section, we must design executable assertions around elementary asserted blocks, in such a way that their combined effect replaces the act of checking the global assertion $s = PST_m(s_0)$ at milestone m.

Specifically, let m and m' be two consecutive milestones (defined on labels L and L') reached during the execution of program p on initial state s_0, and let b be the block of code executed between m and m':

```
L:  ŝ := s;
    b;
    if not a(ŝ, s) then action;
L': ...
```

The question that we ask is: how must we design assertion a so that it reveals the presence of an error in the current state, whenever there is one?

6.2.2   Expressing the Problem as an Equation

Because assertion a cannot check the strict correctness (error freedom) of the current state s against the initial state s_0, we can design it in such a way as to check that if state $\hat{s}$ is s-correct at milestone m then state s is s-correct at milestone m'. A simple inductive proof establishes the validity of this choice: The basis of induction is the strict correctness of s_0; the induction step stems from the very design of assertion a.

Let PST_m and $PST_{m'}$ be the expected past functions of program p at milestones m and m', respectively; and let A be the relation associated with assertion a. For initial state s_0, the set of strictly correct (error-free) states at milestone m is:

$$s_0 \cdot PST_m.$$

Hence the set of states s at milestone m' such that there exists an error free state $\hat{s}$ at milestone m that verifies $a(\hat{s}, s)$ is

$$(s_0 \cdot PST_m) \cdot A.$$

On the other hand, the set of error free states at milestone m' is

$$s_0 \cdot PST_{m'}.$$

Assertion A must be chosen in such a way that, for all s_0,

$$(s_0 \cdot PST_m) \cdot A \subseteq s_0 \cdot PST_{m'}.$$

This is equivalent to

$$s_0 \cdot (PST_m * A) \subseteq s_0 \cdot PST_{m'}.$$

A sufficient condition for this is:

$$PST_m * A \subseteq PST_{m'}.$$

Ideally, we must find the least-defined relation (for a·fixed domain, the largest relation) that verifies this equation.

6.2.3 Solving the Equation

We consider the optimization problem:

Find the least-defined relation A such that

$$PST_m * A \subseteq PST_{m'}. \tag{0}$$

We have the proposition:

- *Proposition 1*. Relation $A = PST_m^\wedge * PST_{m'}$ is an admissible solution for this problem.

Proof. We replace A by its expression in the left-hand side of equation (0):

$$PST_m * A = PST_m * PST_m^\wedge * PST_{m'}. \tag{1}$$

Now, let B be the expected function of block b; we have $PST_{m'} = PST_m * B$. Replacing in equation (1), we get

$$
\begin{aligned}
PST_m * A &= PST_m * PST_m^\wedge * PST_m * B \\
&\subseteq PST_m * (PST_m^\wedge * PST_m) * B &&\text{associativity} \\
&\subseteq PST_m * B &&\text{determinacy of } PST_m \\
&= PST_{m'} &&\text{definition} \qquad \text{[QED]}
\end{aligned}
$$

We shall not prove the optimality of the solution proposed. See Problems 4 and 5.

6.2.4 Illustrative Example

Space:

```
S = set
crt
  n, f, k natural;
sub
  k ≤ n + 1
end.
```

Program:

```
P = begin
```

```
k := 1; f := 1;
k̂ := k; f̂ := f;
while k ≠ n + 1 do
    begin
    f := f * k;
    k := k + 1
    L: if not a(ŝ, s) then action
    k̂ := k; f̂ := f
    end
end.
```

We wish to design assertion a to be checked at the bottom of each loop body such that strict correctness is preserved between two consecutive visits of label L. Let $m = (v, L)$ and $m' = (v + 1, L)$ be two consecutive milestones at label L. Proposition 1 provides that in order to preserve strict correctness, we must check relation

$$A = PST_m^\smallfrown * PST_{m'}.$$

Let TB be the expected function of the loop body b, guarded by the loop condition t. We have

$$PST_m = TB^v,$$
$$PST_{m'} = TB^{v+1}.$$

Hence

$$
\begin{aligned}
A &= (TB^v)^\smallfrown * (TB^{v+1})\\
&= (TB^v)^\smallfrown * (TB^v) * TB\\
&= I(\mathrm{rng}(TB^v)) * TB.
\end{aligned}
$$

This relation is less-defined than

$$
\begin{aligned}
TB\\
&= \{(s, s') \mid k(s) \neq n + 1 \wedge n(s') = n(s) \wedge f(s') = f(s) * k(s)\\
&\qquad \wedge k(s') = k(s) + 1\}.
\end{aligned}
$$

We use the technique of reasoning by equivalence to simplify this relation, on the basis of the remark that all states reached at milestone m (and about to be processed by b) are in the set

$$S_m = \{s \mid k(s) \neq n(s) + 1\}.$$

We choose

$$A' = \{(s, s') \mid n(s') = n(s) \wedge f(s') = f(s) * k(s) \wedge k(s') = k(s) + 1\}.$$

Clearly, all the functional details of the loop body are being checked by this assertion: *strict correctness could not be ensured with less!*

6.2.5   Usage

Once an error is detected in the current state, the following two actions must be taken:

1. The designer must be notified, in a special-purpose file (or output device), so that he can take corrective action (fault removal).
2. A procedure must be invoked to perform damage assessment and take appropriate recovery action.

Let sc be the assertion used to detect strict correctness (error freedom). It must be used in the following calling pattern:

```
procedure error-management;
begin
if not sc(ŝ, s) then
    begin {erroneous state}
    warning(designer-file, error);
    damage-assessment-and-recovery
    end
end.
```

6.2.6   Exercises

1[B]   Let p be the following program on space $S =$ **integer**:

```
p = begin
    L0: ŝ := s;
        b1;
        if not a1(ŝ, s) then action(1);
    L1: ŝ := s;
        b2;
        if not a2(ŝ, s) then action(s);
    L2: end.
```

We define the following milestones:

$$m_0 = (1, L0),$$
$$m_1 = (1, L1),$$
$$m_2 = (1, L2),$$

and we let the expected functions of segments b_1 and b_2 be, respectively,

$$B_1 = \{(s, s') | s' = s^2 + 4\},$$
$$B_2 = \{(s, s') | s' = \log(s)\}.$$

(a) Compute PST_{m_0}, PST_{m_1} and PST_{m_2}.
(b) Determine A_1 and A_2, as shown in Section 6.2.3.
(c) Compare your results with B_1 and B_2.
(d) Design assertions a_1 and a_2 from relations A_1 and A_2; make them as simple as possible.

2[A]   Same as Exercise 1, for

$$B_1 = \{(s,s')\,|\,s' = s^2 - 4\},$$
$$B_2 = \{(s,s')\,|\,s' = \log(s)\}.$$

3[A]   Same as Exercise 1, for

$$B_1 = \{(s,s')\,|\,s' = s^{10}\},$$
$$B_2 = \{(s,s')\,|\,s' = \mathrm{sqrt}(s + 1)\}.$$

6.3 PROBLEMS

1[B]   Let eab_0 be the following elementary asserted block:

```
ŝ := s;
b;
if not a(ŝ, s) then action,
```

and let B be the expected function of block b.
(a) Explain why

$$a(\hat{s}, s) = (\hat{s}, s) \in B$$

is not the strongest assertion that can be checked about this eab (hint: consider that $\mathrm{dom}(B)$ may be different from S).
(b) Propose a stronger assertion. (Hint: $\neg a \vee a \wedge b) = (a \Rightarrow b)$.)

2[A]   Give an example to illustrate the claim that property 'stronger-than' is not synonymous with 'logically implies'.

3[A]   Give an example to illustrate the claim that property 'stronger-than' is not synonymous with 'more-difficult-to-check'.

4[A]   Show that the solution proposed in Section 6.2.3 can be written as:

$$I(\mathrm{rng}(PST_m)) * B,$$

where B is defined as in the proof of Proposition 1. Interpret this result.

5[B]   (a) Show that the solution proposed in Section 6.2.3 is the largest among all the relations whose domain is $\mathrm{rng}(PST_m)$.
(b) In what sense is the solution proposed optimal, i.e. least defined? (Hint: does it make sense that A have a domain that is greater than $\mathrm{rng}(PST_m)$?)

6.4   BIBLIOGRAPHICAL NOTES

The use of executable assertions for the purpose of program validation and error detection is fairly common: Randell (1975) presents executable assertions as the central figure in the design of fault tolerant programs. For more information on error detection, consult Chapter 5 of Anderson and Lee (1981).

CHAPTER 7

Damage assessment: when is recovery necessary?

Once it is established that the current state is erroneous, one must assess the extent of the damage sustained by the state. In particular, one must determine whether a recovery action is necessary. Indeed, the state could be erroneous and still be correct in the large sense (l-correct) or in the specificationwise sense (sp-correct).

7.1 IS THE STATE LOOSELY CORRECT?

In this section we discuss how to design executable assertions that check the preservation of loose correctness from one milestone to the next.

7.1.1 Position of the Problem

Let m and m' be two consecutive milestones in the execution of program p on initial state s_0, and let b be the block of code executed between m and m'. We wish to design an executable assertion $a(\hat{s}, s)$ around block b, in such a way as to be sufficiently strong to ensure that

- If state $\hat{s}$ is l-correct at milestone m
  and
     state s verifies with state $\hat{s}$ the assertion $a(\hat{s}, s)$
  then state s is l-correct at milestone m'.

7.1.2 Expressing the Problem as an Equation

Let

   LC_m be the set of l-correct states at milestone m,

and

$LC_{m'}$ be the set of l-correct states at milestone m'.

We must find relation A such that

$$LC_m \cdot A \subseteq LC_{m'}. \tag{0}$$

Now, for initial state s_0,

$$LC_{m'} = s_0 \cdot P \cdot \widehat{FTR}_{m'}.$$

where P is the expected function of program p, and FTR_m is the expected future function of program p at milestone m. Similarly,

$$LC_{m'} = s_0 \cdot P \cdot \widehat{FTR}_{m'}.$$

Equation (0) can be written as:

$$s_0 \cdot P \cdot \widehat{FTR}_m \cdot A \subseteq s_0 \cdot P \cdot \widehat{FTR}_{m'}.$$

This is equivalent to

$$s_0 \cdot (P * \widehat{FTR}_m * A) \subseteq s_0 \cdot (P * \widehat{FTR}_{m'}).$$

A sufficient condition for this is

$$P * \widehat{FTR}_m * A \subseteq P * \widehat{FTR}_{m'}.$$

Hence our problem can be formulated as follows:

Find the least-defined relation A such that

$$P * \widehat{FTR}_m * A \subseteq P * \widehat{FTR}_{m'}. \tag{1}$$

7.1.3 Solving the Equation

We solve this equation for the two following common program structures:

1. The future path of program p at milestone m is made up of block b, followed by some other block b', and milestones m and m' are of the form (v, L) and (v, L'), where L and L' are the labels surrounding block b (and the visit number is the same).

```
L:  ŝ := s;
    b;
    if not a(ŝ, s) then action;
L': .
```

This situation is captured by the simple equation

$$FTR_m = B * FTR_{m'},$$

where B is the expected function of block b.

2. Block b is the loop body of a while statement, and m and m' are of the form (v, L) and $(v + 1, L)$, where L is the label of the top of the loop body:

```
ŝ := s;
L: while t do
   begin
   b;
   if not a(ŝ, s) then action;
   ŝ := s
   end.
```

This situation is captured by the simple equation

$$FTR_m = FTR_{m'}.$$

Remark 1. Notice that in the iterative statement above, we write the label L before the **while** keyword, whereas the executable assertion is at the bottom of the loop body; for obvious syntactic constraints, we cannot place the executable assertion immediately after label L. Notice, however, that state s is not modified between the executable assertion and label L; so that as far as state s is concerned, the label L could as well be before the executable assertion. We will, in the future, use both positions interchangeably.   □

We discuss these two configurations in turn.

Sequential Configuration. In Equation (1), we replace FTR_m by $B * FTR_{m'}$:

$$P * \hat{FTR_{m'}} * \hat{B} * A \subseteq P * \hat{FTR_{m'}}. \tag{1S}$$

We then have the proposition:

- *Proposition 1.* Relation $A = FTR_m * \hat{FTR_{m'}}$ is an admissible solution of Equation (1S).

Proof. We consider the left-hand side of Equation (1S),

$$P * \hat{FTR_{m'}} * \hat{B} * A$$

in which we replace A by its proposed expression,

$$= P * \hat{FTR_{m'}} * \hat{B} * FTR_m * \hat{FTR_{m'}}.$$

We replace FTR_m by $B * FTR_{m'}$

$$= P * FTR_{m'}^\frown * B^\frown * B * FTR_{m'} * FTR_{m'}^\frown.$$

We invoke associativity:

$$= P * (FTR_{m'}^\frown * (B^\frown * B) * FTR_{m'}) * FTR_{m'}^\frown.$$

Determinacy of B:

$$\subseteq P * (FTR_{m'}^\frown * FTR_{m'}) * FTR_{m'}^\frown.$$

Determinacy of $FTR_{m'}$:

$$\subseteq P * FTR_{m'}^\frown,$$

which is the right-hand side of Equation (1S).   [QED]
We will not prove that the proposed solution is optimal. See Problem 1 for a discussion of this matter.

Iterative Configuration. In Equation (1), we replace $FTR_{m'}$ by FTR_m:

$$P * FTR_m^\frown * A \subseteq P * FTR_m. \tag{1I}$$

We then have the proposition:

- *Proposition 2.* Relation $A = FTR_m * FTR_m^\frown$ is an admissible solution for Equation (1I).

Proof. We consider the left-hand side of Equation (1I), and replace A by $FTR_m * FTR_m^\frown$.

$$P * FTR_m^\frown * FTR_m * FTR_m^\frown$$
$$\subseteq P * FTR_m^\frown, \text{ due to the determinacy of } FTR_m.   \text{[QED]}$$

7.1.4 Illustration

We consider the space defined by the following variable declarations:

n, f, k: **natural**.

We assume further that $1 \le k \le n + 1$. Let p be

```
p = begin
      f := 1; k := 1;
      f̂ := f; k̂ := k;
      while k ≠ n + 1 do
        begin
```

```
f := f * k;
k := k + 1
L: if not a(ŝ, s) then action;
f̂ := f; k̂ := k;
end
end.
```

We wish to derive the assertion that must be checked at the bottom of the loop body to ensure that the program proceeds from one l-correct state to another. By Proposition 2, we take

$$A = FTR_m * FTR_m^\frown.$$

We know from Chapter 4 that

$$FTR_m = W,$$

where W is the expected function of the while statement.
Hence

$$FTR_m = \{(s,s') \mid n(s') = n(s) \land k(s') = n(s) + 1 \\ \land f(s') = f(s) * n(s)!/(k(s) - 1)!\}.$$

Now, we compute A:

$$\begin{aligned} A &= FTR_m * FTR_m^\frown \\ &= \{(s,s') \mid \exists t: (s,t) \in FTR_m \land (s',t) \in FTR_m\} \\ &= \{(s,s') \mid \exists t: n(t) = n(s) \land k(t) = n(s) + 1 \\ &\qquad \land f(t) = f(s) * n(s)!/(k(s) - 1)! \land n(t) = n(s') \\ &\qquad \land k(t) = n(s') + 1 \land f(t) = f(s') * n(s')!/(k(s') - 1)!\} \\ &= \{(s,s') \mid n(s) = n(s') \\ &\qquad \land f(s) * n(s)!/(k(s) - 1)! = f(s') * n(s')!/(k(s') - 1)!\} \\ &= \{(s,s') \mid n(s) = n(s') \land f(s)/(k(s) - 1)! = f(s')/(k(s') - 1)!\}. \end{aligned}$$

Despite its limited practical interest (because it is relatively complex) this relation nevertheless exhibits all the features that pertain to its function (preserving l-correctness): n must be preserved, as well as the ratio $f/(k - 1)!$. Note that there is no indication of the distance between $k(s)$ and $k(s')$, nor even of which is larger; this is an essential feature of loose correctness.   □

7.1.5 Usage

Procedure damage-assessment-and-recovery (Section 6.2.5) is invoked upon finding an error in the current state. When it is invoked, it must take the following actions:

1. Check whether the error in question is maskable.
2. If not, invoke a recovery management routine.

Let lc be the executable assertion used to detect loose correctness. Using this assertion, procedure error-management can be further refined as follows:

```
procedure error-management;
begin
if not sc(ŝ, s) then
  begin {erroneous state}
  warning(designer-file, error);
  if not lc(ŝ, s) then {unmaskable error}
    recovery-management
  end
end.
```

7.1.6 Exercises

1[A] Let p be the following program on space $S = $ **integer**.

```
p = begin
      L0: ŝ := s;
          b1;
          if not a1(ŝ, s) then action(1);
      L1: ŝ := s;
          b2;
          if not a2(ŝ, s) then action(2);
      L2:
      end.
```

Let m be the milestone $(1, L_1)$, and let the expected functions of b_1 and b_2 be, respectively:

$$B_1 = \{(s, s') | s' = s^2 + 4\},$$
$$B_2 = \{(s, s') | s' = \log(s)\}.$$

(a) Using Proposition 1, derive the assertion that we must check at milestone m to ensure loose correctness.
(b) Using the developments of the previous chapter, derive the assertion that we must check at milestone m to ensure strict correctness.
(c) Compare these two assertions, interpret them, and draw conclusions.

2[A]   Same as Exercise 1, for

>   S = **set**
>   a, b, c: **natural**
>   **end**,

and

$$B_1 = \{(s,s') \,|\, a(s') = a(s) \,\wedge\, b(s') = b(s) \,\wedge\, c(s') = a(s)\},$$
$$B_2 = \{(s,s') \,|\, a(s') = a(s) \,\wedge\, b(s') = a(s) + b(s) \,\wedge\, c(s') = c(s)\}.$$

7.2   IS THE STATE SPECIFICATIONWISE CORRECT?

If the success of the program's execution (i.e. freedom from failure) is not measured by the freedom from strict failure, but rather by the freedom from specificationwise failure, then at milestone m an error is considered maskable as soon as the correct state is specificationwise correct. The purpose of the current section is to design an executable assertion at label L which checks for specificationwise correctness of the current state.

7.2.1   Position of the Problem

Let m and m' be two consecutive milestones in the execution of program p on initial state s_0, and let b be the block of code executed between m and m'; we want to design an executable assertion $a(\hat{s}, s)$ around block b which preserves specificationwise correctness; assertion a must be sufficiently strong to ensure that

>   if state $\hat{s}$ is sp-correct at milestone m,
>   and
>   state $\hat{s}$ verifies with state s the assertion $a(\hat{s}, s)$
>   then state s is specificationwise correct at milestone m'.

7.2.2   Expressing the Problem as an Equation

Let

> PC_m be the set of sp-correct states at milestone m,

and

> PC'_m be the set of sp-correct states at milestone m'.

We must find relation A such that

$$PC_m \cdot A \subseteq PC_{m'}. \tag{0}$$

Now, for initial state s_0,

$$PC_m = s_0 \cdot R \cdot FTR\hat{}_m,$$

where R is the specification of the program at hand, and FTR_m is the expected future function of program p at milestone m. Similarly,

$$PC_{m'} = s_0 \cdot R \cdot FTR\hat{}_{m'}.$$

Equation (0) can be written as

$$s_0 \cdot R \cdot FTR\hat{}_m \cdot A \subseteq s_0 \cdot R \cdot FTR\hat{}_{m'}.$$

This is equivalent to

$$s_0 \cdot (R * FTR\hat{}_m * A) \subseteq s_0 \cdot (R * FTR\hat{}_{m'}).$$

A sufficient condition for this is

$$R * FTR\hat{}_m * A \subseteq R * FTR\hat{}_{m'}.$$

Hence our problem can be formulated as follows:

Find the least-defined relation A such that

$$R * FTR\hat{}_m * A \subseteq R * FTR\hat{}_{m'}. \tag{1}$$

7.2.3 Solving the Equation

As in Section 7.1.3 we shall solve this equation for the two following common program configurations:

1. *Sequential configuration:* is characterized by $FTR_m = B * FTR_{m'}$.
2. *Iterative configuration:* is characterized by $FTR_m = FTR_{m'}$.

Sequential configuration. The equation that describes this situation is

$$R * FTR\hat{}_{m'} * B\hat{} * A \subseteq R * FTR\hat{}_{m'}. \tag{1S}$$

We have the proposition:

- *Proposition 3.* If relation R is regular, then relation

$$A = B * FTR_{m'} * R\hat{} * R * FTR\hat{}_{m'}$$

is an admissible solution of Equation (1S).

Proof

$$R * FTR^\wedge_{m'} * B^\wedge * B * FTR_{m'} * R^\wedge * R * FTR^\wedge_{m'}$$
$$\subseteq R * FTR^\wedge_{m'} * FTR_{m'} * R^\wedge * R * FTR^\wedge_{m'} \qquad \text{determinacy of } B$$
$$\subseteq R * R^\wedge * R * FTR_{m'} \qquad\qquad\quad \text{determinacy of } FTR_{m'}$$
$$= R * FTR_{m'} \qquad\qquad\qquad\qquad \text{regularity of } R. \quad \text{[QED]}$$

Iterative Configuration. The equation that describes this situation is

$$R * FTR^\wedge_{m'} * A \subseteq R * FTR^\wedge_{m'}. \tag{1I}$$

We have the proposition:

- *Proposition 4.* If relation R is regular, then relation

  $$A = FTR_m * R^\wedge * R * FTR^\wedge_m$$

  is an admissible solution of Equation (1I).

Proof

$$R * FTR^\wedge_m * FTR_m * R^\wedge * R * FTR^\wedge_m$$
$$\subseteq R * R^\wedge * R * FTR^\wedge_m \qquad \text{determinacy of } FTR_m$$
$$\subseteq R * FTR^\wedge_m \qquad\qquad\quad \text{regularity of } R. \qquad\qquad\qquad \text{[QED]}$$

7.2.4   Illustration

We illustrate, in turn, Propositions 3 and then 4. Let p be the program:

```
p = begin
      L0: ŝ := s;
          b1;
          if not a1(ŝ, s) then action(1);
      L1: ŝ := s;
          b2;
          if not a2(ŝ, s) then action(2);
      L2:
      end,
```

Let the expected function of blocks b_1 and b_2 be

$$B_1 = \{(s, s') \,|\, s' = s^2 + 1\},$$
$$B_2 = \{(s, s') \,|\, s' = s^2\},$$

and let R be

$$R = \{(s, s') \,|\, s' \geq 1\}.$$

We wish to derive the assertion that must be checked at milestone $m_1 = (1, L_1)$ to ensure sp-correctness. By Proposition 3, we have

$$A = B * FTR_{m'} * R\hat{\ } * R * FTR\hat{\ }_{m'}.$$

Now, $B = B_1$ and $FTR_{m'} = B_2$. Hence

$$
\begin{aligned}
A &= B_1 * B_2 * R\hat{\ } * R * B\hat{\ }_2 \\
&= \{(s, s') | s' = (s^2 + 1)^2\} * \{(s, s') | s \geq 1 \wedge s' \geq 1\} * \{(s, s') | s = s'^2\} \\
&= \{(s, s') | \exists t \colon t = (s^2 + 1)^2 \wedge t \geq 1 \wedge s' \geq 1\} * \{(s, s') | s = s'^2\} \\
&= \{(s, s') | \exists t \geq 1 \wedge t = s'^2\} \\
&= \{(s, s') | s'^2 \geq 1\}.
\end{aligned}
$$

The assertion in question is

$$\mathrm{sp}(\hat{s}, s) = \mathrm{abs}(s) \geq 1.$$

Note that it does not refer to the preceding state.

We now illustrate Proposition 4. To do this, we consider the factorial program presented earlier, and we take specification R defined as

$$R = \{(s, s') | k(s') = n(s) + 1\}.$$

Note that R is very weak; it exercises minor aspects of the program's functional properties. By Proposition 4, the following relation preserves sp-correctness:

$$A = FTR_m * R\hat{\ } * R * FTR\hat{\ }_m.$$

We compute

$$
\begin{aligned}
FTR_m &* R\hat{\ } \\
&= \{(s, s') | \exists t \colon n(t) = n(s) \wedge k(t) = n(s) + 1 \\
\wedge f(t) &= f(s) * n(s)!/(k(s) - 1)! \wedge k(t) = n(s') + 1\} \\
&= \{(s, s') | n(s') = n(s) \wedge \exists t \colon n(t) = n(s) \wedge k(t) = n(s) + 1 \\
&\qquad \wedge f(t) = n(s')!\} \\
&= \{(s, s') | n(s') = n(s)\}.
\end{aligned}
$$

Hence

$$
\begin{aligned}
A &= \{(s, s') | \exists t \colon (s, t) \in FTR_m * R\hat{\ } \wedge (s', t) \in FTR_m * R\hat{\ }\} \\
&= \{(s, s') | \exists t \colon n(t) = n(s) \wedge n(t) = n(s')\} \\
&= \{(s, s') | n(s') = n(s)\}.
\end{aligned}
$$

To ensure the preservation of sp-correctness, assertion *spc* must merely check the preservation of n. That k is equal to $n + 1$ in the final state is guaranteed by the very semantics of **while** statements. But that the final value of k is equal to 1 plus the *initial* value of n requires that n be preserved throughout the execution of the program; hence the assertion proposed. See question (e) of Exercise 3 below.

7.2.5 Usage

An assertion that checks the sp-correctness of a state is used in the same manner as one that checks the l-correctness of the state: if the assertion is not valid, one must invoke a recovery management routine. The only possible difference is that if the state is sp-correct without being l-correct, we may want to inform the user of a possible strict failure in the output: he will not obtain the expected output state, but will obtain a correct (with respect to the specification at hand) state nevertheless.

7.2.6 Exercises

1[B]   Consider the first illustrative example of Section 7.2.4. At milestone m_1, compute assertion sc that checks strict correctness, and assertion lc that checks loose correctness. Compare them to assertion spc found in Section 7.2.4 and interpret your results.

2[B]   Re-do the work of the first example of Section 7.2.4, with the following specifications. Interpret your results every time:
(a) $R = \{(s,s')\,|\,s' > 0\}$.
(b) $R = \{(s,s')\,|\,s' = (s^2 + 1)^2\}$.
(c) $R = \{(s,s')\,|\,s^2 + 1 \le s' \le (s^2 + 1)^2\}$.

3[C]   Re-do the work of the second example of Section 7.2.4, with the following specifications. Interpret your result every time:
(a) $R = \{(s,s')\,|\,n(s') = n(s)\}$.
(b) $R = \{(s,s')\,|\,n(s') = n(s) \wedge k(s') = n(s) + 1\}$.
(c) $R = \{(s,s')\,|\,f(s') = n(s)!\}$.
(d) $R = \{(s,s')\,|\,f(s') = n(s)! \wedge n(s') = n(s)\}$.
(Hint: compare with the result of Section 7.1.4.)
(e) $R = \{(s,s')\,|\,k(s') = n(s') + 1\}$.

4[B]   Consider the first example of Section 7.2.4. Construct the proposed Pascal program, along with the executable assertions given. Run the program on ten test data items to show the effect of the executable assertion (whenever a state fails to be sp-correct, procedure *action* is invoked). (Hint: notice that b_1 and b_2 are to be designed at your discretion.)

5[B]   Same as Exercise 4, for the second example of Section 7.2.4.

7.3 PROBLEMS

1[B]   Consider the solution proposed to Equation (1S):
    (a) Show that it can be written as

$$A = B * FTR_{m'} * \hat{FTR}_{m'}.$$

    Compare it with

$$B * I(\text{dom}(FTR_{m'})).$$

    Interpret your comparison.
    (b) Explain why the range of B does not have to be larger than dom($FTR_{m'}$).
    (c) Among all the relations whose range is dom($FTR_{m'}$), is the proposed relation the least-defined relation that is admissible?

2[B]   Interpret the significance of the solution proposed for Equation (1I). In particular, show that it is different from TB (defined in Section 6.2.4), and why.

3[B]   Interpret the result of Proposition 3. In particular, explain the relationship between A and B.

4[B]   What becomes of the assertion proposed in Proposition 4 if specification R is deterministic? Explain.

5[B]   Interpret the result of Proposition 4. In particular, compare it to the result of Proposition 2, and show how it generalizes it (and why it should generalize it).

7.4 BIBLIOGRAPHICAL NOTES

For more on damage assessment, consult Chapter 6 of Anderson and Lee (1981).

CHAPTER 8

Damage assessment: when is recovery sufficient?

Once it is determined that the current state is not maskable, execution may not proceed on to a successful (failure-free) output state unless an external intervention takes place. Some forms of intervention (e.g. backward error recovery, to be discussed in Part V) do not depend on the extent of the damage sustained by the current state; in such cases the recovery action must be triggered, irrespective of the damage, as soon as the error of the state is found to be unmaskable. Other forms of intervention (e.g. forward error recovery, to be discussed in Part IV) depend closely on the extent of the damage; specifically, a recovery action is necessary only if the current state is unmaskable, and is effective only if the current state is recoverable.

The subject of this chapter is to design executable assertions that determine whether the current state is recoverable.

8.1 IS THE STATE LOOSELY RECOVERABLE?

8.1.1 Position of the Problem

Let m and m' be two consecutive milestones in the execution of program p on initial state s_0, and let b be the block of code executed between m and m'. We wish to design an executable assertion $lr(\hat{s}, s)$ around block b, in such a way as to be sufficiently strong to ensure that:

if state $\hat{s}$ is l-correct at milestone m
and
    state s verifies with state $\hat{s}$ the assertion $lr(\hat{s}, s)$
    then
        state s is l-recoverable at milestone m'.

In checking the l-recoverability of state s at milestone m', we take the hypothesis that state $\hat{s}$ at milestone m is l-correct. We prove by induction (on the sequence of milestones) that as long as appropriate recovery actions are taken, all the states visited are l-correct.

Basis of induction. The initial state is l-correct.

Induction step. We assume that state $\hat{s}$ at milestone m is l-correct, and that $lr(\hat{s}, s)$ holds; then state s at milestone m' is l-recoverable. If it is not also l-correct, then action can be taken to map into an l-correct state. Hence the induction hypothesis is proven for state s at milestone m'.

8.1.2 Expressing the Problem as an Equation

Let

LC_m be the set of l-correct states at milestone m

and

$LR_{m'}$ be the set of l-recoverable states at milestone m'.

We must find the least defined relation A such that

$$LC_m \cdot A \subseteq LR_{m'}. \tag{0}$$

We have, by definition,

$$LC_m = s_0 \cdot P \cdot \widehat{FTR_m},$$

where P is the expected function of program p and FTR_m is the expected future function of program p at milestone m.

Because of the clause (in the definition of loose recoverability)

'there exists a Pascal routine r such that . . . ,'

we cannot give a precise expression for set $LR_{m'}$. However, we borrow a result from Part IV, which provides a lower bound for this set:

$$s_0 \cdot P \cdot P\hat{} \subseteq LR_{m'}.$$

This result is only applicable to programs that have the form of an initialized **while** statement:

```
begin
init;
L: while t do b;
end,
```

with m and m' being consecutive visits of the same label L, and such that dom$(P) = S$.

Using the lower-bound provided for $LR_{m'}$, we find a sufficient condition for (0):

$$s_0 \cdot P \cdot FTR_m^\wedge \cdot A \subseteq s_0 \cdot P \cdot P^\wedge.$$

This is equivalent to

$$s_0 \cdot (P * FTR_m^\wedge * A) \subseteq s_0 \cdot (P * P^\wedge).$$

A sufficient condition for this equation is:

$$(P * FTR_m^\wedge * A) \subseteq (P * P^\wedge). \tag{1}$$

8.1.3   Solving the Equation

We must solve the optimization problem:

Find the least-defined relation A such that

$$P * FTR_m^\wedge * A \subseteq P * P^\wedge.$$

We have the following proposition:

- *Proposition 1.* Relation $A = FTR_m * P^\wedge$ is an admissible solution for Equation (1).

Proof

$$P * FTR_m^\wedge * A$$
$$= P * FTR_m^\wedge * FTR_m * P^\wedge \quad \text{expression of } A$$
$$\subseteq P * P^\wedge \quad \text{determinacy of } FTR_m. \qquad \text{[QED]}$$

We shall not prove the optimality of this solution.

8.1.4   Illustrative Example

We take the same space and program as the preceding chapter. We have

$$P = \{(s,s')\,|\,n(s') = n(s) \wedge k(s') = n(s) + 1 \wedge f(s') = n(s)!\}$$

and

$$FTR_m = \{(s,s')\,|\,n(s') = n(s) \wedge k(s') = n(s) + 1$$
$$\wedge f(s') = f(s) * n(s)!/(k(s) - 1)!\}.$$

Hence

$$A = \{(s,s') | \exists t: (s,t) \in FTR_m \wedge (s',t) \in P\}$$
$$= \{(s,s') | \exists t: n(t) = n(s) \wedge k(t) = n(s) + 1$$
$$\wedge f(t) = f(s) * n(s)!/(k(s) - 1)!$$
$$\wedge n(t) = n(s') \wedge k(t) = n(s') + 1 \wedge f(t) = n(s')!\}$$
$$= \{(s,s') | n(s') = n(s) \wedge n(s')! = n(s)! * f(s)/(k(s) - 1)!\}$$
$$= \{(s,s') | f(s) = (k(s) - 1)! \wedge n(s') = n(s)\}.$$

The assertion that we derive from this relation is

$$lr(\hat{s}, s): f(\hat{s}) = (k(\hat{s}) - 1)! \wedge n(s) = n(\hat{s}).$$

This assertion is not cost-effective. We seek a simpler assertion that has the same checking capability. To do so, we simply notice that, by hypothesis, A can only be applied to l-correct states. Hence, if we let A' be the relation associated with the assertion we are seeking, we have

$$I(LC_m) * A = I(LC_m) * A'.$$

From Chapter 5 (Example 1) we remember that

$$LC_m = \{s | f(s) = (k(s) - 1)! \wedge n(s) = n(s_0)\}.$$

It is left to the reader to check, in light of this, that the following relation A' is admissible:

$$A' = \{(s,s') | n(s') = n(s)\}.$$

From this relation we extract the assertion

$$lr(\hat{s}, s) = n(\hat{s}) = n(s).$$

Ensuring the l-recoverability of the current state requires, understandably, that n be preserved.

8.1.5 Usage

Once it is determined that the current state is not loosely correct, a recovery-management routine must be invoked. This routine first checks whether the current state is at least l-recoverable. If it is, then a recovery routine is applied, and the control is given back to the program; if not, then a more drastic action must be taken. Examples of such an action are as follows:

1. *The abort option:* notifying the user of an irretrievable loss of information, and aborting the computation.
2. *The re-try option:* requesting that the user submit an alternate state

instead of the current contaminated state, or taking a pre-defined
default state.
3. *The ignore option:* warn the user of a likely failure (remember, we
are using sufficient conditions of recoverability); then give the
control back to the program.

In the light of this discussion, procedure error-management can be
further refined as follows:

```
procedure error-management;
begin
if not sc(ŝ, s) then {erroneous state}
  begin
  warning(designer-file, error);
  if not lc(ŝ, s) then {unmaskable error}
    begin {recovery management}
    if lr(ŝ, s) then recovery-routine
    else failure-management
    end
  end
end,
```

where failure-management can take three different forms, depending on
the option chosen in case of non-recoverability:
1. *Abort option:*

```
procedure failure-management-abort;
begin
warning(user-file, strict-failure);
goto exit
end.
```

2. *Re-try option:*

```
procedure failure-management-retry;
begin
load-alternate-state {from user terminal or from predefined address}
end.
```

3. *Ignore option:*

```
procedure failure-management-ignore;
begin
warning(user-file, strict-failure)
end.
```

8.1.6 Exercises

1[B] Consider the selection sort program which iteratively places in
$a[i]$ the ith smallest element of array a:
(a) Determine W, the function of the uninitialized **while** statement of this program. We know from Part II that the future
function for such a loop at any milestone attached to the loop
body's top is $FTR_m = W$.
(b) Determine P, the expected function of the whole, initialized,
program.
(c) Apply Proposition 1, to find relation A.
(d) Interpret relation A.
(e) Extract from A a simple, cost-effective, assertion to check.

2[B] Same as Exercise 1, for the insertion sort program, that iteratively
sorts the i first elements of array a by placing $a[i]$ in its proper
place in the subarray $a[1..i]$ and making appropriate shifts.

3[B] Same as Exercise 1, for the linear search program, assuming that
array a is sorted.

4[B] Same as Exercise 1, for the linear search program, assuming that
array a is not necessarily sorted.

5[B] Same as Exercise 1, for the binary search program, assuming of
course that array a is sorted.

8.2 IS THE STATE SPECIFICATIONWISE RECOVERABLE?

8.2.1 Position of the Problem

Let m and m' be two consecutive milestones in the execution of program
p on initial state s_0, and let b be the block of code executed between m
and m'. We want to design an executable assertion $spr(\hat{s}, s)$ around
block b, in such a way as to be sufficiently strong to ensure that:

- if state $\hat{s}$ is sp-correct at milestone m
  and
    state s verifies with state $\hat{s}$ the assertion $spr(\hat{s}, s)$
    then
       state s is sp-recoverable at milestone m'.

Given that such an assertion is found, then whenever p is executed on
initial state s_0, the following claim can be made:

- if at each milestone *spr* holds, and
  whenever at some milestone the state is not sp-correct,
    recovery action is taken to map it into an sp-correct state,
  then
  at each milestone the current state is
    at least sp-recoverable before the recovery action (if any)
    and at least sp-correct after the recovery action.

We prove this result by induction on the sequence of milestones:
Basis of induction. The initial state is l-correct; there is no recovery action.
Induction step. Let $\hat{s}$ be the state of the program at milestone m after (the eventual) recovery. By induction hypothesis, $\hat{s}$ is l-correct. By hypothesis, $spr(\hat{s}, s)$ holds. By design of *spr*, state s is sp-recoverable. After a recovery routine is applied (if any), the state becomes sp-correct.

8.2.2   Expressing the Problem as an Equation

Let

PC_m be the set of sp-correct states at milestone m,

and

$PR_{m'}$ be the set of sp-recoverable states at milestone m'.

We must find the least defined relation A such that

$$PC_m \cdot A \subseteq PR_{m'}. \tag{0}$$

We have, by definition,

$$PC_m = s_0 \cdot R \cdot FTR_m^{\,\hat{}},$$

where R is the specification of program p and FTR_m is the expected future function of program p at milestone m.

Again, the clause (in the definition of specificationwise recoverability)

'there exists a Pascal routine r such that ...,'

prevents us from giving a precise explicit expression for set $PR_{m'}$. However, we borrow again a result from Part IV, which provides a lower bound for this set:

$$s_0 \cdot K(R) \subseteq PR_{m'},$$

where $K(R)$ is the kernel of relation R. This result is applicable only to programs that have the form of an initialized **while** statement:

```
begin
init;
L: while t do b;
end,
```

with m and m' being consecutive visits of the same label L, and such that $\text{dom}(R) = S$.

Using the lower-bound provided for $LR_{m'}$, we find a sufficient condition for (0):

$$s_0 \cdot R \cdot FTR_m^\wedge \cdot A \subseteq s_0 \cdot K(R).$$

This is equivalent to

$$s_0 \cdot (R * FTR_m^\wedge * A) \subseteq s_0 \cdot K(R).$$

A sufficient condition for this equation is:

$$(R * FTR_m^\wedge * A) \subseteq K(R). \tag{1}$$

8.2.3 Solving the Equation

We must solve the optimization problem

Find the least-defined relation A such that

$$R * FTR_m^\wedge * A \subseteq K(R).$$

We have the proposition:

- *Proposition 2.* If specification R is regular, then relation

  $$A = FTR_m * R^\wedge$$

  is an admissible solution for Equation (1).

Proof

$$
\begin{aligned}
&R * FTR_m^\wedge * A \\
&= R * FTR_m^\wedge * FTR_m * R^\wedge \qquad \text{expression of } A \\
&\subseteq R * R^\wedge \qquad\qquad\qquad\quad \text{determinacy of } FTR_m \\
&= K(R) \qquad\qquad\qquad\qquad \text{regularity of } R. \qquad\qquad \text{[QED]}
\end{aligned}
$$

8.2.4 Illustrative Example

We again take the factorial program, and choose, for illustrative purposes, a very weak specification:

$$R = \{(s, s') \mid k(s') = n(s') + 1\}.$$

We leave it to the reader to check that this relation is indeed regular, since it is rectangular (Chapter 1). As we recall, we have

$$FTR_m = \{(s, s') \mid n(s') = n(s) \wedge k(s') = n(s) + 1$$
$$\wedge f(s') = f(s) * n(s)! / (k(s) - 1)!\}.$$

Hence

$$A = \{(s, s') \mid \exists t: (s, t) \in FTR_m \wedge (s', t) \in R\}$$
$$= \{(s, s') \mid \exists t: n(t) = n(s) \wedge k(t) = n(s) + 1$$
$$\wedge f(t) = f(s) * n(s)! / (k(s) - 1)! \wedge k(t) = n(t) + 1\}$$
$$= U(S),$$

the universal relation on S.

The assertion that we extract from this relation is

$$spr(\hat{s}, s) = \textbf{true}.$$

Its interpretation is quite straightforward, in light of the definition of R.

8.2.5 Usage

The assertion derived in this section to ensure sp-recoverability is to be used in essentiality the same manner as that given in Section 8.1.5 to ensure l-recoverability. The only (minor) difference is that error messages sent to the user's file must warn about the possibility of specificationwise failure, rather than strict failure.

8.2.6 Exercises

1[A] Work through the example of Section 8.2.4 with the following specification:

$$R = \{(s, s') \mid k(s') = n(s) + 1\}.$$

Compare your result with that of Section 8.2.4. Compare it also with the result of Section 7.2.4. Interpret your comparisons.

2[A] Work through the example of Section 8.2.4 with the following specification:

$$R = \{(s, s') \mid n(s') = n(s) \wedge k(s') = n(s) + 1\}.$$

Interpret your results; in particular, compare them to those of Section 8.2.4.

3[A]   Work through the example of Section 8.2.4 with the following specification:

$$R = \{(s, s')|f(s') = n(s)!\}.$$

8.3   INTEGRATED DAMAGE ASSESSMENT: ILLUSTRATIVE EXAMPLE

As an illustration of the results of Chapters 6, 7 and 8, we take the factorial program and provide it with an error-management procedure; this procedure is constructed according to the pattern described in Section 8.1.5. For the sake of simplicity, we will limit our attention to deterministic specifications, i.e. we will only check strict correctness, loose correctness, and loose recoverability.

8.3.1   The Fault Tolerant Factorial Program

We take the factorial program discussed in the last three chapters, and augment it with procedures for error detection, damage assessment and (for the purpose of illustration) error recovery. The main body of this program is the following:

```
program Recoverablefactorial;
label 0,1;
type filetype = text;
     errorcodetype = (noerror, maskablerror, recoverablerror, fatalerror);
                     {noerror: strictly correct state;
                      maskablerror: loosely correct state;
                      recoverablerror: loosely recoverable state;
                      fatalerror: non loosely recoverable state}
var
   n, f, : integer; {state s}
   nn, ff, kk: integer; {state ŝ}
   designerfile, userfile: filetype;
   {userfile: echoes input, gives output,
    warns of possible failure whenever applicable;
    designerfile: echoes input,
    gives report on error detection, damage assessment
    and error recovery,
    warns of failure, echoes failure option chosen,
    gives output}
   errorcode: errorcodetype;
```

```
aborting: boolean; {if aborting is set to true
by error management procedure then goto wrapup}
begin {recoverable factorial}
init; {initializes the variables of the program,
         as well as those of additional procedures}
savestate; {included for error control; performs ŝ := s}
1: while k ≤ n do
   begin
   simulaterror(errorcode);
   {included for error control; depending on errorcode,
     can simulate no error, a maskable error,
     a recoverable error or a fatal error; see Section 8.3.2}
   f := f * k;
   k := k + 1;
   errormanagement(aborting); if aborting then goto 0;
   {is written according to pattern of Section 8.1.5, with
     some modifications; see Section 8.3.3}
   savestate {ŝ := s}
   end;
0: wrapup {writes output in designerfile and userfile}
end {recoverable factorial}.
```

8.3.2 Injecting Errors

Procedure *simulaterror*(errorcode) injects an error in the program, according to the value of parameter errorcode: it can simulate no error (state is strictly correct), a maskable error (state is loosely correct), a recoverable error (state is loosely recoverable), or a fatal error (state is not loosely recoverable). The body of this procedure is given below:

```
procedure simulaterror(errorcode: errorcodetype);
{simulates several kinds of errors, of varying degrees of seriousness;
depending on the value of errorcode. The error intervenes at the third
iteration. Variable n must be sufficiently large for the error to appear}
begin
if k = 3 then {error at third teration}
  case errorcode of
  noerror:
    begin
    end;
  maskablerror:
    begin {we assume n > = 4}
```

```
    k := 4; f := 6;
    end;
  recoverablerror:
    begin {we assume n >= 4}
    k := 4; f := 1;
    end;
  fatalerror:
    begin
    n := n + 5;
    end;
  end
  end{simulaterror};
```

8.3.3 Managing Errors

At the end of each iteration, procedure *errormanagement* (aborting) is
invoked to check whether there is an error, assess the extent of the
damage sustained by the program's state, and take appropriate action as
necessary: depending on the seriousness of the damage, this action
ranges from ignoring the error (if it is maskable) to recovering from it (if
it is recoverable) to soliciting external intervention (if it is fatal). The
main body of this procedure is as follows:

```
procedure errormanagement (aborting: boolean);
{does all the administration of error detection, damage assessment and
 (when applicable) error recovery; is written according to the formula
 of Section 8.1.5}
function sc: boolean;
{checks strict correctness, according to formula given in Section 6.2.5}
begin
sc := (nn = n) and (f = ff * kk) and (k = kk + 1)
end{sc};
function lc: boolean;
{checks loose correctness, according to formula given in Section 7.1.5}
var i: integer; {for loop index}
    dif: integer; {carries the ratio of factorial k over factorial kk,
                   or its inverse – depending on which is greater}

begin
dif := 1;
if k < kk then
```

```
      begin
      for i := k to kk − 1 do dif := dif ∗ i;
      lc := (nn = n) and (ff = f ∗ dif)
      end
   else
      begin
      for i := kk to k − 1 do dif := dif ∗ i;
      lc := (nn = n) and (f = ff ∗ dif)
      end
   end{lc};
   function lr: boolean;
   {checks loose recoverability, according to formula given in Section 8.1.5}
   begin
   lr := (nn = n)
   end{lr};
   procedure recover;
   {recovers current state, if it proves to be recoverable; written
     according to formula borrowed from Chapter 9}
   begin
   f := 6; k := 4;
   writeln(designerfile, 'recovery is complete')
   end{recover};
   procedure failuremanagement (aborting: boolean);
   {state is unrecoverable; the error is fatal and drastic action must be
     taken. This procedure handles all the interactions with the user (at the
     terminal) and the designer file and user file. It first solicits the failure
     option (abort, ignore, retry) and, depending on the option selected,
     exits from the program, returns the control to the program, or loads a
     substitute state given by the user. Because it is of limited interest, the
     body of this procedure will not be given}
   begin {failuremanagement}
   end {failuremanagement};
   begin {errormanagement}
   if not sc then {erroneous state}
      begin
      writeln(designerfile, 'strict error detected');
      if lc then {maskable error}
         begin
         writeln(designerfile, 'the error is maskable')
         end
      else {unmaskable error}
```

```
      begin {recovery management}
      writeln(designerfile, 'the error is unmaskable');
      if lr then
        begin
        writeln(designerfile, 'the error is recoverable');
        recover
        end
      else
        begin
        failuremanagement(aborting)
        end
      end {recoverymanagement}
    end {erroneous state}
  end {errormanagement};
```

8.3.4   Running the Program

When all the pieces are put together, we get a program that can spontaneously detect the errors that arise in it, and handle them appropriately according to their gravity. For the sake of illustration, we have run the program several times, with the same input ($n = 7$), varying the errorcode; also, for the fatal error, we have run it three times, once for each failure option. The results of running this program are given below.

------oooOooo------

First Experiment

Input: n = 7   Error code: No error

Designer file:

input is: 7
output is: 5040

User file:

input is: 7
output is: 5040

Here, we witness a normal execution of the program.

------oooOooo------

Second Experiment

Input: n = 7   Error code: Maskable error

Designer file:

input is: 7
strict error detected
the error is maskable
output is: 5040

User file: .

input is: 7
output is: 5040

The designer is informed that an error has been detected; and that it is maskable. So that the current state is loosely correct and the final state is a strict success. As for the user, he has no knowledge of all this activity, as it was altogether a false alert.

------oooOooo------

Third Experiment

Input: n = 7   Error code: Recoverable error

Designer file:

input is: 7
strict error detected
the error is unmaskable
the error is recoverable
recovery complete
output is: 5040

User file:

input is: 7
output is: 5040

The current state is first found not to be strictly correct, then not to be loosely correct; it is found to be recoverable, however, and the recovery routine is invoked. When recovery is complete, the execution of the program resumes. As for the user, he again has no knowledge of all this activity, since the output is not affected by it.

------oooOooo------

Fourth Experiment

Input: $n = 7$ Error code: Fatal error
                                  failure option: abort

Designer file:

input is: 7
strict error detected
the error is unmaskable
the error is recoverable
abort option chosen
output is: −1024

User file:

input is: 7
Unrecoverable error detected. Possible failure in final state
output is: −1024

Here the error that is injected in the program is detected, then it is found to be unmaskable, then unrecoverable. The user chooses the abort option, and the program exits, with an incorrect output. The user is notified of the fatal error, and of the *possibility* that a (strict) failure appear in the output. This is only a possibility, not a certainty, because the assertions that we check are sufficient conditions (for loose correctness, loose recoverability), and it is conceivable that the state does not satisfy the assertions but is still correct or recoverable.

------oooOooo------

Fifth Experiment

Input: $n = 7$ Error code: Fatal error
                                  failure option: retry

Designer file:

input is: 7
strict error detected
the error is unmaskable
the error is unrecoverable
retry option chosen
alternate state is

```
n = 7
f = 5
k = 12
output is: 5
```

User file:

input is: 7
Unrecoverable error detected. Possible failure in final state
output is: 5

Here there is also a fatal error; the failure option selected is *retry*. An alternative state is loaded, and execution resumes; this yields, as it were, a failure on output. But the user has been warned of this possibility.

------oooOooo------

Sixth Experiment

Input: n = 7   Error code: Fatal error
                           failure option: ignore

Designer file:

input is: 7
strict error detected
the error is unmaskable
the error is unrecoverable
ignore option chosen
output is: −1024

User file:

input is: 7
Unrecoverable error detected. Possible failure in final state
output is: −1024

Again, there is a fatal error here; the failure option selected is *ignore*. Execution continues with the current contaminated state; this yields, as it were, a failure on output. But the user has been warned of this possibility.

8.3.5   Exercises

1[B]   Following the pattern of this section, construct an iterative program, along with its error detection and damage assessment procedures, to perform the following function: find element x in array a (of size n), when you know that $x \in a$, and that all the cells of a are distinct. Run your program under similar conditions to those of Section 8.3.4, and show its behavior. (Hint: for the recovery, you may do any of the following: borrow results from Chapter 9; use the definition of loose recovery to informally derive a recovery routine; let the recovery routine load a pre-defined state.)

2[B] Same as Exercise 1, for the following function: compute the sum of the elements of an integer array.

3[B] Same as Exercise 1, for the following function: compute the maximum element of an integer array.

4[C] Let sc, lc, spc, and spr be the executable assertions derived for the factorial program (Section 8.3.1) to detect strict correctness, loose correctness, specificationwise correctness and specification-wise recoverability, with respect to the following specification:

$$R = \{(s, s') \mid k(s') = n(s) + 1\}.$$

Design an error management procedure that uses all these assertions; include it in the program of Section 8.3.1, and run it to show its behavior.

5[C] Same as Exercise 4, for the following specification:

$$R = \{(s, s') \mid n(s') = n(s) \wedge k(s') = n(s) + 1\}.$$

6[C] Same as Exercise 4, for the following specification:

$$R = \{(s, s') \mid f(s') = n(s)!\}.$$

7[C] Let sc, lc, lr, and spr be the executable assertions derived for the factorial program (Section 8.3.1) to detect strict correctness, loose correctness, loose recoverability and specificationwise recoverability, with respect to the following specification:

$$R = \{(s, s') \mid k(s') = n(s) + 1\}.$$

Design an error management procedure that uses all these assertions; include it in the program of Section 8.3.1, and run it to show its behavior.

8[C] Same as Exercise 7, for the following specification:

$$R = \{(s, s') \mid n(s') = n(s) \wedge k(s') = n(s) + 1\}.$$

9[C] Same as Exercise 7, for the following specification:

$$R = \{(s, s') \mid f(s') = n(s)!\}.$$

8.4 PROBLEMS

1[B]   Consider Equation (0) of Section 8.1.2, and consider the sequential configuration as defined in Section 7.1.2. Solve Equation (0) for the sequential configuration.

2[A]   Match the assertion found in Section 7.1.4, against that found in Section 8.1.4. Explain their differences.

3[R]   Discuss the optimality of the relation given in Proposition 1. (Hint: consider the developments of Section 8.1.4.)

4[B]   Solve Equation (0) of Section 8.2.4 for the sequential configuration.

5[R]   Discuss the optimality of the relation given in Proposition 2, in the case of regular specifications. What can be said outside this hypothesis?

6[R]   Discuss what can be done, in the problem of Section 8.2, with specifications that are not regular. In particular, give an example of a non-regular specification and show what happens if the formula of Proposition 2 is applied to it.

7[R]   Propose a detailed error management procedure that makes use of all the damage assessment assertions, namely: *sc* (strict correctness); *sr* (strict recoverability); *lc* (loose correctness); *lr* (loose recoverability); *spc* (specificationwise correctness); and *spr* (specificationwise recoverability).

8.5 BIBLIOGRAPHICAL NOTES

For more information on damage assessment, consult Chapter 6 of Anderson and Lee (1981). Also, consult Wirth (1976) for more details on the sorting and searching programs of Section 8.1.6 (the exercises).

Part IV

Forward Error Recovery

Can Design Faults be tolerated?
YES!
Sometimes, some of them   (Tom Anderson: Montréal, 1985)

When the state of a program is contaminated at run-time, it can be recovered in one of the two following ways:

1. Either by retrieving a previously saved correct state, and re-starting the execution from the point where the state was saved. This process is called *backward error recovery*.
2. Or by modifying the current (contaminated) state, so as to obtain a new correct state, then resuming the execution. This proces is called *forward error recovery*.

Forward error recovery is the subject of this part. Rather than backing up to a previously saved correct state (backward error recovery), forward error recovery attempts instead to generate a (sufficiently) correct state from a (not too) contaminated state.

Forward error recovery is studied with respect to a specification of the program. The equations defining the parameters of forward error recovery depend to some extent on whether the specification at hand is deterministic or non-deterministic. The case of deterministic specifications is discussed in Chapter 9, while non-deterministic specifications are covered in Chapter 10. Chapter 11 illustrates the ideas of forward error recovery, by presenting a program which is developed hand in hand with its forward error recovery capabilities, and showing its behavior.

CHAPTER 9

Forward error recovery: deterministic specifications

The subject of this chapter is the discussion of forward error recovery in programs, i.e. how a program can generate a sufficiently correct state from a contaminated state. We will concentrate on two crucial questions: (i) how do we characterize (by means of sufficient conditions) the level of contamination of the current state; and (ii) how do we characterize (by means of formal specifications) valid recovery routines, i.e. Pascal routines that can map the contaminated state into a correct state. The results we find will be interpreted and then illustrated with examples.

The study of forward error recovery proves to depend critically on whether the specification at hand is deterministic or not: the equations that allow us to extract the parameters of forward error recovery differ, depending on the determinacy of the specification. In Section 9.1, we discuss the significance of considering a deterministic specification, and assess its impact on the discussion of this chapter.

The study of forward error recovery has shown that iterative **while** statements have special self-stabilizing properties. In fact, the most interesting results pertaining to forward error recovery deal with initialized **while** statements, of the form

    begin i; **while** t **do** b **end**

where i stands for the initialization segment, t is the loop condition and b stands for the loop body. Consequently, we focus most of our attention on this kind of program. In Section 9.2, we consider in detail the mechanics of constructing an initialized **while** statement from a deterministic specification, and illustrate them with examples.

In Section 9.3, we give characterizations of loose correctness and loose recoverability, by means of the parameters exhibited in the preceding section, and then we characterize the Pascal routines that can be used for the purpose of error recovery; these routines are designed in such a way as to map a loosely recoverable (not too contaminated) state onto a loosely correct (sufficiently, but not quite correct) state. Using our results, we define the notions of critical information and non-critical information in the state of a program; while the former is critical to the survival of the program's execution, the latter may be lost without jeopardizing its survival.

Finally, in Section 9.4, we discuss the equations of correctness and recoverability of non-iterative programs.

9.1   DETERMINISTIC SPECIFICATIONS

9.1.1   Formulas of Correctness

Let F be a deterministic specification on space S such that $\mathrm{dom}(F) = S$. Let p be a program on space S, which we assume to be correct with respect to specification F. By the formula of program correctness, we have

$$(\forall s, s \in \mathrm{dom}(F) \Rightarrow s \in \mathrm{dom}([p]) \land (s, [p](s)) \in F).$$

Because $\mathrm{dom}(F) = S$, this becomes

$$(\forall s, s \in \mathrm{dom}([p]) \land (s, [p](s)) \in F).$$

Because F is a function, we can rewrite this as

$$(\forall s, s \in \mathrm{dom}([p]) \land [p](s) = F(s)).$$

We simplify this as

$$\mathrm{dom}([p]) = S \land (\forall s, [p](s) = F(s)).$$

We replace S by $\mathrm{dom}(F)$, to obtain

$$\mathrm{dom}([p]) = \mathrm{dom}(F) \land (\forall s, [p](s) = F(s)).$$

This can be written simply as

$$[p] = F.$$

In other words, writing a program *correct with respect* to function F, when $\mathrm{dom}(F) = S$, amounts to writing a program that *computes* F.

Furthermore, a brief glance at the definitions of levels of correctness and recoverability will show that when the specification at hand is deterministic, loose correctness is equivalent to specificationwise correctness, and loose recoverability is equivalent to specificationwise recoverability. Hence, for deterministic specifications, specificationwise correctness and recoverability are of no interest; we will not study them separately.

9.1.2 Exercises

1[A] Let F be a function on space S. If we do not assume $\text{dom}(F) = S$, under what condition is program p correct with respect to F?

2[A] Let F be a function on space S. If we do not assume $\text{dom}(F) = S$, what logical relationship links the properties of
(a) loose correctness of some state s;
(b) specificationwise correctness of state s with respect to F?

3[A] Let F be a function on space S. If we do not assume $\text{dom}(F) = S$, what logical relationship links the properties of
(a) loose recoverability of some state s;
(b) specificationwise recoverability of state s with respect to F?

9.2 DESIGN OF INITIALIZED WHILE STATEMENTS

9.2.1 A Programming Heuristic

Let F be a function on set S which we wish to compute by means of an initialized **while** statement on space S, i.e. a **while** statement of the form:

    begin i; **while** t **do** b **end**,

where i is an initialization segment, and b is a loop body. Following the guidelines of Chapter 3, we should apply the sequence rule to F, yielding the decomposition

$$F = J * W,$$

then we should

(a) find a program i correct with respect to J;
(b) apply the iteration rule to W, to find a **while** statement correct with respect to W.

Below, we present a *programming heuristic* whose purpose is to construct an iterative program of the form proposed above from a deterministic specification F; specifically, this heuristic helps us extract W from F, and then J from W and F. Furthermore, this heuristic readily exhibits all the parameters that we need to discuss the forward error recovery of the iterative program at hand. This heuristic is based on the following theorem:

- *Theorem 1.* Let F be a function on S such that $\text{dom}(F) = S$. Let W be a function on S such that

(a) $S \subseteq \mathrm{dom}(F * F^\wedge * I(\mathrm{dom}(W \cap F)))$,
(b) $I(\mathrm{rng}(W)) * W = I(\mathrm{rng}(W))$,

and let i be a Pascal program correct with respect to $J = F * F^\wedge * I(\mathrm{dom}(W \cap F))$. Then

  (i) there exists a **while** statement w such that $[w] = W$, and
  (ii) the Pascal program $f = (i; w)$ computes F, i.e. $[f] = F$.

Proof. Because W verifies condition (b), we know (by virtue of a theorem due to Mills *et al.*, 1986) that there exists a **while** statement w that computes W, i.e. such that $[w] = W$.

We must now prove that $[i; w] = F$; this is equivalent to $[i] * [w] = F$, which is also equivalent to $[i] * W = F$. In order to prove that $[i] * W = F$, we prove two lemmas:

$$\mathrm{LA}: F = F * F^\wedge * I' * W,$$

and

$$\mathrm{LB}: [i] * W = F * F^\wedge * I' * W,$$

where I' is an abbreviation for $I(\mathrm{dom}(W \cap F))$.

In order to prove LA and LB, we use the following lemma:

- Two functions F and G are equal if:

$$F \subseteq G,$$
$$\mathrm{dom}(G) \subseteq \mathrm{dom}(F).$$

Before we can do so, we must first prove that $F * F^\wedge * I' * W$ is indeed a function. According to the definition of a function, we must prove that

$$(F * F^\wedge * I' * W)^\wedge * (F * F^\wedge * I' * W) \subseteq I.$$

Now,

$$
\begin{aligned}
&(F * F^\wedge * I' * W)^\wedge * (F * F^\wedge * I' * W) \\
&= W^\wedge * I'^\wedge * F * F^\wedge * F * F^\wedge * I' * W && \text{property of operations } * \\
& && \text{and } ^\wedge, \\
&= (W^\wedge * I'^\wedge * F) * (F^\wedge * F) * (F^\wedge * I' * W) && \text{associativity of } *, \\
&\subseteq (W^\wedge * I' * F) * (F^\wedge * I' * W) && \text{determinacy of } F,
\end{aligned}
$$

Now, let us consider

$$
\begin{aligned}
&(W^\wedge * I' * F) \\
&= W^\wedge * I' * I' * F && I' * I' = I', \\
&= (W^\wedge * I'^\wedge) * (I' * F) && \text{associativity of } * \text{ and } I'^\wedge = I', \\
&= (I' * W)^\wedge * (I' * F) && \text{property of operations } * \text{ and } ^\wedge,
\end{aligned}
$$

$$= (I' * W) * (I' * W) \quad \text{by definition of } I', I' * W = I' * F,$$
$$\subseteq I \qquad\qquad\qquad \text{determinacy of } I' * W.$$

The same conclusion can be reached about $(F^\smallfrown * I' * W)$. Hence we deduce $(F * F^\smallfrown * I' * W)^\smallfrown * (F * F^\smallfrown * I' * W) \subseteq I$.

We now prove LA; by the lemma introduced above, LA can be deduced from the following two lemmas:

LAA: $F * F^\smallfrown * I' * W \subseteq F$.
LAB: $\mathrm{dom}(F) \subseteq \mathrm{dom}(F * F^\smallfrown * I' * W)$.

Proof of LAA

$F * F^\smallfrown * I' * W$
$\quad = F * (F^\smallfrown * I' * W) \qquad$ associativity of $*$,
$\quad \subseteq F \qquad\qquad\qquad$ monotonicity of $*$, and discussions above.

Proof of LAB

$\mathrm{rng}(F * F^\smallfrown * I')$
$\quad \subseteq \mathrm{rng}(I') \qquad\qquad$ because $\mathrm{rng}(A * B) \subseteq \mathrm{rng}(B)$,
$\quad = \mathrm{dom}(W \cap F) \qquad$ by definition of I',
$\quad \subseteq \mathrm{dom}(W) \qquad\quad$ monotonicity of function dom.

Hence,

$\mathrm{dom}((F * F^\smallfrown * I') * W) \qquad$ because if $\mathrm{rng}(A) \subseteq \mathrm{dom}(B)$ then
$\quad = \mathrm{dom}(F * F^\smallfrown * I') \qquad \mathrm{dom}(A * B) = \mathrm{dom}(A)$,
$\quad = S \qquad\qquad\qquad\quad$ by virtue of hypothesis (a),
$\quad = \mathrm{dom}(F) \qquad\qquad$ by hypothesis.

Similarly, in order to prove lemma LB, we have to prove the following sublemmas:

LBA: $[i] * W \subseteq F * F^\smallfrown * I' * W$,
LBB: $\mathrm{dom}(F * F^\smallfrown * I' * W) \subseteq \mathrm{dom}([i] * W)$.

Proof of LBA. Segment i is correct with respect to $J = F * F^\smallfrown * I'$; because $\mathrm{dom}(J)$ is equal to S, so is $\mathrm{dom}([i])$. Then the correctness of i with respect to J can be expressed merely as $[i] \subseteq J$. Multiplying this equation on the right by W, we obtain the result sought.

Proof of LBB. Because

$\mathrm{rng}([i])$
$\quad \subseteq \mathrm{rng}(F * F^\smallfrown * I')$
$\quad \subseteq \mathrm{rng}(I')$

$$= \mathrm{dom}(W \cap F)$$
$$\subseteq \mathrm{dom}(W),$$

we have

$$\mathrm{dom}([i] * W) = \mathrm{dom}([i]).$$

Now, because i is correct with respect to $F * F^{\frown} * I'$, $\mathrm{dom}([i])$ equals S; hence so does $\mathrm{dom}([i] * W)$.

From LAA and LAB we deduce LA; from LBA and LBB we deduce LB; from LA and LB we deduce $F = [i] * W$.   [QED]

From the above theorem, we derive the following heuristic:

Heuristic for the Design of Initialized While Statements. Given a function F on S such that $\mathrm{dom}(F) = S$, find a function W such that

(a) $S \subseteq \mathrm{dom}(F * F^{\frown} * I(\mathrm{dom}(W \cap F)))$,
(b) $I(\mathrm{rng}(W)) * W = I(\mathrm{rng}(W))$,

then find a while statement that computes W, and solve specification $J = F * F^{\frown} * I(\mathrm{dom}(W \cap F))$.

Despite its complex expression, specification $J = F * F^{\frown} * I(\mathrm{dom}(W \cap F))$ is usually simple to solve; it is the specification of the initialization segment.

Of course, if F satisfies the equation

$$I(\mathrm{rng}(F)) * F = I(\mathrm{rng}(F)),$$

then choosing W to be equal to F is the most natural option. We check briefly that such a choice of W is valid. Equation (b) of the heuristic is valid, by hypothesis. For Equation (a), we consider

$$\mathrm{dom}(F * F^{\frown} * I(\mathrm{dom}(F \cap W)))$$

$= \mathrm{dom}(F * F^{\frown} * I(\mathrm{dom}(F)))$	because $W = F$,
$= \mathrm{dom}(F * F^{\frown})$	because $\mathrm{dom}(F) = S$,
$= \mathrm{dom}(F)$	a relational identity,
$= S$	by hypothesis.

Note that for such a choice of W, the specification of the initialization segment becomes

$$J = F * F^{\frown}.$$

The reader can readily check that the empty statement (whose functional abstraction is the identity) is correct with respect to J. We then get an iterative statement under the form of an uninitialized **while** statement.

9.2.2   Illustration by Analysis

Because Theorem 1 above and its proof are rather abstract, they give little understanding of this heuristic. We explain this heuristic here; in particular, we explain the significance of Condition (a) and specification J.

Condition (a) expresses that each level set of F contains an element on which F and W coincide. Indeed, Equation (a) can be interpreted by paying attention to the following details:

1. $\text{dom}(W \cap F)$ is the set of states for which W coincides with F, i.e. $\{s \mid F(s) = W(s)\}$.
2. Relation $F * F^\frown$ contain all the pairs (s, s') such that s and s' have the same image by F.
3. $S \subseteq \text{dom}(F * F^\frown * I(\text{dom}(W \cap F)))$
   $\Leftrightarrow (s \in S \Rightarrow \exists s': (s, s') \in F * F^\frown * I(\text{dom}(W \cap F)))$
   $\Leftrightarrow (s \in S \Rightarrow \exists s': (s, s') \in F * F^\frown \wedge s' \in \text{dom}(W \cap F))$
   $\Leftrightarrow (s \in S \Rightarrow \exists s': (s, s') \in F * F^\frown \wedge F(s') = W(s'))$
   $\Leftrightarrow$ for every s in S, there must exist s' in the same level set as s, such that W and F coincide on s'.
   $\Leftrightarrow$ each level set of F contains an element on which F and W coincide.

See Figure 9.1: The spokes delimit the level sets of F; functions W' and W''' are correct choices for W (in the sense that they meet Condition (a) of the heuristic), whereas function W^- is not.

Specification J expresses that the initialization segment must map any state s into a state s' in the same level set as s, and such that F and W coincide on s'; in other words, s' must verify $F(s) = F(s')$ and $F(s') = W(s')$. Let i be a Pascal statement correct with respect to J. Because $\text{dom}(J) = S$ (Condition (a)), so $\text{dom}([i]) = S$; hence the correctness of i with respect to J can be written as $[i] \subseteq J$. Let (s, s') be an element (pair) of $[i]$; then $(s, s') \in J$; then $(s, s') \in F * F^\frown$ and $s' \in \text{dom}(W \cap F)$, then $F(s) = F(s')$ and $W(s') = F(s')$.

The heuristic given above offers us a key to an intriguing question pertaining to the relationship between the function of an initialized **while** statement and that of an uninitialized **while** statement. In order to illustrate the question, we give two brief examples:

Let S be $\{\langle a, b, c \rangle \mid a \in \textbf{integer} \wedge b \in \textbf{natural} \wedge c \in \textbf{integer}\}$, and let F be $\{(s, s') \mid a(s') = a(s) \wedge b(s') = 0 \wedge c(s') = a(s) * b(s)\}$. We assume that we use a subset of Pascal that has no multiplication but does have an addition and a subtraction; then it is natural for a programmer to implement F by

```
begin c := 0; while b ≠ 0 do begin c := c + a; b := b − 1 end end.
```

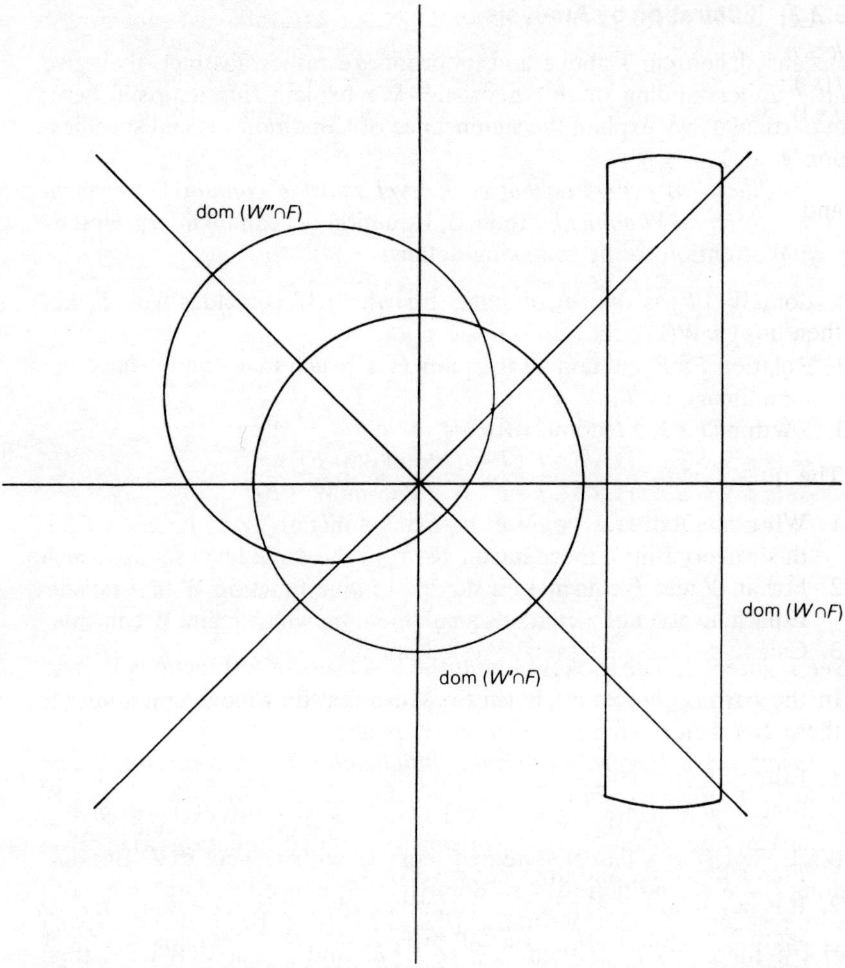

dom $(W''\cap F)$

dom $(W\cap F)$

dom $(W'\cap F)$

Figure 9.1

In effect the programmer has decomposed F into $J * W$, where

$$J = \{(s, s') \mid a(s') = a(s) \wedge b(s') = b(s) \wedge c(s') = 0\}$$

and

$$W = \{(s, s') \mid a(s') = a(s) \wedge b(s') = 0 \wedge c(s') = c(s) + a(s) * b(s)\};$$

then he has implemented J by $(c := 0)$ and W by the **while** statement:

while $b \neq 0$ **do begin** $c := c + a;\ b := b - 1$ **end**.

Let S be $\{\langle n, k, f\rangle\}|n \in$ **natural** $\land$ $k \in$ **natural** $\land$ $f \in$ **integer** $\land$ $k \leq n+1\}$, and let F be $\{(s,s')|n(s') = n(s)$ $\land$ $k(s') = n+1$ $\land$ $f(s') = n(s)!\}$. Then it is natural for a programmer to decompose F into $J * W$, where

$$J = \{(s,s')|n(s') = n(s) \land k(s') = 1 \land f(s') = 1\}$$

and

$$W = \{(s,s')|n(s') = n(s) \land k(s') = n+1 \\ \land f(s') = f(s) * n(s)!/(k(s) - 1)!\},$$

then implement J and W by, respectively:

$i = (k := 1; f := 1),$

$w = ($**while** $k \neq n+1$ **do begin** $f := f * k;\ k := k+1$ **end**$).$

The questions that we pose now are as follows:

1. What mathematical relationships link function W to function F? Is this relationship dependent on J?
2. For any given function F, is there a unique function W that satisfies Equations (a) and (b)?
3. Can W be deduced from F systematically?

In the light of the above heuristic, we offer the following answers to these questions:

1. Equation (b) defines the solution space (i.e. the set of admissible functions W) and Equation (a) defines the solution(s) within that space, for a given F. It is surprising indeed that Equation (a) involves F and W alone, and does not involve J.
2. It is possible to find practical examples when it is not unique. It does seem, though, from practical experience, that there is a unique 'reasonable' solution. The illustrative examples given above offer a hint as to what 'reasonable' might mean.
3. As they are written here, Equations (a) and (b) offer no help as far as extracting W from F.

9.2.3 Illustration by Examples

We illustrate this heuristic with two examples.

Example 1. Let S be the space $\{\langle a, b, c\rangle|a \in$ **integer** $\land$ $b \in$ **natural** $\land$ $c \in$ **integer**$\}$, and let F be the function defined by

$$F = \{(s,s')|a(s') = a(s) \land b(s') = 0 \land c(s') = a(s) * b(s)\}.$$

Determining W. We do not present a systematic way of deriving W from F using Equations (a) and (b) of the proposed programming heuristic; hence, for the purposes of this chapter, we shall content ourselves with proposing a value for W and then verifying that it meets Equations (a) and (b):

$$W = \{(s,s') \,|\, a(s') = a(s) \,\wedge\, b(s') = 0 \,\wedge\, c(s') = c(s) + a(s) * b(s)\}.$$

Equation (a)

$$
\begin{aligned}
W \cap F &= \{(s,s') \,|\, a(s') = a(s) \,\wedge\, b(s') = 0 \,\wedge\, c(s') = c(s) + a(s) * b(s) \\
&\qquad \wedge\, c(s') = a(s) * b(s)\} \\
&= \{(s,s') \,|\, c(s) = 0 \,\wedge\, a(s') = a(s) \,\wedge\, b(s') = 0 \\
&\qquad \wedge\, c(s') = a(s) * b(s)\}.
\end{aligned}
$$

$$\mathrm{dom}(W \cap F) = \{s \,|\, c(s) = 0\}.$$

$$F * \hat{F} = \{(s,s') \,|\, a(s') = a(s) \,\wedge\, a(s) * b(s) = a(s') * b(s')\}.$$

$$
\begin{aligned}
F * \hat{F} * I(\mathrm{dom}(W \cap F)) &= \{(s,s') \,|\, a(s') = a(s) \\
&\qquad \wedge\, a(s) * b(s) = a(s') * b(s') \\
&\qquad \wedge\, c(s') = 0\}.
\end{aligned}
$$

$$\mathrm{dom}(F * \hat{F} * I(\mathrm{dom}(W \cap F))) = S.$$

Equation (b). The range of W is:

$$\mathrm{rng}(W) = \{s \,|\, b(s) = 0\}.$$

$$I(\mathrm{rng}(W)) = \{(s,s') \,|\, s' = s \,\wedge\, b(s) = 0\}.$$

$$
\begin{aligned}
I(\mathrm{rng}(W)) * W \\
&= \{(s,s') \,|\, b(s) = 0 \,\wedge\, a(s') = a(s) \,\wedge\, b(s') = 0 \\
&\qquad \wedge\, c(s') = c(s) + a(s) * b(s)\} \\
&= \{(s,s') \,|\, b(s) = 0 \,\wedge\, a(s') = a(s) \,\wedge\, b(s') = b(s) \,\wedge\, c(s') = c(s)\} \\
&= I(\mathrm{rng}(W)).
\end{aligned}
$$

Hence the choice of W is correct.

Determining J

$$
\begin{aligned}
J &= F * \hat{F} * I(\mathrm{dom}(W \cap F)) \\
&= \{(s,s') \,|\, a(s') = a(s) \,\wedge\, a(s) * b(s) = a(s') * b(s') \,\wedge\, c(s') = 0\}. \quad \square
\end{aligned}
$$

Example 2. Let S be $\{\langle n, f, k \rangle \,|\, n \in \textbf{natural} \,\wedge\, k \in \textbf{natural}\ f \in \textbf{natural} \,\wedge\, k \leq n + 1\}$, and let F be the function on S defined by

$$F = \{(s,s') \,|\, n(s') = n(s) \,\wedge\, k(s') = n(s) + 1 \,\wedge\, f(s') = n(s)!\}.$$

Determination of W. We verify Equations (a) and (b) for function W defined as:

$$
\begin{aligned}
W = \{(s,s') \,|\, n(s') = n(s) \,\wedge\, k(s') = n(s) + 1 \\
\wedge\, f(s') = f(s) * n(s)!/(k(s) - 1)!\}.
\end{aligned}
$$

Equation (a)

$$W \cap F = \{(s,s') | f(s) = (k(s) - 1)! \ \wedge \ n(s') = n(s) \ \wedge \ k(s') = n(s) + 1$$
$$\wedge \ f(s') = n(s)! \}.$$
$$\text{dom}(W \cap F) = \{s | f(s) = (k(s) - 1)! \}.$$
$$I(\text{dom}(W \cap F)) = \{(s,s') | s' = s \ \wedge \ f(s) = (k(s) - 1)! \}.$$
$$F * F^\frown = \{(s,s') | n(s') = n(s) \}.$$
$$F * F^\frown * I(\text{dom}(W \cap F)) = \{(s,s') | n(s') = n(s) \ \wedge f(s') = (k(s') - 1)! \}.$$

Clearly, for all s in S, one can find s' in S such that $n(s') = n(s)$ and $f(s') = (k(s') - 1)!$, e.g. by taking $f(s') = 1$ and $k(s') = 1$. Hence $\text{dom}(F * F^\frown * I(\text{dom}(W \cap F))) = S$.

Equation (b)

$$\text{rng}(W) = \{s | k(s) = n(s) + 1 \}.$$
$$I(\text{rng}(W)) = \{(s,s') | k(s) = n(s) + 1 \ \wedge \ s' = s \}.$$
$$I(\text{rng}(W)) * W$$
$$= \{(s,s') | k(s) = n(s) + 1 \ \wedge \ n(s') = n(s) \ \wedge \ k(s') = n(s) + 1$$
$$\wedge \ f(s') = f(s) * n(s)! / (k(s) - 1)! \}$$
$$= \{(s,s') | k(s) = n(s) + 1 \ \wedge \ n(s') = n(s) \ \wedge \ k(s') = k(s)$$
$$\wedge \ f(s') = f(s) * n(s)! / (n(s) + 1 - 1)! \}$$
$$= \{(s,s') | k(s) = n(s) + 1 \ \wedge \ n(s') = n(s) \ \wedge \ k(s') = k(s)$$
$$\wedge \ f(s') = f(s) \}$$
$$= \{(s,s') | k(s) = n(s) + 1 \ \wedge \ s' = s \}$$
$$= I(\text{rng}(W)).$$

Hence W is a correct choice.

Determination of J.

$$J = F * F^\frown * I(\text{dom}(W \cap F))$$
$$= \{(s,s') | n(s') = n(s) \ \wedge \ f(s') = (k(s') - 1)! \}. \qquad \qquad \square$$

9.2.4 Exercises

1[A] Apply the programming heuristic proposed in this section to the following function:

$$S = \{\langle a,b \rangle | a \in \textbf{integer} \ \wedge \ b \in \textbf{natural} \},$$

$$F = \{(s,s') | a(s') = a(s) + b(s) \ \wedge \ b(s') = 0 \}.$$

Specifically, you must:
(a) propose a possible function W;
(b) check that the function proposed meets Conditions (a) and (b) of the heuristic;

(c) construct specification J;

(d) find a program segment i that is correct with respect to specification J;

(e) find a **while** statement w that computes function W.

Once these steps are followed, you will find that the program

begin i; w **end**

computes function F.

2[A]   Same as Exercise 1:

$$S = \{\langle a, b\rangle \,|\, a \in \text{natural}^* \wedge b \in \text{natural}^*\},$$

where $\text{natural}^* = \text{natural} - \{0\}$,

$$F = \{(s, s') \,|\, a(s') = \gcd(s) \wedge b(s') = \gcd(s)\},$$

where $\gcd(s)$ is the greatest common divisor of $a(s)$ and $b(s)$.

3[A]   Same as Exercise 1:

$$S = \{\langle n, f\rangle \,|\, n \in \text{natural} \wedge f \in \text{natural}^*\},$$

$$F = \{(s, s') \,|\, n(s') = 0 \wedge f(s') = n(s)!\}.$$

4[A]   Same as Exercise 1:

$$S = \{\langle a, b, c\rangle \,|\, a \in \text{integer} \wedge b \in \text{natural} \wedge c \in \text{integer}\},$$

$$F = \{(s, s') \,|\, a(s') = a(s) \wedge b(s') = 0 \wedge c(s') = a(s)^{b(s)}\}.$$

5[B]   Same as Exercise 1:

$$S = \{\langle a, i, x\rangle \,|\, a\!: \text{ array } [1 .. n] \text{ of real};$$
$$i\!: \ 0 .. n + 1;$$
$$x\!: \text{ real}\},$$

$$F = \{(s, s') \,|\, a(s') = a(s) \wedge i(s') = n + 1$$
$$\wedge x(s') = \sum_{i=1}^{n} a(s)[i]$$

6[B]   Same as Exercise 1:

$$S = \{\langle a, i, x\rangle \,|\, a\!: \text{ array } [1 .. n] \text{ of real};$$
$$i\!: \ 0 .. n + 1;$$
$$m\!: \text{ real}\},$$

$$F = \{(s, s') \,|\, a(s') = a(s) \wedge i(s') = n + 1$$
$$\wedge m(s') = \max(a(s))\},$$

where $\max(a)$, for array a, is the largest value contained in array a.

7[B]   Same as Exercise 1:

$$S = \{\langle a,i,x\rangle \,|\, a:\textbf{array } [1 \,..\, n] \textbf{ of real};$$
$$i:\ 0 \,..\, n+1;$$
$$x:\ \textbf{real};$$
$$f:\ \textbf{boolean}\},$$

$$F = \{(s,s')\,|\, a(s') = a(s) \ \wedge\ i(s') = n+1$$
$$\wedge\ x(s') = x(s) \ \wedge\ f(s') = (x(s) \in a(s))\}.$$

8[B]   Same as Exercise 1:

$$S = \{\langle a,i\rangle \,|\, a:\textbf{array } [1 \,..\, n] \textbf{ of real};$$
$$i:\ 0 \,..\, n+1\},$$

$$F = \{(s,s')\,|\, a(s') = \text{sort}(a(s)) \ \wedge\ i(s') = n+1\},$$

where sort(a) is the sorted permutation of array a.

9.3   FORWARD ERROR RECOVERY OF ITERATIVE STATEMENTS

Let F be a function on space S, such that $\text{dom}(F) = S$, and let f be an iterative statement of the form

begin i; L:**while** t **do** b **end**,

which computes F. We assume that f has been derived from F by following the programming heuristic given in the preceding section. We are interested in characterizing levels of correctness/recoverability of state s at label L. We let W be the function of the **while** statement

while t **do** b

and we let D be $\text{dom}(W \cap F)$. Also, we denote by J the relation $F * F^\frown * I(D)$. Note that J is the specification of the initialization segment, introduced above.

9.3.1   Characterizing Levels of Correctness

Specifically, we are interested in three levels: strict correctness (is of limited value, but serves as a reference); loose correctness; loose recoverability.

- *Proposition 1 – necessary and sufficient condition for strict correctness.* State s is strictly correct at milestone (v, L) vis-à-vis s_0 if and only if

$$s = s_0 \cdot ([i] * (I(t) * [b])^{v-1}).$$

Proof. By definition of strict correctness, $s = pst_{v,1}(s_0)$. Due to the form of this particular program, $pst_{v,L} = ([i] * (I(t) * [b])^{v-1})$.   [QED]

The levels of loose correctness and loose recoverability depend on function future (rather than function past). At milestone (v, L), function future depends on label L, and does not depend on the number of visits, v. Consequently, we shall talk interchangeably of a state s being loosely correct/recoverable at label L, or at milestone (v, L). The proposition given below characterizes l-correct states by a sufficient condition.

- *Proposition 2 – sufficient condition of loose correctness.* State s is loosely correct at milestone (v, L) vis-à-vis s_0 if

$$s \in D \wedge (s_0, s) \in F * F^\wedge$$

where $D = \text{dom}(W \cap F)$.

Proof. We must prove that $ftr_{v,L}(s) = F(s_0)$. We compute

$$ftr_{v,L}(s)$$
$= [w](s)$ because of the form of the program,
$= W(s)$ by definition of W,
$= F(s)$ because $s \in D$, and $D = \text{dom}(W \cap F)$,
$= F(s_0)$ because $(s, s_0) \in F * F^\wedge$.   [QED]

Interpretation. This result can be interpreted quite easily, if one rewrites $(s, s_0) \in F * F^\wedge$ as $s \in s_0 \cdot F * F^\wedge$: D is the set of states for which W and F compute the same value; $s_0 \cdot F * F^\wedge$ is the set of states for which application of F yields $F(s_0)$. As long as s belongs to both of these sets, application of W to it yields $F(s_0)$, the desired output result. See Figure 9.2.

Proposition 3 characterizes loosely recoverable states, and its corollary characterizes valid recovery routines.

- *Proposition 3 – sufficient condition of loose recoverability.* State s is loosely recoverable at milestone (v, L) vis-à-vis s_0 if

$$(s, s_0) \in F * F^\wedge.$$

Proof. In order to prove that s is loosely recoverable, we must find a recovery routine r such that $[r](s)$ is loosely correct. Let r be a program correct with respect to specification:

$$J = F * F^\wedge * I(D)$$

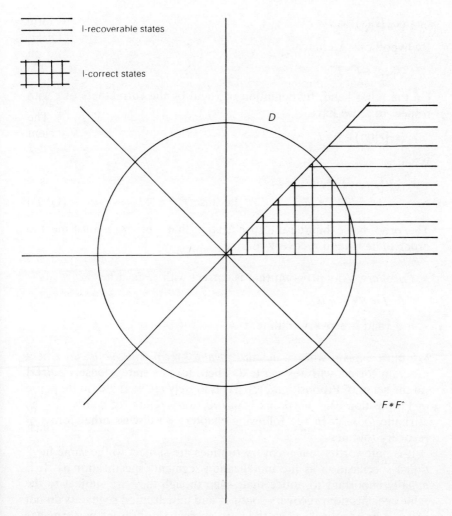

Figure 9.2

(at least one instance of such a program is known to exist: the initialization segment). Because dom(J) = S (see Section 9.2), we also have dom([r]) = S, hence [r](s) is defined. We propose to prove that [r](s) is loosely correct. The assertion

$$[r](s) \in D$$

stems readily from the definition of J, and the correctness of r with respect to J. Now we must prove that

$(s_0, [r](s)) \in F * F^\wedge.$

By hypothesis, we have

$(s_0, s) \in F * F^\wedge.$

On the other hand, by definition of J and by the correctness of r with respect to J, we have

$(s, [r](s)) \in F * F^\wedge.$

Whence

$$(s_0, [r](s)) \in F * F^\wedge * F * F^\wedge$$
$$\subseteq F * F^\wedge \qquad \text{because } F^\wedge * F \subseteq I. \qquad \text{[QED]}$$

This proof has exhibited the specification that a program must meet in order to be a valid recovery routine.

- *Corollary*. Any program that is correct with respect to

  $$J = F * F^\wedge * I(D)$$

  is a valid l-recovery routine.

We must explain what is meant by *valid l-recovery routine*: let r be a program correct with respect to J. Then, for any state s loosely correct (in the sense of Proposition 2), $[r](s)$ is loosely recoverable (in the sense of Proposition 3). The prefix l- in *l-recovery* refers, of course, to the attribute *loosely*. In the following chapter, we discuss other forms of recovery routines.

It is noteworthy that recovery routines are subject to the same functional specification as the initialization segment (specification J). It is equally important to notice that, even though they are subject to the same specification, recovery routines and initialization segments do not have to be identical, since they are subject to different performance requirements due to their different invocation patterns. While initialization segments are invoked systematically before the loop is started, recovery routines are invoked only incidentally, upon deleting an unmaskable error. On the other hand, while initialization segments are invoked on states that are not yet processed by the loop, recovery routines are invoked on states that, except for an eventual error, are partially processed by the loop. Finally, it is important to notice that, even when the recovery routine and the initialization segment of an iterative program are chosen to be identical, they nevertheless have a different effect. While the initialization segment i applies function $[i]$ to

procedure b produces an s-correct state
procedure b' produces an l-correct state
procedure b″ produces an l-recoverable state, which procedure r maps into an l-correct state
procedure b˜ produces an unrecoverable state (causes a fatal error).

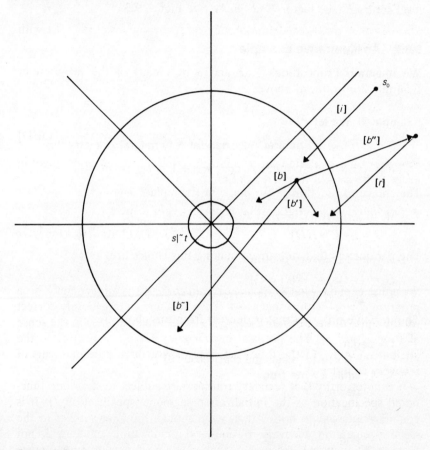

Figure 9.3

the initial state s_0 – yielding $[i](s_0)$, the recovery routine (when it is identical) applies function $[i]$ to a current loosely recoverable state s – yielding $[i](s)$. Hence, even when $r = i$, invocation of r does not necessarily reset the program to its initial state (nor could it, since the initial state is not supposed to be known).

Interpretation. Proposition 3 and its corollary can be interpreted quite easily, if one notes that $s_0 \cdot F * F^{\sim}$ is actually the level set of s_0 by function F. So long as s is in the same level set by F as s_0, it carries sufficient information to retrieve $F(s_0)$. If s is outside D (case where s is loosely recoverable without being loosely correct), the recovery routine will map it back into D (see factor $I(D)$ in J) while keeping it in the same level set by F (see factor $F * F^{\wedge}$ in J). See Figure 9.3.

9.3.2   An Illustrative Example

We illustrate Propositions 1, 2 and 3 by means of the program in Example 2 introduced above.

Example 3. We let

$$S = \{\langle n, f, k\rangle \,|\, n \in \textbf{natural} \land k \in \textbf{natural} \land f \in \textbf{natural} \land k \le n + 1\},$$

$$F = \{(s, s') \,|\, n(s') = n(s) \land k(s') = n + 1 \land f(s') = n(s)!\}.$$

The choice of function W we made in Example 2 was:

$$W = \{(s, s') \,|\, n(s') = n(s) \land k(s') = n + 1$$
$$\land f(s') = f(s) * n(s)!/(k(s) - 1)!\}.$$

The parameters that stem from making this choice are:

$$D = \{s \,|\, f(s) = (k(s) - 1)!\},$$
$$J = \{(s, s') \,|\, n(s') = n(s) \land f(s') = (k(s') - 1)!\}.$$

The iterative program that is derived from this choice is:

```
f = begin
      f := 1; k := 1; {meets the specification J}
    L: while k ≠ n + 1 do
        begin
          f := f * k;
          k := k + 1
        end
      {computes function W}
    end.
```

We consider initial state $s_0 = \langle 7, 3, 5\rangle$, and milestone $m = (3, L)$.

Strictly correct state. The only s-correct state at milestone m is $s = \langle 7, 3, 2\rangle$.

Loosely correct states. State s is loosely correct at milestone m vis-à-vis s_0 if

$$s \in D \land (s, s_0) \in F * F^{\wedge}.$$

$$\Leftrightarrow$$

$$f(s) = (k(s) - 1)! \land n(s) = n(s_0).$$

The strictly correct state verifies this condition; so do several other states, such as $\langle 7,1,1 \rangle$, $\langle 7,2,1 \rangle$, $\langle 7,4,6 \rangle$, $\langle 7,5,24 \rangle$, $\langle 7,6,120 \rangle$, $\langle 7,7,720 \rangle$, which are not strictly correct.

Loosely recoverable states. State s is loosely recoverable at milestone m vis-à-vis s_0 if

$$(s, s_0) \in F * F^{\hat{}}$$
$$\Leftrightarrow$$
$$n(s) = n(s_0).$$

All the loosely correct states verify this condition; so do several other states, such as $\langle 7,1,2 \rangle$, $\langle 7,2,3 \rangle$, $\langle 7,3,4 \rangle$, $\langle 7,4,12 \rangle$, $\langle 7,5,720 \rangle$, which are not strictly correct. The specification of recovery routines is

$$J = \{(s, s') \mid n(s') = n(s) \wedge f(s') = (k(s') - 1)!\}.$$

Any routine that preserves n while setting f to the factorial of $(k - 1)$ is a valid recovery routine. An example of such is

r0 = **begin** f := 1; k := 1 **end**,

which is the initialization segment. Another example might be

```
r1 = begin
     if n > 4 then
        begin
        f := 6; k := 4
        end
     else
        begin
        f := 1; k := 1
        end
     end.
```

Note that this particular recovery routine r_0 meets a special property: for any loosely recoverable state s,

$$[r_0](s) = [r_0](s_0),$$

which means that when we apply the recovery routine to state s, we actually reinitialize it; of course, this is by no means general. See the exercises given below.

Summary. The factorial program shows how a program can lose two out of its three variables (namely f and k), and still be recoverable. Of course, it is unusual for a program to be able to afford to lose two-thirds of its space, but it is usual for programs to be so redundant that much damage can be done to their state without jeopardizing their survival. □

9.3.3 Critical and Non-critical Information

The discussions of Section 9.3.1 have shown that l-correct states can be characterized in terms of the conjunction of two predicates:

(a) a predicate involving s_0, namely

$$(s_0, s) \in F * F\hat{};$$

(b) a predicate that does not involve s_0, but involves s alone, namely

$$s \in D.$$

The first predicate characterizes recoverable states; hence it is critical to the survival of the execution of the program. In effect, it carries the information that must be known about s_0 to make recovery possible (s_0 need not necessarily be known itself; some information about it may suffice, namely its equivalence class by $F * F\hat{}$). This predicate is said to carry the *critical information* of the state of the program; any damage done to s which results in this predicate no longer holding is generally an irretrievable loss of information.

The second predicate makes no reference to s_0 and does not appear in the characterization of l-recoverable states. It is said to carry the *non-critical information* of the state of the program; any damage done to s which results in this predicate no longer holding is generally a retrievable loss of information. The predicate carries information that reflects which function was applied to the initial state; since this information is, by definition, contained in the very text of the program, it can be retrieved.

The success of forward error recovery in generating correct states from incorrect states lies in its ability to characterize the property of l-correctness by the conjunction of two predicates, one of them involving s and reflecting properties of the program only, the other reflecting properties of the program as well as its initial state. The former being known at program design time, provisions can be made to recover from damage done to it.

It is instructive to recognize critical and non-critical information in the state of the program discussed in the preceding section. Critical information is carried by the predicate

$$n(s) = n(s_0).$$

Any alteration to the value of n constitutes an irretrievable loss of information. Non-critical information is carried by the predicate

$$f(s) = (k(s) - 1)!.$$

Any damage done to variables f and k constitutes a retrievable loss of information. Note that in the factorial program, critical information is geographically separated from non-critical information, in that they are carried by different variables. This is by no means general.

In the study of program analysis and design by function manipulation (a similar approach to that used here), it is often useful to distinguish between the following:

(a) *preservation equations*, i.e. equations that express what must remain unchanged as the program executes; and
(b) *termination equations*, i.e. equations that express how the program progresses towards a final state.

There is some analogy between critical information and preservation equations, as well as between non-critical information and termination equations. This analogy can be explained as follows. If we fail to progress toward termination (i.e. we lose non-critical information), then there is still hope that we will eventually succeed. If, on the other hand, we fail to preserve the information needed to compute the final correct state (i.e. we lose critical information), then there is no way to recover (loosely) the loss (specificationwise recovery may still be possible; see next chapter).

9.3.4 Exercises

1[A] Given that you have worked Exercise 1 of Section 9.2.4, give characterizations of the following:
(a) strictly correct states,
(b) loosely correct states,
(c) loosely recoverable states,
using the formulas given in Propositions 1, 2 and 3. Interpret the results you find, and give examples of states in each level of correctness.
2[A] Same as Exercise 1, in reference to Exercise 2 of Section 9.2.4.
3[A] Same as Exercise 1, in reference to Exercise 3 of Section 9.2.4.
4[A] Same as Exercise 1, in reference to Exercise 4 of Section 9.2.4.
5[B] Same as Exercise 1, in reference to Exercise 5 of Section 9.2.4.
6[B] Same as Exercise 1, in reference to Exercise 6 of Section 9.2.4.
7[B] Same as Exercise 1, in reference to Exercise 7 of Section 9.2.4.

8[B] Same as Exercise 1, in reference to Exercise 8 of Section 9.2.4.

9[B] Same as Exercise 1, in reference to the program given in Example 1, Section 9.2.3.

10[A] The exercise illustrates loosely correct states. Type the following program and run on Turbo Pascal.

```
program fact(input,output);
label 0;
const n = 7;
var k, f: integer;
    done: boolean;
    procedure lcorrectstate;
    var ch: char;
    begin
    writeln('current state is:', n,k,f);
    writeln('c: continue; r: replace state');
    readln(ch);
    if ch = 'r' then
        begin
        writeln('give alternate state ⟨k, f⟩, k≤', n);
        writeln('n=', n);
        readln(k); readln(f)
        end;
    done := true
    end;
begin
done := false; {to invoke lcorrectstate}
k := 1; f := 1; {meets the specification J}
0: while k⟨⟩n + 1 do
    begin
    if ((k = 3) and (not done)) then lcorrectstate;
    f := f * k;
    k := k + 1
    end
{computes function W};
writeln('final state ⟨n, k, f⟩ |,n,',|,k,',',f);
end.
```

Whenever it arrives to milestone $(3, 0)$, it posts the message

    c: continue; r: replace state

you may either let it continue with its current s-correct state, or you may replace its current state by an alternate l-correct state. If you choose the latter option, it will post the message give alternate state $\langle k, f \rangle$, $k \le 7$.

Run the program as many times as necessary to feed it all the possible l-correct states at milestone $(3, 0)$. Notice that at the end it will always post the final state:

final state $\langle n, k, f \rangle = 7, 8, 5040$.

9.4   FORWARD ERROR RECOVERY IN SEQUENCE STATEMENTS

9.4.1   Motivation

In Section 9.3, we have discussed forward recovery in **while** statements, i.e. how one or more executions of the loop body of a **while** statement can smooth out an error caused by a previous execution of the loop body. One may be tempted to say that the results of Propositions 3 and 4 can be applied to all programs, since virtually all programs have the pattern

    begin initialization; **while** t **do** body **end**

as an outer control structure. In practice, the results of Propositions 3 and 4 apply best when a faulty execution of the loop body has least chance of throwing the state outside the (loose or specificationwise) recoverability domain. Now, as the loop body grows larger and more complex, it becomes less and less reasonable to assume that an error appearing during the execution of the loop body does not cause the state to be damaged beyond sp-recoverability by the time the end of the loop body (i.e. the next milestone) is reached. The need to discuss forward error recovery in sequence statements follows from this remark; we shall discuss how a statement can smooth out an error caused by the statement which precedes it in the sequence.

9.4.2   Parameters of the Sequence Statement

We are given a function F on space S. We suppose that $\text{dom}(F) = S$ and that F can be written as

$$F = F_1 * F_2,$$

where $\text{dom}(F_2) = S$. We assume that there exist statements st_1 and st_2, and a subset D_2 of S such that

$$[st_1] = F_1,$$
$$\text{rng}(F_1) \subseteq D_2,$$
$$I(D_2) * [st_2] = I(D_2) * F_2.$$

Then function F can be computed by the sequence statement

st = **begin** st1; st2 **end**.

Further, we assume that there exists a statement r_2 that is correct with respect to the specification

$$J_2 = F_2 * F_2' * I(D_2).$$

Example 4. We take

S = **real**,

$$F = \{(s, s') \mid s' = \text{sqrt}(s^2 + 1)\},$$

where sqrt stands for the square root.
  We do have $\text{dom}(F) = S$. We choose

$$F_1 = s^2 + 1,$$
$$F_2 = \text{sqrt}(|s|),$$

where $|s|$ stands for the absolute value of s. We do have $\text{dom}(F_2) = S$, and also,

$$F = F_1 * F_2.$$

We define st_1, st_2 and D_2 as follows:

st1 = **begin** s := s * s + 1 **end**,
st2 = **begin** s := sqrt(s) **end**,

$$D_2 = \{s \mid s \geq 0\}.$$

One can check readily that:

$$[st_1] = F_1,$$
$$\text{rng}([st_1]) = \{s \mid s \geq 1\} \subseteq D_2,$$
$$I(D_2) * [st_2] = \{(s, s') \mid s \geq 0 \wedge s' = \text{sqrt}(s)\}$$
$$= \{(s, s') \mid s \geq 0 \wedge s' = \text{sqrt}(|s|)\}$$
$$= I(D_2) * F_2.$$

Indeed, function F can be computed by the sequence statement

st = **begin** s := s * s + 1; L: s := sqrt(s) **end**.

We consider specification J_2:

$$J_2 = F_2 * \hat{F_2} * I(D_2)$$
$$= \{(s,s')\,|\,\mathrm{sqrt}(|s|) = \mathrm{sqrt}(|s'|)\ \wedge\ s' \geq 0\}$$
$$= \{(s,s')\,|\,|s| = |s'|\ \wedge\ s' \geq 0\}$$
$$= \{(s,s')\,|\,s' = |s|\}.$$

We propose a Pascal routine r_2 that is correct with respect to J_2:

r2 = **begin** s := abs(s) **end**. □

9.4.3 Characterizing Levels of Correctness

We consider the sequence statement

st = **begin** st1; L: st2 **end**,

and we characterize its correctness level at milestone $(1, L)$.

- *Proposition 4 – necessary and sufficient condition of strict correctness, sequences.* State s is strictly correct at milestone $(1, L)$ vis-à-vis initial state s_0 if and only if

$$s = F_1(s_0).$$

Proof. This stems directly, of course, from the definitions of strict correctness and function past.   [QED]

- *Proposition 5 – sufficient condition of loose correctness, sequences.* State s is loosely correct at milestone $(1, L)$ vis-à-vis initial state s_0 if

$$s \in D_2\ \wedge\ F_2(s) = F(s_0).$$

Proof. The future function of this program at milestone $(1, L)$ is

$$ftr = [st_2].$$

Because $s \in D_2$, $[st_2](s) = F_2(s)$. By hypothesis, $F_2(s) = F(s_0)$.   [QED]

- *Proposition 6 – sufficient condition of loose recoverability, sequences.* State s is loosely recoverable at milestone $(1, L)$ vis-à-vis initial state s_0 if

$$F_2(s) = F(s_0).$$

Proof. By hypothesis, there exists a routine r_2 that is correct with respect to J_2. Because $\mathrm{dom}(J_2)$ equals S, so does $\mathrm{dom}([r_2])$. Hence

$[r_2](s)$ is defined. Also, from the correctness of r_2 with respect to J_2, we deduce two results:

$$F_2(s) = F_2([r_2](s)),$$
$$[r_2](s) \in D_2$$

(the reader may look at the expression of J_2 to convince himself). The crux of this proof is to show that state s which verifies

$$F_2(s) = F(s_0)$$

is l-recoverable, by means of routine r_2; in other words, we must prove that $ftr([r_2](s)) = F(s_0)$. Now,

$$
\begin{array}{ll}
ftr([r_2](s)) & \\
= [st_2]([r_2](s)) & ftr = [st_2], \\
= F_2([r_2](s)) & [r_2](s) \in D_2, \\
= F_2(s) & F_2(s) = F_2([r_2](s)), \\
= F(s_0) & \text{hypothesis.} \qquad\qquad \text{[QED]}
\end{array}
$$

See Figure 9.4 for an illustration of the results of Propositions 4, 5 and 6.

Example 5. We consider the program presented in Example 4. State s is strictly correct at milestone $(1, L)$ if and only if

$$s = s_0^2 + 1.$$

State s is loosely correct at milestone $(1, L)$ if

$$s \geq 0 \wedge \text{sqrt}(|s|) = \text{sqrt}(s_0^2 + 1).$$

This can be rewritten as

$$s = s_0^2 + 1.$$

There exists a unique l-correct state, namely the s-correct state. This is due to the injectivity of function future ($[st_2]$, in this case). As we know from the definitions, l-correctness depends in general on the non-injectivity of function future. State s is loosely recoverable at milestone $(1, L)$ if

$$\text{sqrt}(|s|) = \text{sqrt}(s_0^2 + 1)$$
$$\Leftrightarrow$$
$$|s| = s_0^2 + 1.$$

There exists two l-recoverable states at milestone $(1, L)$: state $(s_0^2 + 1)$, which is loosely and strictly correct; and state $-(s_0^2 + 1)$, which is not l-correct, but which can be mapped by r_2 into an l-correct state. At this milestone, we cannot afford to lose the absolute value of s. We can,

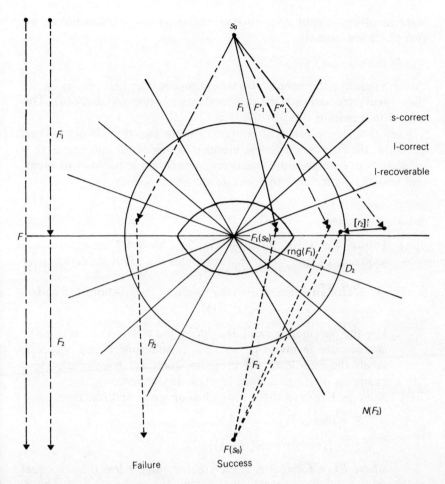

s-correct

l-correct

l-recoverable

Failure   Success

Figure 9.4

however, lose the sign of s and still recover: procedure r_2 will retrieve it and pass the control back to function future.   □

In summary, the equations of forward error recovery in sequence statements exhibit much the same features as those of **while** statements: loose correctness is characterized by the conjunction of two predicates, of the form

$$u(s) \wedge b(s_0, s),$$

where u is a unary predicate involving s alone, while b is a binary predicate involving s_0 and s; and loose recoverability is characterized by one predicate, namely

$b(s_0, s)$.

As with iterative statements, it is natural to consider that $b(s_0, s)$ carries the critical information of the program's state, while $u(s)$ carries its non-critical information.

Even though the practical interest of these equations is not beyond question, they are nevertheless useful in terms of the mechanics they exhibit about how program functions interact in a sequence statement, and how they contribute to generate state redundancy.

9.4.4 Exercises

1[A] Follow the steps described in Section 9.4.2 to construct a sequence of statements that computes the following function:

> S = **real**,
>
> $F = \{(s, s') | s' = \log(s^2 + 1)\}$.

Use the parameters exhibited during the construction process to characterize levels of correctness at milestone $(1, L)$, where L labels the middle of the program. Interpret your results; give examples of states in each level of correctness.

2[B] Same as Exercise 1, for the following space and function:

> S = **real**,
>
> $F = \{(s, s') | s' = E(s^3 - 1)\}$,

where $E(x)$, for real x, is the greatest integer less than or equal to x.

3[B] Same as Exercise 1, for the following space and function:

> S = **natural**,
>
> $F = \{(s, s') | s' = (s + 5) \bmod 4\}$.

4[B] Same as Exercise 1, for the following space and function:

> S = $\{\langle a, b \rangle : a \in \textbf{natural} \wedge b \in \textbf{natural}\}$,
>
> $F = \{(s, s') | a(s') = (a(s) + b(s)) \text{ div } 6\}$.

9.5 PROBLEMS

1[R]   This exercise demonstrates the necessity of the conditions of l-correctness and l-recoverability. Discuss whether the sufficient condition of l-correctness, given in Proposition 2, and the sufficient condition of l-recoverability, given in Proposition 3, are necessary.

2[R]   This exercise discusses the generality of the programming heuristic. Consider the programming heuristic given in Section 9.2.3. It is natural to consider that any function F can be computed by an initialized **while** statement. Yet, it does not seem that any function F can be processed by the heuristic proposed; hence this heuristic lacks generality:

   (a) Give a brute force characterization of functions that can be processed by this heuristic.
   (b) Find simple sufficient conditions that ensure that a given function can be processed by this heuristic.

3[B]   Examples of recoverable sequence programs. Find a function F, a decomposition $F = F_1 * F_2$, and a sequence statement:

   begin st1; L: st2 **end**

   such that the sets of s-correct states, l-correct states and l-recoverable states are identical. Show a method for finding it.

4[B]   Examples of recoverable sequence programs. Find a function F, a decomposition $F = F_1 * F_2$, and a sequence statement

   begin st1; L: st2 **end**

   such that the set of s-correct states is identical to the set of l-correct states, and is a proper subset of the set of l-recoverable states. Show a method for finding it.

5[B]   Examples of recoverable sequence programs. Find a function F, a decomposition $F = F_1 * F_2$, and a sequence statement

   begin st1; L: st2 **end**

   such that the set of s-correct states, l-correct states, and l-recoverable states are distinct. Show a method for finding it.

6[R]   In Section 9.2.2, three questions were asked about the relationship between functions F and W in the programming heuristic. Two of these questions remain open, namely: for any given function F, is there a unique ('reasonable') function W that works? How do we extract W from F? Study this question in detail.

9.6 BIBLIOGRAPHICAL NOTES

The results of this chapter are derived from Mili (1985), equations of recoverability, and Mili *et al.* (1987), programming heuristics, to which the interested reader is referred for further details. The notions of preservation equations and termination equations (used in Section 9.3) are borrowed from Linger *et al.* (1979) and Mills *et al.* (1986).

CHAPTER 10

Forward error recovery: non-deterministic specifications

We saw in Chapter 4 that a state may fail to be loosely correct, yet be mapped by the function future onto a state that is considered correct by the specification; we then say that the state is specificationwise correct. Similarly, a state may fail to be loosely recoverable, yet contain sufficient information to be mapped by a recovery routine onto a specificationwise correct state; we then say that the state is specificationwise recoverable.

In this chapter, more so than in the preceding chapter, we focus our attention on initialized **while** statements. In Section 10.1, we present a heuristic for deriving an initialized **while** statement from a non-deterministic specification, prove its validity, and illustrate it with examples. This heuristic offers the priviledge of exhibiting the parameters we need to discuss forward error recovery. In Section 10.3, we give sufficient conditions of specificationwise correctness and specificationwise recoverability, discuss their significance, and illustrate their use with graduated examples. The equations in Section 10.3 involve the kernel of R rather intensively; now, it is usually difficult to compute the kernel of a relation using the definition (Chapter 1) and in Section 10.2, we discuss ways to compute it efficiently.

10.1 THE DESIGN OF INITIALIZED WHILE STATEMENTS

10.1.1 A Programming Heuristic

Let R be a specification (relation) on space S such that $\mathrm{dom}(R) = S$. We propose to write an initialized **while** statement that is correct with respect to R. If R is deterministic, then the heuristic given in Chapter 9 can be applied to it. For non-deterministic specifications, we must devise an alternative heuristic.

- *Theorem 1 – derivation of an initialized **while** statement for nondeterministic specifications.* Let R be a relation on space S such that $\text{dom}(R) = S$, and let J and W be functions on S such that

  (a) $I(\text{rng}(W)) * W = I(\text{rng}(W))$,
  (b) $\text{dom}(J) = S$,
  (c) $\text{rng}(J) \subseteq \text{dom}(W \cap R)$,
  (d) $J * R \subseteq R$.

  Then $J * W$ is more-defined than R, whence it stems that if program i computes J and **while** statement w computes W, then the program

  > **begin** i;w **end**

  is correct with respect to R.

Proof. In order to prove that $J * W$ is more-defined than R, we prove the two following lemmas:

(i) $\text{dom}(R) \subseteq \text{dom}(J * W)$;
(ii) $\forall s, s \in \text{dom}(R) \Rightarrow s \cdot (J * W) \subseteq s \cdot R$.

Proof of (i). In order to prove $\text{dom}(R) \subseteq \text{dom}(J * W)$, we will prove $\text{dom}(J * W) = S$. Now, if $\text{rng}(J) \subseteq \text{dom}(W)$, then (relational identity) $\text{dom}(J * W)$ equals $\text{dom}(J)$, which by Hypothesis (b) equals S. Hence all we have to do is prove $\text{rng}(J) \subseteq \text{dom}(W)$, which stems readily from Hypothesis (c).

Proof of (ii). Because $\text{dom}(R) = S$, (ii) can be written as

$$\forall s, s \cdot (J * W) \subseteq s \cdot R$$
$$\Leftrightarrow$$
$$J * W \subseteq R.$$

Now,

$$
\begin{aligned}
J * W &= J * I(\text{rng}(J)) * W && \text{postrestriction of } J \text{ to its range,}\\
&\subseteq J * I(\text{dom}(W \cap R)) * W && \text{by hypothesis (c),}\\
&= J * I(\text{dom}(W \cap R)) * R && \text{an identity,}\\
&\subseteq J * R && \text{because } I(S') \subseteq I, \text{ for all } S',\\
&\subseteq R && \text{by hypothesis (d).} \qquad \text{[QED]}
\end{aligned}
$$

10.1.2   An Illustrative Example

We use a simple example to illustrate the mechanics of the programming heuristic given above:

Example 1. Let S be the space defined by

$$S = \{\langle a, k, x \rangle \,|\, a\text{: \textbf{array} } [1 .. n] \textbf{ of real};$$
$$k\text{: \textbf{integer}};$$
$$x\text{: \textbf{real}}\}$$

and let $0 \le k \le n + 1$, where $n \ge 1$. Let R be the relation

$$R = \{(s,s') \,|\, x(s') = \sum_{i=1}^{n} a(s)[i]\},$$

where sum(a') is 0 if the array is empty, and equal to the sum of all the elements of the array if it is not empty. We propose

$$W = \{(s,s') \,|\, a(s') = a(s)$$
$$\wedge\ k(s') = n + 1 \wedge x(s') = x(s) + \sum_{i=k(s)}^{n} a(s)[i]\}$$
$$J\ = \{(s,s') \,|\, a(s') = a(s) \wedge k(s') = 1 \wedge x(s') = 0\},$$

where

a'[i .. j] is: if i > j then the empty array
else the subarray (a'[i], a '[i + 1], ... a'[j])
a'[1 .. n] will be abbreviated by a'.

Function W can be computed by

w = while k ≠ n + 1 **do begin** x := x + a[k]; k := k + 1 **end**,

and function J can be computed by

i = **begin** k := 1; x := 0. **end**.

We verify in turn that Conditions (a), (b), (c) and (d) of Theorem 1 are satisfied.

Condition (a). The range of W is $\text{rng}(W) = \{s \,|\, k(s) = n + 1\}$.

$$I(\text{rng}(W)) * W = \{(s,s') \,|\, k(s) = n + 1 \wedge a(s') = a(s) \wedge k(s') = n + 1$$
$$\wedge\ x(s') = x(s) + \sum_{i=n+1}^{n} a(s)[i]\}$$
$$= \{(s,s') \,|\, k(s) = n + 1 \wedge s' = s\}$$
$$= I(\text{rng}(W)).$$

Condition (b)

$$\text{dom}(J) = \{ss'\text{: } a(s') = a(s) \wedge k(s') = 1 \wedge x(s') = 0\}$$
$$= S.$$

Condition (c)

$$W \cap R = \{(s,s') \,|\, a(s') = a(s) \wedge k(s') = n + 1$$

$$\wedge\; x(s') = x(s) + \sum_{i=k(s)}^{n} a(s)[i]$$

$$\wedge\; x(s') = \sum_{i=1}^{n} a(s)[i]$$

$$= \{(s,s') \mid \sum_{i=1}^{n} a(s)[i] = x(s) + \sum_{i=k(s)}^{n} a(s)[i]$$

$$\wedge\; a(s') = a(s) \wedge k(s') = n + 1$$

$$\wedge\; x(s') = \sum_{i=1}^{n} a(s)[i]\}$$

$$= \{(s,s') \mid x(s) = \sum_{i=1}^{k(s)-1} a(s)[i]\}.$$

$$\wedge\; a(s') = a(s) \wedge k(s') = n + 1$$

$$\wedge\; x(s') = \sum_{i=1}^{n} a(s)[i]\}.$$

$$\text{dom}(W \cap R) = \{s \mid x(s) = \sum_{i=1}^{k(s)-1} a(s)[i]\}.$$

$$\text{rng}(J) = \{s \mid k(s) = 1 \wedge x(s) = 0\}.$$

Clearly, $\text{rng}(J) \subseteq \text{dom}(W \cap R)$.
  Condition (d)

$$J * R = \{(s,s') \mid a(s') = a(s) \wedge k(s') = 1 \wedge x(s') = 0\}$$

$$* \;\{(s,s') \mid x(s') = \sum_{i=1}^{n} \mathbf{a}(s)[i]\}$$

$$= \{(s,s') \mid x(s') = \sum_{i=1}^{n} \mathbf{a}(s)[i]\}$$

$$= R$$

$$\subseteq R.$$

10.1.3 Exercises

1[A] Apply the programming heuristic proposed in this section to the following specification:

$$S = \{\langle a, b\rangle \mid a \in \textbf{integer} \wedge b \in \textbf{natural}\},$$

$$R = \{(s,s') \mid a(s') = a(s) + b(s)\}.$$

Specifically, you must:

(a) propose possible functions J and W,
(b) check that the functions proposed meets Conditions (a), (b), (c) and (d) of the heuristic,

(c) find a program segment i that is correct with respect to specification J,

(d) find a **while** statement w that computes function W.

Once these steps are followed, you will find that the program

> **begin** i; w end

is correct with respect to specification R.

2[A] Same as Exercise 1:

$$S = \{\langle a,b\rangle | a \in \textbf{integer} \wedge b \in \textbf{natural}\},$$

$$R = \{(s,s')|b(s') = 0\}.$$

3[A] Same as Exercise 1:

$$S = \{\langle a,b\rangle | a \in \textbf{natural}^* \wedge b \in \textbf{natural}^*\},$$

where $\textbf{natural}^* = \textbf{natural} - \{0\}$,

$$R = \{(s,s')|a(s') = \gcd(s)\},$$

where $\gcd(s)$ is the greatest common divisor of $a(s)$ and $b(s)$.

4[A] Same as Exercise 1:

$$S = \{\langle a,b\rangle | a \in \textbf{natural}^* \wedge b \in \textbf{natural}^* \},$$

where $\textbf{natural}^* = \textbf{natural} - \{0\}$,

$$R = \{(s,s')|a(s') = b(s')\}.$$

5[A] Same as Exercise 1:

$$S = \{\langle n,f\rangle | n \in \textbf{natural} \wedge f \in \textbf{natural}^*\},$$

$$R = \{(s,s')|f(s') = n(s)!\}.$$

6[A] Same as Exercise 1:

$$S = \{\langle a,b,c\rangle | a \in \textbf{integer} \wedge b \in \textbf{natural} \wedge c \in \textbf{integer}\},$$

$$R = \{(s,s')|c(s') = a(s)^{b(s)}\}.$$

7[B] Same as Exercise 1:

$$S = \{\langle a,i,x\rangle | \text{a: } \textbf{array } [1 .. \text{n}] \textbf{ of real};$$
$$\text{i: } 0 .. \text{n} + 1;$$
$$\text{x: } \textbf{real}\},$$

$$R = \{(s,s')|x(s') = \sum_{i=1}^{n} a(s)[i]$$

8[B] Same as Exercise 1:

$$S = \{\langle a,i,x\rangle \,|\, a: \textbf{array } [1\,..\,n]\textbf{ of real};$$
$$i:\ 0\,..\,n+1;$$
$$x: \textbf{real}\},$$
$$R = \{(s,s')\,|\,a(s') = a(s) \wedge x(s') = \sum_{i=1}^{n} a(s)[i]$$

9[B]   Same as Exercise 1:

$$S = \{\langle a,i,x\rangle \,|\, a: \textbf{array } [1\,..\,n]\textbf{ of real};$$
$$i:\ 0\,..\,n+1;$$
$$x: \textbf{real}\},$$
$$R = \{(s,s')\,|\,i(s') = n+1 \wedge x(s') = \sum_{i=1}^{n} a(s)[i]$$

10[B]   Same as Exercise 1:

$$S = \{\langle a,i,m\rangle \,|\, a: \textbf{array } [1\,..\,n]\textbf{ of real};$$
$$i:\ 0\,..\,n+1;$$
$$m: \textbf{real}\},$$
$$R = \{(s,s')\,|\,a(s') = a(s) \wedge m(s') = \max(a(s))\},$$

where $\max(a)$, for array a, is the largest value contained in array a.

11[B]   Same as Exercise 1:

$$S = \{\langle a,i,m\rangle \,|\, a: \textbf{array } [1\,..\,n]\textbf{ of real};$$
$$i:\ 0\,..\,n+1;$$
$$m: \textbf{real}\},$$
$$R = \{(s,s')\,|\,i(s') = n+1 \wedge m(s') = \max(a(s))\},$$

where $\max(a)$, for array a, is the largest value contained in array a.

12[B]   Same as Exercise 1:

$$S = \{\langle a,i,m\rangle \,|\, a: \textbf{array } [1\,..\,n]\textbf{ of real};$$
$$i:\ 0\,..\,n+1;$$
$$m: \textbf{real}\},$$
$$R = \{(s,s')\,|\,a(s') = a(s) \wedge i(s') = n+1\}.$$

13[B]   Same as Exercise 1. Even though this specification is deterministic, it is recommended that you apply the heuristic that is proposed for non-deterministic specifications:

$$S = \{\langle a,i,m\rangle \,|\, a: \textbf{array } [1\,..\,n]\textbf{ of real};$$
$$i:\ 0\,..\,n+1;$$
$$m: \textbf{real}\},$$

$$R = \{(s,s') \mid a(s') = a(s) \land i(s') = n+1$$
$$\land \ m(s') = \max(a(s))\}.$$

where $\max(a)$, for array a, is the largest value contained in array a.

14[B] Same as Exercise 1:

$S = \{\langle a, i, x, f \rangle \mid a:$ **array** $[1..n]$ **of real**;
   $\quad i:\ 0..n+1;$
   $\quad x:$ **real**;
   $\quad f:$ **boolean**$\}$,

$$R = \{(s,s') \mid a(s') = a(s) \land i(s') = n+1$$
$$\land \ x(s') = x(s) \land f(s') = (x(s) \in a(s))\}.$$

15[B] Same as Exercise 1:

$S = \{\langle a, i, x, f \rangle \mid a:$ **array** $[1..n]$ **of real**;
   $\quad i:\ 0..n+1;$
   $\quad x:$ **real**;
   $\quad f:$ **boolean**$\}$,

$$R = \{(s,s') \mid a(s') = a(s) \land x(s') = x(s)$$
$$\land \ f(s') = (x(s) \in a(s))\}.$$

16[B] Same as Exercise 1:

$S = \{\langle a, i, x, f \rangle \mid a:$ **array** $[1..n]$ **of real**;
   $\quad i:\ 0..n+1;$
   $\quad x:$ **real**;
   $\quad f:$ **boolean**$\}$,

$$R = \{(s,s') \mid i(s') = n+1 \land x(s') = x(s)$$
$$\land \ f(s') = (x(s) \in a(s))\}.$$

17[B] Same as Exercise 1:

$S = \{\langle a, i, x, f \rangle \mid a:$ **array** $[1..n]$ **of real**;
   $\quad i:\ 0..n+1;$
   $\quad x:$ **real**;
   $\quad f:$ **boolean**$\}$,

$$R = \{(s,s') \mid a(s') = a(s) \land i(s') = n+1$$
$$\land \ f(s') = (x(s) \in a(s))\}.$$

18[B] Same as Exercise 1:

$S = \{\langle a, i, x, f \rangle \mid a:$ **array** $[1..n]$ **of real**;
   $\quad i:\ 0..n+1;$

x: **real**;
f: **boolean**},

$$R = \{(s,s')\,|\,a(s') = a(s) \land i(s') = n + 1 \\ \land\ x(s') = (x(s)\}.$$

19[B]   Same as Exercise 1:

S = {⟨a, i, x, f⟩ | a: **array** [1 .. n] **of real**;
i: 0 .. n + 1;
x: **real**;
f: **boolean**},

$$R = \{(s,s')\,|\,f(s') = (x(s) \in a(s))\}.$$

20[B]   Same as Exercise 1:

S = {⟨a, i, x, f⟩ | a: **array** [1 .. n] **of real**;
i: 0 .. n + 1;
x: **real**;
f: **boolean**},

$$R = \{(s,s')\,|\,a(s') = a(s) \land i(s') = n + 1\}.$$

21[B]   Same as Exercise 1:

S = {⟨a, i, x, f⟩ | a: **array** [1 .. n] **of real**;
i: 0 .. n + 1;
x: **real**;
f: **boolean**},

$$R = \{(s,s')\,|\,i(s') = n + 1 \land f(s') = (x(s) \in a(s))\}.$$

22[B]   Same as Exercise 1:

S = {⟨a, i, x, f⟩ | a: **array** [1 .. n] **of real**;
i: 0 .. n + 1;
x: **real**;
f: **boolean**},

$$R = \{(s,s')\,|\,i(s') = n + 1 \land f(s') = (x(s') \in a(s'))\}.$$

23[B]   Same as Exercise 1:

S = {⟨a, i⟩ | a: **array** [1 .. n] **of real**;
i: 0 .. n + 1};

$$R\ \{(s,s')\,|\,a(s') = \text{sort}(a(s))\},$$

where sort(a) is the sorted permutation of array a.

24[B]   Same as Exercise 1:

$$S = \{\langle a,i\rangle | a: \textbf{array } [1 \ .. \ n] \textbf{ of real};$$
$$i: \ 0 \ .. \ n+1\};$$

$$R \ \{(s,s') | \text{sorted}(a(s')) \ \wedge \ i(s') = n+1\},$$

where sorted(a) means that array a is sorted.

25[B]   Same as Exercise 1:

$$S = \{\langle a,i\rangle | a: \textbf{array } [1 \ .. \ n] \textbf{ of real};$$
$$i: \ 0 \ .. \ n+1\};$$

$$R = \{(s,s') | \text{perm}(a(s'), a(s)) \ \wedge \ i(s') = n+1\},$$

where perm(a,a') means that array a is a permutation of array a'.

10.2   COMPUTING KERNELS

In order to characterize levels of specificationwise correctness and specificationwise recoverability, one must compute the kernel of the specification at hand. In practice, computing $K(R)$ proves to be a difficult task. However, we have found that for regular relations, the kernel takes a special form. In this section, we first discuss the form that $K(R)$ takes when R is regular, and then we study the impact of this property on our study.

10.2.1   The Kernel of Regular relations

As a reminder (from Chapter 1), let's mention that the kernel of a relation R is:

$$K(R) = \{(s,s') | \varnothing \neq s' \cdot R \subseteq s \cdot R\},$$

and that the nucleus of relation R is:

$$N(R) = R * R^\wedge.$$

We have the proposition:

- *Proposition 1.* Let R be a regular relation. Then the kernel of R equals its nucleus.

Proof. Given a regular relation R, we compute its kernel:

$$K(R) = \{(s,s') | \varnothing \neq s' \cdot R \subseteq s \cdot R\} \quad \text{by definition,}$$

$$\subseteq \{(s,s')|s' \cdot R \cap s \cdot R \neq \emptyset\} \quad \text{since } s' \cdot R \neq \emptyset,$$
$$= \{(s,s')|\exists s'': (s,s'') \in R \wedge (s',s'') \in R\} \quad \text{by definition of}$$
$$\text{intersection,}$$
$$= \{(s,s')|\exists s'': (s,s'') \in R \wedge (s'',s') \in R^{\hat{}}\} \quad \text{by definition of}$$
$$\text{inversion,}$$
$$= R * R^{\hat{}} \quad \text{by definition of relative product,}$$
$$= N(R) \quad \text{by definition of nucleus.}$$

On the other hand,

$$R * R^{\hat{}} = \{(s,s')|\exists s'': (s,s'') \in R \wedge (s'',s') \in R^{\hat{}}\} \quad \text{by definition of}$$
$$\text{relative product,}$$
$$= \{(s,s')|\exists s'': (s,s'') \in R \wedge (s',s'') \in R\} \quad \text{by definition of}$$
$$\text{inversion,}$$
$$= \{(s,s')|s' \cdot R \cap s \cdot R \neq \emptyset\} \quad \text{due to the existence of } s'',$$

$$\subseteq \{(s,s')|\emptyset \neq s' \cdot R \wedge s \cdot R' = s \cdot R\} \quad \text{due to the regularity}$$
$$\text{or } R,$$
$$\subseteq \{(s,s')|\emptyset \neq s' \cdot R \subseteq s \cdot R\} \quad \text{by generalization,}$$
$$= K(R) \quad \text{by definition.}$$

Hence $K(R = N(R)$. [QED]

The interest of Proposition 1 stems from $N(R)$ being easier to compute than $K(R)$: whenever R is regular, we can compute $N(R)$ instead of $K(R)$. Proposition 1 yields an interesting corollary which we present below.

- *Proposition 2*. If R is regular, then its kernel is an equivalence relation on dom(R).

Proof. We admit that, for any relation R, $K(R)$ is transitive, and $N(R)$ is symmetric and reflexive on dom(R). If R is regular, then $K(R) = N(R)$ is an equivalence relation on dom(R). [QED]

Example 2. Let space S be defined by

$$S = \{\langle n,f,k \rangle | n \in \text{natural} \wedge f \in \text{natural} \wedge k \in \text{natural}\},$$

where $k(s) \leq n(s) + 1$. Let R be the specification

$$R = \{(s,s')|f(s') = n(s)!\}.$$

Given that we must compute $K(R)$, let us check whether R is regular. Clearly, dom(R) = S. To prove the regularity of R, we prove that R is uniform (by virtue of Proposition 12 of Chapter 1); let x and y be such that

$$x \cdot R \cap y \cdot r \neq \emptyset.$$

By definition,

$$\exists s_0: f(s_0) = n(x)! \wedge f(s_0) = n(y)!.$$

Now,

$$x \cdot R = \{s \mid f(s) = n(x)!\},$$

and

$$y \cdot R = \{s \mid f(s) = n(y)!\}.$$

Hence

$$x \cdot R = \{s \mid f(s) = f(s_0)\} = y \cdot R.$$

Therefore, R is regular, whence we deduce by virtue of Proposition 1 that

$$\begin{aligned} K(R) &= R * R^\wedge \\ &= \{(s,s') \mid \exists s'': f(s'') = n(s)! \wedge f(s'') = n(s')!\} \\ &= \{(s,s') \mid n(s)! = n(s')!\}. \end{aligned} \qquad \Box$$

Example 3. We define space S by:

$$\begin{aligned} S = \{\langle a, k, x \rangle \mid &a: \textbf{array } [1 \ldots n] \textbf{ of natural}; \\ &k: 0 \ldots n+1; \\ &x: \textbf{natural}\}, \end{aligned}$$

where n is some positive integer. We admit that all the cells of array a are distinct. Let R be

$$R = \{(s,s') \mid x(s') = \max(a(s))\}.$$

Given that we must compute $K(R)$, let us check whether R is regular. Clearly, $\mathrm{dom}(R) = S$. Again, we prove the uniformity of R instead; we take u and v such that

$$u \cdot R \cap v \cdot r \neq \emptyset.$$

By definition,

$$\exists s_0: x(s_0) = \max(a(u)) \wedge x(s_0) = \max(a(v)).$$

Now,

$$u \cdot R = \{s \mid x(s) = \max(a(u))\},$$

and

$$v \cdot R = \{s \,|\, x(s) = \max(a(v))\}.$$

Hence

$$u \cdot R = \{s \,|\, x(s) = x(s_0)\} = v \cdot R.$$

Hence we deduce, by Proposition 1, that

$$K(R) = R * R\hat{}$$
$$= \{(s, s') \,|\, \max(a(s)) = \max(a(s'))\}. \qquad \square$$

10.2.2   Exercises

1[A]   Compute the kernel of the following specifications, using the results of Chapter 1, and Proposition 1 of this chapter; use Proposition 2 to check your result.

$$S = \{\langle a, b \rangle \,|\, a \in \textbf{integer} \wedge b \in \textbf{natural}\},$$

$$R = \{(s, s') \,|\, a(s') = a(s) + b(s)\}.$$

2[A]   Same as Exercise 1:

$$S = \{\langle a, b \rangle \,|\, a \in \textbf{integer} \wedge b \in \textbf{natural}\},$$

$$R = \{(s, s') \,|\, b(s') = 0\}.$$

3[A]   Same as Exercise 1:

$$S = \{\langle a, b \rangle \,|\, a \in \textbf{natural}^* \wedge b \in \textbf{natural}^*\},$$

where $\textbf{natural}^* = \textbf{natural} - \{0\}$,

$$R = \{(s, s') \,|\, a(s') = \gcd(s)\},$$

where $\gcd(s)$ is the greatest common divisor of $a(s)$ and $b(s)$.

4[A]   Same as Exercise 1:

$$S = \{\langle a, b \rangle \,|\, a \in \textbf{natural}^* \wedge b \in \textbf{natural}^*\},$$

where $\textbf{natural}^* = \textbf{natural} - \{0\}$,

$$R = \{(s, s') \,|\, a(s') = b(s')\}.$$

5[A]   Same as Exercise 1:

$$S = \{\langle n, f \rangle \,|\, n \in \textbf{natural} \wedge f \in \textbf{natural}^*\},$$

$$R = \{(s, s') \,|\, f(s') = n(s')!\}.$$

6[A]   Same as Exercise 1:

$S = \{\langle a, b, c \rangle \mid a \in \textbf{integer} \wedge b \in \textbf{natural} \wedge c \in \textbf{integer}\}$,

$R = \{(s, s') \mid c(s') = a(s)^{b(s)}\}$.

7[B]   Same as Exercise 1:

$S = \{\langle a, i, x \rangle \mid$ a: **array** $[1 .. n]$ **of real**;
                i: $0 .. n + 1$;
                x: **real**$\}$,

$R = \{(s, s') \mid x(s') = \sum\limits_{i=1}^{n} a(s)[i]$

8[B]   Same as Exercise 1:

$S = \{\langle a, i, x \rangle \mid$ a: **array** $[1 .. n]$ **of real**;
                i: $0 .. n + 1$;
                x: **real**$\}$,

$R = \{(s, s') \mid a(s') = a(s) \wedge x(s')$

$= \sum\limits_{i=1}^{n} a(s)[i]$

9[B]   Same as Exercise 1:

$S = \{\langle a, i, x \rangle \mid$ a: **array** $[1 .. n]$ **of real**;
                i: $0 .. n + 1$;
                x: **real**$\}$,

$R = \{(s, s') \mid i(s') = n + 1 \wedge x(s')$

$= \sum\limits_{i=1}^{n} a(s)[i]$

10[B]   Same as Exercise 1:

$S = \{\langle a, i, m \rangle \mid$ a: **array** $[1 .. n]$ **of real**;
                i: $0 .. n + 1$;
                m: **real**$\}$,

$R = \{(s, s') \mid a(s') = a(s) \wedge m(s') = \max(a(s))\}$,

where $\max(a)$, for array a, is the largest value contained in array a.

11[B]   Same as Exercise 1:

$S = \{\langle a, i, m \rangle \mid$ a: **array** $[1 .. n]$ **of real**;
                i: $0 .. n + 1$;
                m: **real**$\}$,

$R = \{(s, s') \mid i(s') = n + 1 \wedge m(s') = \max(a(s))\}$,

where $\max(a)$, for array a, is the largest value contained in array a.

12[B]   Same as Exercise 1:

$$S = \{\langle a,i,m\rangle \,|\, a\text{: \textbf{array} }[1..n]\text{ \textbf{of real}};$$
$$i\text{:   } 0..n+1;$$
$$m\text{: \textbf{real}}\},$$
$$R = \{(s,s')\,|\, a(s') = a(s) \wedge i(s') = n+1\}.$$

13[B]   Same as Exercise 1:

$$S = \{\langle a,i,m\rangle \,|\, a\text{: \textbf{array} }[1..n]\text{ \textbf{of real}};$$
$$i\text{:   } 0..n+1;$$
$$m\text{: \textbf{real}}\},$$
$$R = \{(s,s')\,|\, a(s') = a(s) \wedge i(s') = n+1$$
$$\wedge\, m(s') = \max(a(s))\},$$

where $\max(a)$, for array a, is the largest value contained in array a.

14[B]   Same as Exercise 1:

$$S = \{\langle a,i,x,f\rangle \,|\, a\text{: \textbf{array} }[1..n]\text{ \textbf{of real}};$$
$$i\text{:   } 0..n+1;$$
$$x\text{: \textbf{real}};$$
$$f\text{: \textbf{boolean}}\},$$
$$R = \{(s,s')\,|\, a(s') = a(s) \wedge i(s') = n+1 \wedge x(s') = x(s)$$
$$\wedge\, f(s') = (x(s) \in a(s))\}.$$

15[B]   Same as Exercise 1:

$$S = \{\langle a,i,x,f\rangle \,|\, a\text{: \textbf{array} }[1..n]\text{ \textbf{of real}};$$
$$i\text{:   } 0..n+1;$$
$$x\text{: \textbf{real}};$$
$$f\text{: \textbf{boolean}}\},$$
$$R = \{(s,s')\,|\, a(s') = a(s) \wedge x(s') = x(s)$$
$$\wedge\, f(s') = (x(s) \in a(s))\}.$$

16[B]   Same as Exercise 1:

$$S = \{\langle a,i,x,f\rangle \,|\, a\text{: \textbf{array} }[1..n]\text{ \textbf{of real}};$$
$$i\text{:   } 0..n+1;$$
$$x\text{: \textbf{real}};$$
$$f\text{: \textbf{boolean}}\},$$
$$R = \{(s,s')\,|\, i(s') = n+1 \wedge x(s') = x(s)$$
$$\wedge\, f(s') = (x(s) \in a(s))\}.$$

17[B]   Same as Exercise 1:

$$S = \{\langle a,i,x,f\rangle \,|\, a\text{: \textbf{array} }[1..n]\text{ \textbf{of real}};$$
$$i\text{:   } 0..n+1;$$

x: **real**;

f: **boolean**},

$$R = \{(s,s') \mid a(s') = a(s) \land i(s') = n + 1$$
$$\land f(s') = (x(s) \in a(s))\}.$$

18[B]   Same as Exercise 1:

S = {⟨a, i, x, f⟩ | a: **array** [1 .. n] **of real**;

i: 0 .. n + 1;

x: **real**;

f: **boolean**},

$$R = \{(s,s') \mid a(s') = a(s) \land i(s') = n + 1 \land x(s') = x(s)\}.$$

19[B]   Same as Exercise 1:

S = {⟨a, i, x, f⟩ | a: **array** [1 .. n] **of real**;

i: 0 .. n + 1;

x: **real**;

f: **boolean**},

$$R = \{(s,s') \mid f(s') = (x(s) \in a(s))\}.$$

20[B]   Same as Exercise 1:

S = {⟨a, i, x, f⟩ | a: **array** [1 .. n] **of real**;

i: 0 .. n + 1;

x: **real**;

f: **boolean**},

$$R = \{(s,s') \mid a(s') = a(s) \land i(s') = n + 1\}.$$

21[B]   Same as Exercise 1:

S = {⟨a, i, x, f⟩ | a: **array** [1 .. n] **of real**;

i: 0 .. n + 1;

x: **real**;

f: **boolean**},

$$R = \{(s,s') \mid i(s') = n + 1 \land f(s') = (x(s) \in a(s))\}.$$

22[B]   Same as Exercise 1:

S = {⟨a, i, x, f⟩ | a: **array** [1 .. n] **of real**;

i: 0 .. n + 1;

x: **real**;

f: **boolean**},

$$R = \{(s,s') \mid i(s') = n + 1 \land f(s') = (x(s') \in a(s'))\}.$$

23[B]   Same as Exercise 1:

S = {⟨a, i⟩ | a: **array** [1 .. n] **of real**;

i: 0 .. n + 1},

$$R = \{(s,s') \mid a(s') = \text{sort}(a(s))\},$$

where sort(*a*) is the sorted permutation of array *a*.

24[B]   Same as Exercise 1:

$S = \{\langle a,i \rangle | a: \textbf{array } [1 .. n] \textbf{ of real};$
$\qquad i: 0 .. n + 1\},$
$R = \{(s,s') | \text{sorted}(a(s')) \wedge i(s') = n + 1\},$

where sorted(*a*) means that array *a* is sorted.

25[B]   Same as Exercise 1:

$S = \{\langle a,i \rangle | a: \textbf{array } [1 .. n] \textbf{ of real};$
$\qquad i: 0 .. n + 1\},$
$R = \{(s,s') | \text{perm}(a(s'), a(s)) \wedge i(s') = n + 1\},$

where perm(*a*, *a'*) means that array *a* is a permutation of array *a'*.

10.3   EQUATIONS OF SPECIFICATIONWISE RECOVERY

10.3.1   Sufficient Conditions for Specificationwise Recovery

Let *R* be a specification on space *S* and let *p* be an initialized **while** statement

begin i; L: **while** t **do** b **end**

correct with respect to *R* which is derived according to the equations of Theorem 1. We are interested in characterizing sp-correctness and sp-recoverability with respect to some specification *R* for intermediate states at milestone (v, L) in the execution of the **while** statement, vis-à-vis some initial state s_0.

- *Proposition 3 – sp-correctness.* State *s* is sp-correct with respect to *R* at milestone (v, L) vis-à-vis s_0 *if*

$$s \in D \wedge (s_0, s) \in K(R).$$

Proof. State *s* is sp-correct at milestone (v, L) with respect to *R* vis-à-vis s_0 if and only if

$$ftr(s) \in s_0 \cdot R,$$

where *ftr* is the *future* function of the program at milestone (v, L). Now, in Chapter 4 we have established that for any value of *v*, the *future* function of a **while** statement *w* at milestone (v, L) equals $[w]$. Hence the formula of sp-correctness can be written in this case as

$[w](s) \in s_0 \cdot R,$

or, equivalently,

$W(s) \in s_0 \cdot R.$

Let s' be $W(s)$; by definition, $(s, s') \in W$. Because $s \in D$, we have $(s, s) \in I(D)$; hence

$(s, s') \in I(D) * W.$

Because $D = \operatorname{dom}(W \cap R)$ we can write $I(D) * W \subseteq I(D) * R$. Thus

$(s, s') \in I(D) * R,$

from which we deduce $(s, s') \in R$, or $s' \in s \cdot R$. Because $s \cdot R \subseteq s_0 \cdot R$, we have $s' \in s_0 \cdot R$; because $s' = W(s)$, we get $s \cdot W \subseteq s_0 \cdot R$, which can also be written as $W(s) \in s_0 \cdot R$.   [QED]

- *Proposition 4 – sp-recoverability for **while** statements.* State s is sp-recoverable with respect to R at milestone (v, L) vis-à-vis s_0 if

  $(s_0, s) \in K(R).$

  Furthermore, any program that is correct with respect to $K(R) * I(D)$ is a valid recovery routine.

Proof. State s is sp-recoverable if there exists a routine r, independent of s, such that

$ftr([r](s)) \in s_0 \cdot R.$

For routine r, we take the initialization segment i. By virtue of the definition of sp-recoverability and of our choice of recovery routine, we must prove that

$s \cdot [i] * ftr \subseteq s_0 \cdot R.$

Because $ftr = [w] = W$, what we must prove can be written as:

$s \cdot [i] * W \subseteq s_0 \cdot R.$

Now, since i is correct with respect to J, and since $\operatorname{dom}([i]) = \operatorname{dom}(J)$,

$[i] \subseteq J,$

whence

$s \cdot [i] * W \subseteq s \cdot J * W.$ (0)

On the other hand, we have by definition

$J = J * I(\operatorname{rng}(J)),$

whence we deduce, by virtue of Condition (c) of Theorem 1, and of the definition of D,

$J = J * I(D).$

Replacing the left-hand side by the right-hand side in Equation (0), we obtain

$s \cdot [i] * W \subseteq s \cdot J * I(D) * W.$

By the definition of D, $I(D) * W \subseteq I(D) * R$, hence

$$\begin{aligned} s \cdot [i] * W &\subseteq s \cdot J * I(D) * R \\ &\subseteq s \cdot J * R && \text{because } I(D) \subseteq I \\ &= s \cdot R && \text{by Hypothesis (d) of Theorem 1} \\ &\subseteq s_0 \cdot R && \text{by Hypothesis of this proposition.} \end{aligned}$$

Now, let r be a program correct with respect to $K(R) * I(D)$. We must prove that if

$(s_0, s) \in K(R)$

(i.e. if s is sp-recoverable), then $[r](s)$ is sp-correct, i.e. that

$ftr([r](s)) \in s_0 \cdot R.$

Due to the structure of the program at hand, $ftr = [w]$, hence

$s \cdot [r] * ftr = s \cdot [r] * [w].$

Because r is correct with respect $K(R) * I(D)$,

$s \cdot [r] \subseteq s \cdot K(R) * I(D).$

Hence

$s_1[r] * ftr \subseteq s \cdot K(R) * I(D) * [w].$

By definition of D, $I(D) * [w] \subseteq I(R) * R$, hence

$s_1[r] * ftr \subseteq s \cdot K(R) * I(D) * R.$

Because $I(D) \subseteq I$,

$s_1[r] * ftr \subseteq s \cdot K(R) * R.$

Because $(s_0, s) \in K(R)$, we have $s \in s_0 \cdot K(R)$. Hence,

$s_1[r] * ftr \subseteq s_0 \cdot K(R) * K(R) * R.$

By transitivity of $K(R)$,

$s_1[r] * ftr \subseteq s_0 \cdot K(R) * R.$

We analyse

$$
\begin{aligned}
K(R) * R &= \{(s,s') \mid \exists x \colon (s,x) \in K(R) \wedge (x,s') \in R\} \\
&\subseteq \{(s,s') \mid \exists x \colon x \cdot R \subseteq s \cdot R \wedge s' \in x \cdot R\} \\
&\subseteq \{(s,s') \mid s' \in s \cdot R\} \\
&= \{(s,s') \mid (s,s') \in R\} \\
&= R.
\end{aligned}
$$

Hence,

$$
s_1[r] * ftr \subseteq s_0 \cdot R. \qquad\qquad \text{[QED]}
$$

In order to illustrate Propositions 3 and 4, we build on the work of Example 1 and discuss the sp-correctness and sp-recoverability of the sum program with respect to the specification proposed.

Example 4. Consider the program and the specification of Example 1:
Space:

$$
S = \{\langle a, k, x \rangle \colon a \colon \textbf{array } [1 .. n] \textbf{ of real};
$$
$$
k \colon \textbf{integer};
$$
$$
x \colon \textbf{real}\}.
$$

Specification:

$$
R = \{(s,s') \mid x(s') = \sum_{i=1}^{n} a(s)[i]\},
$$

Program:

```
f = begin
    x := 0.0; k := 1;
    L: while k ≠ n + 1 do
        begin x := x + a[k]; k := k + 1 end
    end.
```

Initial state:

$$
s_0 = \langle a_0, k_0, x_0 \rangle,
$$

where

$$
a_0[i] = 2.0 * i, \qquad \text{for all } i \text{ such that } 1 \le i \le n,
$$
$$
k_0 = 0,
$$

and

$$
x_0 = 0.0.
$$

A state s is sp-correct vis-à-vis s_0 with respect to the specification given if

$$s \in \mathrm{dom}(W \cap R) \wedge (s_0, s) \in K(R)$$

In order to compute $K(R)$, we check whether R is regular. We write R as the relative product of a function,

$$\{(s, s') \mid a(s') = a(s) \wedge k(s') = k(s) \wedge x(s') = \sum_{i=1}^{n} a(s)[i]\},$$

with an equivalence relation,

$$\{(s, s') \mid x(s') = x(s)\},$$

and we invoke Proposition 10 of Chapter 1 to deduce that R is regular. Hence the condition above can be written as

$$s \in \mathrm{dom}(W \cap R) \wedge (s_0, s) \in N(R)$$

$\Leftrightarrow$

$$x(s) = \sum_{i=1}^{n} a(s)[i]$$

$$\sum_{i=1}^{n} a(s)[i] = n * (n + 1).$$

A state is sp-correct with respect to R if $x(s)$ contains the partial sum between 1 and $k(s) - 1$ and the total sum of $a(s)$ is identical to the total sum of $a(s_0)$; there is no mention in this condition of the fact that $a(s)$ should be equal to $a(s_0)$ (a necessary condition of l-correctness), nor should there be, since the specification is interested only in the sum of $a(s_0)$ rather than in $a(s_0)$ itself.

• A state s is sp-recoverable vis-à-vis s_0 with respect to R if

$$\sum_{i=1}^{n} a(s)[i] = n * (n + 1).$$

An acceptable recovery routine is any routine that will map s into D without affecting $\sum_{i=1}^{n} a(s)[i]$, but possibly affecting $a(s)$, $k(s)$ and $x(s)$; a trivial recovery routine will merely apply function J, but is not the only routine that will do so.   □

Remark 1. As one would expect, the characterizations given in Propositions 3 and 4 are generalizations of the characterizations given in Chapter 9 for deterministic specifications. Indeed, if R is deterministic, then it is regular and its kernel equals its nucleus. Now, the equations given for deterministic specifications provide precisely that the condition of (loose) recoverability is

$$(s_0, s) \in N(R).$$

As for D, it has the same expression ($\mathrm{dom}(W \cap R)$) in both cases.   □

10.3.2   Illustrative Examples

We further illustrate the formulas of specificationwise recovery by means of three examples, using specifications with varying degrees of determinacy.

In the first example, the specification is moderately non-deterministic. In this case, the characterization of sp-recoverability is identical to that of l-recoverability. In fact, even though this specification is not deterministic, it captures enough of the functional properties of the program at hand.

In the second example, the specification is fairly non-deterministic. Here, the formula of sp-recoverability imposes the condition that the current state carry some information related to the initial state.

In the third and last example, the specification is 'very' non-deterministic. Here, the formula of sp-recoverability makes no mention of the initial state. Consequently, any state is sp-recoverable, regardless of what little relationship it has to the initial state.

These three examples cover, to some extent, the range of possible situations that may arise. First, we start with the moderately non-deterministic specification.

Example 5. Let space S be defined by:

$$S = \{\langle n, f, k \rangle \,|\, n \in \textbf{natural} \,\wedge\, f \in \textbf{natural} \,\wedge\, k \in \textbf{natural}\},$$

where $1 \le k(s) \le n(s) + 1$. Let R be the specification

$$R = \{(s, s') \,|\, f(s') = n(s)!\}.$$

Note that R is non-deterministic because it does not specify values for $n(s')$ and $k(s')$; it does, however, reflect what a user may realistically want from a factorial program with three variables. We have seen in Example 2 above that

$$K(R) = \{(s, s') \,|\, n(s)! = n(s')!\}.$$

Let J and W be the following functions on space S:

$$W = \{(s, s') \,|\, n(s') = n(s) \,\wedge\, k(s') = n(s) + 1 \\ \wedge\, f(s') = f(s) * n(s)!/(k(s) - 1)!\}$$
$$J = \{(s, s') \,|\, n(s') = n(s) \,\wedge\, k(s') = 1 \,\wedge\, f(s') = 1\}.$$

Function W can be computed by

$$w = \textbf{while } k \ne n + 1 \textbf{ do begin } f := f * k;\ k := k + 1 \textbf{ end,}$$

and function J can be computed by

$i =$ **begin** $k := 1$; $f := 1$ **end**.

Equation (a)

$$I(\text{rng}(W)) * W$$
$$= \{(s,s')\,|\,k(s) = n(s) + 1 \,\wedge\, n(s') = n(s) \,\wedge\, k(s') = n + 1$$
$$\wedge\, f(s') = f(s) * n(s)!/(k(s) - 1)!\}$$
$$= \{(s,s')\,|\,k(s) = n + 1 \,\wedge\, n(s') = n(s) \,\wedge\, k(s') = k(s)$$
$$\wedge\, f(s') = f(s)\}$$
$$= I(\text{rng}(W)).$$

Condition (b). Can be readily checked.

Condition (c). First, we have

$$\text{rng}(J) = \{s\,|\,k(s) = 1 \,\wedge\, f(s) = 1\}.$$

On the other hand,

$$W \cap R$$
$$= \{(s,s')\,|\,n(s') = n(s) \,\wedge\, k(s') = n(s) + 1$$
$$\wedge\, f(s') = f(s) * n(s)!/(k(s) - 1)! \,\wedge\, f(s') = n(s)!\}$$
$$= \{(s,s')\,|\,f(s) = (k(s) - 1)! \,\wedge\, n(s') = n(s) \,\wedge\, k(s') = n(s) + 1$$
$$\wedge\, f(s') = n(s)!\}$$

Hence

$$\text{dom}(W \cap R) = \{s = |f(s) = (k(s) - 1)!\}.$$

Clearly, $\text{rng}(J) \subseteq \text{dom}(W \cap R)$.

Condition (d)

$$J * R = \{(s,s')\,|\,n(s') = n(s) \,\wedge\, k(s') = 1 \,\wedge\, f(s') = 1\}$$
$$*$$
$$\{(s,s')\,|\,f(s') = n(s)!\}$$
$$= \{(s,s')\,|\,\exists s'': n(s'') = n(s) \,\wedge\, k(s'') = 1 \,\wedge\, f(s'') = 1$$
$$\wedge\, f(s') = n(s'')!\}$$
$$= \{(s,s')\,|\,f(s') = n(s)! \,\wedge\, \exists s'': n(s'') = n(s) \,\wedge\, k(s'') = 1$$
$$\wedge\, f(s'') = 1\}$$
$$= \{(s,s')\,|\,f(s') = n(s)!\}$$
$$= R.$$

According to Theorem 1, the program

begin $k := 1$; $f := 1$; **while** $k \neq n + 1$ **do begin** $f := f * k$; $k := k + 1$ **end end**,

is correct with respect to specification R.

By Proposition 3, a state is sp-correct vis-à-vis s_0 with respect to specification R if:

$$f(s) = (k(s) - 1)! \,\wedge\, (s_0, s) \in K(R)$$

$\Leftrightarrow$

$$f(s) = (k(s) - 1)! \wedge n(s)! = n(s_0)!.$$

In other words, state s is sp-correct if $f(s)$ is the factorial of $(k(s) - 1)$, and if the factorial of $n(s)$ is preserved. Notice a subtle difference between this condition and the condition of loose correctness found in Example 3 of the preceding chapter; the preceding example provides that s is loosely correct if

$$f(s) = (k(s) - 1)! \wedge n(s) = n(s_0).$$

Now, the conditions $n(s)! = n(s_0)!$ and $n(s) = n(s_0)$ are not quite equivalent, because if $n(s)! = 1$, then $n(s) = 1$ or $n(s) = 0$; for all other values of n, these conditions are equivalent.

If we restrict our attention to non-zero values of n, then the conditions of loose correctness and specificationwise correctness are identical. This calls for the following remark: even though the specification is non-deterministic, the condition of sp-correctness happens to be the same as the condition of l-correctness. This is merely the result of the particular form that the function computed by the program has:

$$J * W = \{(s, s') \mid n(s') = n(s) \wedge k(s') = n(s) + 1 \wedge f(s') = n(s)!\}.$$

Because the final values of all the variables are expressed in terms of a unique initial variable, namely $n(s)$, the non-determinacy of relation R that comes from focusing on a single final variable ($f(s')$, whose expression, $n(s)!$, is invertible) does not result in any difference between sp-correctness and l-correctness.

State s is sp-recoverable with respect to R vis-à-vis s_0 if

$$n(s)! = n(s_0)!.$$

For non-zero values of n, this condition is identical to the condition of loose recoverability, given in the preceding chapter for this same program.   □

We now consider the case of a specification that is fairly non-deterministic. As we shall see, the condition of sp-recoverability will not be as tight as that of Example 5; it will nevertheless require that the current state carry some information pertaining to the initial state, s_0.

Example 6. We define space S by

$S = \{\langle a, k, x \rangle \mid a: \textbf{array } [1 . . n] \textbf{ of natural};$
$\qquad k: 0 . . n + 1;$
$\qquad x: \textbf{natural}\},$

where n is some positive integer. We admit that all the cells of array a are distinct. Let R be

$$R = \{(s,s')\,|\,x(s') = \max(a(s))\}.$$

If we follow a similar pattern as the preceding example, we find

$$K(R) = \{(s,s')\,|\,\max(a(s)) = \max(a(s'))\}.$$

We propose

$$W = \{(s,s')\,|\,a(s') = a(s) \wedge k(s') = n + 1$$
$$\wedge\, x(s') = \max(x(s), \max(a(s)[k(s)\,..\,n]))\},$$
$$J = \{(s,s')\,|\,a(s') = a(s) \wedge k(s') = 1 \wedge x(s') = 0\},$$

where $a'[i\,..\,j]$ is defined as in Example 3, and $\max(a')$, for an array (or subarray) a', is zero if the array is empty, or the maximum value in the array (or subarray) a' if the array is not empty.

Function W can be computed by the following Pascal program:

```
w = while k ≠ n + 1 do
    begin
    if x < a[k] then x := a[k];
    k := k + 1
    end,
```

and function J can be computed by the Pascal program

```
i = begin
    k := 1; x := 0
    end.
```

We check Conditions (a), (b), (c) and (d) of Theorem 1.
Condition (a). The range of W is

$$\mathrm{rng}(W) = \{s\,|\,k(s) = n + 1\}.$$

Now,

$$I(\mathrm{rng}(W)) * W$$
$$= \{(s,s')\,|\,k(s) = n + 1 \wedge a(s') = a(s) \wedge k(s') = n + 1$$
$$\wedge\, x(s') = \max(x(s), \max(a(s)[n + 1\,..\,n]))\}$$
$$= \{(s,s')\,|\,k(s) = n + 1 \wedge a(s') = a(s) \wedge k(s') = k(s)$$
$$\wedge\, x(s') = x(s)\}$$
$$= \{(s,s')\,|\,k(s) = n + 1 \wedge s' = s\}$$
$$= I(\mathrm{rng}(W)).$$

Condition (b)

$$\mathrm{dom}(J) = S.$$

Condition (c)

$$W \cap R = \{(s, s') \mid a(s') = a(s) \wedge k(s') = n + 1 \wedge x(s') = \max(a(s))$$
$$\wedge \; x(s') = \max(x(s), \max(a(s)[k(s) \ .. \ n]))\}$$
$$= \{(s, s') \mid \max(a(s)) = \max(x(s), \max(a(s)[k(s) \ .. n]))$$
$$\wedge \; a(s') = a(s) \wedge k(s') = n + 1 \wedge x(s') = \max(a(s))\}$$
$$\mathrm{dom}(W \cap R) = \{s \mid \max(a(s)) = \max(x(s), \max(a(s)[k(s) \ .. \ n]))\}.$$

On the other hand,

$$\mathrm{rng}(J) = \{s \mid k(s) = 1 \wedge x(s) = 0\}.$$

Let s be an element of $\mathrm{rng}(J)$; s satisfies the condition

$$k(s) = 1 \wedge x(s) = 0.$$

Then,

$$\max(x(s), \max(a(s)[k(s) \ .. \ n]))$$
$$= \max(0, \max(a(s)[1 .. n]))$$
$$= \max(a(s)).$$

Hence

$$s \in \mathrm{dom}(W \cap R).$$

Condition (d)

$$J * R = \{(s, s') \mid a(s') = a(s) \wedge k(s') = 1 \wedge x(s') = 0\}$$
$$*$$
$$\{(s, s') \mid x(s') = \max(a(s))\}$$
$$= \{(s, s') \mid \exists s'' \colon a(s'') = a(s) \wedge k(s'') = 1 \wedge x(s'') = 0$$
$$\wedge \; x(s') = \max(a(s''))\}$$
$$= \{(s, s') \mid x(s') = \max(a(s)) \wedge \exists s'' \colon a(s'') = a(s) \wedge k(s'') = 1$$
$$\wedge \; x(s'') = 0\}$$
$$= \{s, s') \mid x(s') = \max(a(s))\}$$
$$= R.$$

We consider the initial state $s_0 = \langle a_0, k_0, x_0 \rangle$, where

$a_0[i] = i$, for all i between 1 and n,
$k_0 = 1$,
$x_0 = 0$.

State s is sp-correct with respect to R vis-à-vis s_0 if

$$\max(a(s)) = \max(x(s), \max(a(s)[k(s) \ .. \ n]))$$
$$\wedge$$
$$(s_0, s) \in K(R).$$

Because $\max(a(s_0)) = n$, we get

$$\max(a(s)) = \max(x(s), \max(a(s)[k(s) \ .. \ n]))$$
$$\wedge$$
$$\max(a(s)) = n.$$

The first conjunct can be interpreted as follows: the right-hand side of the conjunct expresses what the **while** statement would compute in x if it were executed on state s, while the left-hand side expresses what it must compute. The second conjunct expresses that the max of array $a(s)$ must be the same as that of array $a(s_0)$, so that when the **while** statement is executed on s, it will generate the max of $a(s_0)$.

- State s is sp-recoverable with respect to R vis-à-vis s_0 if

$$\max(a(s)) = n.$$

As long as the information that R is interested in (namely the max of $a(s_0)$) is found in $a(s)$ (by computing the max), then we have an sp-recoverable state.   □

Finally, we consider a specification which is so non-deterministic that any state is sp-recoverable with respect to it. Note that even though it is very non-deterministic, this specification still captures an important functional property of the program.

Example 7. We consider the space defined by:

$$S = \{\langle a, k \rangle \,|\, a: \textbf{array} \ [1 .. n] \ \textbf{of real};$$
$$k: \textbf{integer}\},$$

where n is greater than or equal to 1. We restrict our attention to values of k between 0 and $n + 1$. Let R be the specification defined as

$$R = \{(s, s')\,|\,\text{sorted}(a(s'))\}$$

where sorted(a') means that the array (or subarray) a' is sorted in increasing order. This specification is regular because it is rectangular. We compute its kernel:

$$
\begin{aligned}
K(R) &= N(R) \\
&= R * R\hat{\ } \\
&= (S \times A) * (A \times S), \\
&\quad \text{where } A = \{s\,|\,\text{sorted}(s)\} \\
&= (S \times S) \\
&= U(S).
\end{aligned}
$$

Specification R is doubly non-deterministic: first, it specifies no value for $k(s')$; second, it makes no mention of s; in particular, it does not specify that $a(s')$ is a permutation of $a(s)$. We propose

$$W = \{(s, s') \mid k(s') = n + 1 \wedge a(s)[1 .. k(s) - 1] = a(s')[1 .. k(s) - 1]$$
$$\wedge \text{ sorted}(a(s')[k(s) .. n]) \wedge \text{perm}(a(s), a(s'))\},$$
$$J = \{(s, s') \mid a(s') = a(s) \wedge k(s') = 2\}.$$

Function W captures the behavior of a *selection sort* program. We verify the conditions of Theorem 1.

Condition (a) $\text{rng}(W) = \{s \mid k(s) = n + 1\}$.

$$I(\text{rng}(W)) * W = \{(s, s') \mid k(s) = n + 1 \wedge a(s') = a(s)$$
$$\wedge \; k(s') = n + 1\}$$
$$= \{(s, s') \mid k(s) = n + 1 \wedge s' = s\}$$
$$= I(\text{rng}(W))$$

Condition (b)

$\text{dom}(J) = S$.

Condition (c)

$R \cap W$
$$= \{(s, s') \mid k(s') = n + 1 \wedge a(s)[1 .. k(s) - 1] = a(s')[1 .. k(s) - 1]$$
$$\wedge \text{ sorted}(a(s')[k(s) .. n]) \wedge \text{sorted}(a(s'))$$
$$\wedge \text{ perm}(a(s), a(s'))\}$$
$\text{dom}(W \cap R)$
$$= \{s \mid \exists s': k(s') = n + 1 \wedge a(s)[1 .. k(s) - 1] = a(s')[1 .. k(s) - 1]$$
$$\wedge \text{ sorted}(a(s')[k(s) .. n]) \wedge \text{sorted}(a(s'))$$
$$\wedge \text{ perm}(a(s), a(s'))\}$$
$$= \{s \mid \text{sorted}(a(s)[1 .. k(s) - 1]) \wedge \exists s': k(s') = n + 1$$
$$\wedge \; a(s)[1 .. k(s) - 1] = a(s')[1 .. k(s) - 1]$$
$$\wedge \text{ sorted}(a(s')[k(s) .. n]) \wedge \text{sorted}(a(s'))$$
$$\wedge \text{ perm}(a(s), a(s'))\}$$
$$= \{s \mid \text{sorted}(a(s)[1 .. k(s) - 1])\}.$$
$\text{rng}(J) = \{s \mid k(s) = 2\}$.

Clearly, $\text{rng}(J) \subseteq \text{dom}(W \cap R)$.

Condition (d)

$$J * R = \{(s, s') \mid a(s') = a(s) \wedge k(s') = 2\} * \{(s, s') \mid \text{sorted}(a(s'))\}$$
$$= \{(s, s') \mid \text{sorted}(a(s'))\}$$
$$= R.$$

Now we can apply Propositions 3 and 4. State s is sp-correct with respect to R vis-à-vis s_0 if

$$s \in \text{dom}(W \cap R) \wedge (s_0, s) \in K(R)$$

$\Leftrightarrow$

$$s \in \text{dom}(W \cap R) \wedge (s_0, s) \in U(S)$$

$\Leftrightarrow$

$$s \in \text{dom}(W \cap R).$$

$\Leftrightarrow$

$$\text{sorted}(a(s)[1 \mathinner{.\,.} k(s) - 1]).$$

Because R merely imposes the condition that the final array be sorted, any partially sorted array is sp-correct.

State s is sp-recoverable if
$$(s_0, s) \in K(R)$$

$\Leftrightarrow$

true.

Any state is sp-recoverable with respect to R vis-à-vis s_0: Since R only requires that the final array be sorted, and requires no relationship to the initial array, one can always generate a sorted output array from scratch. $\qquad\qquad\square$

10.3.3 Exercises

1[A]   Use the results of Exercise 1 of Section 10.1.3 and Exercise 1 of Section 10.2.3 to characterize levels of specificationwise recovery for the program constructed from the following specification:

$$\mathsf{S} = \{\langle \mathsf{a}, \mathsf{b}\rangle \,|\, \mathsf{a} \in \textbf{integer} \wedge \mathsf{b} \in \textbf{natural}\},$$

$$R = \{(s, s') \,|\, a(s') = a(s) + b(s)\}.$$

2[A]   Same as Exercise 1, in reference to Exercises 2 of Sections 10.1.3 and 10.2.3:

$$\mathsf{S} = \{\langle \mathsf{a}, \mathsf{b}\rangle \,|\, \mathsf{a} \in \textbf{integer} \wedge \mathsf{b} \in \textbf{natural}\},$$

$$R = \{(s, s') \,|\, b(s') = 0\}.$$

3[A]   Same as Exercise 1, in reference to Exercises 3 of Sections 10.1.3 and 10.2.3:

$$\mathsf{S} = \{\langle \mathsf{a}, \mathsf{b}\rangle \,|\, \mathsf{a} \in \textbf{natural}^* \wedge \mathsf{b} \in \textbf{natural}^*\},$$

where $\textbf{natural}^* = \textbf{natural} - \{0\}$,

$$R = \{(s, s') \,|\, a(s') = \gcd(s)\},$$

where $\gcd(s)$ is the greatest common divisor of $a(s)$ and $b(s)$.

4[A]   Same as Exercise 1, in reference to Exercises 4 of Sections 10.1.3 and 10.2.3:

$S = \{\langle a,b \rangle \,|\, a \in \textbf{natural}^* \wedge b \in \textbf{natural}^*\}$,

where $\textbf{natural}^* = \textbf{natural} - \{0\}$,

$R = \{(s,s') \,|\, a(s') = b(s')\}$.

5[A]   Same as Exercise 1, in reference to Exercises 5 of Sections 10.1.3 and 10.2.3:

$S = \{\langle n,f \rangle \,|\, n \in \textbf{natural} \wedge f \in \textbf{natural}^*\}$,

$R = \{(s,s') \,|\, f(s') = n(s)!\}$.

6[A]   Same as Exercise 1, in reference to Exercises 6 of Sections 10.1.3 and 10.2.3:

$S = \{\langle a,b,c \rangle \,|\, a \in \textbf{integer} \wedge b \in \textbf{natural} \wedge c \in \textbf{integer}\}$,

$R = \{(s,s') \,|\, c(s') = a(s)^{b(s)}\}$.

7[B]   Same as Exercise 1, in reference to Exercises 7 of Sections 10.1.3 and 10.2.3:

$S = \{\langle a,i,x \rangle \,|\, a\text{: } \textbf{array } [1..n] \textbf{ of real};$
$\qquad\qquad i\text{: } 0..n+1;$
$\qquad\qquad x\text{: } \textbf{real}\}$,

$$R = \{(s,s') \,|\, x(s') = \sum_{i=1}^{n} a(s)[i]$$

8[B]   Same as Exercise 1, in reference to Exercises 8 of Sections 10.1.3 and 10.2.3:

$S = \{\langle a,i,x \rangle \,|\, a\text{: } \textbf{array } [1..n] \textbf{ of real};$
$\qquad\qquad i\text{: } 0..n+1;$
$\qquad\qquad x\text{: } \textbf{real}\}$,

$$R = \{(s,s') \,|\, a(s') = a(s) \wedge x(s')$$
$$= \sum_{i=1}^{n} a(s)[i]$$

9[B]   Same as Exercise 1, in reference to Exercises 9 of Sections 10.1.3 and 10.2.3:

$S = \{\langle a,i,x \rangle \,|\, a\text{: } \textbf{array } [1..n] \textbf{ of real};$
$\qquad\qquad i\text{: } 0..n+1;$
$\qquad\qquad x\text{: } \textbf{real}\}$,

$$R = \{(s,s') \,|\, i(s') = n+1 \wedge x(s')$$
$$= \sum_{i=1}^{n} a(s)[i]$$

10[B] Same as Exercise 1, in reference to Exercises 10 of Sections 10.1.3 and 10.2.3:

$$S = \{\langle a,i,m\rangle\,|\,a:\textbf{ array }[1\,..\,n]\textbf{ of real};$$
$$i:\ 0\,..\,n+1;$$
$$m:\textbf{ real}\},$$

$$R = \{(s,s')\,|\,a(s') = a(s) \wedge m(s') = \max(a(s))\},$$

where $\max(a)$, for array a, is the largest value contained in array a.

11[B] Same as Exercise 1, in reference to Exercises 11 of Sections 10.1.3 and 10.2.3:

$$S = \{\langle a,i,m\rangle\,|\,a:\textbf{ array }[1\,..\,n]\textbf{ of real};$$
$$i:\ 0\,..\,n+1;$$
$$m:\textbf{ real}\},$$

$$R = \{(s,s')\,|\,i(s') = n+1 \wedge m(s') = \max(a(s))\},$$

where $\max(a)$, for array a, is the largest value contained in array a.

12[B] Same as Exercise 1, in reference to Exercises 12 of Sections 10.1.3 and 10.2.3:

$$S = \{\langle a,i,m\rangle\,|\,a:\textbf{ array }[1\,..\,n]\textbf{ of real};$$
$$i:\ 0\,..\,n+1;$$
$$m:\textbf{ real}\},$$

$$R = \{(s,s')\,|\,a(s') = a(s) \wedge i(s') = n+1\}.$$

13[B] Same as Exercise 1, in reference to Exercises 13 of Sections 10.1.3 and 10.2.3:

$$S = \{\langle a,i,m\rangle\,|\,a:\textbf{ array }[1\,..\,n]\textbf{ of real};$$
$$i:\ 0\,..\,n+1;$$
$$m:\textbf{ real}\},$$

$$R = \{(s,s')\,|\,a(s') = a(s) \wedge i(s') = n+1$$
$$\wedge\, m(s') = \max(a(s))\},$$

where $\max(a)$, for array a, is the largest value contained in array a.

14[B] Same as Exercise 1, in reference to Exercises 14 of Sections 10.1.3 and 10.2.3:

$$S = \{\langle a,i,x,f\rangle\,|\,a:\textbf{ array }[1\,..\,n]\textbf{ of real};$$
$$i:\ 0\,..\,n+1;$$

x: **real**;

f: **boolean**},

$$R = \{(s,s')| a(s') = a(s) \wedge i(s') = n + 1 \\ \wedge x(s') = x(s) \wedge f(s') = (x(s) \in a(s)))\}.$$

15[B] Same as Exercise 1, in reference to Exercises 15 of Sections 10.1.3 and 10.2.3:

S = {⟨a, i, x, f⟩ | a: **array** [1 .. n] **of real**;

i: 0 .. n + 1;

x: **real**;

f: **boolean**},

$$R = \{(s,s')| a(s') = a(s) \wedge x(s') = x(s) \\ \wedge f(s') = (x(s) \in a(s)))\}.$$

16[B] Same as Exercise 1, in reference to Exercises 16 of Sections 10.1.3 and 10.2.3:

S = {⟨a, i, x, f⟩ | a: **array** [1 .. n] **of real**;

i: 0 .. n + 1;

x: **real**;

f: **boolean**},

$$R = \{(s,s')| i(s') = n + 1 \wedge x(s') = x(s) \\ \wedge f(s') = (x(s) \in a(s)))\}.$$

17[B] Same as Exercise 1, in reference to Exercises 17 of Sections 10.1.3 and 10.2.3:

S = {⟨a, i, x, f⟩ | a: **array** [1 .. n] **of real**;

i: 0 .. n + 1;

x: **real**;

f: **boolean**},

$$R = \{(s,s')| a(s') = a(s) \wedge i(s') = n + 1 \\ \wedge f(s') = (x(s) \in a(s)))\}.$$

18[B] Same as Exercise 1, in reference to Exercises 18 of Sections 10.1.3 and 10.2.3:

S = {⟨a, i, x, f⟩ | a: **array** [1 .. n] **of real**;

i: 0 .. n + 1;

x: **real**;

f: **boolean**},

$$R = \{(s,s')| a(s') = a(s) \wedge i(s') = n + 1 \\ \wedge x(s') = x(s)\}.$$

19[B]   Same as Exercise 1, in reference to Exercises 19 of Sections
10.1.3 and 10.2.3:

$$S = \{\langle a, i, x, f \rangle \,|\, a\colon \textbf{array } [1\,..\,n] \textbf{ of real};$$
$$i\colon \ 0\,..\,n+1;$$
$$x\colon \textbf{ real};$$
$$f\colon \textbf{ boolean}\},$$

$$R = \{(s, s') \,|\, f(s') = (x(s) \in a(s))\}.$$

20[B]   Same as Exercise 1, in reference to Exercises 20 of Sections
10.1.3 and 10.2.3:

$$S = \{\langle a, i, x, f \rangle \,|\, a\colon \textbf{array } [1\,..\,n] \textbf{ of real};$$
$$i\colon \ 0\,..\,n+1;$$
$$x\colon \textbf{ real};$$
$$f\colon \textbf{ boolean}\},$$

$$R = \{(s, s') \,|\, a(s') = a(s) \ \wedge \ i(s') = n+1\}.$$

21[B]   Same as Exercise 1, in reference to Exercises 21 of Sections
10.1.3 and 10.2.3:

$$S = \{\langle a, i, x, f \rangle \,|\, a\colon \textbf{array } [1\,..\,n] \textbf{ of real};$$
$$i\colon \ 0\,..\,n+1;$$
$$x\colon \textbf{ real};$$
$$f\colon \textbf{ boolean}\},$$

$$R = \{(s, s') \,|\, i(s') = n+1 \ \wedge \ f(s') = (x(s) \in a(s))\}.$$

22[B]   Same as Exercise 1, in reference to Exercises 22 of Sections
10.1.3 and 10.2.3:

$$S = \{\langle a, i, x, f \rangle \,|\, a\colon \textbf{array } [1\,..\,n] \textbf{ of real};$$
$$i\colon \ 0\,..\,n+1;$$
$$x\colon \textbf{ real};$$
$$f\colon \textbf{ boolean}\},$$

$$R = \{(s, s') \,|\, i(s') = n+1 \ \wedge \ f(s') = (x(s') \in a(s'))\}.$$

23[B]   Same as Exercise 1, in reference to Exercises 23 of Sections
10.1.3 and 10.2.3:

$$S = \{\langle a, i \rangle \,|\, a\colon \textbf{array } [1\,..\,n] \textbf{ of real};$$
$$i\colon \ 0\,..\,n+1\},$$

$$R = \{(s, s') \,|\, a(s') = \text{sort}(a(s))\},$$

where sort(a) is the sorted permutation of array a.

24[B]   Same as Exercise 1, in reference to Exercises 24 of Sections
        10.1.3 and 10.2.3:

$$S = \{\langle a,i\rangle | a: \textbf{array } [1\,..\,n] \textbf{ of real};$$
$$i: 0\,..\,n+1\},$$

$$R = \{(s,s') | \text{sorted}(a(s')) \wedge i(s') = n+1\},$$

where sorted(a) means that array a is sorted.

25[B]   Same as Exercise 1, in reference to Exercises 25 of Sections
        10.1.3 and 10.2.3:

$$S = \{\langle a,i\rangle | a: \textbf{array } [1\,..\,n] \textbf{ of real};$$
$$i: 0\,..\,n+1\},$$

$$R = \{(s,s') | \text{perm}(a(s'), a(s)) \wedge i(s') = n+1\},$$

where perm(a, a') means that array a is a permutation of
array a'.

10.4   PROBLEMS

1[R]   Discuss the necessity of the conditions given by Propositions 3
       and 4 for sp-correctness and sp-recoverability.

2[R]   Propose a set of equations for specificationwise recovery in
       sequence statements. To this effect, consider the developments
       of Sections 10.1 and 10.3, as well as Section 9.4.

10.5   BIBLIOGRAPHICAL NOTES

The results of Sections 10.1 and 10.3 are due to Mili *et al.* (1987). The
results of Section 10.2 are due to Jaoua (1987) and Boudriga *et al.*
(1989). The selection sort program studied in Example 7 is due to Wirth
(1976).

CHAPTER 11

Hybrid program validation

The study of forward error recovery has enabled us to distinguish between two kinds of information in a program's state: (i) critical information, i.e. information that must be present in the current state in order for it to be recoverable; and (ii) non-critical information, i.e. information that can be damaged without jeopardizing the recoverability of the current state.

In this chapter we discuss a hybrid validation method which consists of the following two criteria:

1. *Proving* that the critical information is preserved throughout the execution of the program.
2. *Ensuring* that the non-critical information is recovered whenever it is damaged, using forward error recovery techniques.

In Sections 11.1 and 11.2, we discuss this method for deterministic, then for non-deterministic specifications. In Section 11.3 we take a critical look at this method, and assess its potential and limitations.

11.1 HYBRID PROGRAM VALIDATION: DETERMINISTIC SPECIFICATIONS

In the context of deterministic specifications, the critical information of state s is defined by the equation

$$(s_0, s) \in F * F^\frown,$$

while the non-critical information is defined by the predicate

$$s \in \mathrm{dom}(W \cap F).$$

Also, the specification of the recovery routine is

$$F * F^\frown * I(D).$$

11.1.1   How Do We Preserve Critical Information?

We address this question under two possible fault hypotheses.

H1: Anticipated faults. The program is possibly faulty, while the virtual machine on which the program runs is assumed fault-free.

It is usually very simple to prove using, for example, Hoare's logic, that the program preserves its critical information. Specifically, it suffices to prove that the assertion

$$(s_0, s) \in F * F^\frown$$

is invariant throughout the program.

There is both empirical evidence and experimental evidence to the effect that it is easy to prove the preservation of critical information:

1. *Empirical evidence:* while non-critical information expresses what has been done to the state as execution progresses, and is a dynamic measure of the progress of execution toward termination, critical information expresses what has not been undone to the state of the program, and is a static measure of the limits within which the state evolves toward termination.
2. *Experimental evidence:* it can be seen from the examples treated in Sections 11.1.5, 11.2.2 and 11.2.3 (below) that it is very easy to prove the preservation of critical information.

H2: Unanticipated faults. The program is supposed correct, while the virtual machine is possibly faulty.

It does not seem reasonable to assume that even though the virtual machine is faulty, it can only contaminate non-critical information of the program. Hence a combination of partial solutions must be used under Hypothesis H2; these depend on the specific conditions at hand. We briefly mention three of these solutions:

1. Saving the variables that are involved in the critical information in special high-security memories. This solution is most attractive when critical information is limited to few variables. Cases where this solution is disadvantageous include assertions whose preservation requires more space than is strictly necessary. As an example, consider an array of size n, and consider the assertion

   $$\text{perm}(a(s_0), a(s)). \tag{e0}$$

   In order to ensure the preservation of (e0), we need to store all of a, which is as much as we need to store to preserve the much stronger assertion,

$$a(s) = a(s_0). \tag{e1}$$

2. Protecting the space against suspicious-looking modifications, by means of *watchdog processor* techniques.
3. Damage confinement techniques, using executable assertions to ensure that the program evolves from a correct state to a correct state.

11.1.2   How Do We Assess Damage?

Given that the critical information of the current state is preserved, the current state is provably l-recoverable. However, it may or may not be l-correct, depending on whether its non-critical information is damaged. The assertion that defines non-critical information is

$$s \in D,$$

where $D = \mathrm{dom}(W \cap F)$. Interestingly, this assertion involves s alone, and does not involve s_0. This feature is critical in hybrid validation, for we take the hypothesis that no previous state of the program is available to us when we attempt to assess the damage and take a recovery action. Under the hypothesis that the critical information is preserved, the l-correctness of the current state is assessed by inspection of it alone.

11.1.3   How Do We Recover Non-critical Information?

The specification of the recovery routine is

$$J = F * F^\wedge * I(D).$$

Again, the main interest of this specification is that it does not refer to s_0; a recovery routine r that is correct with respect to J will produce a loosely correct state out of the (possibly contaminated, but still) loosely recoverable current state.

11.1.4   Constructing a Fault Tolerant Program

Given the boolean Pascal function *detect* which checks whether the current state is in D, and returns **true** if and only if it is not; and given the recovery routine *recover* which is correct with respect to the specification J, we augment the given iterative program as follows:

```
p =
begin
i; {initialization}
```

```
1: while t do
   begin
   b; {loop body}
   if detect then recover {added feature}
   end
end.
```

Such a program is said to be *H-valid* (H stands for: hybrid).

11.1.5   Example of Application

As an illustrative example, we consider the bubblesort program. For the sake of parsimony, and because this is of no interest to us in this section, we do not show all the details of how to make this program H-valid. Rather, we content ourselves with giving the parameters, referring the interested reader to the bibliography for more details.

The space

```
S = set
       a: array [1 .. n] of integer;
       i, j: 0 .. n + 1
    end.
```

The function

$$F = \{(s,s') \,|\, a(s') = \text{sort}(a(s)) \,\wedge\, i(s') = n \,\wedge\, j(s') = n - 1\},$$

where sort(a) is the sorted permutation of array a.

The program

```
p =
program bubblesort (input, output);
label 1;
const n = 10;
      lower = 0;
      upper = 11;
type
      itemtype = integer;
      indextype = lower .. upper;
      arraytype = array [indextype] of itemtype;
var
      a: arraytype;
      i,
```

```
            j: indextype;
            {auxiliary variable}
            x: itemtype;
begin
for i := 1 to n do read(a[i]);
i := 1;
1:  while i ≤ (n − 1) do
    begin
    j := n;
    while j ≥ i + 1 do
      begin
      if a[j − 1] > a[j] then
        begin
        x := a[j − 1];
        a[j − 1] := a[j];
        a[j] := x
        end;
      j := j − 1
      end;
    i := i + 1
    end;
for i := 1 to n do write(a[i], ' '); writeln
end.
```

The critical information. First, we compute $F * F^\wedge$.

$$F * F^\wedge = \{(s, s') \mid \text{sort}(a(s)) = \text{sort}(a(s'))\}.$$

If we sort $a(s)$, we find the same result as if we sort $a(s')$. Hence $a(s)$ and $a(s')$ are permutations of each other. This is abbreviated as

$$\text{perm}(a(s), a(s')).$$

$$F * F^\wedge = \{(s, s') \mid \text{perm}(a(s), a(s'))\}.$$

Hence the critical information of state s for initial state s_0 is

$$(s_0, s) \in F * F^\wedge \Leftrightarrow \text{perm}(a(s_0), a(s)).$$

Proving the preservation of critical information. Under Hypothesis H1 (faulty program) we must prove the invariance of assertion

$$\text{perm}(a(s), a(s_0))$$

throughout the text of the program. The only place in the program when this assertion is likely to be affected is the **begin–end** block that modifies a, namely

```
begin
x := a[j − 1];
a[j − 1] := a[j];
a[j] := x
end.
```

Now, it is clear that

{perm(a(s0), a(s))}

```
begin
x := a[j − 1];
a[j − 1] := a[j];
a[j] := x
end.
```
{perm(a(s0), a(s))}

is a theorem of Hoare's logic of program correctness. Hence, under the hypothesis of anticipated faults, the critical information is preserved.

Under the hypothesis of unanticipated faults, we assume that proper measures are taken for the following purposes:

(a) to protect the array from memory contaminations;
(b) to ensure that all the modifications to the array occur as a swap of two cells.

Set D. We find

$$D = \{s \mid \text{sorted}(a(s)[1 .. i(s) − 1])$$
$$\wedge \ (\forall k, i(s) \le k \le n \Rightarrow a(s)[i(s) − 1] \le a(s)[k])$$
$$\wedge \ 1 \le i(s) \le n\}.$$

Detecting Errors. Because the critical information is (provably) preserved, the current state is necessarily l-recoverable. It may or may not be l-correct. A (Pascal) boolean function is needed to determine whether the current state is l-correct, and to trigger a recovery routine in case it is not.

On the basis of the definition of D given above, we propose the following function:

```
function detect: boolean;
const greatint = 32767;
var
  ord,
  lt,
  rng: boolean; {first, second and third conjunct
                 characterizing set D}
  k: indextype;
begin
a[0] := − greatint;
```

```
ord := true; for k := 1 to i − 2 do ord := ord and (a[k] ≤ a[k + 1]);
lt := true; for k := i to n do lt := lt and (a[i − 1] ≤ a[k]);
rng := (1 ≤ i) and (i ≤ n);
detect := not (ord and lt and rng)
end;
```

Recovering from errors. If the boolean function *detect* returns **true**, the current state is known not to be l-correct. However, because the critical information is preserved, the current state is known to be l-recoverable. Hence if a recovery routine is applied to it, it will map it into an l-correct state. The specification of the recovery routine is:

$$J = F * F^\smallfrown * I(D)$$
$$= \{(s, s') \,|\, \mathrm{perm}(a(s), a(s')) \wedge \mathrm{sorted}(a(s')[1 \,..\, i(s') - 1])$$
$$\wedge \; (\forall k, i(s') \le k \le n \Rightarrow a(s')[i(s') - 1] \le a(s')[k]$$
$$\wedge \; 1 \le i(s') \le n\}.$$

In order to satisfy this specification, we keep array a intact (hence satisfying $\mathrm{perm}(a(s), a(s'))$), and we set i to 1, to satisfy the last three conjuncts. However, for the sake of efficiency (and also to preclude the possibility that the program iterate infinitely through the cycle: fault manifestation; error detection; error recovery), we assign to i the greatest possible value that still keeps s' in D. Hence the following routine.

```
procedure recover;
const greatint = 32767;
var
  k: indextype;
  min: itemtype;
begin
i := 1; a[n + 1] := − greatint {sentinel};
while a[i] ≤ a[i + 1] do i := i + 1;
{computing the min of a[i .. n]}
min := greatint; for k := i to n do if a[k] < min then min := a[k];
{adjusting index i}
while a[i] > min do i := i − 1
end.
```

Constructing the Fault Tolerant Program. Using **procedures** *detect* and *recover*, we obtain the following program.

```
program bubblesort (input, output);
label 1;
```

```
const n = 10;
      lower = 0;
      upper = 11;
type
      itemtype = integer;
      indextype = lower .. upper;
      arraytype = array [indextype] of itemtype;
var
      a: arraytype;
      i,
      j: indextype;
      {auxiliary variable}
      x: itemtype;
      function detect: boolean;
      {not shown here}
      procedure recover;
      {not shown here}
begin
for i := 1 to n do read(a[i]);
i := 2;
1: while i ≤ (n − 1) do
   begin
   j := n;
   while j ≥ i + 1 do
     begin
     if a[j − 1] > a[j] then
       begin
       x := a[j − 1];
       a[j − 1] := a[j];
       a[j] := x
       end;
     j := j − 1
     end;
   i := i + 1;
   if detect then recover; {added feature}
   end;
for i := 1 to n do write(a[i], ' ')
end.
```

Fault Tolerant Behaviour: Vis-à-vis Anticipated Faults. We introduce in turn three errors in the program, and watch how the program recovers spontaneously from the contaminations caused by these errors. Of course, in keeping with our hypotheses, these errors do not affect the critical information of the program.

Error 1:

$i := 1$

is replaced by

$i := 2$

in the initialization segment. The experimental results are as follows. Note: the figures in parentheses represent the number of times that **procedure** *recover* was invoked:

INPUT	OUTPUT		
	WITHOUT RECOVERY	WITH RECOVERY	
0 1 2 3 4 5 6 7 8 9	0 1 2 3 4 5 6 7 8 9	0 1 2 3 4 5 6 7 8 9	(0)
9 8 7 6 5 4 3 2 1 0	9 0 1 2 3 4 5 6 7 8	0 1 2 3 4 5 6 7 8 9	(1)
9 0 8 1 7 2 6 3 5 4	9 0 1 2 3 4 5 6 7 8	0 1 2 3 4 5 6 7 8 9	(1)
0 9 1 8 2 7 3 6 4 5	0 1 2 3 4 5 6 7 8 9	0 1 2 3 4 5 6 7 8 9	(0)
5 6 7 8 9 0 1 2 3 4	5 0 1 2 3 4 6 7 8 9	0 1 2 3 4 5 6 7 8 9	(1)
0 2 4 6 8 9 7 5 3 1	0 1 2 3 4 5 6 7 8 9	0 1 2 3 4 5 6 7 8 9	(0)

The rows that have 0 as the number of invocations of the recovery routine represent cases where error 1 prevents the state from being s-correct, while it does not prevent it from being l-correct. As for rows that have 1 between parentheses, they represent cases where the state generated is l-recoverable, but is not l-correct.

Error 2:

$j \geq i + 1$

is replaced by

$j > i + 1$

in the condition of the inner loop. The experimental results are as follows.

INPUT	OUTPUT		
	WITHOUT RECOVERY	WITH RECOVERY	
0 1 2 3 4 5 6 7 8 9	0 1 2 3 4 5 6 7 8 9	0 1 2 3 4 5 6 7 8 9	(0)
9 8 7 6 5 4 3 2 1 0	9 0 1 2 3 4 5 6 7 8	0 1 2 3 4 5 6 7 8 9	(1)

```
9 0 8 1 7 2 6 3 5 4    9 0 1 2 3 4 5 6 7 8    0 1 2 3 4 5 6 7 8 9    (1)
0 9 1 8 2 7 3 6 4 5    0 1 2 3 4 5 6 7 8 9    0 1 2 3 4 5 6 7 8 9    (0)
5 6 7 8 9 0 1 2 3 4    5 0 1 2 3 4 6 7 8 9    0 1 2 3 4 5 6 7 8 9    (1)
0 2 4 6 8 9 7 5 3 1    0 1 2 3 4 5 6 7 8 9    0 1 2 3 4 5 6 7 8 9    (0)
```

Error 3:

$$i := i + 1$$

is replaced by

$$i := i + 2$$

at the bottom of the outer loop. The experimental results are as follows.

INPUT   OUTPUT

	WITHOUT RECOVERY	WITH RECOVERY

```
0 1 2 3 4 5 6 7 8 9    0 1 2 3 4 5 6 7 8 9    0 1 2 3 4 5 6 7 8 9    (1)
9 8 7 6 5 4 3 2 1 0    0 9 1 8 2 7 3 6 4 5    0 1 2 3 4 5 6 7 8 9    (5)
9 0 8 1 7 2 6 3 5 4    0 9 1 2 3 8 4 5 6 7    0 1 2 3 4 5 6 7 8 9    (5)
0 9 1 8 2 7 3 6 4 5    0 1 2 9 3 4 5 8 6 7    0 1 2 3 4 5 6 7 8 9    (4)
5 6 7 8 9 0 1 2 3 4    5 0 1 6 2 7 3 8 4 9    0 1 2 3 4 5 6 7 8 9    (3)
0 2 4 6 8 9 7 5 3 1    0 1 2 3 4 5 6 7 8 9    0 1 2 3 4 5 6 7 8 9    (1)
```

Fault Tolerant Behaviour: Vis-à-vis Unanticipated Faults. We simulate two errors that could conceivably result from a faulty virtual machine; in keeping with our assumptions, these errors do not affect critical information of the program. Whether they are likely to occur is not the object of our discussion; rather, we are interested in their illustrative potential.

Error 1: we assume that the virtual machine affects the index *i* of the array. This is simulated by the following **procedure**:

```
procedure error1;
begin
if i = 7 and not err1 then
  begin
  i := 9; err1 := true
  end
end.
```

This procedure is placed right after the update of index *i* in the outer loop body; it requires that err1 be declared as global and initialized to false. The experimental results are as follows:

INPUT	OUTPUT		
	WITHOUT RECOVERY	WITH RECOVERY	
0 1 2 3 4 5 6 7 8 9	0 1 2 3 4 5 6 7 8 9	0 1 2 3 4 5 6 7 8 9	(0)
9 8 7 6 5 4 3 2 1 0	0 1 2 3 4 5 9 8 6 7	0 1 2 3 4 5 6 7 8 9	(1)
9 0 8 1 7 2 6 3 5 4	0 1 2 3 4 5 9 6 7 8	0 1 2 3 4 5 6 7 8 9	(1)
0 9 1 8 2 7 3 6 4 5	0 1 2 3 4 5 6 9 7 8	0 1 2 3 4 5 6 7 8 9	(1)
5 6 7 8 9 0 1 2 3 4	0 1 2 3 4 5 6 7 8 9	0 1 2 3 4 5 6 7 8 9	(0)
0 2 4 6 8 9 7 5 3 1	0 1 2 3 4 5 6 7 8 9	0 1 2 3 4 5 6 7 8 9	(0)

Error 2: we assume that the virtual machine affects the array, while keeping the critical information preserved; specifically, it intervenes at some time during run-time to swap two cells of the array. We propose the following **procedure**.

```
procedure error2;
var
  x: itemtype;
begin
if (i = 6) and not (err2) then
  begin
  x := a[4]; a[4] := a[8]; a[8] := x;
  err2 := true
  end
end.
```

This procedure is placed right after the update of index i in the outer loop body; it requires that err2 be declared as global and initialized to false. The experimental results are as follows:

INPUT	OUTPUT		
	WITHOUT RECOVERY	WITH RECOVERY	
0 1 2 3 4 5 6 7 8 9	0 1 2 7 4 3 5 6 8 9	0 1 2 3 4 5 6 7 8 9	(1)
9 8 7 6 5 4 3 2 1 0	0 1 2 7 4 3 5 6 8 9	0 1 2 3 4 5 6 7 8 9	(1)
9 0 8 1 7 2 6 3 5 4	0 1 2 8 4 3 5 7 8 9	0 1 2 3 4 5 6 7 8 9	(1)
0 9 1 8 2 7 3 6 4 5	0 1 2 6 4 3 5 7 8 9	0 1 2 3 4 5 6 7 8 9	(1)
5 6 7 8 9 0 1 2 3 4	0 1 2 7 4 3 5 6 8 9	0 1 2 3 4 5 6 7 8 9	(1)
0 2 4 6 8 9 7 5 3 1	0 1 2 7 4 3 5 6 8 9	0 1 2 3 4 5 6 7 8 9	(1)

The essence of the behavior of this fault tolerant program is exhibited in the column labelled 'OUTPUT / WITH RECOVERY': In this column, the output is always

   0 1 2 3 4 5 6 7 8 9,

for all the errors and for all the inputs.

11.1.6   Exercises

1[B]   Let S be the space defined by

   a: **array** [1 .. n] **of real**;
   i: 0 .. n + 1;
   x: **real**,

   and let F be the function defined by

$$F = \{(s, s') \,|\, a(s') = a(s) \wedge i(s') = n + 1 \wedge x(s') = \sum_{i=1}^{n} a(s)[i]\},$$

   where $\sum_{i=1}^{n} a'[i]$ is the sum of the elements of array a':
   (a) Following the heuristics of Chapter 9, derive an iterative program that computes function F on S.
   (b) Derive an expression for the critical information of this program, and discuss means to ensure its preservation under the two hypotheses presented in this chapter.
   (c) Derive an expression of the non-critical information of this program, and use it to write procedure *detect* that detects when a state is no longer loosely correct.
   (d) Derive an expression of the specification of the recovery routine, and use it to derive a procedure that recovers from errors to the state of the program.
   (e) Construct the fault tolerant program so obtained, and experiment it on appropriately chosen input data, for appropriately chosen anticipated faults and unanticipated faults. Comment your results in terms of the (natural) redundancy of the program.

2[B]   Same space and same questions as Exercise 1, with function

$$F = \{(s, s') \,|\, a(s') = \text{Min}(s) \wedge i(s') = n + 1 \wedge x(s') = \min(s)\},$$

   where $\min(s)$ is the smallest value of array $a(s)$, and $\text{Min}(s)$ is the array of dimension n containing n times $\min(s)$.

3[B]   Same space and same questions as Exercise 1, with function

$$F = \{(s, s') \,|\, a(s') = N \wedge i(s') = n + 1 \wedge x(s') = x(s)\},$$

   where N is the array of dimension n that has value k at the cell of index k.

4[C]   If you have done all Exercises 1, 2 and 3 (or any two of them), compare your results as far as the ratio critical information/non-critical information. Give an explanation for these ratios in terms of the injectivity of function F.

11.2   HYBRID PROGRAM VALIDATION: NON-DETERMINISTIC SPECIFICATIONS

11.2.1   Position of the Problem

The three aspects of the method are as follows:

1. What is the expression of the critical information? (to know what must be provably preserved to ensure that the current state is sp-recoverable).
2. What is the expression of the non-critical information? (to know how to detect that the current state is not sp-correct).
3. What is the specification of the recovery routine? (to know how to generate an sp-correct state from the current sp-recoverable state).

We address these aspects in turn below.

For a non-deterministic specification R, the *critical information* of current state s vis-à-vis initial state s_0 is captured in the equation

$$(s_0, s) \in K(R).$$

We use the same approach as Section 11.1.1, and take the same hypotheses, to prove the preservation of critical information.

For a non-deterministic specification R, the *non-critical information* of current state s is captured in the equation

$$s \in D,$$

where $D = \text{dom}([w] \cap R)$. We must derive a Pascal boolean function *detect* that returns **true** if and only if the current state s is outside D, hence is not sp-correct. Because the critical information is known to be preserved, s is known to be sp-recoverable.

If the boolean function *detect* returns **true**, then the current state is known not to be sp-correct, while being sp-recoverable. A recovery routine will then map it to a sp-correct state; the recovery routine must be correct with respect to specification

$$J = K(R) * I(D).$$

In Sections 11.2.2 and 11.2.3 we discuss specificationwise recovery by means of illustrative examples: in Section 11.2.2, we take a specification that is an equivalence relation; while in Section 11.2.3 we take a specification that is rectangular, i.e. merely expresses a property of the output. These examples are sufficiently different to span a wide range of possibilities.

11.2.2   An Equivalence Specification

We take the same program as Section 11.1.5, and the specification

$$R = \{(s, s') | \text{perm}(a(s), a(s'))\}.$$

For the sake of brevity, we skip the computations, leaving it to the interested reader to check their validity.

The critical information of the program with respect to R is

$$\text{perm}(a(s_0), a(s)).$$

Provided that this information is preserved by the compendium program/virtual machine, we can make the program fault tolerant by means of the following **procedures** *detect* and *recover*:

```
function detect: boolean;
begin detect := not ((1 ≤ i) and (i ≤ n)) end.
procedure recover;
begin i := n end.
```

Note that the **procedures** detect and recover are extremely simple. Due to the form of the specification at hand, this program has virtually no non-critical information to check and retrieve.

11.2.3   A Rectangular Specification

We take the same program as Section 11.1.5 and the specification

$$R = \{(s, s') | \text{sorted}(a(s'))\}.$$

Because this relation is rectangular, its kernel equals $R * R\hat{\,}$. A quick check reveals that $R * R\hat{\,} = U(S)$. Hence this program has no critical information with respect to R.

On the other hand, its non-critical information proves to be the same as that found in Section 11.1.5. Hence **procedures** *detect* is the same as that of Section 11.1.5.

```
function detect: boolean;
const greatint = 32767;
```

```
var
  ord,
  lt,
  rng : boolean; {first, second and third conjunct
                       characterizing set D}
  k: indextype;
begin
a[0] := − greatint;
ord := true; for k := 1 to i − 2 do ord := ord and (a[k] ≤ a[k + 1]);
lt := true; for k := i to n do lt := lt and (a[i − 1] ≤ a[k]);
rng := (1 ≤ i) and (i ≤ n);
detect := not (ord and lt and rng)
end;
```

As for **procedure** *recover*, it must be correct with respect to the specification

$$J = K(R) * I(D)$$
$$= U(S) * I(D)$$
$$= \{(s, s') | s' \in D\}.$$

A trivial recovery routine for this case is:

```
procedure recover;
begin
for i := 1 to n do a[i] := i;
i := n
end.
```

11.2.4 Exercises

1[B]   Let S be the space defined by

```
a: array [1..n] of real;
i: 0..n + 1;
x: real,
```

and let R be the relation defined by

$$R = \{(s, s') | x(s') = \sum_{i=1}^{n} a(s)[i]\},$$

where $\sum_{i=1}^{n} a'[i]$ is the sum of the elements of array a':

(a) Following the heuristics of Chapter 10, derive an iterative program that solves specification R on S.

(b) Derive an expression for the (specificationwise) critical information of this program, and discuss means to ensure its preservation under the two hypotheses presented in this chapter.

(c) Derive an expression of the non-critical information of this program, and use it to write procedure detect that detects when a state is no longer loosely correct.

(d) Derive an expression of the specification of the recovery routine, and use it to derive a procedure that recovers from errors to the state of the program.

(e) Construct the fault tolerant program so obtained, and experiment it on appropriately chosen input data, for appropriately chosen anticipated faults and unanticipated faults. Comment your results in terms of the (natural) redundancy of the program and the non-determinacy of the specification-wise at hand. In particular, if you have done Exercise 1 of Section 11.1.6, compare it with your results, and explain the differences you find in terms of the determinacy of R.

2[B]   Same space and questions as Exercise 1, for the specification

$$R = \{(s,s') \mid a(s') = \text{Min}(s)\},$$

Compare your results with Exercise 2 of Section 11.1.6.

3[B]   Same space and same questions as Exercise 1, with specification

$$R = \{(s,s') \mid a(s') = N\},$$

Compare your results with Exercise 3 of Section 11.1.6.

4[C]   If you have done all of Exercises 1, 2 and 3 (or any two of them), compare your results as far as the ratio critical information/non-critical information. Give an explanation for these ratios in terms of the determinacy of specification R.

5[B]   Take the program of Section 11.1.5; complete it with the fault tolerant functions designed in Section 11.2.2. Illustrate its behavior in the manner of Section 11.1.5.

6[B]   Take the program of Section 11.1.5; complete it with the fault tolerant functions designed in Section 11.2.3. Illustrate its behavior in the manner of Section 11.1.5.

11.3   AN ASSESSMENT OF HYBRID VALIDATION

11.3.1   Potentials and Limitations

The hybrid validation method of programs depends on the distinction between critical information and non-critical information in the state of a program. Its fundamental principle is to preserve critical information throughout the execution of the program, while ensuring that non-critical information is retrieved whenever it is damaged.

Experiments similar to those of Section 11.1.5 have exhibited a great tolerance to faults within the limits of our hypotheses.

Notice that by taking an equivalence specification and a rectangular specification in turn we have found, respectively, no non-critical information to retrieve, then no critical information to preserve.

The hybrid program validation method discussed in this chapter provides effective means of tolerance to errors that affect non-critical information. Thanks to its boolean function *detect* and its **procedure** *recover*, the program at hand tolerates errors; perhaps we could say that the program *defies* errors, to better describe the situation. Experiments similar to those of Section 11.1.5 have been made for non-deterministic specifications, and have exhibited a great tolerance to faults within the limits of our hypotheses. The non-determinacy of specifications contributes an additional source of redundancy in the state of the program, hence an additional source of fault tolerance.

Notice that by taking an equivalence specification and a rectangular specification in turn we have found, respectively, no non-critical information to retrieve, then no critical information to preserve.

Nevertheless, the validation method proposed has the three following weaknesses, as we discuss below:

1. Hypothesis H2, which provides that the virtual machine does not affect critical information, is not totally satisfactory. To make it more reasonable, one needs special equipment (high-security memories, watchdog processors, ...); this limits its scope of application.
2. H-valid programs have a *partial correctness* flavor about them. All we can claim is that when the program terminates, its final state is correct; but we have no guarantee that it does terminate. In fact, the backtracking features of the compendium

   if detect **then** recover

   can sometimes prevent a program from terminating. There are instances of a contamination to non-critical information which terminates in an incorrect final state in the absence of a recovery routine, but fails to terminate when the recovery routine is active.
3. Even though hybrid validation is functionally valid, its cost-effectiveness is not established. In the example of Section 11.1.5, **procedures** *detect* and *recover* are not very simple, and are rather voluminous. One would expect that for larger programs, the ratio of complexity

and size between the recovery software (procedures detect and recover) and the program is much smaller than it is in this particular example, but we have no ground on which to lay this claim.

11.3.2 Exercises

1[B] Is it always the case that sp-recovery with respect to an equivalence (relation as) specification yields no non-critical information to retrieve? Give a general result.

2[B] Is it always the case that sp-recovery with respect to a rectangular (relation as) specification yields no critical information to preserve? Give a general result.

11.4 PROBLEMS

1[B] Explain the exact relationship that exists between predicate $s \in D$ used in this chapter (Section 11.1.2) for damage assessment and those introduced in Part III for (what seems like) the same purpose.

2[B] Explain the exact relationship that exists between predicate $s \in D$ used in this chapter (Section 11.2.1) for damage assessment and those introduced in Part III for (what seems like) the same purpose.

3[B] One way to show the value of an array $[1 .. n]$ that carries values $\{1, 2, .. n\}$ is to use a cartesian plane, where

(a) the X coordinates represent the indices of the array $[1 .. n]$,
(b) the Y coordinates represent the values of the array $\{1 .. n\}$.

Then a sorted array is represented by the diagonal, while an array that is not sorted will have dots scattered around the plane. We call this the $X-Y$ representation of the array.

In the context of the program discussed in Section 11.1.5, the effect of an error on some input array can be represented by the $X-Y$ representation of the corresponding output array. For a given set of input data, the effect (graveness) of an error can then be represented by the superposition of the $X-Y$ representations of the outputs corresponding to these input vectors. We call the superposition of these $X-Y$ representations the diagnostics of the error.

Write a procedure that, for each error, runs the program on a set of data and prints its diagnostics. Hook this procedure to the program of Section 11.1.5 (with, then without, its fault tolerance capability) and run it in turn with all five errors defined in Section 11.1.5.

4[B]   Give a general treatment for specificationwise hybrid validation, given that the specification at hand is:
  (a) an equivalence;
  (b) rectangular on its range;
  (c) the intersection of an equivalence with a range-rectangular relation;
  (d) rectangular on its domain;
  (e) the intersection of an equivalence with a domain-rectangular relation.

5[B]   Complete the computations of Section 11.2.2.

6[B]   Complete the computations of Section 11.2.3.

11.5   BIBLIOGRAPHICAL NOTES

For detailed information on the construction of hybrid programs, consult Jaoua (1987). For information on the Hoare logic of program proving (used in the hybrid validation method), consult Hoare (1969), Manna (1974) and Mili (1984). For references on the use of high-security memories consult Schlichting (1980); for references on the use of watchdog processors consult Mahmood *et al.* (1983). The bubblesort program used in the illustrative examples of this chapter is taken from Wirth (1976).

Part V

Backward Error Recovery

Can it be used in practice?
YES!
Examples exist.
  Defensive programming
  Multi-version software
  Recovery blocks.   (TOM ANDERSON: Montréal, 1985)

Forward error recovery offers reasonably slick means with which to generate a sufficiently correct state from a contaminated state, provided it is not too contaminated (i.e. is still recoverable). It is fairly efficient, in terms of the time and overhead space that it involves. On the other hand, the mathematics that it uses are both elegant and instructive – in the sense that they elucidate important properties of the programs at hand. But efficiency and elegance is not the whole story, and forward error recovery performs poorly on two fronts: first, its power is limited, since it can do nothing if the state is contaminated beyond specificationwise recoverability; second, it lacks generality, in that it tailors its solution to the program at hand, by means of potentially involved computations.

Backward error recovery addresses precisely these two issues: it can be applied irrespective of the damage sustained by the state; and the pattern of error detection/error recovery is uniform, i.e. it does not change from one program to another.

Chapter 12 presents a general structuring pattern that we apply to programs for the purposes of backward error recovery. Chapter 13 discusses the mathematics of backward error recovery, and derives its main equations. Finally, Chapter 14 discusses a special use of recovery blocks, emphasizing on the self-checking capability that these blocks afford at run-time.

CHAPTER 12

Program structuring for backward error recovery

Because of its program-dependent nature, forward error recovery could only be studied in a rigid framework, which we characterize as follows: we apply it to initialized **while** statements only; the milestones considered are attached to the top of the loop body; the loop body is the basic block on which detection and recovery is applied; the specifications considered, when they are not deterministic, are at least regular. Note that these constraints are not intrinsic to forward error recovery; rather they are imposed by the results we have found (see Chapters 9 and 10).

By contrast, backward error recovery is, to a large extent, a free-format arrangement: it can be applied to programs or program parts of any structure; the granularity of the detection and recovery actions is defined arbitrarily (i.e. arbitrarily large or small); the milestones where detection is performed are chosen arbitrarily. This new freedom is, actually, a mixed blessing: while it gives us potentially more power, it is also more complex.

The subject of this chapter is to discuss the form and significance of the control structures that are needed to implement backward error recovery.

12.1 RECOVERY BLOCKS: THEIR STRUCTURE

Let P be a Pascal program. For the purposes of backward error recovery, we structure program P into what we call *recovery blocks* (following Randell, 1975). A recovery block is essentially an elementary asserted block (Chapter 6) where the action invoked in case of failure of the executable assertion consists in calling zero or more alternate segments of code, before declaring an error.

12.1.1 Definitions

In their simplest form, recovery blocks are defined by the following BNF syntax:

⟨generalized statement⟩ ::= ⟨statement⟩|⟨recovery block⟩
⟨recovery block⟩ ::= **ensure** ⟨acceptance test⟩ **by**
          ⟨alternate list⟩ **else error**
⟨alternate list⟩ ::= ⟨alternate⟩|
          ⟨alternate⟩ **else by** ⟨alternate list⟩
⟨alternate⟩ ::= ⟨statement⟩
⟨acceptance test⟩ ::= ⟨expression⟩

The first ⟨alternate⟩ in the ⟨alternate list⟩ corresponds to the block of code we would have if there were no recovery blocks at all; the other alternates would typically be less and less desirable alternate blocks, which we invoke in turn if the first alternate fails, as long as the acceptance test is not satisfied.

An example of recovery block is

ensure acceptance-test
by primary-block
else by secondary-alternate
else by tertiary-alternate
....
else error,

where *acceptance-test* is a boolean function, while *primary-block*, *secondary-block* and *tertiary-block* are procedures. The execution of such a block proceeds as follows: the current state, say s, is saved in some backup state, say $\hat{s}$, then the primary-block is invoked, modifying s while keeping $\hat{s}$ intact. Upon exit from the primary-block, the (boolean-valued) acceptance test involving $\hat{s}$ and s is checked; if it returns **true**, then the recovery block is exited, else state $\hat{s}$ is loaded onto s and the secondary block is invoked, modifying s while keeping $\hat{s}$ intact, etc. If upon exit from the last alternate the acceptance test is true, then the recovery block is exited; else procedure **error** is invoked to cast the necessary warning and take corrective action.

It is reasónable to assume that any program is made up of recovery blocks, since any block can be written as:

ensure true
by b
else error.

Let a program with recovery blocks be given; if we use the above artifact for all blocks that are not embedded in a recovery block, then we get a program made up of nothing but recovery blocks. This assumption may be made, in the future, to simplify our developments. The program that we then obtain is called an *asserted program*.

12.1.2 Exercises

1[A]   Rewrite the following recovery block as an elementary asserted block:

> **ensure** $a(\hat{s}, s)$
> **by** b
> **else error.**

2[A]   Rewrite the following recovery block as elementary asserted blocks:

> **ensure** $a(\hat{s}, s)$
> **by** b1
> **else by** b2
> **else error.**

12.2   RECOVERY BLOCKS: THEIR USAGE

Let *rb* be the following recovery block:

> L: **ensure** $a(\hat{s}, s)$
> **by** b1
> **else by** b2
> **else by** b3
> . . . .
> **else error**;
> L':,

and let *m* and *m'* be the milestones (v, L) and (v, L') attached at both ends of this recovery block, for some visit number *v*. We will discuss, in turn, the use of boolean function *acceptance test* then the use of the alternates.

12.2.1   Acceptance Tests

In forward error recovery, it is important to perform an accurate damage assessment before taking recovery action, precisely because the action to take depends on the level of damage: if the state is maskable (assertion *lc*, Chapter 7), then no recovery is necessary; else, if the state is recoverable (assertion *lr*, Chapter 8), then a recovery procedure must be applied; else a failure management procedure (Chapter 8) must be invoked.

By contrast, the recovery action that one must take upon detecting an error, under a backward error recovery policy, is independent of the level of damage sustained by the state; this is due to the availability, at milestone *m*, of a correct state $\hat{s}$, from which we can (hopefully) derive a correct state *s* at milestone *m'*. Hence, for a given recovery block, there is a unique assertion to be checked about the function computed by the alternates: the acceptance test.

The strength of the acceptance test (as an executable assertion, see Chapter 6) depends on the following three factors:

1. Whether we are dealing with a deterministic or a non-deterministic specification; the assertion is stronger in the first case than in the second.
2. Whether we are interested in strict success or specificationwise success of the output state; the assertion is stronger in the first case than in the second.
3. Whether we are interested in detecting errors (and, thereby diagnosing or removing the faults that cause them) or in making the best use of the program (never mind the faults, provided we can recover from the errors that result from them); the assertion is stronger in the first case than in the second.

In the design of acceptance tests, we recognize the three following possible situations:

1. *We are interested in having the program proceed from a strict correct state (at milestone m) to the next (at milestone m'):* then each recovery block must ensure that if the state at *m* is strictly correct, then so is the state at *m'*. This kind of assertion is discussed in Chapter 6; we review it briefly in Section 13.1, and illustrate its use in our context. This case is rather unlikely in practice, and is of little interest; we include it for the sake of completeness.
2. *We are interested in strict success (of the output state):* then the acceptance test must ensure that the recovery block proceeds from an l-correct state (at milestone *m*) to an l-correct state (at milestone *m'*). The mathematics that capture the construction of such assertions are discussed in Chapter 7; we review them in Section 13.2, and illustrate them with an example.
3. *We are interested in specificationwise success, and the specification at hand is non-deterministic:* then the acceptance test must ensure that

the recovery block proceeds from a sp-correct state to the next. The mathematics that capture the construction of such assertions are discussed in Chapter 8; we review them in Section 13.3, and illustrate them with an example.

The design of alternates is also dependent on which of these situations prevails; it is the subject of the next section.

12.2.2   Alternate Blocks

We discuss the construction of alternate blocks in each of the three situations defined above.

Preserving strict correctness. In this case, the primary alternate and the other alternates must compute the exact function. Typically, the consecutive alternates are less and less efficient versions of the primary alternate, possibly earlier and earlier releases of it. This simple situation is illustrated by the following example:

```
L:  ensure s = sort(ŝ)
    by quickersort(s)
    else by quicksort(s)
    else by bubblesort(s)
    else error;
L':
```

In this case, the alternates are different, but they compute the same function.

Preserving loose correctness. To ensure strict success in the output. In this case the alternates may not only be different, they may also compute different functions; provided that for any given state at milestone $m = (v, L)$, these alternates produce loosely correct states at milestone $m' = (v, L')$.

As an example, we assume that we must write a recovery block rb that inserts an element in a list; this block is to be followed by another block that sorts the global list. Because of the sorting procedure downstream of rb, the order of elements in the list is immaterial. Let there be three procedures to insert an element in a list:

```
insert-at-head(i, l) {inserts item i at the head of list l}
insert-at-tail(i, l) {inserts item i at the tail of list l}
insert-at-current(i, l) {inserts item i at the current pointer of
                         list l – assuming its existence}
```

Then we propose the following recovery block:

L: **ensure** inserted (i(ŝ), l(ŝ), l(s))
     by insert-at-current(i, l)
     else by insert-at-head(i, l)
     else by insert-at-tail(i, l)
     else error;
L':,

where *inserted*(i', l', l) means that l is obtained by inserted i' into l', at some position. The alternatives compute different functions, but they all produce loosely correct states.

Preserving Specificationwise correctness. To ensure specificationwise success of the output. In this case the alternates not only do not compute the same function, their difference can be propagated to the output; provided the different output states so obtained cause no specification-wise failure.

As an example, let's consider a recovery block that must insert an element in a list; this block is to be followed by another block that sorts the global list. We are interested in specificationwise success in the output, with respect to a specification that requires the output to be sorted (it imposes no relationship to the input), that it includes at least the last element inserted in the list, and that this element is preserved. Using the procedure of the example above, and procedure

   construct-sequence(i, l)

which constructs list l from the single item i, we propose the following recovery block:

L: **ensure** (i(s) ∈ l(s) and i(ŝ) = i(s))
     by insert-at-head(i, l)
     else by construct-sequence(i, l)
     else error;
L':.

The results produced by the alternates are nowhere near similar; but both of them, when mapped by the future function, produce results that are acceptable by the specification at hand.

12.2.3 Exercises

1[B]   We consider an elementary asserted block, and we let *sc*, *lc* and *lr* be the executable assertions checking the strict correctness, loose correctness, and loose recoverability of the state after execution of the block. Let these assertions be used as

```
L:
    ŝ := s;
    b;
L': if not sc then
    begin {action}
    if not lc then
       if lr then recover
       else error
    end.
```

Write a recovery block that performs the same function as the asserted block above.

2[B]   Same question as Exercise 1, for assertions

       sc, defined above,
       spc, for specificationwise correctness,
       spr, for specificationwise recoverability.

12.3 PROBLEMS

1[C]   There is one phase of program fault tolerance that we are not considering in this book; it is *fault removal*. In the current state of the art, this phase cannot be carried out on-line; the best way to cope with this shortcoming is to prevent faults from getting in the way of the subsequent phases of damage assessment and error recovery.

     (a) Devise an instance where backward error recovery performs better than forward error recovery in bringing a solution to this shortcoming.

     (b) Devise an instance where forward error recovery performs better.

     (c) Which is generally better?

2[C]   We consider two recovery options for a given program:

     (a) backward error recovery, with acceptance tests that measure strict correctness (Section 12.2);

     (b) forward error recovery, with a concern for specificationwise success (Chapter 8).

   To fix our ideas, we define the following six parameters:

     (i) The space overhead of forward error recovery is a ratio,

R_s, of the space requirement of the program; we assume, $0 \le R_s \le 1$.

(ii) The time overhead of forward error recovery is a ratio, R_t, of the time requirement of the program; we assume, $0 \le R_t \le 1$.

(iii) The space overhead of backward error recovery is equal to its original space requirement.

(iv) The space overhead of backward error recovery is equal to its original time requirement.

(v) Out of every n executions of the program, one yields a state that is not strictly correct.

(vi) Out of every m executions of the program that yield a non-strictly correct state, one yields a state that is not sp-recoverable.

Using these parameters, express the time-and-space vs. quality tradeoffs that one must consider before choosing one of the policies proposed.

12.4 BIBLIOGRAPHICAL NOTES

The recovery block structuring device is presented in Randell (1975). It is also discussed in textbook form in Anderson and Lee (1981).

CHAPTER 13

Mathematics for backward error recovery

In this chapter we discuss the mathematics that guide the construction of acceptance tests and alternate blocks for backward error recovery. The acceptance tests and the alternate blocks are combined, as we recall, in the following structure:

```
L:  ensure acceptance-test
    by primary-alternate
    else by secondary-alternate
    else by tertiary-alternate
    . . . . . . . . .
    else error;
L':.
```

An important remark, which is implicit in the significance and usage of this structure, needs to be made explicit: the alternate blocks must, by construction, be correct with respect to the specification defined by the acceptance test. This has an immediate practical consequence: whereas in forward error recovery we need to specify in turn the detection procedures and the recovery procedures, in backward error recovery we use a single specification for both purposes. As we have seen in the preceding chapter, this specification typically takes three forms depending on whether we are interested in:

(a) strict correctness of the current state;
(b) strict success of the final state (hence loose correctness of the current state);
(c) or specificationwise success of the final state (hence specificationwise correctness of the current state).

These three cases are discussed in turn in Sections 13.1, 13.2 and 13.3. Given a relation A, we say that a recovery block is *valid* with respect to A if and only if the following hold:

1. The block's acceptance test checks for $(\hat{s}, s) \in A$ (or for $(\hat{s}, s) \in A'$, where A' is obtained from A by reasoning by equivalence);
2. The block's alternates are all correct with respect to A.

13.1   STRICT CORRECTNESS OF THE CURRENT STATE

13.1.1   The Equations

We consider a recovery block rb between milestones $m = (v, L)$ and $m' = (v, L')$ and we let PST_m and $PST_{m'}$ be the past functions of the program at hand, at milestones m and m'.

We take an identical argument to that of Chapter 6 to deduce that the executable assertion to be used as the acceptance test is defined by the relation A such that

$$PST_m * A \subseteq PST_{m'}.$$

As we have seen in Chapter 6, a solution of this problem is:

$$A = PST_m^\frown * PST_{m'}.$$

The acceptance test checks

$$(\hat{s}, s) \in A,$$

and all the alternates must be correct with respect to A.

It is instructive to express this relation A in terms of B, the expected function of the recovery block at hand. If we simply notice that $PST_{m'} = PST_m * B$, we get

$$A = I(\mathrm{rng}(PST_m)) * B.$$

It is worth noting that even the assertion that preserves strict correctness does not necessarily check for the expected function of the block; this is illustrated in the next section; see also Problem 2.

13.1.2   Illustration

We are to design a recovery block rb between milestones m and m', whose expected function B is defined on the set of lists by

$$B = \{(s, s') | s' = \mathrm{sort}(s)\},$$

where $\mathrm{sort}(s)$ is the sorted permutation of list s.

The relation that defines the acceptance test and the specification of the alternates depends on the range of the past function at milestone m. We consider three possible cases, for illustration:

1. *The past path yields a sorted array.* Let the past path be

```
for i: = 1 to n do s[i]: = i.
```

Then

$$PST_m = \{(s,s') \mid \forall i: 1 \leq i \leq n, s'[i] = i\}$$

and

$$rng(PST_m) = \{s' \mid \forall i: 1 \leq i \leq n, s'[i] = i\}$$

Whence we obtain

$$
\begin{aligned}
A &= I(rng(PST_m)) * B \\
&= \{(s,s') \mid \forall i: 1 \leq i \leq n, s[i] = i \wedge s' = \text{sort}(s)\} \\
&= \{(s,s') \mid \forall i: 1 \leq i \leq n, s[i] = i \wedge s' = s\}.
\end{aligned}
$$

Because s is sorted, $\text{sort}(s) = s$

$$= I(\text{sorted}(s)).$$

Procedure *skip* (the empty procedure) is correct with respect to A. Using the method of reasoning by equivalence (Section 6.1.4), we transform this relation into $A' = I$. We then get the trivial recovery block

```
ensure ŝ = s
by skip
else error.
```

2. *The past path yields any array.* Let the past path be

```
for i: = 1 to n do read(s[i]).
```

Then

$$rng(PST_m) = S$$

and

$$I(rng(PST_m)) = I.$$

Whence,

$$B = A.$$

An example of recovery block is then

```
ensure s = sort(ŝ)
by quickersort(s)
else by quicksort(s)
```

    else by bubblesort(s)
    else error.

  3. *The past path yields a reverse ordered array*. Let the past path be

    for i := 1 **to** n **do** s[i] := n − i.

Then

$$\text{rng}(PST_m) = \{s' \mid \forall i: 1 \leq i \leq n, s'[i] = n - i\}.$$

Whence we obtain

$$\begin{aligned}
A &= I(\text{rng}(PST_m)) * B \\
&= \{(s, s') \mid \forall i: 1 \leq i \leq n, s[i] = n - i \wedge s' = \text{sort}(s)\} \\
&= \{(s, s') \mid \forall i: 1 \leq i \leq n, s[i] = n - i \wedge s' = \text{reverse}(s)\}.
\end{aligned}$$

Because s is reverse-sorted, sort(s) = reverse(s).
Procedures:

    init(s) {sets s[i] to i, for all i}
    quickersort(s) {sorts s}
    rev(s) {reverses s}

are all correct with respect to A; we use them as alternates. Also, we use reasoning by equivalence to obtain the following assertion:

$$\begin{aligned}
A' &= \{(s, s') \mid \forall i: 0 \leq i \leq n - 1, s'[i] = i\} \\
&= \{(s, s') \mid \text{id}(s')\}.
\end{aligned}$$

Whence we deduce the following recovery block

    ensure id(s)
    by init(s)
    else by quickersort(s)
    else by rev(s)
    else error.

The three cases above (the first and third of which are rather pathological) show to what extent a recovery block depends on its context, even when it deals with strict correctness.

13.1.3 Exercises

[1B] Let *rb* be a recovery block we must write between milestones m and m', whose expected function B is defined on the space

       S = **set**
          x: itemtype;

```
    loc: 0 .. n;
    a: array [loc] of itemtype
end
```

by

$$B = \{(s,s')\,|\,a(s)[0] = x(s) \land a(s')[\text{loc}(s')] = x(s)$$
$$\land\ x(s') = x(s)$$
$$\land\ (\forall j: \text{loc}(s') < j \le n \Rightarrow a(s')[j] \ne x(s))$$
$$\land\ a(s') = a(s)\}.$$

Design three distinct past paths at milestone m, with distinct ranges. From each, deduce an appropriate recovery block to preserve strict correctness.

2[B]   Same as Exercise 1, for the same space, and expected function

$$B = \{(s,s')\,|\,x(s) \in a(s) \land a(s')[\text{loc}(s')] = x(s)$$
$$\land\ x(s') = x(s) \land a(s') = a(s)$$
$$\land\ (\forall j: \text{loc}(s') < j \le n \Rightarrow a(s')[j] \ne x(s))\}.$$

3[B]   Same as exercise 1, for the same space, and expected function

$$B = \{(s,s')\,|\,x(s) \in a(s) \land a(s')[\text{loc}(s')] = x(s)$$
$$\land\ x(s') = x(s) \land a(s') = \text{sort}(a(s))$$
$$\land\ (\forall j: \text{loc}(s') < j \le n \Rightarrow a(s')[j] \ne x(s))\}.$$

4[B]   Same as Exercise 1, for the same space, and expected function

$$B = \{(s,s')\,|\,a(s')[\text{loc}(s')] = x(s)$$
$$\land\ x(s') = x(s) \land a(s') = a(s)$$
$$\land\ (\forall j: 1 \le j < n \Rightarrow a(s)[j] \le a(s)[j+1])\}.$$

13.2   LOOSE CORRECTNESS OF THE CURRENT STATE

13.2.1   The Equations

We consider a recovery block rb between milestones m and m' and we let FTR_m and $FTR_{m'}$ be the future functions at milestones m and m'.

We take a similar argument to that of Chapter 7; and deduce that the executable assertion to be used as the acceptance test is captured by relation A, which satisfies the following equation:

$$P * \hat{FTR_m} * A \subseteq P * \hat{FTR_{m'}}.$$

Also, following Chapter 7, we adopt the admissible solution

$$A = FTR_m * FTR_{m'}^{\frown}.$$

We express this assertion in terms of the expected function of the block, say B, so as to highlight that the executable assertion is much less defined than the expected function of the block. From the identity $FTR_m = B * FTR_{m'}$, we derive

$$A = B * (FTR_{m'} * FTR_{m'}^{\frown}).$$

While function B maps each argument s to a single image, $B(s)$, relation A maps s into the level set of $B(s)$ by $FTR_{m'}$; as $FTR_{m'}$ grows less and less injective, A grows less and less deterministic.

Given relation A, the acceptance test is defined by $(\hat{s}, s) \in A$ (modulo *reasoning by equivalence*, see Chapter 6) and all the alternates must be correct with respect to A.

13.2.2 Illustration

We take a quantitative approach to the example given in Section 12.2.2, dealing with preserving loose correctness. We define the space as

```
S = set
     i: itemtype;
     l: listtype
  end
```

where listtype includes lists of type itemtype, and itemtype is a totally ordered type. We let function B be

$$B = \{(s, s') \mid i(s') = i(s) \wedge l(s') = \text{insert}(i(s), l(s))\},$$

where $\text{insert}(i, l)$ is the list obtained by inserting item i at the head of list l. We let the future function at milestone m' be

$$FTR_{m'} = \{(s, s') \mid i(s') = i(s) \wedge l(s') = \text{sort}(l(s))\},$$

where $\text{sort}(l)$ is the sorted permutation of list l. The assertion that defines this recovery block is

$$A = B * N(FTR_{m'}).$$

It is easy to see that

$$N(FTR_{m'}) = \{(s, s') \mid i(s') = i(s) \wedge \text{perm}(l(s), l(s'))\},$$

where $\text{perm}(l, l')$ means that l and l' are permutations of each other. Whence

$$A = \{(s, s') \mid i(s') = i(s) \wedge \text{perm}(\text{insert}(i(s), l(s)), l(s'))\}.$$

If we let

insert-at-head(i, l),
insert-at-tail(i, l),
insert-at-current(i, l)

be the procedures given in the preceding chapter, then the following is a valid structure for the recovery block at hand:

ensure $(\hat{s}, s) \in A$
by insert-at-head(i, l)
else by insert-at-current(i, l)
else by insert-at-tail(i, l)
else error

13.2.3 Exercises

1[B] Study the problem of Section 13.2.2, with

$$FTR_{m'} = \{(s, s') \mid i(s') = i(s) \land l(s') = M(l(s))\},$$

where $M(l)$, for list l, is a list with the same length as l, whose all elements are the maximal element of l.

2[B] Same as Exercise 1, for

$$FTR_{m'} = \{(s, s') \mid i(s') = i(s) \land l(s') = \text{reverse}(l(s))\}.$$

3[B] Let rb be a recovery block on space S = listtype, whose expected function is

$$B = \{(s, s') \mid s' = \text{sort}(s)\}.$$

Propose a construction for this recovery block, using

$$FTR_{m'} = \{(s, s') \mid s' = \text{reverse}(s)\}.$$

4[B] Same as Exercise 3, for

$$FTR_{m'} = \{(s, s') \mid s' = M(s)\}.$$

5[B] Same as Exercise 3, where the future path at milestone m' is a binary search program.

13.3 SPECIFICATIONWISE CORRECTNESS OF THE CURRENT STATE

13.3.1 The Equations

We consider the same problem as Sections 13.1 and 13.2; but this time we are interested in preserving specificationwise correctness from milestone m to milestone m'. Using a similar argument to that of Chapter 7, we deduce that the executable assertion to be used as the acceptance test is captured by relation A, which satisfies the following equation:

$$R * FTR_m^\wedge * A \subseteq R * FTR_m^\wedge.$$

Also, following Chapter 7, we adopt the following admissible solution:

$$A = FTR_m * R^\wedge * R * FTR_{m'}^\wedge,$$

assuming (as we do) that R is regular.

As in the preceding sections, we express relation A in terms of the expected function B, which the recovery block is supposed to compute. We easily find

$$A = B * FTR_{m'} * R^\wedge * R * FTR_{m'}^\wedge;$$

clearly, this a *very* non-deterministic (and non-defined) relation.

Given A, the acceptance test is defined as

$$(\hat{s}, s) \in A$$

and the alternates must all be correct with respect to A.

13.3.2 Illustration

We take the example of Section 12.2.2, which we quantify in this section. As we recall, we have to construct a recovery block rb, with the following four parameters:

1. The space is

    S = **set**
        l: listtype;
        i: itemtype
    end.

2. The expected function, B, is

    $$B = \{(s, s') \,|\, i(s') = i(s) \land l(s') = \text{insert}(i(s), l(s))\}.$$

3. The future function at milestone m' is

    $$FTR_{m'} = \{(s, s') \,|\, i(s') = i(s) \land l(s') = \text{sort}(l(s))\}.$$

4. The specification of the aggregate made up of the recovery block and the future path is

    $$R = \{(s, s') \,|\, i(s') = i(s) \land \text{sorted}(l(s')) \land i(s') \in l(s')\},$$

where sorted(l') means that l' is sorted.

We have

$$FTR_{m'} * R^{\char94}$$
$$= \{(s,s')|\exists t: i(t) = i(s) \land l(t) = \text{sort}(l(s)) \land i(t) = i(s')$$
$$\land \text{ sorted}(l(t)) \land i(t) \in l(t)\}$$
$$= \{(s,s')|i(s') = i(s) \land i(s') \in \text{sort}(l(s))\}$$
$$= \{(s,s')|i(s') = i(s) \land i(s) \in l(s)\},$$

whence

$$FTR_{m'} * R^{\char94} * R * FTR^{\char94}_{m'}$$
$$= \{(s,s')|\exists t: i(t) = i(s) \land i(t) \in l(s) \land i(t) = i(s')$$
$$\land i(t) \in l(s')\}$$
$$= \{(s,s')|i(s') = i(s) \land i(s) \in l(s) \land i(s') \in l(s')\}.$$

We find

$$A = B * FTR_{m'} * R^{\char94} * R * FTR^{\char94}_{m'}$$
$$= \{(s,s')|i(s') = i(s) \land l(s') = \text{insert}(i(s), l(s))\}$$
$$* \{(s,s')|i(s') = i(s) \land i(s) \in l(s) \land i(s') \in l(s')\}$$
$$= \{(s,s')|\exists t: i(t)\, i(s) \land l(t) = \text{insert}(i(s), l(s)) \land i(s') = i(t)$$
$$\land i(t) \in l(t) \land i(s') \in l(s')\}$$
$$= \{(s,s')|i(s') = i(s) \land i(s') \in l(s')\}.$$

The executable assertion

$$i(s) \in l(s) \text{ and } i(\hat{s}) = i(s)$$

does capture relation A, as the reader can see. Also, if we consider
that functions

$$[\text{insert-at-head}(i, l)] = \{(s, s')|i(s') = i(s) \land l(s') = \text{insert}(i(s), l(s))\}$$

and

$$[\text{construct-sequence}(i, l)] = \{(s, s')|i(s') = i(s) \land l(s') = \text{contruct}(i(s))\}$$

are both more-defined than A, we can conclude that the recovery block
rb is

    ensure $(i(s) \in l(s)$ **and** $i(\hat{s}) = i(s))$
    by insert-at-head(i, l)
    else by construct-sequence(i, l)
    else error

is valid with respect to relation A.

13.3.3 Exercises

1[B]   Consider the example of Section 13.3.2. Find a valid recovery block for the specification

$$R = \{(s,s') | \text{sorted}(l(s')) \wedge i(s) \in l(s')\}.$$

Interpret your results.

2[B]   Same as Exercise 1, for the specification

$$R = \{(s,s') | \text{sorted}(l(s')) \wedge i(s') \in l(s')\}.$$

Interpret your results.

3[B]   Same as Exercise 1, for the specification

$$R = \{(s,s') | i(s') \in l(s')\}.$$

Interpret your results.

4[B]   Same as Exercise 1, for the specification

$$R = \{(s,s') | \text{sorted}(l(s'))\}.$$

Interpret your results.

5[B]   Consider the example of Section 13.3.2. Find a valid recovery block, for the specification

$$R = \{(s,s') | i(s') = i(s) \wedge i(s) \in l(s')\},$$

and the future function

$$FTR_{m'} = \{(s,s') | i(s') = i(s) \wedge l(s') = \text{reverse}(l(s))\}.$$

Interpret your results.

6[B]   Same as Exercise 5, for the same future function, and the specification

$$R = \{(s,s') | i(s') \in l(s')\}.$$

Interpret your results.

13.4 PROBLEMS

1[B]   Consider the problem of, e.g., loose recovery. In backward recovery, the same relation is used to define the executable assertion, and the specification of the recovery routine (Section 13.2. In forward error recovery, two different relations are used. Using the results of parts III and IV:

(a) give the relation that preserves loose correctness;

(b) give the relation that defines the specification of recovery routines.

Discuss their difference, and explain it in terms of the opposition between the two error recovery policies.

2[B]   We consider the executable assertions derived in Sections 13.1, 13.2 and 13.3, and we let B be the expected function of the recovery block.

(a) Show that relation A_1, derived in Section 13.1, is less defined than B.

(b) Show that relation A_2, derived in Section 13.2, is less defined than B.

(c) Show that relation A_3, derived in Section 13.3, is less defined than B.

(d) What definedness properties exist between the relations A_1, A_2 and A_3?

(e) Contrast the way in which A_1 on one hand, and A_2 and A_3 on the other hand, are less defined than B.

3[C]   Consider the relation proposed in Section 13.3. Show that when R is deterministic we find (as we should) the relation proposed in Section 13.2. (Hint: consider the following:

$$PST_{m'} * FTR_{m'} \subseteq P$$
$$\text{rng}(R * R') \subseteq \text{rng}(R')$$
$$F^\wedge * F \subseteq I \Rightarrow F^\wedge * F = I(\text{rng}(F)).)$$

13.5   BIBLIOGRAPHICAL NOTES

For more on backward error recovery, consult Randell (1975) or Anderson and Lee (1981).

CHAPTER 14

Self-checking programs

A recovery block runs an acceptance test, then, in case of failure, calls several alternate procedures in turn; in case all the alternates fail the acceptance test, an error routine is invoked. So far, we have concentrated on the design of acceptance tests and alternate procedures; in this chapter, we discuss the design and use of the **else error** branch of recovery blocks. Because of this emphasis, we will, without loss of generality, restrict our attention to recovery blocks of the form

    ensure a($\hat{s}$, s)   {acceptance test}
    by b   {primary, and unique, alternate}
    else message   {**error** routine}

which we write, rather, as elementary asserted blocks

    $\hat{s}$: = s;
    b;
    if not a($\hat{s}$, s) **then** message.

It is also without loss of generality (see Section 12.1.1) that we restrict our attention to programs that are made up of nothing but elementary asserted blocks; as we recall, such programs are called *asserted programs*. The purpose of this chapter is to discuss the analysis, and verification of asserted programs.

The problem of *analyzing* asserted programs can be formulated as follows: let p be an asserted program containing assertions $a_1, a_2, \ldots, a_k$ throughout its text, and let s be an initial state on which p is executed; if execution of p on s terminates in a final state s' and all the assertions checked during the execution turned out to be valid, what can be said for the pair (s, s')? In fact, we must deduce a global assertion from the local assertions $a_1, a_2, \ldots, a_k$.

The problem of *verifying* asserted programs can be formulated as follows: let p be an asserted program containing assertions $a_1, a_2, \ldots, a_k$ in its text and let R be a specification expressing a relationship between the initial states and the final states of p. We say that p is *self-checking* with respect to R if and only if whenever p is executed on an initial state s, causes no assertion to be false and terminates in a state s', then the pair (s, s') is in R.

Section 14.1 discusses the architecture of asserted programs and lays the ground for the following sections. Sections 14.2 and 14.3 discuss, respectively, the analysis and verification of asserted programs.

14.1   ON THE ARCHITECTURE OF ASSERTED PROGRAMS

14.1.1   Asserted Programs

Elementary asserted blocks can be combined together using Pascal-like constructs of sequence, alternation and iteration to form asserted programs. Below is an (schematic) example of an asserted program:

Example 1

```
ap = begin
       ŝ: = s;;
       b1;
       L1: if not a1(ŝ, s) then message(1);
       ŝ: = s;
       while t do
         begin
         b2;
         L2: if not a2(ŝ, s) then message(2);
         ŝ: = s;
         if u then
           begin
           b3;
           L3: if not a3(ŝ, s) then message(3);
           ŝ: = s;
           end
         else
           begin
           b4;
           L4: if not a4(ŝ, s) then message(4);
           ŝ: = s;
           end
         end
     end.                                                    □
```

14.1.2 Self-Checking Programs

Let p be an asserted program on space S, containing assertions a_1, a_2, a_3, ..., a_k. We denote by $nm(s)$, where $s \in S$, the predicate that is true if and only if execution of p on state s generates no message, i.e. causes none of the assertions to be false.

We say that program p is *self-checking* with respect to relation R if and only if

$$s \in \mathrm{dom}(R) \wedge s \in \mathrm{dom}([p]) \wedge nm(s) \Rightarrow (s, [p](s)) \in R.$$

Informally, this can be expressed as follows: for all initial state s verifying the input condition $(s \in \mathrm{dom}(R))$, if program p terminates normally $(s \in \mathrm{dom}([p]))$ without generating messages $(nm(s))$, then the final state $([p](s))$ verifies with the initial state (s) the specified output condition $((s, [p](s)) \in R)$.

It is worthwhile noticing the presence of the clause $(s \in \mathrm{dom}([p]))$ on the left of the $\Rightarrow$ sign in the definition above; this gives the self-checking property a *partial correctness* connotation. This connotation can be explained as follows: an assertion in a program is useful only to the extent that the control of the execution reaches it; when it does, the assertion can check that the block under its control has executed properly; however, there is nothing it can do to check that the block in question terminates, for if it does not terminate, the assertion won't even be reached!

Before we close this section, we need to make a remark on the functional abstraction of an elementary asserted block. Let

```
eab: ŝ: = s;
     b;
     if not a(ŝ, s) then message.
```

We propose to compute [eab]. If we are interested in s only, then the first instruction does not affect s (rather, it affects $\hat{s}$) and the third instruction does not affect it either (rather, it affects the message file). Hence, for our purposes, $[eab] = [b]$.

14.1.3 Exercises

1[A] Show that a program that is partially correct is necessarily self-checking. Is self-checkingness sufficient to establish partial correctness? Illustrate your answer with an example.

2[A] Consider an asserted program whose executable assertions are all equal to the predicate

false,

and consider a specification R. Is this program self-checking with respect to specification R? Note: we assume that the program is entirely made up of elementary asserted blocks.

3[A] Can a program be defined and self-checking with respect to some relation R at the same time? Can a program be self-checking without being defined? Justify your answers.

4[B] Consider the following statement on space S = **integer**:

```
b = begin
    s: = s * s + 1;
    s: = s − 4;
    s: = abs(s) + 2
    end.
```

Propose five assertions in increasing order of strength, that one can check about this block. Prove that they are ordered by strength (the relational more-defined is transitive).

5[B] Same question as Exercise 4.

```
Space S = real.
b = begin
    s: = s * s − 4;
    s: = log(s)
    end.
```

6[B] Let P be a program on space S = **integer**, which is self-checking with respect to the following specification:

$$R = \{(s, s') | 3 \leq s \wedge s + 1 \leq s' \leq s * s + 2\}.$$

What can you say about the output state, in each of the following cases:

(a) The initial state is $s = 4$; the program terminates normally and sends no messages.

(b) The initial state is $s = 2$; the program terminates normally and sends no messages.

(c) The initial state is $s = 10$; the program terminates normally and sends a message.

(d) The initial state is $s = 2$; the program does not terminate normally and sends no messages.

(e) The initial state is $s = 6$; the program does not terminate normally and sends messages.

7[B] Let P be a program on space S = **real**, and let R be the following specification:

$$R = \{(s,s')|0\le s\le 100 \wedge s<s'\le s^2\}.$$

Compute the domain of this specification (be careful). For each scenario given below, say whether it is inconsistent with the self-checkingness of P with respect to R:

(a) Input state is 3; execution of P terminates normally, and generates no messages; output state is 7.

(b) Input state is 0; execution of P terminates normally, and generates no messages; output state is 1.

(c) Input state is 5; execution of P terminates normally, and generates no messages; output state is 31.

(d) Input state is 5; execution of P terminates normally, and generates a message; output state is 20.

(e) Input state is 2; execution of P terminates normally, and generates several messages; output state is 4.

8[B]   Same as Exercise 7, with the same space and specification.

(a) Input state is 1; execution of P does not terminate normally, and generates messages.

(b) Input state is 1; execution of P terminates normally, and generates no messages; output state is 1.

(c) Input state is 4; execution of P terminates normally, and generates no messages; output state is 25.

(d) Input state is 4; execution of P terminates normally, and generates no messages; output state is 15.

(e) Input state is 4; execution of P terminates normally, and generates no messages; output state is 5.

14.2   THE ANALYSIS OF ASSERTED PROGRAMS

The problem of analyzing an asserted program can be formulated as follows: let p be an asserted program; find the strongest assertion with respect to which p is self-checking. In this section, we present a bottom−up approach to this problem: the analysis of a complex asserted program is based on the analyses of its components.

14.2.1   Analysis of an Elementary Asserted Block

- *Proposition 1.* The elementary asserted block

```
eab: ŝ: = s;
     b;
```

if not a(ŝ, s) **then** message

is self-checking with respect to $R = \{(s, s') | a(s, s')\}$.

Proof. Let $\hat{s}$ be an element of dom(R) such that $\hat{s} \in$ dom([b]) and $nm(\hat{s})$; because $\hat{s} \in$ dom([b]), execution of b terminates and the assertion is reached; because $nm(s)$ holds, the **then** branch was not taken, hence $a(\hat{s}, [b](\hat{s}))$ holds; whence $(\hat{s}, [b](\hat{s})) \in R$.   [QED]

Among all the relations, R is not necessarily the most defined relation with respect to which eab is self-checking. We use an example to prove this claim.

```
S = integer;
eab: ŝ: = s;
     b;
     if not (ŝ > 3 ∧ s = ŝ + 1) then message.
```

The relation defined by this assertion is $R = \{(s, s') | s > 3 \wedge s' = s + 1\}$. Let R' be the relation $R' = \{(s, s') | s' = s + 1\}$; then R' is more defined than R, yet eab is self-checking with respect to R', as can be seen from the following: Let s' be an element of dom(R') such that $s \in$ dom([b]) and $nm(s)$; then from $nm(s)$ we deduce $(s, [b](s)) \in R$, whence $(s, [b](s)) \in R'$.

If we restrict ourselves to relations whose domain is S (Chapter 6 shows we can do so without loss of generality), then R is indeed the most-defined relation with respect to which eab is self-checking.

14.2.2 Analysis of a Sequence

- *Proposition 2.* Let p_1 and p_2 be asserted programs. If p_1 is self-checking with respect to R_1 and p_2 is self-checking with respect to R_2 and rng(R_1) $\subseteq$ dom(R_2) then $p = (p_1; p_2)$ is self-checking with respect to $R = R_1 * R_2$.

Proof. To the asserted program p_1 is associated the predicate $nm_1(s)$, indicating the absence of messages; to the asserted program p_2 is associated the predicate $nm_2(s)$. Clearly, the predicate associated to p is $nm(s) = (nm_1(s) \wedge nm_2([p_1](s)))$. Now, let $\hat{s}$ be a state in dom(R) such that $\hat{s} \in$ dom([p]) and $nm(\hat{s})$; we must prove that $(\hat{s}, [p](\hat{s})) \in R$. From $\hat{s} \in$ dom(R) and $R = R_1 * R_2$ we deduce that $\hat{s} \in$ dom(R_1); from $\hat{s} \in$ dom([p]) and $p = (p_1; p_2)$ we deduce $\hat{s} \in$ dom([p_1]); from $nm(\hat{s})$ and $nm(s) = (nm_1(s) \wedge nm_2([p_1](s)))$ we deduce $nm_1(\hat{s})$. From $\hat{s} \in$ dom(R_1) $\wedge \hat{s} \in$ dom([p_1]) $\wedge nm_1(\hat{s})$ and the self-checkingness of p_1 with respect to R_1 we deduce $(\hat{s}, [p_1](\hat{s})) \in R_1$; by virtue of the hypothesis $\mathrm{rng}(R_1) \subseteq \mathrm{dom}(R_2)$, we deduce $[p_1](\hat{s}) \in \mathrm{dom}(R_2)$. From $\hat{s} \in \mathrm{dom}([p_1; p_2])$ we deduce $[p_1](\hat{s}) \in \mathrm{dom}([p_2])$ and from $nm(\hat{s})$ we deduce $nm_2([p_1](\hat{s}))$. From $[p_1](\hat{s}) \in \mathrm{dom}(R_2) \ \wedge \ [p_1](\hat{s}) \in \mathrm{dom}([p_2]) \ \wedge \ nm_2([p_1](\hat{s}))$ we deduce – by virtue of the self-checkingness of p_2 with respect to R_2 – that $([p_1](\hat{s}), [p_2]([p_1](\hat{s}))) \in R_2$. Because $p = (p_1; p_2)$ we rewrite this formula as $([p_1](\hat{s}), [p_1; p_2](\hat{s})) \in R_2$; this combined with the formula $(\hat{s}, [p_1](\hat{s})) \in R_1$ yields $(\hat{s}, [p_1; p_2](\hat{s})) \in R_1 * R_2$; whence $(\hat{s}, [p](\hat{s})) \in R$.　　　　　　　　　　　　　　　　　　　　　[QED]

14.2.3　Analysis of Alternation

- *Proposition 3.* If p_1 is self-checking with respect to R_1 and p_2 is self-checking with respect to R_2 then p = (if t **then** p1 **else** p2) is self-checking with respect to $R = I(t) * R_1 \cup I(\neg t) * R_2$.

Proof. Clearly, if nm_1 is the predicate associated to p_1 and nm_2 the predicate associated to p_2, then $nm = (t \ \& \ nm_1 \ \vee \ \neg t \ \& \ nm_2)$ is the predicate associated with p. Let $\hat{s}$ be an element of $\mathrm{dom}(R)$ such that $\hat{s} \in \mathrm{dom}([p])$ and $nm(\hat{s})$. We distinguish between two cases, depending on whether $t(\hat{s})$ holds or not. Because these cases are strictly symmetric, we consider but one.

　　Case. $t(\hat{s})$ holds. Then, by the formula of R, $\hat{s} \in \mathrm{dom}(R_1)$. On the other hand, from $\hat{s} \in \mathrm{dom}([p])$ and $t(\hat{s})$ stems $\hat{s} \in \mathrm{dom}([p_1])$. Finally, $nm_1(\hat{s})$ stems from $nm(\hat{s})$ and $t(\hat{s})$. By virtue of the self-checkingness of p_1 with respect to R_1, we have $(\hat{s}, [p_1](\hat{s})) \in R_1$; from which we deduce, because $t(\hat{s})$ holds, that $(\hat{s}, I(t) * [p_1](s)) \in I(t) * R_1$. Due to the semantics of (**if-then-else**) and the formula of R, we get $(\hat{s}, [p](\hat{s})) \in R$.
　　　　　　　　　　　　　　　　　　　　　[QED]

14.2.4　Analysis of Iteration

- *Proposition 4.* If b is self-checking with respect to B and $\mathrm{dom}(B) = S$, then p = (**while** t **do** b) is self-checking with respect to $R = (I(t) * B)^* * I(\neg t)$.

Proof. If nm' is the predicate associated to b to indicate the absence of messages, then the predicate associated to p is

$$nm(s) = \neg t(s) \ \vee \ \forall j, \ 0 \le j \le k: nm'(s \cdot (I(t) * [b])^j)$$

where k is the number of iterations required to process s. Let $\hat{s}$ be an element of dom(R) such that $\hat{s} \in$ dom($[p]$) and $nm(\hat{s})$. If $\neg t(\hat{s})$ holds, then $[p](\hat{s}) = \hat{s}$ and $(\hat{s}, [p](\hat{s})) \in I(\neg t) \subseteq R$. If $t(\hat{s})$ holds, let k be the number of iterations needed to process $\hat{s}$; k is defined since $\hat{s} \in$ dom($[p]$). Let x_j be the sequence defined as follows

$$x_j - \hat{s} \cdot (I(t) * [b])^j, \text{ for } 0 \le j \le k.$$

We have – by definition – $x_0 = \hat{s}$ and $x_k = [p](\hat{s})$. Let j be an index between 0 and $k - 1$ inclusive. Because dom(B) = S, we have $x_j \in$ dom(B); because $\hat{s} \in$ dom($[p]$), we have $x_j \in$ dom($[b]$); from $nm(\hat{s})$ we deduce $nm'(x_j)$. By virtue of the self-checkingness of b with respect to B we have $(x_j, x_{j+1}) \in B$; because $t(x_j)$ holds, we have $(x_j, x_{j+1}) \in I(t) * B$. By the definition of sequence (x_j), we have $(\hat{s}, [p](\hat{s})) \in (I(t) * B)^k$; because $\neg t([p](\hat{s}))$, we have

$$(\hat{s}, [p](\hat{s})) \in (I(t) * B)^k * I(\neg t)$$
$$\subseteq (I(t) * B)^* * I(\neg t)$$
$$= R. \qquad\qquad\qquad\qquad\qquad\qquad\qquad\qquad\qquad\qquad \text{[QED]}$$

When relation R is derived from asserted program p by means of Propositions 1, 2, 3 and 4, we say that R is the *associated relation* of program p.

14.2.5 Examples of Application

We give two examples of application of the propositions above. Both are simple: they are primarily illustrative. The statements added for the purpose of checking assertions are marked with (**); the declarations of $\hat{s}$ are implicit.

Example 2

```
S = {⟨x, y⟩ | x ∈ integer ∧ y ∈ integer ∧ y ≥ 0}.
p =
begin
(**) ŷ := y;
while y ≠ 0 do
   begin
   x := x + 1;
   y := y – 1;
   (**) if not (y = ŷ – 1) then message;
   (**) ŷ := y
   end
end.
```

Let $B = \{(s,s')\,|\,y(s') = y(s) - 1\}$. The asserted program is self-checking with respect to $R = (I(t) * B)^* * I(\neg t)$. We have

$$I(y \neq 0) * B = \{(s,s')\,|\,y(s) \neq 0 \wedge y(s') = y(s) - 1\}$$
$$(I(y \neq 0) * B)^* = \{(s,s')\,|\,y(s) \neq 0 \wedge y(s') < y(s)\} \cup I.$$
$$R = \{(s,s')\,|\,y(s) \neq 0 \wedge y(s') < y(s) \wedge y(s') = 0\}$$
$$\cup \ \{(s,s')\,|\,s' = s \wedge y(s) = 0\}$$
$$= \{(s,s')\,|\,y(s) > 0 \wedge y(s') = 0\} \cup \{(s,s')\,|\,y(s) = 0 \wedge s' = s\}.$$
$$= \{(s,s')\,|\,(y(s) > 0 \vee s' = s) \wedge y(s') = 0\}$$
$$= \{(s,s')\,|\,(y(s) = 0 \Rightarrow s' = s) \wedge y(s') = 0\}$$

Upon analysis, this relation seems to carry very little information on the functional behavior of the program since both conjuncts stem from the semantics of iteration – rather than from the assertion included; it is then clear that this assertion is a waste of resources.

How about if the assertion checked were $a'(\hat{s}, s) = (x = \hat{x} + 1)$? Then we would find the program self-checking with respect to the relation

$$R' = \{(s,s')\,|\,(y(s) \neq 0 \wedge x(s') > x(s) \vee s' = s) \wedge y(s') = 0\}.$$

Clearly, this relation carries more information than relation R. Two lessons can be learned from this remark. First, two local assertions (a and a') that are seemingly symmetric produce global relations that look quite distinct. Second, two local assertions that appear to be equally strong (a and a') can yield global relations that are not equally defined (i.e. global relations that do not carry the same amount of information). As to whether relation R' is worth the cost of run-time checking assertion a', one needs to look at the third assertion before making a judgement.

We consider $a''(\hat{s}, s) = (x = \hat{x} + 1 \wedge y = \hat{y} - 1)$. Then we find the following relation:

$$R'' = \{(s,s')\,|\,y(s) \geq 0 \wedge a(s') = a(s) + b(s) \wedge b(s') = 0\}.$$

This relation is very informative; it does seem as though the cost of checking a'' versus a' is well worth the advantage of R'' over R' (though the simplicity of the example makes the comparison shallow). This discussion is an example of how the strength of an assertion can be decided at design time.   □

Example 3

$$S = \{\langle x, y, p, q, r\rangle\,|\,x \in \textbf{integer} \wedge$$
$$y \in \textbf{integer} \wedge$$
$$p \in \textbf{integer} \wedge$$

$$q \in \textbf{integer} \wedge$$
$$r \in \textbf{integer} \wedge$$
$$x > 0 \wedge y > 0 \wedge p > 0\}.$$

p =
begin
(∗∗) x̂ := x; ŷ := y;
p := 1;
(∗∗) **if not** (p = 1 ∧ x = x̂ ∧ y = ŷ) **then** message(1); (∗R1∗)
(∗R1∗)
(∗∗) x̂ := x; ŷ := y; p̂ := p;
while y ≠ 0 **do**
  begin
  p := y **div** 2;
  r := y **mod** 2;
  if r = 0 **then**
    begin
    y := y **div** 2;
    x := x ∗ x
    end
  else
    begin
    p := p ∗ x;
    y := y − 1
    end
  (∗∗) **if not** (log(p) + y ∗ log(x) = log(p̂) + ŷ ∗ log(x̂))
      then message(2); (∗R2∗)
  (∗∗) x̂ := x; ŷ := y; p̂ := p;
  end
end.

This program is self-checking with respect to the relation

$$R = R_1 * (I(y(s) \neq 0) * R_2)^* * I(y(s) = 0).$$
$$I(y(s) \neq 0) * R_2$$
$$= \{(s, s') \mid y(s) \neq 0 \wedge \log(p(s)) + y(s) * \log(x(s))$$
$$= \log(p(s')) + y(s') * \log(x(s'))\}.$$

Because this relation is transitive, it is equal to its own transitive closure. Hence its reflexive transitive closure is equal to its union with I:

$$(I(y \neq 0) * R_2)^* = I(y \neq 0) * R_2 \cup I.$$
$$R = \{(s, s') \mid p(s') = 1 \wedge x(s') = x(s) \wedge y(s') = y(s)\}$$
$$* \{(s, s') \mid y(s) \neq 0$$

$$\wedge \; \log(p(s)) + y(s) * \log(x(s)) = \log(p(s')) + y(s') * \log(x(s'))\}$$
$$* \; \{(s,s') \, | \, s' = s \, \wedge \, y(s) = 0\}$$
$$\cup$$
$$\{(s,s') \, | \, p(s') = 1 \, \wedge \, x(s') = x(s) \, \wedge \, y(s') = y(s)\}$$
$$* \; \{(s,s') \, | \, s' = s \, \wedge \, y(s) = 0\}.$$
$$= \{(s,s') \, | \, y(s) \neq 0 \, \wedge \, y(s) * \log(x(s)) = \log(p(s')) \, \wedge \, y(s') = 0\}$$
$$\cup$$
$$\{(s,s') \, | \, x(s') = x(s) \, \wedge \, y(s') = 0 \, \wedge \, p(s') = 1\}$$
$$= \{(s,s') \, | \, y(s) \neq 0 \, \wedge \, p(s') = x(s)^{y(s)} \, \wedge \, y(s') = 0\}$$
$$\cup$$
$$\{(s,s') \, | \, y(s) = 0 \, \wedge \, p(s') = 1 \, \wedge \, y(s') = 0 \, \wedge \, x(s') = x(s)\}.$$

This is how much we can say about (s, s') any time the program executes on s and terminates in s' without sending messages!   □

14.2.6 Exercises

1[A] Using Propositions 1, 2, 3 and 4, compute the relation associated with the following asserted program. The blocks of code in each elementary asserted block are not shown explicitly, for they play no role in determining the required relation.

(a) Space S = **integer**;
   Program,

```
p = begin
      ŝ := s;
      b1;
      if not ŝ − 2 ≤ s ≤ ŝ + 2 then message(1);
      ŝ := s;
      b2;
      if not s = ŝ + 3 then message(2)
    end.
```

(b) Space S = **integer**;
   Program,

```
p = begin
      ŝ := s;
      b1;
      if not s = ŝ + 3 then message(1);
      ŝ := s;
      b2;
      if not ŝ − 2 ≤ s ≤ ŝ + 3 then message(2)
    end.
```

(c) Space s = **real**;
     Program,

```
p = begin
    ŝ := s;
    b1;
    if not ((ŝ + 1) ≤ s ≤ (ŝ + 1)² and s > 0) then message(1);
    ŝ := s;
    b2;
    if not (ŝ > 0 and s = log(ŝ)) then message(2)
    end.
```

(d) Space s = **real**;
     Program,

```
p = begin
    ŝ := s;
    b1;
    if not (s = ŝ + 1 and s > 0) then message(1);
    ŝ := s;
    b2;
    if not (ŝ > 0 and log(ŝ) < s ≤ 2 * log(ŝ)) then message(2)
    end.
```

(e) Space S = **integer**;
     Program,

```
p = begin
    ŝ := s;
    b1;
    if not s > 0 then message(1);
    ŝ := s;
    b2;
    if not ŝ + 1 ≤ s ≤ ŝ + 3 then message(2)
    end.
```

2[B]   Consider the following asserted programs on space S = **integer**:

```
p1 = begin
     ŝ := s;
     b1;
     if not (s = ŝ + 2) then message(1);
     ŝ := s;
     b2;
```

```
                if not ((1 ≤ ŝ ≤ 3) and (s = s²)) then message(2)
                end.
        p2 = begin
                ŝ := s;
                b1;
                if not ((1 ≤ s ≤ s) and (s = ŝ + 2)) then message(1);
                ŝ := s;
                b2;
                if not (s = s²) then message(2)
                end.
```

(a) Can we apply Proposition 2 to program p_1?
(b) In what sense are these programs similar?
(c) Can we apply Proposition 2 to program p_2?
(d) Compute the resulting relation; call it R.
(e) What property does p_1 verify with respect to R?

3[A] Same as Exercise 1, for the following programs:

(a) Space S = **integer**;
Program,

```
        p = begin
                ŝ := s;
                if s > 0 then
                    begin
                    b1;
                    if not (s = ŝ − 5) then message(1)
                    end
                else
                    begin
                    b2;
                    if not true then message(2)
                    end
                end.
```

Note: $((a \wedge b) \vee \neg a) = (a \Rightarrow b)$.
(b) Space S = **real**;
Program,

```
        p = begin
                ŝ := s;
                if s > 0 then
```

```
       begin
       b1;
       if not s = log(ŝ + 1) then message(1)
       end
     else
       begin
       b2;
       if not s = log(−ŝ − 1) then message(2)
       end
     end.
```

(c) Space S = **integer**;
    Program,

```
p = begin
    ŝ := s;
    if s mod 2 = 0 then
       begin
       b1;
       if not (s = ŝ/2) then message(1)
       end
     else
       begin
       b2;
       if not (s = (ŝ − 1)/2) then message(2)
       end
     end.
```

Note: Use function **div**.

(d) Space S = **real**;
    Program,

```
p = begin
    ŝ := s;
    if s ≠ 0 then
       begin
       b1;
       if not (s > ŝ) then message(1)
       end
     else
       begin
       b2;
```

```
                          if not (s > 0) then message(2)
                          end
                       end.
```

(e) Space S = **real**;
     Program,

```
           p = begin
               ŝ := s;
               if s > 2 then
                  begin
                  b1;
                  if not (s − log(ŝ − 2)) < e then message(1)
                  end
               else
                  begin
                  b2;
                  if not |s − log(ŝ − 2)| < e then message(2)
                  end
               end,
```

for some e > 0.

4[B]   Same as Exercise 1. Beware: some cases are degenerate.
(a) Space,

```
          S = set
              a, b, c: integer
          end
       Program,
       p = begin
          ŝ := s;
          b0;
          if not (a(s) = a(ŝ) and b(s) = b(ŝ) and c(s) = 0)
                                          then message(0);

          ŝ := s;
          while b ≠ 0 do
             begin
             b1;
             if not (a(s) = a(ŝ) and b(s) = b(ŝ) − 1 and c(s) = c(ŝ) + a(ŝ))
                                          then message(1);
             ŝ := s
             end
          end.
```

(b) Space,

```
S = set
    a, b, c: integer
end
Program,
p = begin
    ŝ := s;
    b0;
    if not (a(s) = a(ŝ) and b(s) = b(ŝ) and c(s) = 0)
                                    then message(0);
    ŝ := s;
    while b ≠ 0 do
      begin
      b1;
      if not (a(s) = a(ŝ) and c(s) + a(s) * b(s) = c(ŝ) + a(ŝ) * b(ŝ))
                                    then message(1);

      ŝ := s
      end
    end.
```

(c) Space,

```
S = set
    a, b, c: integer
end
Program,
p = begin
    ŝ := s;
    b0;
    if not (a(s) = a(ŝ) and c(s) + a(s) * b(s) = c(ŝ) + a(ŝ) * b(ŝ))
                                    then message(0);
    ŝ := s;
    while b ≠ 0 do
      begin
      b1;
      if not (a(s) = a(ŝ) and c(s) + a(s) * b(s) = c(ŝ) + a(ŝ) * b(ŝ))
                                    then message(1);
      ŝ := s
      end
    end.
```

(d) Space,

```
S = set
```

```
                  a, b, c: integer
              end
          Program,
       p = begin
              ŝ := s;
              b0;
              if not (s = ŝ) then message(0);
              ŝ := s;
              while b ≠ 0 do
                  begin
                  b1;
                  if not (a(s) = a(ŝ) and c(s) + a(s) * b(s) = c(ŝ) + a(ŝ) * b(ŝ))
                                                then message(1);
                  ŝ := s
                  end
              end.
```

(e) Space,

```
          S = set
                a, b, c: integer
              end
          Program,
       p = begin
              ŝ := s;
              b0;
              if not true then message(0);
              ŝ := s;
              while b ≠ 0 do
                  begin
                  b1;
                  if not (a(s) = a(ŝ) and c(s) + a(s) * b(s) = c(ŝ) + a(ŝ) * b(ŝ))
                                                then message(1);
                  ŝ := s
                  end
              end.
```

5[B]   Same as Exercise 4.
       (a) Space,

```
          S = set
                a, b, c: integer
              end
          Program,
```

```
p = begin
  ŝ := s;
  b0;
  if not (a(s) = a(ŝ) and b(s) = b(ŝ) and c(s) = 0)
                                      then message(0);
  ŝ := s;
  while b ≠ 0 do
    begin
    b1;
    if not (a(s) = a(ŝ) then message(1);
    ŝ := s
    end
  end.
```

(b) Space,

```
S = set
  a, b, c: integer
end
Program,
p = begin
  ŝ := s;
  b0;
  if not (a(s) = a(ŝ) and b(s) = b(ŝ) and c(s) = 0)
                                      then message(0);
  ŝ := s;
  while b ≠ 0 do
    begin
    b1;
    if not b(s) = b(ŝ) − 1 then message(1);
    ŝ := s
    end
  end.
```

(c) Space,

```
S = set
  a, b, c: integer
end
Program,
p = begin
  ŝ := s;
  b0;
  if not (a(s) = a(ŝ) and b(s) = b(ŝ) and c(s) = 0)
```

```
                                              then message(0);
        ŝ := s;
        while b ≠ 0 do
          begin
          b1;
          if not c(s) = c(ŝ) + a(s) then message(1);
          ŝ := s
          end
        end.
```

(d) Space,

```
        S = set
          a, b, c: integer
        end
      Program,
      p = begin
        ŝ := s;
        b0;
        if not (a(s) = a(ŝ) and b(s) = b(ŝ) and c(s) = 0)
                                              then message(0);
        ŝ := s;
        while b ≠ 0 do
          begin
          b1;
          if not (b(s) = b(ŝ) − 1 and c(s) = c(ŝ) + a(s))
                                              then message(1);
          ŝ := s
          end
        end.
```

(e) Space,

```
        S = set
          a, b, c: integer
        end
      Program,
      p = begin
        ŝ := s;
        b0;
        if not (a(s) = a(ŝ) and b(s) = b(ŝ) and c(s) = 0)
                                              then message(0);
        ŝ := s;
```

```
while b ≠ 0 do
    begin
    b1;
    if not c(s) + a(s) * b(s) = c(ŝ) + a(ŝ) * b(ŝ) then message(1);
    ŝ := s
    end
end.
```

6[A]   Consider the following programs on space S = **integer**.

```
p1 = begin
    ŝ := s;
    s := s + 2;
    if not (s = ŝ + 2) then message(1);
    ŝ := s;
    s := s + 2;
    if not (s = ŝ + 2) then message(2)
    end.
p2 = begin
    ŝ := s;
    s := s + 1;
    if not (s = ŝ + 2) then message(1);
    ŝ := s;
    s := s + 3;
    if not (s = ŝ + 2) then message(2)
    end.
```

(a) Compute the relations associated with each one of these programs.
(b) What self-checking property do these programs have in common?
(c) What correctness property do these programs have in common?
(d) In what way are they different?
(e) Draw general conclusions.

14.3 VERIFYING ASSERTED PROGRAMS

The question that we address in this section is: given an asserted program p and a specification R, how can we prove that p is self-checking with respect to R?

14.3.1 Formula of Consistency

In the analysis of programs (Chapter 3), one computes the function of the program at hand, then matches it against a given specification. Similarly, in the analysis of asserted programs, one derives the associated relation with respect to which the program is self-checking, say A, then matches it against the given specification, say R. While the preceding section shows how to derive A, this section shows how to match A against R. We have the following proposition:

- *Proposition 5*. Let p be an asserted program on space S, and let R be a relation on S. Let A be the associated relation of program p. If A is more-defined than R, *then* p is self-checking with respect to R.

Proof. By virtue of Propositions 1, 2, 3, and 4 (and by construction of relation A) p is self-checking with respect to A, i.e.

$$\hat{s} \in \text{dom}(A) \wedge \hat{s} \in \text{dom}([p]) \wedge nm(\hat{s}) \Rightarrow (\hat{s}, [p](\hat{s})) \in A.$$

Let $\hat{s}$ be an element of $\text{dom}(R)$ such that $\hat{s} \in \text{dom}([p])$ and $nm(\hat{s})$; because A is more-defined than R, $\hat{s} \in \text{dom}(A)$; by virtue of the self-checkingness of p with respect to A, $(\hat{s}, [p](\hat{s}) \in A$; because A is more-defined than R, $(\hat{s}, [p](\hat{s})) \in R$. [QED]

Note that this proposition offers a sufficient condition for self-checkingness, not a necessary condition. In order to prove that an asserted program is not self-checking with respect to a specification, one must refer to the definition of the self-checking property and resort to counterexamples.

14.3.2 Illustrative Example

Example 5. We consider the same space and asserted program as Example 4, namely:

$$S = \{\langle x, y, p, q, r \rangle : \ x \in \textbf{integer} \wedge$$
$$y \in \textbf{integer} \wedge$$
$$p \in \textbf{integer} \wedge$$
$$q \in \textbf{integer} \wedge$$
$$r \in \textbf{integer} \wedge$$
$$x > 0 \wedge y \geq 0 \wedge p > 0\}.$$

$$p =$$
begin
$$(**) \ \hat{x} := x; \ \hat{y} := y;$$

(∗∗) **if not** $(p = 1 \wedge x = \hat{x} \wedge y = \hat{y})$ **then** message(1); (∗R1∗)

   (∗∗) $\hat{x} := x; \hat{y} := y; p := p;$

  while $y \neq 0$ **do**

    begin

     $p := y$ **div** 2;

     $r := y$ **mod** 2;

     if $r = 0$ **then**

      begin

       $y := y$ **div** 2;

       $x := x * x$

      end

     else

      begin

       $p := p * x;$

       $y := y - 1$

      end

     (∗∗) **if not** $(\log(p) + y * \log(x) = \log(p) + \hat{y} * \log(\hat{x}))$

         then message(2); (∗R2∗)

    (∗∗) $\hat{x} := x; \hat{y} := y; p := p;$

    end

  end.

This program is self-checking with respect to the relation

$$R = R_1 * (I(y(s) \neq 0) * R_2)^* * I(y(s) = 0),$$

which we have found, in Example 4, to be equal to

$$A = \{(s, s') \,|\, y(s) \neq 0 \wedge p(s') = x(s)^{y(s)} \wedge y(s') = 0\}$$
$$\cup$$
$$\{(s, s') \,|\, y(s) = 0 \wedge p(s') = 1 \wedge y(s') = 0 \wedge x(s') = x(s)\}.$$

It is left to the reader to check that this asserted program is self-checking with respect to the following relations:

$$R_0 = \{(s, s') \,|\, y(s) \neq 0 \wedge p(s') = x(s)^{y(s)} \wedge y(s') = 0\},$$
$$R_1 = \{(s, s') \,|\, y(s) = 0 \wedge p(s') = 1 \wedge y(s') = 0 \wedge x(s') = x(s)\},$$
$$R_2 = \{(s, s') \,|\, p(s') = x(s)^{y(s)} \wedge y(s') = 0\},$$
$$R_3 = \{(s, s') \,|\, y(s) = 0 \wedge x(s') = x(s)\};$$

and that it is not self-checking with respect to the following relations (Proposition 5 is not applicable: one must find counter examples):

$$T_0 = \{(s, s') \,|\, y(s') = 0 \wedge x(s') = x(s)\},$$
$$T_1 = \{(s, s') \,|\, p(s') = x(s)^{y(s)} \wedge x(s') = x(s)\}. \qquad \square$$

14.3.3 Exercises

1[A] Consider the following asserted program:
Space S = **integer**;
Program,

```
p = begin
    ŝ := s;
    b1;
    if not ŝ - 2 ≤ s ≤ ŝ + 2 then message(1);
    ŝ := s;
    b2;
    if not s = ŝ + 3 then message(2)
    end.
```

For each specification given below, state whether it is self-checking (using Proposition 5) or not (using the definition, and counterexamples):
(a) $R_a = \{(s,s') \mid s - 5 \le s' \le s - 1\}$.
(b) $R_b = \{(s,s') \mid s - 6 \le s' \le s\}$.
(c) $R_c = \{(s,s') \mid s - 4 \le s' \le s - 2\}$.
(d) $R_d = \{(s,s') \mid s \ge 3 \wedge s - 5 \le s' \le s - 1\}$.
(e) $R_e = \{(s,s') \mid s - 6 \le s' \le s \wedge s' \ge 0\}$.

2[B] Same as Exercise 1, for the following program and specification:
Space S = **real**;
Program,

```
p = begin
    ŝ := s;
    b1;
    if not (ŝ + 1 ≤ s ≤ (ŝ + 1)² and s > 0) then message(1);
    ŝ := s;
    b2;
    if not (ŝ > 0 and s = log(ŝ)) then message(2)
    end.
```

(a) $R_a = \{(s,s') \mid \log(s + 1) \le s' \le \log((s + 1)^2)\}$.
(b) $R_b = \{(s,s') \mid \log(s + 1) \le s' \le 2 * \log(s + 1)\}$.
(c) $R_c = \{(s,s') \mid s' \le \log((s + 1)^2)\}$.
(d) $R_d = \{(s,s') \mid \log(\mid s + 1 \mid) \le s' \le 2 * \log(\mid s + 1 \mid)\}$.
(e) $R_e = \{(s,s') \mid s + 1 > 0 \wedge \log(s + 1) \le s' \le \log((s + 1)^2)\}$.

3[B] Same as Exercise 2, for the same set of specifications, and the following program:

Space S = **real**;
Program,

```
p = begin
    ŝ := s;
    b1;
    if not (ŝ > 0 and log(ŝ) ≤ s ≤ 2 * log(ŝ)) then message(2)
    b2;
    if not (ŝ > 0 and log(ŝ) ≤ s ≤ 2 * log(ŝ)) then message(2)
    end.
```

4[A]   Same as Exercise 1, for the following program and specifications: Space S = **integer**;
Program,

```
p = begin
    ŝ := s;
    if s mod 2 = 0 then
        begin
        b1;
        if not (s = ŝ/2) then message(1)
        end
    else
        begin
        b2;
        if not (s = (ŝ − 1)/2) then message(2)
        end
    end.
```

(a) $R_a = \{(s,s') | s \le 2*s' \le s+1\}$.
(b) $R_b = \{(s,s') | s \bmod 2 = 0 \land s' = s \text{ div } 2\}$.
(c) $R_c = \{(s,s') | s \bmod 2 = 1 \land s' = s \text{ div } 2\}$.
(d) $R_d = \{(s,s') | s > 2 \land s' > s\}$.
(e) $R_e = \{(s,s') | s \le 2 \land s' \le s\}$.

5[A]   Same as Exercise 1, for the following program and specifications:
Space,

```
S = set
        a, b, c: integer
    end
```

Program,

```
p = begin
    ŝ := s;
    b0;
    if not (a(s) = a(ŝ) and b(s) = b(ŝ) and c(s) = 0)
                                  then message(0);
    ŝ := s;
    while b ≠ 0 do
      begin
      b1;
      if not (a(s) = a(ŝ) and c(s) + a(s) * b(s) = c(ŝ) + a(ŝ) * b(ŝ))
                                    then message(1);

      ŝ := s
      end
    end.
```

(a) $R_a = \{(s, s') \mid b(s) \geq 0 \wedge c(s') = a(s) * b(s)\}$.
(b) $R_b = \{(s, s') \mid b(s) \geq 0 \wedge a(s') = a(s)\}$.
(c) $R_c = \{(s, s') \mid b(s) \geq 0 \wedge c(s') = c(s) + a(s) * b(s)\}$.
(d) $R_d = \{(s, s') \mid a(s') = a(s) \wedge b(s') = 0 \wedge c(s') = a(s) * b(s)\}$.
(e) $R_e = \{(s, s') \mid b(s) \geq 0 \wedge c(s) = 0 \wedge c(s') = a(s) * b(s)\}$.

6[B]   Same as Exercise 5, with the same specifications and the following program:

Space,

```
S = set
      a, b, c: integer
    end
```

Program,

```
p = begin
    ŝ := s;
    b0;
    if not (a(s) = a(ŝ) and c(s) + a(s) * b(s) = c(ŝ) + a(ŝ) * b(ŝ))
                                    then message(0);
    ŝ := s;
    while b ≠ 0 do
      begin
      b1;
      if not (a(s) = a(ŝ) and c(s) + a(s) * b(s) = c(ŝ) + a(ŝ) * b(ŝ))
                                    then message(1);

      ŝ := s
      end
    end.
```

7[B]   Same as Exercise 5, with the same specifications and the
following program:
Space,

```
S = set
      a, b, c: integer
    end
```

Program,

```
p = begin
    ŝ := s;
    b0;
    if not (a(s) = a(ŝ) and b(s) = b(ŝ) and c(s) = 0)
                                            then message(0);
    ŝ := s;
    while b ≠ 0 do
      begin
      b1;
      if not (a(s) = a(ŝ)) then message(1);
      ŝ := s
      end
    end.
```

8[B]   Same as Exercise 5, with the same specifications and the
following program:
Space,

```
S = set
      a, b, c: integer
    end
```

Program,

```
p = begin
    ŝ := s;
    b0;
    if not (a(s) = a(ŝ) and b(s) = b(ŝ) and c(s) = 0)
                                            then message(0);
    s := s;
    while b ≠ 0 do
      begin
      b1;
      if not b(s) = b(ŝ) − 1 then message(1);
```

```
        ŝ := s
        end
    end.
```

9[B] Same as Exercise 5, with the same specifications and the
following program:
Space,

```
    S = set
            a, b, c: integer
        end
```

Program,

```
    p = begin
        ŝ := s;
        b0;
        if not (a(s) = a(ŝ) and b(s) = b(ŝ) and c(s) = 0)
                                        then message(0);
        ŝ := s;
        while b ≠ 0 do
            begin
            b1;
            if not (c(s) = c(ŝ) + a(s)) then message(1);
            ŝ := s
            end
        end.
```

10[B] Same as Exercise 5, with the same specifications and the
following program:
Space,

```
    S = set
            a, b, c: integer
        end
```

Program,

```
    p = begin
        ŝ := s;
        b0;
        if not (a(s) = a(ŝ) and b(s) = b(ŝ) and c(s) = 0)
                                        then message(0);
        ŝ := s;
        while b ≠ 0 do
            begin
```

```
b1;
if not (b(s) = b(ŝ) − 1 and c(s) = c(ŝ) + a(s))
                                then message(1);

ŝ := s
end
end.
```

14.4 PROBLEMS

1[B] Discuss the impact (in terms of loss of generality, practical interest, significance) of taking the hypothesis that the relations associated with each executable assertion has its domain equal to S.

2[C] Discuss the inheritance of definedness by the relative product rule. Specifically, discuss whether if R_1 is the most-defined relation with respect to which p_1 is self-checking, and R_2 is the most-defined relation with respect to which p_2 is self-checking, then the relation given in Proposition 2 is the most-defined relation with respect to which

$$P_1; P_2$$

is self-checking.

3[C] Discuss the inheritance of definedness by the union rule. See Problem 2, and use Proposition 3.

4[C] Discuss the inheritance of definedness by the transitive closure rule. See Problem 2, and use Proposition 4.

5[B] Find an example of
(a) asserted program,
(b) specification R,
such that p is self-checking with respect to R, yet the associated relation of program p is not more-defined than R.

6[R] Investigate the problem of how to construct a self-checking program from a specification.

14.5 BIBLIOGRAPHICAL NOTES

The use of executable assertions in conjunction with backward error recovery is discussed in Anderson and Lee (1981).

Bibliography

Abrial, J.R., S.A. Schuman and B. Meyer (1980) *The Specification Language Z: Syntax and Semantics*, Oxford: Oxford University Computing Laboratory, Programming Research Group.

Agrawal, V. (ed.) (1985) *Proceedings, Colloquium on Fault Tolerance*, Montréal, Canada: Centre de Recherche en Informatique de Montréal.

Anderson, T. and P.A. Lee (1981) *Fault Tolerance: Theory and practice.* Englewood Cliffs, NJ: Prentice Hall.

Babb, R. and A. Mili (eds.) (1984) *Workshop Notes, International Workshop on Models and Languages for Software Specification and Design*, Québec, Canada: Research Report, Département d'Informatique, Université Laval.

Balzer, R. and N. Goldman (1979) 'Principles of good software specification and their implications for specification languages', IEEE Symposium on Software Specifications, IEEE Press, pp. 58–67.

Berg, H.K., W.E. Boebert, W.R. Franta and T.G. Moher (1981) *Formal Methods of Program Verification and Specification*, Englewood Cliffs, NJ: Prentice Hall.

Boudriga, N., J-L Durieux, A. Jaoua and A. Mili (1989) 'Specifying by regular relations', *Theoretical Computer Science*, December.

Caplain, M. (1978) Langage de Spécifications. Thèse de Doctorat és-Sciences d'Etat, France: Institut National Polytechnique de Grenoble.

DeBakker, J.W. (1980) *Mathematical Theory of Program Correctness*, Englewood Cliffs, NJ: Prentice Hall.

Dijkstra, E.W. (1976) *A Discipline of Programming*, Englewood Cliffs, NJ: Prentice Hall.

Gries, D. (ed.) (1978) *Programming Methodology: a collection of articles by members of IFIP WG 2.3*, New York: Springer-Verlag.

Gries, D. (1981) *The Science of Programming*, New York: Springer-Verlag.

Harandi, M.T. (ed.) (1987) *Proceedings, Fourth International Workshop on Software Specification and Design*, Monterey, CA, Piscataway, NJ: IEEE Press.

Hennell, M.A. (ed.) (1985) *Proceedings, Third International Workshop on Software Specification and Design*, London, Piscataway, NJ: IEEE Press.

Hoare, C.A.R. (1969) 'An axiomatic basis for computer programming', *Comm. ACM*, **12**(10), 576–83.

IEEE Symposium on Software Specification (1979), Piscataway, NJ: IEEE Press.

Jaoua, A. (1987) Etude du Recouvrement Avant sous les Hypothéses de Spécifications Déterministes et non-Déterministes. Dissertation of Doctorat-és-Sciences d'Etat, Toulouse: Université Paul Sabatier, Octobre.

Jaoua, A., S. Guemara, A. Mili and P. Torrés (1987) 'On the use of executable assertions in structured programs', *The Journal of Systems and Software*, New York: North Holland, March.

Jensen, K. and N. Wirth (1974) *Pascal User Manual and Report*, Heidelberg: Springer-Verlag.

Jones, C.B. (1986) *Systematic Software Development Using VDM*, London Prentice Hall.

Kleene, S.C. (1968) *Mathematical Logic*, New York: John Wiley.

Larson, L.C. (1983) *Problem Solving through Problems*, New York: Springer-Verlag.

Linger, R.C., H.D. Mills and B.I. Witt (1979) *Structured Programming: Theory and practice*, Reading, MA: Addison Wesley.

Liskov, B. and S. Zilles (1977) 'An introduction to formal specifications of data abstractions'. In: *Current Trends in Programming Methodology*, vol I: *Software Specification and Design* (ed. R.T. Yeh), Prentice Hall.

Liu, C.L. (1977) *Elements of Discrete Mathematics*, New York: McGraw-Hill.

Loeckx, J., K. Siebert and R.D. Stansifer (1984) *The Foundations of Program Verification*, Stuttgart: Wiley-Teubner.

Mahmood, A., E.J. McCluskey and D.J. Lu (1983) Concurrent Fault Detection Using a Watchdog Processor and Assertions, private correspondence, Center for Reliable Computing, Computer Systems Laboratory, Stanford University, June.

Manna, Z. (1974) *Mathematical Theory of Computation*, New York: McGraw-Hill.

Mendelson, E. (1964) *Introduction to Mathematical Logic*, Princeton, NJ: Van Nostrand.

Metze, G. and A. Mili (1981) 'Self checking programs: An axiomatization of program validation by executable assertions', *Proceedings, FCTS-11*, pp. 84–6, Portland (ME), Piscataway, NJ: IEEE Press.

Meyer, B. (1985) 'On formalism in specifications', *IEEE Software*, **2**(1), 6–26.

Mili, A. (1983) 'A relational approach to the design of deterministic programs', *Acta Informatica*, December.

Mili, A. (1984) *An Introduction to Formal Program Verification*, New York: Van Nostrand Reinhold.

Mili, A. (1985) 'Toward a theory of forward error recovery', *IEEE Trans. on Soft. Eng.*, **SE-11**(8), 735–48.

Mili, A., X-Y. Wang and Q. Yu (1986) 'Specification methodology: An integrated relational approach', *Software – Practice and Experience*, November.

Mili, A., J. Desharnais, and F. Mili (1987) 'Relational heuristics for the design of deterministic programs', *Acta Informatica*, vol 24.

Mills, H.D., V.R. Basili, R.H. Hamlet, J.D. Gannon and B. Schneiderman (1986) *Principles of Computer Programming: A mathematical approach*, Boston: Allyn and Bacon.

Ohno, Y. (ed.) (1982) *Requirements of Engineering Environments*, Amsterdam: North Holland.

Parnas, D.L. (1972) 'A technique for software module specification with examples', *Communications of the ACM*, **12**(10), 330–6.

Potts, C. (1989) *Workshop Notes, the Fifth International Workshop on Software Specification and Design*, Pittsburgh, PA, 19–20 May, Piscataway, NJ: IEEE Press.

Quine, W.V.O. (1961) *Methods of Logic*, New York: Holt, Rinehart and Winston.

Randell, B. (1975) 'System structure for software fault tolerance', *IEEE-Trans. on Soft. Eng.* **SE1**(2), 220–32. (Also: Chapter 25 of Gries, 1978.)

Sanderson, G. (1980) A Relational Theory of Computing: *Lecture notes in computer science*, vol 100, Heidelberg: Springer-Verlag.

Schlichting, R.D. and F.B. Schneider (1980) *Verification of Fault Tolerant Software*, Department of Computer Science, Cornell University, Rep. TR-80-446, November.

Stanat, D.F. and D.F. McAllister (1977) *Discrete Mathematics in Computer Science*, New York: Prentice Hall.

Stone, H.S. (1973) *Discrete Mathematical Structure and Their Applications*, Science Research Associates.

Stoy, J. (1977) *Denotational Semantics: The Scott–Strachey approach to programming language theory*, Boston: MIT Press.

Suppes, P. (1957) *Introduction to Logic*, Princeton: Van Nostrand.

Suppes, P. (1972) *Axiomatic Set Theory*, New York: Dover Publications.

Tarski, A. (1941) 'On the calculus of relations', *The Journal of Symbolic Logic*, **6**(3), 73–98.

Tremblay, J.P. and R.P. Manohar (1975) *Discrete Mathematical structures with Applications to Computer Science*, New York: McGraw-Hill.

Wirth, N. (1976) *Algorithms + data Structures = Programs*, New York: Prentice Hall.

Yeh, R.T. (1977) *Current Trends in Programming Methodology*, vol I, Englewood Cliffs, NJ: Prentice Hall.

Index